12

Do write & tell me what you are doing
& what your plans —
Have you heard from
L—? — I hope you
are not starving as he
does —

Your plans seem vague
Did you see Cecile
the day & then
Hank as to whether
Howard has made
the mortgage or not —
Mrs Schneider could
not place the book
and has gone to
Italy — Our only
hope is the American
Serial — but no
word yet —

The endpapers reproduce Isadora's last letter, written to the author: "Darling Vitia . . . I miss you dreadfully . . . . we are in a H—— of a fix here . . . . no way of getting out unless I can sell the furniture . . . . Think of me and play Scriabine—perhaps you will be nearer to my spirit when the body with all its material nuisance is not there—There are a few inspired moments in life & the rest is Chipuka—I kiss you tenderly with all my love. . . ."

The Real
ISADORA

*The author with Isadora, Nice, 1926. They took each other's
photos and had them printed as one, a copy for each. This together with a
photo of Gordon Craig was kept by Isadora on her dressing table.*

The Real

ISADORA

by Victor Seroff

THE DIAL PRESS · NEW YORK · 1971

Grateful acknowledgment is made to the following publishers for permission to quote from copyrighted material:
Alfred A. Knopf for selections from *Gordon Craig: The Story of His Life* by Edward Craig, copyright © 1968 by Edward A. Craig; The Viking Press, Inc., for selections from *Index to the Story of My Days* by Edward Gordon Craig, copyright © 1957 by Edward Gordon Craig; Liveright Publishing Corp., for selections from *My Life* by Isadora Duncan, copyright © 1927 by Horace Liveright Inc., renewal ©R 1955 by Liveright Publishing Corporation; Wesleyan University Press, for selections from *Duncan Dancer; an Autobiography* by Irma Duncan, copyright © 1965, 1966 by Irma Duncan Rogers; Thomas Nelson Inc. for selections from *Isadora: A Revolutionary in Art and Love* by Allan Ross Macdougall, copyright © 1960 Thomas Nelson & Sons; The New York Public Library for "Isadora Duncan, Pioneer in the Art of Dance." Our special thanks to Mr. Walter Lippmann for permission to quote from his letter to Mabel Dodge Luhan. Quotations from the Russian and French, unless otherwise indicated, are the author's own translations.

Library of Congress Catalog Card Number: 75-144385

PRINTED IN THE UNITED STATES OF AMERICA

FIRST PRINTING

TO MY DEAR FRIEND
Emile Capouya

Illustrations

facing page 158

((7))

The endpapers reproduce Isadora Duncan's last letter, written to the author from Nice, 1927, the full text of which appears in the book, pp. 428–429.

The Real
ISADORA

Art gives form and harmony to what in life is chaos and discord.

ISADORA DUNCAN

PART ONE

Chapter I

Isadora Duncan was the greatest performing artist that the United States ever produced. Beyond that, she had gifts as an artistic creator that amounted to genius—in fact, she invented an art form of profound significance, in which, save for her six adopted pupils, she has had no successful direct heirs though she was to influence generations of later dancers. Yet this most unique American artist has been, on the whole, badly served by those who have undertaken to give us accounts of her life, her personality, and her achievement. During the years following her death in 1927, I read several books about her written by people whom I knew, and I was surprised by their fictional character. Moreover, Isadora's own autobiography—*My Life*, published by Horace Liveright in 1927—did not wholly escape the effects of romancing. Indeed, her autobiography, for reasons that will be presented in this book, gives an impression that departs in important respects from the true facts, and presents a life, an artist, a woman, that are diminished reflections of a great original.

It is in part to set the record straight that I have at last undertaken to write the biography of a woman I knew very well, whose real memoirs were the many conversations we had in the years before her tragic death. It is also easier for me to write this story now—certainly easier than it was for her at that time, when she was under so many pressures. Also, since so many of the people who figure in her story, and were later to embroider it according to their individual fancy, are no longer alive, to give truth to their fictions, invented out of private needs, will hurt no one now. Even more important than this are the new materials now available about less well known or unrecorded parts of Isadora's history. This is particularly true of what may be, historically speaking, the most significant part of her career—material dealing with her sojourn in the Soviet Union, both as dancer and dance teacher, and as the wife of a famous Russian poet. This material gives us new insight not only into Isadora's story, but into a strangely poignant early time in the history of Soviet Russia.

But the weightiest reason for writing this biography now is the great need for it: a new generation of young people, many of them nourished without their knowledge on the very ideas of free expression and personal liberation which were so dear to Isadora, know nothing of the real Isadora. They know the legend, but know nothing of the woman. They are a truth-loving generation, too, and fabrications do not suit them. It is time for a biography that is true to the facts of Isadora's life and true to the spirit that animated her art.

Although I was intimately acquainted with Isadora, I will not claim that I read the complete manuscript of her book. But I read many chapters, and in fact many sections handed to me by her as she completed each page; the composition of some of these I actually "accompanied," so to speak, for Isadora, beset by the demands of her publisher, her literary agent, and well-wishing friends, sometimes needed the prompting of an appropriate background, and asked me to create the desired atmosphere by playing the piano for her.

One example will, I believe, sufficiently illustrate her predicament. With tears in her eyes that sprang from embarrassment even more than from annoyance, she once told me that her publisher was insisting that she describe in detail how she had felt while losing her virginity. Faced at that time with a truly desperate economic situation, Isadora felt that she had to comply. And since the episode had occurred many years earlier in Budapest, Isadora asked me to play one of Liszt's Hungarian rhapsodies to suggest the proper "Hungarian atmosphere."

During the early spring of 1926, when I went to see Isadora at her apartment in the Studio-Hotel in the rue Delambre in Paris, I found her sitting by the fireplace with a gentleman I did not know.

"I want you to meet M. Eduard Schneider," she said. "He has been telling me wonderful stories, so please sit down for a few minutes until he finishes the one. . . ." I noticed that Isadora had been crying; Schneider, too, appeared deeply moved. Although he was telling his story to Isadora almost in a whisper, I gathered that he was speaking of Eleonora Duse, whose biographer he was, for he mentioned the name of the famous actress several times. Duse's performance in London in June 1923, in Ibsen's *Ghosts* and *The Lady from the Sea*, and in a new play by Emilio Praga, *La Porta Chiusa (The Closed Door)* had stirred such enthusiasm that she had agreed to go to the United States during the spring of the following year. In the middle of her second tour across the country, having visited San Francisco, she was appearing in Pittsburgh. One cold, wet day, the driver who brought her to the theater left her before a door that he took for the stage door. It was locked. Duse knocked at it for some time, standing in the wind and pouring rain, before she was heard and admitted into the theater. She caught a cold that proved fatal. She died two weeks later, on April 21, 1924. With these details Eduard Schneider ended his story.

After a few moments of silence during which Isadora wiped away her tears, she said to me, "M. Schneider was a great friend of Duse, and he has been telling me about her." Then, smiling, she added, "Just as you will be telling people about me someday."

No one, myself least of all, could have taken Isadora's words as prophetic at that time. I was a pianist, with a concert career before me, and I should have been very much surprised if someone had told me at that time that in addition to being a musician I would eventually become a journalist, a music critic, and a biographer.

And yet that evolution has in fact occurred. During the years in which those unanticipated stages of my life were coming to pass, many persons were writing articles about Isadora, and even full-length books about her. To one who knew her, the greater part of these productions are shocking indictments of their authors' ignorance, and sometimes of their malevolence—attitudes that history will surely come to treat with contempt. But these writings exist, and have helped to form the public's view of Isadora Duncan. For that reason I have been concerned to present a truer picture of that remarkable woman, and in that spirit I have written the following pages.

In *My Life*, Isadora fell into fictionalizing not only when meeting her publisher's demand for sensational material but also out of a naive desire to heighten the colors of certain events—and occasionally to make up for the scantiness of her own information, or the haziness of her recollection.

In this way, she presented a fairly good picture of her mother, but spoke of her father only in vague terms, most probably because she scarcely knew him from their few meetings during her childhood, since he had left her mother before she was born. In actual fact, none of the authors who wrote about Isadora's father could have known anything about him until Allan Ross Macdougall undertook thorough researches in San Francisco. As a result, he was able to give a detailed account of Isadora's background, especially as regards her father, in his book, *Isadora*, published in 1960.

Joseph Charles Duncan, Isadora's father, was born in Philadelphia, but he went West as a young man, attracted by the Gold Rush of 1849. After various engagements as a journalist, he settled in San Francisco, where he became editor and proprietor of the California *Home Journal*, and invoice clerk at the Custom House. Because of the destruction of documents and records during the great earthquake and fire in San Francisco in 1906, there is little information available concerning Duncan's various other activities. Even the date of his marriage to Thomas Gray's youngest daughter, Mary Dora, is unknown.

In 1819, at the age of sixteen, Thomas Gray had emigrated from Ireland. After serving in Illinois in the Black Hawk War, in which he achieved the rank of colonel, he was granted the post of federal collector of the Port of St. Louis. Like Duncan, he also eventually settled in San Francisco, where he served as Naval Officer of the Port—an appointment he owed to his personal acquaintance, during the Black Hawk War, with Abraham Lincoln. He later represented San Francisco in the California State Legislature.

Colonel Gray disapproved of his daughter's marriage to Duncan, not only because Duncan was much older than Mary Dora, but because Duncan had already had a wife who had given him four children. From Gray's viewpoint, too, Duncan's frequent changes of occupation did not promise sufficient financial security for Mary Dora's future. But no doubt even the Colonel could not foresee the dramatic entanglements that marked the climax of Duncan's business career in San Francisco.

A journalist, a dabbler in poetry, and a member of San Francisco's Art Association, Duncan had also become involved in the banking business as early as 1870. He served as promotor and officer of various banking organizations until 1877, when he organized the Union Bank, a venture that was apparently stillborn. About one month later, he inaugurated the Fidelity Savings Bank; its financial affiliates failed within another month. The Fidelity Savings Bank was forced to close. Duncan, and Benjamin Le Warne, a son-in-law who was his associate in these ventures, absconded. Charges of forgery and felony were brought against them, and they were hunted by the police. Eventually, after attempting to flee to Nicaragua on a swift sailing ship, the two were captured—Duncan in San Francisco and Le Warne in Oakland. Duncan was tried, but the jury could not agree on a verdict, for the evidence was confusing and the witnesses' testimony inconclusive. He was tried a second time, with the same outcome, and then a third time. The third jury was as puzzled as its predecessors had been. There was a fourth and final trial, which ended with a verdict of not guilty.

These events could not fail to have a profound effect on the fortunes of Duncan's new family, and upon those of Isadora. Here, however, before beginning to recount the events of her life, I must deal with the matter of her age and of her unusual first name—for the destruction of San Francisco's records have left areas of shadow around both of these matters.

As a rule, establishing a woman's exact birthday poses a delicate question. But thanks to inquiries made by Isadora's elder brother, Augustin, in San Francisco in 1947, concerning the birth dates of his brother, his two sisters, and himself, it was established that Isadora was born on May 27, 1878, although during her lifetime the exact year changed to suit the demands of a given situation. Isadora told me that, depending on the circumstances, she was sometimes made four or five years older than she really was. As an example, she mentioned rather vaguely the difficulties the Duncan family had had with the authorities in the United States when they wished to leave the country and go to England.

In her memoirs she said: "I went to public school at the early age of five. I think my mother prevaricated about my age." And a few pages farther on: "When I was ten years old the classes were so large that I informed my mother that it was useless for me to go to school any more. I put up my hair on the top of my head and said that I was sixteen. As I was very tall for my age everyone believed me." It may be worth remarking in this connection that Isadora was generally thought to be a very tall woman—even by persons who had met her; in fact, she was of average woman's height, about five feet five inches.

Isadora seemed to have so little respect for official documents that she was constantly losing them or leaving them behind. For a long time, her American passport was lost in one of the innumerable Soviet government offices, and yet she always was issued new documents to facilitate her traveling in Europe. After her death, it appeared from the evidence of her American passport that she was forty-nine. Only two years previously, Isadora had told me that that document made her "four or five years older" than she really was.

The origin of her first name has never been firmly established. At her birth, she was named Dora Angela; Dora, after her mother's name, Mary Dora. In her memoirs she never speaks of herself except as Isadora, even when quoting remarks addressed to her when she was still in her early teens, that is, before she had acquired that name. Now, according to her memoirs, Augustin Daly, the manager who eventually engaged her for his show in New York, had said, when she first had met him in Chicago: "Isadora. That is a pretty name." But Macdougall told me that Daly had billed her as Sara Duncan in his Broadway production in New York. Macdougall also told me that he thought it was Daly who eventually suggested to her the name of Isadora, a name which she made immortal all over the world—except in Russia, where purely because of mistaken phonetic spelling she was and still is known as Aisedora.

Among Isadora's books, which she asked me to rescue from the rat-infested attic in an apartment she once occupied in Paris, I found a volume, which I still have, *Life and Times of Girolamo Savonarola*, by Professor Pasquale Villari, with the following curious dedication: "To Isadora Duncan from her mother, also Isadora."

Be that as it may, Isadora was the youngest child in her family. Of her brothers, Raymond was nearly four years older than she (he was born on November 1, 1874), and Augustin nearly five years older (born on April 17, 1873); her sister, Mary Elizabeth, was seven years Isadora's senior (born on November 8, 1871).

Isadora was born in a "fine house" on the corner of Gary and

Taylor streets in San Francisco, but she was not destined to grow up in it.

Since the time that their father had deserted the family, their sole means of support was their mother. She was a musician, but her meager earnings from giving piano lessons were not sufficient to keep them living in this fine mansion. Among other unattractive features, poverty has the power to enforce a nomadic existence on its victims. And the Duncan family soon learned its classic pattern. Whether evicted for nonpayment of rent, or moving voluntarily in order to escape the claims of creditors, the Duncan family shifted their belongings constantly from one two-room apartment to the next.

Unlike Prince Charles of England, who, when recently interviewed, said that as a child he thought that all children lived in palaces, Isadora learned at an early age the difference between "having" and "not having" for mere survival. Of the four children, she had the most adventurous spirit, was able to face the butchers and the bakers to whom they were already indebted, and to return home happily with an armful of trophies gained by her glib tongue and childish diplomacy. Years later, when writing her autobiography, she remembered observing her mother bent over knitting, which she did in order to supplement her meager income from teaching. On one occasion the shop rejected her work, and Isadora, having seen her mother crying, snatched the basket of finished knitting and, after peddling her wares from door to door, returned home with more money than the shop would have paid her mother.

One thing was certain—poverty did not succeed in dampening the children's courage and happy dispositions. The lack of playthings did not prevent them from inventing their own games, but their greatest enjoyment was supplied by their mother. If she was not too exhausted, upon her return home after going from house to house giving lessons, she would play the piano for them or she would read them poetry or stories. These sessions were not only an education but also the first stimulus to awaken their creative spirits. Chopin's waltzes and mazurkas, and Mendelssohn's "Songs without Words" inspired the first dancing steps; what in the beginning was mere fun soon was turned to practical effect, for the girls started teaching the children in their neighborhood. Elizabeth and Isadora began to have regular paying pupils, whom they taught the popular drawing room dances called "society dances"—waltzes, mazurkas, and polkas. After their father's brief return to San Francisco, on his moving the family into a new house, they not only opened a regular school for dancing, but also joined their brothers in giving theatrical performances in the spacious barn in back of the house. Their performances were so successful in the neighborhood that the "company"—the two sisters and two brothers—went on the road to Santa Clara, Santa Rosa, and Santa Barbara. Although Isadora failed to mention their repertory in her memoirs, one can easily imagine that they found their material in the local public library, where they were frequent visitors.

Ina Golbrith, the librarian, took a special interest in Isadora and was responsible for guiding her through the works of Dickens, Thackeray, and Shakespeare, while on her own Isadora read a great many "inspired books and trash," as she said. This voracious reading prompted her to write a novel, start a homemade newspaper for which she wrote editorials, news, and short stories. Most important of all, she began a diary written in a secret language. For by this time, she had a secret.

She was eleven years old when she fell in love with a young man who worked in a drugstore, and who was, of course, very beautiful and had the beautiful name of Vernon. He was one of the pupils in Elizabeth and Isadora's classes for grownups. Isadora went to balls with him, and in order to appear older, she wore long dresses. In her diary she referred to their dancing together as "floating in his arms." During the following two years she never knew whether Vernon was aware of how "madly" in love with him she was, but one day she received that first cruel, inevitable shock—"her Vernon" was going to marry a young society girl in Oakland.

By the time Isadora saw Vernon again, almost thirty years later, she had had many such shocks in her life, and she had learned to be philosophical about them. But when he came to see her in her dressing room after a performance in San Francisco, and she tried to tell him of her passionate love for him when she had been eleven, "he became frightened and talked about his wife, the plain girl from whom his affections had never deviated." And adding, "How simple some people's lives can be," she closed her account of this first episode in her love life.

Chapter II

Whenever Isadora was asked when she had begun to dance, she invariably said, "most probably in my mother's womb." By way of explaining this rather startling statement, she always added that her mother, while expecting Isadora's birth, was so distressed because of her husband's desertion that she could survive only on iced oysters and champagne—the food of Aphrodite. And, since Isadora herself firmly believed that the character of a child is already formed in its mother's womb, it is fair to assume that the roots of her highly emotional nature were in evidence during her teens.

Isadora was growing up in San Francisco, which at that time was enjoying a remarkable influx of theatrical companies and world-famous artists: German and Italian operatic companies, Sarah Bernhardt and her colleagues from the Comédie Française, Constant Coquelin and Jane Harding, Tomasso Salvini and his company from Italy, and the London Lyceum Theater Company of Henry Irving and Ellen Terry. Having witnessed from top seats in the gallery at least some of the performances given by these artists, Isadora dreamed of a brilliant career for herself with some similar theatrical company, a desire that had already been kindled in her imagination by the books she had been reading since her childhood. Her lack of success with the local theatrical managers was no doubt the main reason for her determination to seek her career elsewhere than in San Francisco. And yet it is reasonable to suppose that her emotional state—the grief caused by her first unhappy infatuation—provided an additional impulse for her decision to leave San Francisco.

In this case, after a family council, it was decided that the Duncans would all go East, to Chicago, to New York, or perhaps even to Europe. At first, however, only Isadora was to go to Chicago with her mother, who was indispensable to her as her piano accompanist. Her sister and brothers would join them later, after Isadora had made her fortune, for there was not the slightest doubt in their minds about immediate success. They all firmly believed that Isadora had something new to offer in dance form, something different from ballroom dancing, and different from doing formal pirouettes on a stage. Although Isadora sometimes denied any influence on the "something new she had to offer" by the *Delsarte System of Expression*, first published in 1885, it is highly improbable that Isadora was completely ignorant of François Delsarte, whom many acknowledge as a master teacher of principles of flexibility and body grace.

Delsarte is generally thought to have had a more than casual influence on what was later to be called modern dance, especially through American teachers of his principles; on Ruth St. Denis, for example, that other great American revolutionary woman of dance. Nevertheless, it is probably true that Isadora Duncan taught herself to be a dancer, gradually molded by exposure to the dance, art, music, and even the literature of several cultures. But she was most truly an American artist, in her spirit of willingness to try new forms, her optimism, the generosity and even the fervor of her presence.

No study was ever made, and now probably cannot be, of the influence on Isadora of historical forms of American pageantry, the tableaux, for instance, that became standard small town entertainment on national holidays, when extroverted amateurs conceived living pictures in pantomime, and struck poses to illustrate the memorable events which created and then, in their mythic guise, bound a nation into a people. It is no wonder that Isadora was to become so great an admirer of Walt Whitman, celebrating in her way some of the same American impulses; and it is perhaps even more appropriate that she came from the West, from California which in so many ways has always exemplified the "new."

But the twenty-five dollars and the heirlooms consisting of

some jewelry and old lace, with which Isadora and her mother arrived in Chicago, soon went in paying for cheap rooms in boardinghouses and their meager meals. They were practically stranded in the strange city which offered them a life no different from their former drab existence in Oakland. But, undaunted, Isadora continued making the rounds of theatrical managers for whom she danced Chopin's waltzes and mazurkas. "You are a pretty girl," was their general reaction, "but in our business we need some peppery stuff, something with frills and kicks." However, if she could provide these, Charles Fair, the manager of the Masonic Roof Garden, was ready to offer her an engagement in his vaudeville show. Isadora could not refuse the offer, for she and her mother had come to the end of their resources. Still, when after she had been entertaining the audiences for three weeks as "The Californian Faun," the manager offered to prolong her engagement, even promising a tour on the road, Isadora refused. Thoroughly disgusted with this forced labor, which went against her ideas of art, she naively believed that this was the first and last time that she would have to compromise in order to survive.

In addition to the salary she received, and the respite that it gave her from immediate financial worries, she had the opportunity of meeting Ivan Miroski, a forty-five-year-old Polish poet and painter, whose courtship must have assuaged the ego wounded by the unsuspecting Vernon. Far from chaperoning her daughter, Isadora's mother left her alone to enjoy her tête-à-têtes with Miroski, and their long walks in the woods on the outskirts of the city. Unable at last to deny his feelings, Miroski asked Isadora to marry him, and Isadora did believe that this was to be her "great love."

And perhaps it would have been, had she not read in the newspapers that Augustin Daly, the great man among theater managers, happened to be in Chicago with his company. After many long afternoons and evenings at the stage door trying to waylay Daly, Isadora was finally lucky enough to attract his attention, and after he saw her dance for not more than the few minutes he could spare, he engaged her for his show in New York. She was to report there for rehearsals.

This was the great opportunity of her career, she thought, and on the wings of her success with Daly, she wired to a friend in San Francisco asking for not less than one hundred dollars. Apparently miracles do happen. The money arrived—plus her two brothers and sister, to whom an engagement with Daly meant a fortune already made. Their happy reunion did not include Miroski, who was distressed by their future separation. As lovers have done and always will do, Isadora and Miroski swore eternal love, and she left him with the classical promise to return and marry him as soon as she had made her fortune in New York.

The hundred dollars did not go very far in New York, and since during the six weeks of rehearsals the company received no salary, the Duncans were several times put out of boardinghouses for the same reason—nonpayment of rent. Eventually they landed in two bare rooms way uptown. For lack of carfare, Isadora often had to go on foot all the way to 29th Street, where the rehearsals were being held.

She had a small part in *Miss Pygmalion,* a pantomime with music by Francis Thome which Daly had brought from France; Mlle. Jane May was the leading actress. Only the constant threat of destitution made Isadora accept the part, for she believed that there was no art in pantomime, and that it was not worthy of her ideas and her ideals. "If you want to speak, why don't you speak? Why all this effort to make gestures as if in a deaf and dumb asylum?" she thought. But she controlled herself, and behaved as she was told, that is, to point with exaggerated gestures when saying "you," to press her heart to express love, and to beat her chest when speaking of herself.

After three weeks in New York, the company went on the road and Isadora received a first taste of theatrical life that she never forgot. During this tour of one-night stands, Isadora was constantly exhausted from searching for cheap boardinghouses that were safe for a young lady's virtue, so that she could economize and send some money to her mother in New York. But during the two months of the tour, though Isadora wrote long letters to Miroski every day, her letters contained no complaints. In fact, despite Jane May's violent outbursts of temper, Isadora actually learned to admire the actress and even thought that she could have become a great dancer had the scope of her expression not been so limited. And, although she herself never changed her opinion of pantomime as falling beneath the level of true art, she may have acquired some of the techniques of pantomime during this time. While she never made pantomime a part of her own art, she did become an extraordinary mimic and in later years amused her admirers with that talent. She also became exceptionally good at impersonating others as well as herself while illustrating some of her experiences. But these were merely her parlor tricks, as it were.

Personally, I was even more impressed by Isadora's imitating with her two fingers a performance of two ballet dancers. She did not do it often; apparently she had to be in a special mood. As a rule, and I am speaking of the later years in her life, she was extremely patient with slow service in restaurants, for she was always in sympathy with the hard-working waiters. It was during one long wait in a restaurant that she first entertained me, as well as herself, by imitating this ballet performance. Placing her arm on the tablecloth, she raised her wrist just high enough to give her fingers freedom of movement. Then her index finger suddenly turned into a ballerina coming on stage, while her second finger, the ballerina's male partner, remained in the background. After a few bows to the public, the ballerina performed a few runs, skips and kicks, and ended her performance by leaning on the shoulder of her partner. All this was done with extreme agility and finesse.

Isadora had small, sensitive hands. She never wore rings or bracelets, or any other ornaments; they would only have marred the beauty of her arms and fingers. In fact, she almost never wore any jewelry.

The tour of *Miss Pygmalion* was a dismal failure. Jane May went back to Paris and Isadora would have again been making the rounds with the managers had Daly not offered her a small part in *A Midsummer Night's Dream*, with Ada Rehan in the leading role. This time Isadora was to appear in one of the fairy scenes. And, since she actually danced on the stage, this should be considered as Isadora Duncan's debut—in January 1896. But her first triumphal success lasted only one night. The audience's enthusiastic applause stopped the show. Daly was enraged, for he did not think it proper that a single dance should interrupt the play, since it was not a music hall performance. From then on Isadora performed her dance on a darkened stage, so that only "a white fluttering thing" could be seen by the audience.

After two weeks in New York, the show went on the road, and once again Isadora suffered the dreary life of a traveling company, to which she could never get accustomed. However, she was happy at least for a short while when they reached Chicago and she saw Miroski again. It was summer, and, whenever Isadora was free from rehearsals, they were together. This time it was agreed that Miroski would follow her to New York, where they would be married. But upon her return to New York, an unexpected revelation put an end to her romance. Her brother Augustin had discovered that Miroski was already married—his wife was living in London.

Again, as had happened after her unsuccessful romance with Vernon, she was offered an opportunity to escape from the scene of her thwarted love, or at least the chance of diversion—*"pour changer les idées"* (literally, to change one's ideas, but Isadora meant: to get a fresh perspective), as she used to say in her later years, when speaking of the necessity of solving some problem.

While Isadora was still enjoying watching Ada Rehan and, as she claimed later, learning a great deal from her both at rehearsals and during her performances as Rosalind, Beatrice, and Portia, Daly announced that he intended to send the company on tour in England. It has never been definitely established whether Daly sent Isadora to England by herself, or whether she went there with his company, but she did arrive in London in the spring of 1897. There she took lessons in dancing from Ketti Lenner, the leading dancer at the Empire Theater. In her youth in Vienna, Ketti Lenner was supposed to have been a pupil of the famous ballerina Fanny Elssler. But Isadora herself never spoke of her training, either with Ketti Lenner, or later in New York with Marie Bonfanti. In fact, she seemed to prefer leaving in doubt the matter of whether she had ever had formal training as a dancer. I remember well that, a year before her death, we saw a performance of Rudolph Friml's operetta *Rose Marie* at the Théâtre de Mogador in Paris. While the audience was breathlessly watching a dancer perform ballet steps, Isadora whispered to me: "That is a real dancer. I have never had such technique, not even in my youth. I could never do what you see her doing."

Be that as it may, after spending the summer months studying with Ketti Lenner, Isadora returned to New York, and, apparently tired of the small parts offered her in Daly's theatrical productions, resigned from the company after having been a member of it for two years.

By that time, the Duncans—except for Augustin, who had joined a theatrical company and was on the road most of the time—had settled in one of the Carnegie Hall studios. They covered the bare walls with curtains and slept on the floor on mattresses that were put up behind the curtains during the day. Elizabeth opened a dancing school in the studio, while Raymond tried his hand at journalism. But their combined efforts at making a living did not allow them to meet their expenses, so they rented their studio by the hour to music teachers and to singers. This meant that they had to leave the premises and either occupy themselves elsewhere or try to enjoy the enforced pleasure of long walks in Central Park, regardless of the weather or the temperature.

At about this time, Isadora became interested in the music of Ethelbert Nevin, who, upon his return from Europe, had rented for his living quarters a studio next to the Duncans. At first, on hearing that Isadora was using his compositions for her dances, he was furious, but after seeing her perform them—"Narcissus," "Ophelia," and "Water Nymphs"—he was so delighted that he went to the piano and improvised a piece for her, which he called "Spring." Isadora always regretted that, although he frequently played it for her, it was never written down, for she had great faith in Nevin's musical talent, and even believed that he could have developed into the Chopin of America had he not died while still very young.

Nevin was so enthusiastic about Isadora's dancing that he immediately proposed their giving concerts together and, in fact, made all the arrangements for a concert on March 24, 1898, at the Carnegie Hall Music Room, or Carnegie Lyceum, as it was then called.

But, while Nevin was busy with preparations for the concert, Isadora took part in a program called "An Afternoon with Omar Khayyam, the Astronomer-Poet of Persia," offered by Justin Mac-Carthy. An author who later—in the early 1900s—became famous for his play *If I Were King*, MacCarthy gave a lecture about Omar Khayyam at the Lyceum Theater on March 14, 1898, ten days before Nevin's scheduled concert. To illustrate some of the verses from the *Rubáiyát*, MacCarthy engaged Isadora.

Outside of her participation in Daly's Broadway productions, this was one of Isadora's first public appearances in New York, and it provoked a mixed reaction in the press, as well as in the audience, mostly composed of typical matinee patronesses, well dressed, well fed, and highly moral.

It was reported that "when Isadora stood still, she was like a graceful Greek statue of classic outlines. But she had neither the color nor the immobility of marble. Her arms were bare to the shoulder, as were her legs to the knee." Apparently, that was sufficient to cause some forty women to leave the theater. They did not blame Mac-Carthy, who was "properly garbed," and conducted himself as a "perfect gentleman," but Isadora's "nudity" was altogether shocking to them. To understand their attitude it is sufficient to recall that in that era women went bathing in a costume covering their bodies from neck to ankle, and that to her audience Isadora's exposure of her "limbs" was nothing less than a shameless challenge to their moral standards.

And, if her performance had not been appraised by the more intelligent in the audience as "well within the limits of good art," Isadora's debut before the New York public could have damaged Nevin's concert. But the concert was a great success. Isadora believed that it could have meant the beginning of her career, but it was not exploited by an enterprising manager.

Nevertheless, the concert did bring Isadora to the attention of patronesses of the arts, then very influential in New York society. During the summer months, the members of the so-called "400" migrated to their large estates, either at Newport by the sea, or at Lenox in the Berkshires. Isadora who, after her concert with Nevin, had already danced in their New York drawing rooms, now danced on the lawns of their estates before the Astors, Vanderbilts, and Belmonts. But, while she was referred to as "the only real society pet," Isadora soon learned that this was merely an honorary title and, as such, brought her no material gain. By the time she paid for her trips, and sometimes those of her mother, Augustin, Raymond, or Elizabeth, there was barely enough money left for their tickets back to New York.

Still, Isadora's alfresco performances indirectly had a beneficial effect on Elizabeth's dancing school. The number of pupils from wealthy families was growing so rapidly that, despite the high rent involved, they moved from the Carnegie Hall studio to two spacious rooms on the ground floor of the fashionable Windsor Hotel, on Fifth Avenue between 46th and 47th streets.

Not quite a year had passed since Isadora's first concert with Nevin and her introduction to New York society, and the Duncans' financial situation seemed to have improved, when, on March 17, 1899, at three o'clock in the afternoon, the hotel caught on fire. Isadora and Elizabeth, with their mother at the piano, were giving a dancing lesson to the children, but they were interrupted by one of the chaperoning maids, who whispered to Elizabeth that she thought there must be something wrong at the hotel, perhaps a fire. The rapidity with which the fire engulfed the building caught the hotel guests so completely by surprise that some of them jumped out of the windows to certain death. Though fully aware of the danger, without alarming the children, the Duncans told them to hold hands and walk in pairs as in a dance; they led them out of the hotel to the street, and on to a nearby house, where eventually their distressed parents came to collect them.

Once more the Duncans had to move—this time to the Buckingham, another fashionable Fifth Avenue hotel. Practically all their possessions had been lost in the fire. This time Isadora insisted that it was fate, and that they should make every effort to leave New York and go to England. But the old problem—lack of funds—kept them from carrying out this plan for over six weeks after the fire at the Windsor Hotel.

With her characteristic determination, Isadora began to call upon all the millionaires at whose homes and estates she had danced, asking them to donate enough money for her trip to England. She was still young and naive enough to believe that her request would find a generous response. Often after having been graciously received before she disclosed the reason for her visit, she would find herself sent off with a "bon voyage" and a minuscule check—hardly sufficient for a "bon voyage" for the whole Duncan family.

Actually, one member of the family, Augustin, was not ready to join them, because while playing Romeo on the road with a small company, he had not only fallen in love with his sixteen-year-old Juliet but had married her. This was far from pleasing to the family. In fact everyone except Isadora plainly showed his hostility. But Isadora visited the young bride and discovered that, besides being in a very precarious financial situation, the newly married couple were expecting a child. Unfortunately, Isadora could offer only love and sympathy.

Even her participation in performances "Given in Aid of Miss Isadora Duncan and Other Sufferers from the Windsor Hotel Fire" resulted in unpleasant complications. Only after she had threatened a lawsuit was her claim for her professional fee settled. Her plans to leave the country found little support in the press, which ridiculed her performance at one of the fund-raising occasions. The following New York newspaper report appeared on April 19, 1899:

> Under the patronage of sixty-seven society women from the inner ranks of the One hundred and Fifty of New York . . . an impressive function was held yesterday. Miss Isadora Duncan, assisted by her sister, Miss Elizabeth Biroen Duncan, her brother, Mr. Augustin Duncan, with a large mama in a blue gown that was monstrous and unnatural, and a diaphanous younger brother distributing strophes from Ovid in the background, gave, for the first time in New York, some idyls from Theocritus and Bion, done into dance under the name of "The Happier Age of Gold. . . ."

> Miss Duncan has recently had the misfortune to lose her wardrobe by the Windsor Hotel fire, which probably accounts for and excuses the fact that her sole costume for yesterday's dance was a species of surgical bandage of gauze and satin of the hue of raspberry ice, with streamers of various lengths, which floated merrily or mournfully as the dancer illustrated the bridal of Helene or the burial of Adonis.

> Miss Duncan's melancholy brother kindly read extracts from Theocritus and Ovid as an accompaniment to the writhings and painful leaps and hops of his sister, while a concealed orchestra discoursed doleful music and the audience of tortured souls gazed at one another and blushed or giggled, according to the individual form of nervousness.

> When the final dance was finished, there was a sigh of relief that it was over and that Miss Duncan's bandages hadn't fallen off, as they threatened to do during the entire show. Then the audience of sixty-seven solemnly filed upon the stage to kiss Miss Duncan, her mama, and her sister, and wish them success in introducing "The Happier Age of Gold" to London drawing rooms in May.

> Miss Duncan has fully determined on this reckless course, which is sad, considering we are at peace with England at present.

Such was the "bon voyage" Isadora received from the press in her native country.

Chapter III

It was risky to venture all the way to Europe with only about three hundred dollars in their pockets—even the romantic Duncans could see that. Rather than have the family travel as steerage passengers, which would have cost them their last penny, Raymond managed to persuade the captain of a cattleboat to take them along free of charge. They were young and their hearts were gay, and, apparently, their adventurous spirit was so contagious that even their mother took the rough voyage in her stride.

Many years later, while speaking of artists venturing into a country where they are completely unknown, Raymond told me the advice he would give them, something he had learned in his youth. An artist, he said, even at the sacrifice of his last penny, should invest in a luxurious first-class cabin, see to it that his presence on the ship and later his landing should excite attention, and in his first interview with the press, he should criticize everything in the country even before he has set foot on its soil. In this way, he maintained, that artist could insure that he would be admired, listened to, and treated with great respect.

But, since at the time of their departure for England the Duncans did not have the funds to invest in luxurious shipboard cabins, they were in no position to adopt any such scheme. In order to avoid adverse publicity, Raymond appears to have suggested another romantic plan, which the rest of the family readily adopted

—to travel incognito, like royalty. They sailed as the O'Gormans, a name derived from the name of their maternal grandmother, Gorman. And Isadora became Maggie O'Gorman.

In referring in her memoirs to their arrival in England, Isadora had an amusing sally worthy of Cervantes' Sancho Panza: "The O'Gormans landed in Hull on a May morning, took a train, and a few hours later the Duncans arrived in London."

London, and everything about English life, was a new world to them, except for Isadora, since it was her second visit there. The English accent delighted them, and, like good American tourists, always hungry for culture, they spent their days in sightseeing and in visiting the historical landmarks of the city from Westminster Abbey and the British Museum to the Tower of London and Richmond Park, completely unmindful of their dwindling resources.

It is impossible to say whether Isadora's descriptions of the hardships of their initial life in London, with which in later years she regaled her friends, were true to the facts or were merely romantic embellishments, as in a Dickens novel. She told, with intended pathos, of their spending days on park benches, and, not without good-natured humor, of a desperate escapade in which they went to an expensive hotel and got one good meal and a good night's rest in comfortable beds, escaping early the next morning without paying their bill.

Unlike the rest of the family, Isadora was not only thoroughly acquainted with the city from her previous long sojourn there, but she had a number of friends from that period. In addition to those friends, she could also count on introductions to the English public by such well-established personnages in London society as MacCarthy and his wife Cissie Loftus, the famous Shakespearean actress and mimic of the music hall stage. It often happens in the beginning of artists' careers that they eventually reach *the* person or group of people who either launch them on the road to success, or, by advising them, play an important role in the development of their art. But nothing of the kind had so far happened to the Duncans.

In July, as is customary, the London musical and theatrical season closed, and the following three months threatened the Duncans with the same dreary, penniless existence they had been experiencing.

Having kept in touch with the mothers of her former pupils in

New York, Elizabeth decided to return and reopen her dancing school, so that she could financially sustain Isadora, Raymond, and their mother, who were determined to remain in London although nothing very promising was in the offing. In fact, to add to Isadora's already depressed state of mind, she had received a letter from a friend in Chicago telling her that Ivan Miroski had died. A year had passed since Isadora had last seen him. Miroski had volunteered for the Spanish-American War, but had died on his way abroad from typhoid fever, which he caught in a military camp in Florida. This prompted Isadora to call on Miroski's wife, in whose home, adorned with Ivan's portraits and pictures, she relived her association with the woman's husband. They shed tears together, and Isadora wept even more when she was returning home on top of a penny bus. Isadora said later, "Up to then I had been sleeping with Ivan Miroski's photograph and letters under my pillow, but from that day I consigned them to a closed packet in my trunk."

Then, at the moment when their spirits reached their lowest ebb, when even the British Museum had lost its magnetic power, and they would just as soon keep warm in bed and not leave their unpaid-for rooms, Raymond and Isadora, purely by chance, met Mrs. Patrick Campbell who, after seeing Isadora dancing for her own amusement in Kensington Gardens, invited the Duncans to her house.

At Mrs. Campbell's beautiful home, where the famous actress entertained them by playing the piano, singing old English songs, and reciting poetry, the Duncans forgot the gloom of their icy rooms, the London fog, and what they had begun to believe was a hopeless situation. It always took little to revive the Duncan spirits, and, when Mrs. Campbell gave Isadora a letter of introduction to Mrs. George Wyndham, Isadora was convinced that this was the first step toward a change in her fortunes. And in a way it was, for at Mrs. Wyndham's home, where nearly everybody in the artistic and literary world came to see Isadora dance, she met Charles Hallé: if he did not succeed in launching her career in London, he certainly played one of the most important roles in Isadora's development of her art.

The tall, slender, gray-haired Charles Hallé was the son of Sir Charles Hallé, the famous German musician, who had made his career in England as a pianist and conductor, and in 1857 had founded an orchestra in Manchester which bore his name. Isadora was at once attracted to the younger Charles Hallé, a well-known painter, and she formed such a close friendship with him that hardly a day passed without her visiting his studio. During the traditional English tea, her host entertained her with his personal recollections of Burne-Jones, Rossetti, Whistler, and Tennyson. Through Charles Hallé, Isadora met most of the men prominent in literature and the arts, and was courted by young poets. Her new friends read to her the poems of Swinburne, Keats, Browning, Rossetti, and works of Oscar Wilde.

But Hallé did more than introduce the young American dancer to the wealth of English culture. As director of the New Gallery in Regent Street, where contemporary painters exhibited their works, Hallé conceived a plan for a series of performances in the court of the gallery. For these "Evenings with Isadora Duncan," under the patronage of Queen Victoria's daughter, the Princess of Schleswig-Holstein, he enlisted his friends to give lectures: Sir William Richmond, the painter, on the relation of dancing to painting, Andrew Lang on Greek mythology, and Sir Hubert Parry on music.

The first of these functions was held on March 16, 1900.

Although her dancing in the courtyard, with a fountain in the center and potted palms and flowers for a background, did not create a sensation, it received some notices in the press. One of them, "An American Dancer," describing Isadora's unusual attire, was obviously written by a woman.

Miss Isadora Duncan is the very latest in the way of plastic dancers. She does not undertake the terpsichorean art in the ordinary way, but illustrates poems or poetic ideals to music of what seems to be perfectly artless and natural dance movements. For instance, she dances Mendelssohn's musical poem "A Welcome to Spring," with frolicsome, laughing grace that makes one think of flowers and birds and lambs at play. Her costume for this is appropriately copied from Botticelli's "Primavera." The robe appears to consist of several gauze slips worn one over another. The upper one has angel sleeves and is dim, pale green color, painted here and there with delicate flowers. The draperies reach to the feet, and are full enough to blow about outlining the figure as she dances.

Very Botticelli-like is the long, dark hair crowned with roses, and falling in curls to the waist. Ropes of roses wind about her body and the feet are shod with gold sandals. Not a single routine step is taken and the whole dance seems like something that might have happened in ancient Greece. . . . She has been analyzing and memorizing the steps and attitudes of the classic nymphs of antique art. Her work thus is the result of the application of poetic intelligence to the art of dancing. Her aim is to study nature and the classics and to avoid the conventional.

In appearance Miss Duncan is graceful and slender with a small oval face, good features and a mass of thick dark hair. She is beautiful and has particularly graceful arms and hands.

Another reviewer was of the opinion that the advent of Isadora Duncan in 1900, when Queen Victoria was in the last year of her reign, heralded a more liberal and enlightened attitude toward, not merely the dance, but life in general. When speaking of her performance, he made an even more important observation: "Until Isadora Duncan appeared and gave the dance a new form and life, helping us to realize that the dance can be an art, it had no validity other than as a mere diversion. No one who considered himself an intellectual gave the dance as it was serious consideration. It either appeared in the guise of social dancing and, therefore, could not be pronounced an art, or it represented ballet dancing—a diversion for the less intelligent-minded and for old gentlemen known as balletomanes."

J. Fuller-Maitland, in his favorable review published on March 17 in *The Times*, described in detail the performance of "a young dancer of remarkable skill whose art, though it may fail to satisfy the average ballet master, has wonderful eloquence of its own." A distinguished musicologist and critic, he was one of the first to suggest a much wider field for Isadora's art. He also wrote: "Miss Duncan's exceptional beauty of face and figure fits her for the self-appointed task of illustrating such passages as were chosen from the *Homeric Hymn to Demeter* and the *Idylls of Theocritus.*"

But when Fuller-Maitland spoke to her after the performance, he raised an important technical point, telling her how anxious he was to have the rubato in the Chopin compositions reflected in her dance. He said later, "She went through one or two of the Chopin pieces until she could get the right elasticity of rhythm," but it is doubtful that Isadora quickly adopted the rubato, which is indeed of the essence in performing Chopin's works. Rubato is an art that is indispensable in playing the cantilena in Chopin, an art of which most pianists, unfortunately, are ignorant even today. Not marked with metronomic precision, rubato demands complete freedom of expression within the rhythmically written measure of the composition, and is entirely individual. However, it requires sound musical knowledge and, above all, good taste, for otherwise it can lead to a rhapsodizing quality, which would produce an entirely inappropriate effect.

But, even if Isadora, as might well have been the case with a far more accomplished musician, could not grasp its full significance on the spur of the moment, the question of rubato expression must have sunk deeply into her consciousness. In fact, she must have developed the idea even further, for many years later she told me that the Argentine tango should be danced, not following the rhythm of the music, but against it.

On Fuller-Maitland's advice, apparently, and accompanied by him on the harpsichord at her second and third performances on July 4 and 6, 1900, at the New Gallery, she dispensed with the reading of verse as an accompaniment to her dancing, substituting music for it. She danced three Chopin preludes, the Waltz in C sharp minor, a Mazurka in A minor, Mendelssohn's "Spring Song" and, as an encore, the minuet from Gluck's *Orfeo*.

In addition to these public appearances, Isadora danced in Benson's production of *A Midsummer Night's Dream*, the same part in the fairy scene that she had previously danced in the Daly production. But she never "got any further," as she said, in the Benson Company, and, although with her performances at the New Gallery and through personal introductions by Charles Hallé, she came into contact with "the highest intellectual and artistic personalities of the day in London," the theatrical and concert managers did not show any interest in promoting her art.

With their financial situation only slightly improved, the Duncans passed a pleasanter year than perhaps expected, during which Charles Hallé took Isadora to see Henry Irving and Ellen Terry in their Shakespearean repertory, and the visiting Italian company starring Eleonora Duse. Isadora's unbounded admiration for these personalities, and later her intimate friendship with Terry and Duse, stemmed from those first introductions to their art. But for his part, Raymond was impatient, and in the spring of 1900, he left for Paris.

Victor Seroff

Having quickly acclimatized himself to Paris, which included the traditional acquisition of a *midinette*, a working-class girlfriend, Raymond kept urging Isadora and their mother to join him. With no definite prospects for engagements, Isadora also had become restless, even though she had gained experience and enrichment by her association with the prominent men of the London artistic world. At last, at the close of summer 1900, she and her mother packed their few belongings, and went to Paris—the city that despite frequent travels elsewhere in Europe and several visits to the United States, was to be her home for the rest of her life.

Chapter IV

Their first surprise was the appearance of "my little brother Raymond," as Isadora used to call him, when he met them at the station. Most probably to harmonize with his lodgings in the Latin Quarter, where he was presently to take them, he had grown long hair, curling behind his ears, and was attired in a loose blouse, a flowing tie, and corduroy trousers.

Because none of them knew French, and since Raymond's vocabulary consisted of two words, *chercher* and *atelier*, the latter of which does not necessarily mean an artist's studio, but can be any kind of workshop, they landed at the end of the day in a loft above a printing establishment in the Montparnasse quarter. Only during the night, when the machines of the printing press kept waking them up, did they realize the reason for the extremely low price for their furnished abode. But they had already paid for a month in advance, and so they were to remain there for at least that long. The nightly racket of the machines had one beneficial effect. From five in the morning, Isadora and Raymond set out to explore the city, which enchanted them even more than had London. They found their way to the Louvre, where they subsequently spent their days examining the masterpieces, particularly in the rooms with collections of Greek vases. "But I was especially entranced by the Carpeaux group before the Opéra," Isadora still remembered, when she spoke to me about it many years later.

She became very interested when I told her about the origin of this *Groupe de Danse*. The day after its unveiling, the Parisians were so indignant at the "frivolity" of the subject that they claimed the figures represented exhaustion after a wild bacchanal, and, therefore, the group was not fit to remain among seven other dignified statues in front of the entrance to the Opéra.

They even staged a demonstration, and a woman from the crowd threw an inkwell that splattered the sculpture. After emphatic demands were sent to the mayor of Paris, the statue was to have been removed and would have been had the order not been signed in July 1870—the beginning of the Franco-Prussian War. After the war no one thought of it again. Actually, Isadora said she was not at all surprised at the public outcry, considering the reaction her own early performances had provoked in New York. She was only surprised at the French, whom she regarded as far less puritanical than Americans and far more advanced in their morality.

Later that spring, Charles Hallé came to Paris to see the 1900 *Exposition Universelle* and Raymond, to his grief, lost his companion to Hallé, with whom Isadora wandered all over Paris from early morning to late at night.

Most of all, they were drawn to the Champs de Mars, where like a dream from *A Thousand and One Nights* come true, the Orient rose on what had been a vast barren ground. They examined the white stucco palaces with their marble-floored patios and mosaic fountains, Cambodian temples, and Chinese pagodas surrounded by palm-roofed Tahitian huts and Tunisian bazaars. Often, they lost each other in the teeming crowds of merchants and artisans in their national dress—brocaded saris, tiger skins, loincloths, and kimonos—who were singing, yelling, and dancing to attract the visitors' attention. Isadora and Hallé saw the voodoo priests from Martinique and watched Annamese snake charmers and prancing Arabian thoroughbreds. They explored the streets where natives from distance lands bivouacked, as if at home, and where proud camels and bored elephants barely moved. They spent hours browsing in the Oriental shops and country theaters and listening to the popular musicians, whose free—rubato—renditions of their national music seemed to flow as if inspired.

They found their way to the Javanese village, transplanted from the Indian Ocean to the Esplanade des Invalides right in the heart of

Paris. There the gamelan, a weird orchestra, accompanied the performances of the Bedayas, the native dancers, now swaying in their voluptuous undulations, now emphasizing their stiff, hieratical gestures.

At the Trocadero they saw Mounet-Sully, in the Comédie Française version of *Oedipus Rex*, and they returned over and over again to Loie Fuller's small theater. This extraordinary artist became a favorite of the Parisian audiences at the Folies Bergères, where she performed her unique numbers consisting mostly of swinging-skirt dances illuminated by a special kind of lighting of her own invention. "A luminous vision," and an "extraordinary genius," Isadora used to call her. At the exposition, Loie Fuller introduced to her public Sada Yacco, an actor and dancer who headed the Japanese theatrical group. "Charles Hallé and I," Isadora said, "were thrilled by the wondrous art of this great tragedian."

From all their wanderings through the exposition, Isadora carried away one of the impressions she enjoyed the most. With Hallé, she had seen the masterpieces of Auguste Rodin at the Rodin Pavilion, where the sculptor's works were on display. Later, Isadora met the sixty-year-old sculptor and, although he made a series of pen-and-ink drawings of her, he did not include her in any of his major works.

Before Charles Hallé returned to London, he left Isadora in the care of his nephew Charles Noufflard and his friend Jacques Beaugnies. Meanwhile, the Duncans had twice changed their domicile. From the loft over the printing establishment they moved to a studio on the rue de la Gaieté, and then to a large studio in the Avenue Villiers. With their young friend André Beaunier, Noufflard and Beaugnies became constant admiring visitors at Isadora's studio. And it seems that each one of this trio had his own assignment in "taking care of Isadora." While the more erudite Beaunier took it upon himself to introduce Isadora to the works of Molière, Flaubert, Théophile Gautier, and Maupassant by reading them aloud to her, his two friends took charge of furthering Isadora's career as a dancer. Beaugnies' mother was married to Saint-Marceau, the sculptor, and entertained in her salon in the Boulevard Malesherbes to which, it was said in Paris, no one was admitted unless he was of great personal distinction. And so it was only natural that Charles Noufflard was proud to introduce Isadora, the young American dancer, to Madame Saint-Marceau.

At Madame Saint-Marceau's "Friday evenings," Isadora charmed the select audiences with her dancing to Chopin's preludes and waltzes. *"Quel ravissement! Quel charme! Quel joli enfant!"* exclaimed André Messager, the composer, while accompanying Isadora, or *"Tu es adorable,"* as Victorien Sardou, the famous dramatist, said, kissing her after she had danced for them, with the twenty-six-year-old Maurice Ravel at the piano. These remarks heard and quoted in Paris salons were not empty words, but led to a succession of performances at the homes of the Countess Greffule, and the Prince and Princesse Edmond de Polignac. Among the members of the French haut monde, the Polignacs were known as patrons of the arts. To them more than to anybody else, perhaps, Isadora was indebted for the launching of her career.

Princesse Edmond de Polignac's first meeting with Isadora typified her attitude toward her future protégées. Unannounced, at the end of an afternoon, she introduced herself at Isadora's studio, briefly spoke of the impression Isadora had made upon the prince and herself at one of the "Friday evenings," patiently listened to Isadora's exposition of her theories, invited her to her home, and, after leaving an envelope containing two thousand francs, departed as unobtrusively as she had entered.

In Prince Edmond de Polignac, Isadora found a most sensitive musician, an amateur composer, who hailed her as "a vision and a dream for which he had long been waiting." Isadora danced for him, and they contemplated collaborating in composing dances, a project that to Isadora's disappointment never materialized because of the prince's death.

But while he was still alive, the concert at the Polignac home was particularly successful and pleasing to Isadora because the Princesse made it public and not merely for a select audience, thus providing the occasion for the development of a wider interest in Isadora's dancing. This permitted Isadora to arrange some subscription performances at her own studio, which could accommodate about thirty persons.

"There exists an amusing announcement in her own handwriting for a soirée she planned to give at her studio during these early years.

Dated December 12, 1901, it says: 'Miss Duncan will dance to the sound of harp and flute in her Studio next Thursday Evening and, if you feel that seeing this small person dancing against the waves of an overpowering destiny is of ten francs' benefit to you—why come along!' "*

After dancing at the Duchesse d'Uze's salon, Isadora declared: "When I am rich I shall rebuild the Temple of Paestum and open a college of priestesses, a school of the dance. I shall teach an army of young girls who will renounce as I have done, every other sensation, every other career. The Dance is a religion and should have its worshippers."

At the beginning of Isadora's career, and in fact during many following years, she puzzled not only her audiences but also the professional critics, who felt compelled to enlighten the public in their newspaper and magazine columns with their individual analytical understanding of Isadora's "new" and perhaps even "revolutionary" approach to the dance. In their reviews they emphasized those aspects of Isadora's performances that were most familiar to them. André Levinson, the French author, a great admirer of ballet, wrote about Isadora's performances in 1901:**

> The dance of Isadora Duncan, who finds inspiration for some of her dances in fifteenth century Italian paintings, reveals itself as a mimic art. In the "Angel Playing the Viol," she reproduces the arm movement of the bow. In the "Primavera," a choreographic copy of Botticelli's painting, she simulates the act of sowing flowers with her open hand. In Gretchaninoff's "Berceuse," she pretends to lean over the cradle of a child. In her "Narcissus," wearing a tucked-in white tunic showing an admirable knee, and bending over an imaginary spring, the spectator seems to see her reflection in the clear water. And, when she dips her hand in the water, one actually feels the refreshing contact of the hand with the liquid element.

> The eloquent illusion, the gift of plastic suggestion, is one of her strongest points. As in Goethe's Ballad where water caught in the hollow of her hand by a Hindu girl transforms itself into a crystal ball, so do Isadora's imitative gestures draw from space imaginary objects which she animates with concrete life, more realistic often than real objects. This juggling with the shadows of things, this

---

* "Isadora Duncan—Pioneer in the Art of Dance," by Irma Duncan (published by the New York Public Library), *Dance* magazine, June, 1969.
** *Ibid.*

visual illusion, is the triumph of the great mime. Whenever she uses ferns, or a scarf, or autumn leaves, as in Tchaikovsky's "Romance," she moves away from her original intention, and it becomes an unjustifiable infraction of her pure style as a mime.

Now she was being admired, congratulated, and cheered, and yet her happiness was not complete. She longed to be loved.

From among her three young admirers, at first Isadora chose André Beaunier, who was the least physically attractive. He was fat and short, and had small eyes; one had to be a *"cérébrale"* to realize that those eyes were sparkling with wit and intelligence, according to Isadora. And throughout her life, she insisted on herself as being *"cérébrale,"* especially in the choice of her lovers—although some deviations from the rule might throw doubt on the assertion. It was only to be expected that, after two years of a close *"cérébrale"* association, based on the reading of French literature, and discussions, during their long walks in the country, of books that André was writing, her mind and body should be filled with a desire to crown this Platonic relationship with a more intimate one. But, despite her offering him ample chances to take the final step, he fled from each opportunity, leaving Isadora in anguish—and even in such despair that she turned her interest to Charles Noufflard, whose not too cerebral behavior held a more tangible promise. This time, as if following the program prescribed by most of the French popular novels, after a champagne supper in a *cabinet particulier* in an expensive restaurant, and in the hotel room reserved for *Monsieur et Madame,* her passionate suitor having covered Isadora with kisses and caresses, which left her "trembling but happy," Charles suddenly fell to his knees by the bed, crying that he could not commit a crime, that Isadora must remain pure, and therefore she should dress and be taken home.

According to Isadora, these were two experiences which had a decided effect upon her emotional nature, "thus turning all its force toward [her] Art, which gave [her] the joys that love withheld."

Chapter V

"I spent long days and nights in the studio seeking what might be the divine expression of the human spirit through the medium of the body's movement." And in the following paragraph in her memoirs, Isadora talks of the discovery and the meaning of her dance just as she tried to explain it in so many words to those who asked her about the basic theory of her art:

> For hours I would stand quite still, my two hands folded between my breasts, covering the solar plexus. I was seeking and finally discovered the central spring of all movement, the creator of motor power, the unity from which all diversities of movement are born, the mirror of vision for the creation of the dance—it was from this discovery that was born the theory on which I founded my school.

To explain how her theory differed from that of a regular ballet school, she said:

> The ballet school taught the pupils that this spring was found in the center of the back at the base of the spine. From this axis, says the ballet master, arms, legs and trunk must move freely, giving the result of an articulated puppet. This method produces an artificial mechanical movement not worthy of the soul. I, on the contrary, sought the source of the spiritual expression to flow into the channels of the body, filling it with vibrating light—the centrifugal force reflecting the spirit's vision.
> After many months, when I had learned to concentrate all my force

to this one Centre, I found that thereafter when I listened to music, the rays and vibrations of the music streamed to this one fount of light within me—there they reflected themselves in Spiritual Vision, not the brain's mirror, but the soul's, and from this vision I could express them in dance.

And she used to say to her pupils: "Listen to the music with your soul. Now, while listening, do you not feel an inner self awakening deep within you?" Perhaps this was the best way she could express in words what she actually felt herself. I was often with Isadora when she was listening to music, and she always seemed to resemble a harmonium that was being softly filled with its own music, while the expression of her face mirrored the music that was flowing through her mind and body, which is what she apparently meant by "soul." At those moments, her transfiguration, when listening to the music, was so great that it seemed as if she were completely oblivious to everything else in the world.

She firmly believed that children especially could profit by her advice to "listen to the music with your soul." "From then on, even in walking, and in all their movements, they would possess spiritual power and grace which do not exist in any movements born from the physical frame, or created from the brain." Looking back in her memoirs upon her rich experience in teaching children to dance, she said, "This is the reason why quite small children in my school appearing in the Trocadero or the Metropolitan Opera House before vast audiences have been able to hold those audiences with a magnetism generally possessed only by very great artists." What is beyond doubt is that Isadora herself possessed that power. "The peculiar environment of my childhood and youth had developed this power in me to a very great degree, and in different epochs of my life I have been able to shut out all outside influences and to live in this force alone," she said in this connection. Had it been that simple, the world and the history of art would have had dozens of Isadoras, but there was in her something else that made her unique, something that cannot be taught or transferred to another person. "They think they can do as I do," Isadora often told me when, in later years, for one reason or another, she was vexed with her former pupils, those who had been the closest to her and to whom, if to anyone, she might have been able to "teach" her art. But it was not a question of "doing something," as she was doing it herself.

And, although she would add, "They think they are me!" I doubt that, in her modest way, she was ever ready to use the words "my personality," which she had in the highest degree, and which the others lacked.

Just as the term "genius" is applied to a creator of works that defy explanation, so the qualities that form "personality" are so individual that they cannot be strictly defined. Personality is not confined to artists, politicians, and persons in the public eye generally, but can be encountered in men and women in every walk of life; some possess it in greater measure than others. Isadora was among those who possessed it in the highest degree, and she was utterly unconscious of it. And yet, as soon as she walked into a room her presence was immediately felt—she filled the room, so to speak, and drew attention as the center of a picture does. Thus it was a combination of her "personality" and her inner "force" that made her performances unique.

Despite her frequent performances in Parisian salons, despite the stir she created among the literati and artists in Paris, as she previously had done in London, there was not a single theatrical manager interested in professionally managing her career—with one exception. She was approached by an enterprising theatrical manager from Berlin, who offered her a contract to appear in a music hall in the German capital. Although she indignantly refused his suggestion, he renewed it on several occasions, each time doubling the fee he had last proposed. While Isadora's financial situation was far from comfortable and, in fact, there were no prospects for immediate improvement, Isadora was adamant. "My art is not for a musichall among acrobats and trained animals."

During the last years of her life when, in spite of being worldfamous, she was very nearly destitute, I heard her refuse with the same indignation not only offers from directors of well-known music halls, but also the most lucrative proposals to appear in motion pictures. I was present at an after-dinner conference in the Paris drawing room of William Bradley, her literary agent, when Cecil B. De Mille tried to persuade her to appear in motion pictures. There were several possibilities for acting and dancing in specially written scripts, and finally, backed up by Bradley, De Mille spoke of her "playing herself" when her memoirs would be filmed.

Sipping a glass of champagne, Isadora smiled sweetly at both men, professed great interest in what they were saying, and promised to "think about it."

But after we left the party she said to me, "I would not consent to lower my art by exhibiting it in a musichall when I was a mere beginner, and I certainly will not do it now by appearing in their motion pictures where you are entirely at the mercy of their script writers, director, and producers. I can easily imagine what they would do to me, if they should ever decide to film my memoirs!" When speaking of herself, she was seldom mistaken in her prophecies.

The only interesting offer came, at the end of 1901, from Loie Fuller who, having successfully managed the Japanese actors at the Paris Exposition, thought that she could also include Isadora's performances. She suggested that Isadora join her in Berlin, and Isadora accepted.

Except for enjoying Loie Fuller's own performances, and living in the luxurious hotels provided by her during their stay in Berlin, and later on their tour from Berlin to Vienna via Leipzig and Munich, Isadora could only claim to be learning something "new" about "life." In her memoirs, she tried to describe Loie Fuller's Lesbian entourage as "a dozen or so beautiful young girls grouped about her, alternately stroking her hands and kissing her." "Although my mother certainly loved us all," Isadora continued, "in my simple upbringing, she rarely caressed us, and so I was completely taken aback by coming upon this extreme attitude of expressed affection, which was quite new to me." But when one night in Vienna, one of the members of the Fuller entourage made direct advances to her, Isadora figuratively screamed, "Mama" by telegraphing her mother to come immediately to Vienna.

Besides her dissatisfaction at the unsavory atmosphere of the troupe, Isadora realized that Loie Fuller had sustained financial losses in presenting the Japanese actors to the German public, and that, therefore, she could not expect much help from her in the future—although Fuller did arrange for her a matinee and evening performance at the Hotel Bristol in Vienna. But again, unlike what had happened in London and Paris, such performances could only produce a roster of men and women prominent in society, whose enthusiasm, or adverse criticisms, could merely furnish themes for gossip in their otherwise inconsequential conversations. Nevertheless, it was in Vienna that a decisive step was taken in furthering Isadora's career.

To launch that career, Isadora did not need the wife of the British Ambassador, or the Princess Metternich, "an all-powerful member of Viennese society," or the American Ambassador, who was a member of the McCormick dynasty in Chicago—all of whom she met in Vienna. She simply needed a theatrical manager, a businessman, who, not over-burdened by sentimentality, would see in Isadora a salable product that could earn a profit.

After seeing Isadora dance at the Künstler Haus, an art theater, a man of that description came to see her. What he said was brief and to the point: "When you wish to find a future, call on me."

Alexander Gross was in fact a Hungarian impresario. He offered to present Isadora in Budapest, dancing the whole evening alone on the stage of the Urania Theater. The contract called for thirty such evenings. Isadora was hesitant about accepting because, as she told Gross, she believed that her dancing was more appropriate for an audience of artists and intellectuals than for the general public. But Gross brushed aside her scruples, saying that if artists, the most critical of audiences, liked her dancing, she could be sure that the general public would be even more enthusiastic.

Isadora's debut in April 1902 at the sold-out Budapest theater included improvisations to such native compositions as Strauss's "Blue Danube Waltz" and Liszt's "Rakoczy March." The wild enthusiasm of the Budapest audiences never abated during the following twenty-nine performances.

Chapter VI

Isadora was enchanted with Budapest. She thought it was the most beautiful city she had ever seen. This time she did not rush about the city to examine its museum, monuments, and art galleries, as she had done upon her arrival in Paris and London. Nor did she return to her hotel room disappointed, as in Berlin, because that city did not in the least resemble Athens, which for some reason she had expected, but whose architecture was "purely Germanic, pedantic, an archeological professor's conception of Greece." She was perfectly satisfied to enjoy the original beauty of Budapest, with its luxurious gardens and wide avenues always crowded with men and women dressed in their colorful national costumes. Although she did not understand a single word of Hungarian, she was fascinated by the sound of the language—as she was by Hungarian music. Dining on rich food and the heavy local wines, she listened to the gypsy orchestras; having discovered rubato in their playing, she was ready to announce that "one gypsy playing on a dusty road in Hungary was worth more than all the musicians in the world."

And, if to all these impressions one adds the triumphal success of her performances—such success as she had never dreamed of—and the fact that she had come to Budapest in the spring, when the soft nights were perfumed with blossoming flowers, it can easily be understood that Isadora felt almost delirious with expectation of the love she had longed for. And, indeed, Budapest not only marked the beginning of her career, but was also the place where, at last, she was to have her first love affair.

It was at this place in her memoirs that Isadora felt particularly embarrassed when she tried to satisfy her publishers. Those gentlemen, after receiving some parts of her manuscript, had cabled the following instructions to her: "Enough of your hifalutin ideas send love chapters make it spicy." Isadora showed me this message at the time she received it. The last person on earth to discuss the intimate aspects of other peoples' lives, she certainly was not going to violate her own privacy. This was not a question of her puritan upbringing, nor of her *pudeur*, her sexual shyness. She simply considered it in bad taste.

But, since she was repeatedly told that the success of her memoirs would depend entirely on frank descriptions of her love affairs, and since she was driven to write them by a desperate need for money, she tried to revive in her memory the emotions that had stirred her almost twenty-five years earlier. It was then that she asked me to play for her Liszt's Hungarian rhapsodies—to create, as she said, a Hungarian atmosphere, or perhaps better still, "an aphrodisiac atmosphere," while, reclining on the sofa, she wrote the details of losing her virginity. She was merely pretending, as I was convinced, to give an authentic description, and I remember well its graphic character, for she let me read this chapter page by page. Fortunately, it must have been too spicy even for her publishers, for the chapter was completely rewritten before publication.

She gave fictitious names to some of the men with whom she had intimate relationships, because as she said, it was bad taste to disclose publicly their feelings and behavior, and even worse taste to intrude into their family lives. There are two slightly different versions of her meeting "Romeo," as she called him in her book. According to Oscar Beregi himself, then a talented young actor in the Hungarian National Theater, he was asked to one of the previews of Isadora's performances. After seeing her dance, he went backstage and invited her and her mother to see him play Romeo in Shakespeare's *Romeo and Juliet*. Their friendship and, eventually, their love affair stemmed from that time.

But Isadora's recollections, as given in her memoirs, are far more romantic and glamorous. To prepare the reader for later details, this rewritten version describes Isadora's physical and emo-

tional state: "My breasts, which until now had been hardly perceptible, began to swell softly and astonish me with charming but embarrassing sensations. My hips, which had been like a boy's, took on
another undulation, and through my whole body I felt one great
surging, longing, unmistakable urge, so that I could no longer sleep
at night, but tossed and turned in feverish, painful unrest."

Having thus set the stage for action, so to speak, this version
continues: "One afternoon, at a friendly gathering, over a glass of
golden Tokay, I met two large black eyes that burned and glowed
into mine with such ardent adoration and Hungarian passion that in
that one look was all the meaning of the spring in Budapest. He was
tall, of magnificent proportions, a head covered with luxurious curls,
black, with purple lights in them. . . . From our first look, every
power of attraction we possessed rushed from us in a mad embrace.
From that first gaze, we were already in each other's arms, and no
power on earth could have prevented this."

In the following pages in her memoirs, she described her impression of Beregi as an actor—which was that he was the greatest
actor in Hungary. She also described his passionate courting of her,
and at last she gave a detailed account of losing her virginity. But
she did so within the limits of contemporary literary discretion in
spite of her frankness.

The height of their passion did not last as long as Isadora might
have expected, however. Beregi never doubted that, after they were
married, Isadora's role as his wife would not require from her any
more than watching his performances from an especially reserved
seat of honor in a loge. He even went so far as showing Isadora
several apartments from which to choose their future home. But
that was not at all in the cards for Isadora, for whom, if there was
to be a choice between art and love, art had the preference. And so,
after completing her tour through the smaller cities in Hungary,
and after seeing Oscar Beregi for the last time as Mark Antony on
the stage, she left for Vienna to fulfill her contract with Alexander
Gross. There is no doubt that escaping from the scene of her love
affair helped to relieve her emotions at first. And yet it is also clear
that eventually she suffered so much emotionally and physically
from this separation that she became so ill that Alexander Gross
had to place her in a hospital. She spent several weeks there in utter
prostration, although Beregi came to stay with her right in her room,

where a cot was brought in for him. "He was tender and considerate," Isadora later recalled. In the end, he went back to Budapest and his art, and Gross took Isadora to convalesce in Franzensbad.

Carlsbad, Marienbad, and Franzensbad, situated about 1,200 feet above sea level in northern Bohemia, have been famous health resorts for several centuries. That Gross chose Franzensbad from among these three spas indicates that Isadora was not suffering merely from "love sickness." Franzensbad, with its mineral springs, is reputed to have beneficial effects in the treatment of women's ailments. Except for saying in her memoirs that her "journey from Budapest to Vienna was one of the bitterest and saddest [she] had ever experienced," and that "all joy seemed suddenly to have left the Universe," Isadora never spoke of what had happened to cause her so much suffering. One might conjecture that it was a miscarriage, but there is no documentary evidence for the supposition.

Alexander Gross's wife came to Franzensbad to keep Isadora company, but, despite her long convalescence, Isadora was still "languid and sad, refusing to be interested either in the beautiful country, or the kind friends about her." The fact that by now her discomforts were caused more by her mental rather than her physical state can be assumed from her almost sudden realization that her finances were rapidly being drained by expensive doctors' and nurses' bills, and that she had better fulfill the three performances Gross was only too glad to arrange for her. These were to take place before fashionable audiences in Carlsbad, Marienbad, and Franzensbad, which during the summer months tripled their population with an influx of notables from all over Europe.

At one time Isadora's attitude had been characterized accurately enough by her own exclamation: "Let those judge me who can, but rather blame Nature or God, that He has made this one moment of the act of love to be worth more, and be more desirable, than all else in the Universe that we, who know, can experience." But now, after kissing her dancing dress, which had been reposing in her trunk, she swore never again to desert art for love—a vow that ever after she tried to keep, but in vain.

Her next engagements were to be in Munich, but before these performances, accompanied by her sister Elizabeth, she went to Abazia, a beautiful winter health resort on the Adriatic. This trip is worth mentioning only because Isadora claimed that there she had

"inaugurated a bathing costume which had since become popular—
a light blue tunic of fine crêpe de chine, low necked, with little
shoulder straps, skirt just above the knees, with bare legs and feet,"
thus substituting for the blouse, with its skirt between the knee and
ankle, and stockings and swimming shoes, all in black. She also
claimed to have discovered there the original source of the "light
fluttering of her arms, hands, and fingers," which she later developed
in her dance, in the trembling of the leaves of the palm trees in the
early morning breeze outside her room. In her memoirs, she remarked
that these movements had been abused by her imitators because
"they forgot to go to the original source and contemplate the movements of the palm tree, to receive them inwardly before giving them
outwardly."

In November 1902, Elizabeth and Isadora went to Munich,
where Gross was arranging for her debut at the Künstler Haus. At
that time, Munich was the center of the artistic and intellectual life
of Germany, and Isadora was pleased to see "every young girl carrying a portfolio or music roll under her arm, every shopwindow a
veritable treasury of rare books and old prints, and the streets
crowded with students." Many prominent painters, sculptors, and
authors, as well as professors of philosophy, resided in the city. It
was autumn, the beginning of a new year of studies, and Isadora
was caught up by the students' spirit of learning. Since the original
excitement of her introduction to the literature of London and
Paris, she had felt deprived of just this spirit. She began to study
German, not only because she wanted to read in the original the
works of the German philosophers—Schopenhauer, Kant, and
Nietzsche—but because she wanted to attend and understand the
long discussions held by artists and scholars at the Künstler Haus.
Later, Nietzsche's *Also Sprach Zarathustra* became one of her
favorite books, and to the last days of her life, she kept a copy of it
in an English translation by her bedside. I have the book, with her
own extensive annotations in the margins.

While she was encouraged in her intellectual pursuits by her
newly acquired scholarly friends, the idea of her dancing at the
Künstler Haus did not receive an enthusiastic welcome. It took her
some time to convince her critics that her dancing would not be a
sacrilege to their temple of art. In fact, her debut at the Künstler Haus
was so successful that it launched her triumphs throughout Germany.

Her main audiences were young people, students as serious in their university studies as they were in their drinking in the famous Munich beer halls. And Isadora for the first time experienced their traditional mode of expressing appreciation for a favorite artist. After each performance, they would unhitch the horses from her carriage and pull it through the streets to her hotel, where they would remain below her windows, serenading her until she threw them flowers or other mementos.

Among her enthusiastic spectators was Richard Wagner's son, Siegfried, then in his early thirties. Eventually they met and formed a close friendship. At last Isadora had met in the flesh a direct descendant of the composer whose music she so greatly admired. She said of him that his "conversation was brilliant, with frequent recollections of his great father, which seemed to be always about his person as a sacred halo." On his part, Siegfried was so impressed by Isadora's performances that he immediately suggested that she go to Bayreuth to take part in *Tannhäuser* at the music and drama festival. The invitation, however, had to be sanctioned by Siegfried's mother, since Cosima had the last word in everything concerning Bayreuth. Eventually, after Isadora's success was followed by even greater triumphs at the Berlin Opera House during March 1903, and after the German public had added to Isadora's name such adjectives as *die Göttliche* and *die Heilige* (goddess-like and sacred), thus substantiating her son's impressions, Cosima wrote to Isadora in August 1903 inviting her to visit them at Bayreuth in order to discuss her appearance at the festival during the following season.

By then, Isadora was far away from Germany, and far from any thoughts of taking part in *Tannhäuser* at Bayreuth. After her success in Berlin, she hoped to conquer Paris, where she had arrived in May 1903. But several performances at the Sarah Bernhardt Theater, which, with her earnings from Germany, she could easily afford to hire, brought no favorable reaction from the Parisian public. She heard again the old criticism that her dancing had a "certain plastic charm," and perhaps some "interesting feeling for art," but that it could not be taken seriously, except by the dilettantes, whose opinion did not count.

Disappointed, she returned to Munich where, after the arrival of Augustin and Raymond, the whole family was reunited once again. Isadora was tired. Her performances in Munich and Berlin, although extremely happy events in her career, had left her exhausted since they had come at a time when she still had not regained her health completely. Her failure in Paris again brought on the depression from which she had been suffering. She needed a rest. And what could have been a better idea than to visit Greece, a visit which had been the family's dream even before they had left the United States.

This Greece worship of the Duncans, particularly Isadora and Raymond, has since become legendary. Some of it stemmed from a general American interest in (and version of!) an ancient culture, resulting at that time in many a popular lecture series from many a highbrow podium in which Americans tended to congratulate themselves as direct heirs of Athenian democracy and its attendant arts. Slides and illustrations of the Acropolis were popular in many homes, though what was known of the real ancient Greece was rather limited. Isadora's study of Greek art, in books and museums, and the movements she developed from the paintings on vases, was much more serious, though the Duncans too always had their own imaginative version of what was popularly supposed to be derived from the Greek and also what was genuinely Greek.

Chapter VII

Raymond, the most Greek-minded of the Duncans, was to be at the helm for this expedition, and he devised a route to Athens that would have dumbfounded any ordinary tourist. The journey began in a normal enough way. They were first to pass through Venice, where they were to spend a week or two, long enough to acquaint themselves with the charm and art treasures of this unique city, and then on to the seaport of Brindisi at the heel of the Italian peninsula. There they were to embark on a small steamer, which would bring them to the island of Santa Maura. Raymond's itinerary was based on two principles: their voyage was to resemble that of Ulysses in the *Odyssey*, and be as primitive as possible, avoiding all comforts.

After solemnly paying respect to the spot where Sappho was supposed to have plunged to her death in the waters of the Ionian Sea, they hired a small sailing boat to take them to the village of Karvassaras in Greece. The two Greek fishermen who manned the small vessel, well versed in tempting the treacherous Ionian waters, were more concerned with a threatening storm than with Ulysses' experiences, of which they were ignorant. For their part, the Duncans busied themselves with bringing aboard food supplies for the passage. A large piece of goat cheese, and an ample amount of ripe black olives and dried fish, under the light breeze of the blazing July day, provided an exotic aroma for the travelers, while they were gently rocked by the waves into dreams of ancient Greece. Reaching

Karvassaras at the end of the day, they were greeted by practically the whole population of the village, who were somewhat surprised to see Raymond and Isadora kneel down and kiss the soil in the most reverent manner.

The Duncans spent the night in one room at the only inn in the village—a sleepless one, as Isadora related later, because Raymond talked incessantly about the wisdom of Socrates, and the celestial compensation of Platonic love, and because they could not escape from the bites of the insects, in their first intimate contact with this native fauna. There was no railroad at Karvassaras—traveling by rail would not have been acceptable in Raymond's plans anyway—and they started off on foot, at dawn, toward Agrinion, following their mother in a carriage in which she tried to make herself comfortable among the luggage. They took the route that "Philip of Macedon had tramped with his army over two thousand years before," or so Raymond informed them. They reached Agrinion late at night, exhausted, but in an exhilarated mood; on the following morning they took the stagecoach to Missolonghi to pay tribute to the memory of Lord Byron, who had died there in 1824. They continued their journey by taking a small boat to Patras where, finally, they boarded a train to Athens. Here ended the first part of their odyssey.

"We arrived at violet-crowned Athens in the evening, and the daybreak found us, with trembling limbs and hearts faint with adoration, ascending the steps of her Temple," Isadora recalled later. "As we mounted, it seemed to me that all the life I had known up to that time had fallen away from me as a motley garment; that I had never lived before, that I was born for the first time in that long breath and first gaze of pure beauty. . . . We mounted the last step of the Propylaea and gazed on the Temple shining in the morning light."

And, although they were speechless in their admiration for what they saw, one thought seemed to have communicated itself among the Duncans. "We were all together, my mother and her four children. We decided that the Clan Duncan was quite sufficient unto itself and that other people had only led us astray from our ideals. Also, upon viewing the Parthenon, it seemed to us that we had reached the pinnacle of perfection. We asked ourselves why we should ever leave Greece, since we found in Athens everything which satisfied our aesthetic sense."

And to summarize this mutual feeling, Isadora had added, "The spirit which I sought was the invisible Goddess Athena who still inhabited the ruined Parthenon. Therefore we decided that the Clan Duncan should remain in Athens eternally, and there build a temple that should be characteristic of us."

One thing must be said about the Duncan family—when they were together, they were indeed self-sufficient and they made little effort to seek out other people. Here in Athens, they were entirely preoccupied with their *idée fixe*—to build their own temple—and to find suitable ground they explored Coloros, Phaleron, and the valleys of Attica. Finally, Raymond, "laying his staff upon the ground," announced to them that they were on the perfect spot to build their temple—practically on a level with the Acropolis, and less than two miles east of it. It was a barren hill called Kopanos, which belonged to five peasant families. These owners, as soon as they heard that there was a prospective buyer, called a council at which it was decided that they had always been wrong to consider the ground worthless, when actually it was priceless, and they accordingly set a high figure for the land. But the Duncans were still determined to buy the ground, so at a sumptuous banquet arranged by them, the deal was closed.

Raymond, of course, was to draw up the plans, which were to take as a model the Palace of Agamemnon. As for the material, red stone from Mount Pentelicus was to be brought in carts drawn by donkeys. When the day arrived for laying the cornerstone of their future home, the Duncans insisted on making it a festive occasion, according to old Greek tradition. They invited the peasants from the surrounding neighborhood and engaged a priest to perform the ceremony, presumably "handed down through the Byzantine priests from the time of the Temple of Apollo."

Isadora apparently rose to the occasion, for she did not flinch when the black-hatted priest, attired in black robes with a large silver cross hanging loosely on his chest, decapitated a black cock with one stroke of his sacrificial knife. Moreover, caught up by this barbarous rite, she joined Raymond in a dance in a square, which the priest kept sprinkling with the blood that streamed from the throat of the slaughtered bird.

This, I would think, was the most authentic Greek dance Isadora had ever performed. Then the priest blessed the future inhabitants of the temple in prayer and incantation, thus completing the sacrificial rite, and he left the peasants, who had been arriving in carts with barrels of wine and *ouzo*, to celebrate the occasion around a huge bonfire, by drinking, singing, and dancing throughout the night.

Isadora's participation in the building of the temple was purely financial. However, since to duplicate the two-foot-thick walls of the Palace of Agamemnon required a large quantity of red stone, Isadora came to realize that the cost was seriously draining her bank account in Berlin. But such a prosaic calculation was not to be considered when their ideal of teaching their gospel of the Good, the True, and the Beautiful was about to be realized. Nothing seemed to mar their enthusiasm until suddenly they were dealt a terrible blow. It was discovered that there was no water, neither on the hill nor for miles around. Raymond's courageous attempt to have his workmen dig an artesian well was in vain. There was no water, and their cherished dream had to be abandoned.

Fortunately, their pilgrimage to Greece, which had turned into a romantic adventure, bore more fruit than the mere adoption of the ancient Greek dress—handwoven chitons and sandals—with which they startled the Athenians of the twentieth century on the streets of their city. During the months spent on the building of their temple, Isadora studied ancient Greek art, passing whole days in museums and filling her notebooks with a wealth of new ideas. She had become more and more convinced that the ancient Greeks not only appreciated the beautiful in nature, but that their artists must have constantly observed the beautifully moving human form, for as she said, "of all the thousands of figures of Greek sculptors, bas-reliefs and vases, there it not one but is in exquisite bodily proportion and harmony of movement."

With the rest of the family, Isadora became very much interested in Byzantine music in the Greek church. After examining the ancient manuscripts in the library at the seminary, the Duncans arrived at the conclusion, also held by many distinguished scholars, that "the hymns of Apollo, Aphrodite and all the pagan gods had found their way through transformation into the Greek Church."

This discovery led them to the idea of forming a boys' chorus, which Isadora could use as a background for her performances, and they proceeded to select ten boys in a rather professional way: They engaged a professor of Byzantine music to help them choose boys with the most beautiful voices by means of a competition offering prizes.

They held the competition in the Theater of Dionysus after having received permission from the city authorities.

In a large salon at the Hotel d'Angleterre, where the Duncans were staying, with the help of a young seminarist, Isadora rehearsed her dance, accompanied by the boys, who sang the choruses from Aeschylus' tragedy *The Suppliants*. Later, Isadora gave a public performance at the Municipal Theater, which had such success with the enthusiastic young audience that King George of Greece requested a repeat performance at the smaller Royal Theater. However, although the royal family seemed to be pleased with the spectacle, Isadora felt that the regular ballet would have been more to their taste. In fact, speaking of her first visit to Greece, Isadora often said that, after that performance at the Royal Theater, she spent a sleepless night and at dawn went to the Theater of Dionysus where she danced by herself.

Later, as she stood before the Parthenon, after reviewing in her mind everything that had happened since their arrival in the country, she came to the conclusion that their "dream" was doomed to failure —they could not revive the ancient Greek arts and ways of living. "We could not have the feeling of the ancient Greeks. . . . I was, after all, but a Scotch-Irish-American. Perhaps, through some affinity, nearer allied to the Red Indians than to the Greeks."

In addition to Isadora's disappointment on that score, she now found that her funds were getting very low, and so, taking along with them the ten-boy chorus, and their Byzantine priest-professor, the Duncans tearfully bade good-bye to Athens and to Greece and left by train for Vienna. But the final touch to their romantic journey in search of ancient Greece did not come until six months later. In Vienna, Isadora offered to her public her revival of the Greek tragedy, but her audience remained cool—even after Isadora had delivered a speech, trying to explain in words what she and her supporting boy-chorus had tried to present on the stage. She told them about the "fright of the maidens who gathered around the altar of Zeus, seeking protection from their incestuous cousins coming across the sea," a scene from *The Suppliants*. "Never mind the ancient Greeks and their tragedies. You had better dance *Die Blaue Donau* for us," Isadora heard from the audience, which was usually delirious at her performances because she danced their favorite Blue Danube Waltz.

She fared better in Munich, where the professors at the university discussed Isadora's ideas with their students, but in Berlin her audiences resembled those of Vienna. "Forget the Greeks, let them alone, dance the Blue Danube." Again and again, Isadora made speeches explaining that she was trying her best to convey the feelings of twenty maidens all by herself, but that some day she would have her school and then would return with her dancers to give a truer performance.

Besides having to perform for unresponsive audiences, Isadora was faced with unexpected difficulties with her Greek chorus. It seemed that the boys, far from acting as representatives of ancient Greek culture, were behaving like modern Athenians, demanding in restaurants to be served the food they were used to at home: black bread, ripe olives, and raw onions. When they failed to get satisfaction, they were not above sending schnitzels flying into the waiters' faces, or even attacking them with knives, as was actually reported on one occasion.

After they had been thrown out of several first-class hotels, Isadora decided to keep them under supervision at close range, and she installed them in the drawing room of her own Berlin apartment. Still treating them as children, Isadora and Elizabeth used to take them for their daily walks in the Tiergarten, completely oblivious to the fact that the pious little boys, after they had been put to bed, were climbing out of the windows and going about "Berlin by night," in pursuit of their own pleasures.

Since they were at that stage of adolescence, their voices changed so rapidly that the chorus sounded more off key at each performance and could "no longer be excused on the ground that it was Byzantine." Their master, the Byzantine seminarian, showed a definite loss of interest in ancient Greek art, and appeared vague and distracted as a result of his frequent excursions into the *mondaine* life of the capital.

The situation became a bit "too Greek," even for Isadora, and so the boys were taken to a department store where they were reclad in knickerbockers or long trousers, according to their ages and sizes. On the following day, they were sent back home, not by the route of Ulysses, but in the second-class compartment of the train to Athens.

Chapter VIII

Having brought her "Greek period" to a close in this manner, Isadora returned to her old repertory. But, since she was now without a Greek chorus for a background, she began dreaming of having a school, from which she could choose some pupils to join her as companions in certain dances. In fact, when she danced, in her imagination she already saw such an "orchestra" of dancers—"the white supple forms of [her] companions: sinewy arms, tossing heads, vibrant bodies, swift limbs environing [her] . . ."

She was willing to give performances in Hamburg, Hanover, and Leipzig, but declined all her manager's proposals for a world tour. She felt that she had not completed her studies for the creation of an entirely new form of dance. This feeling stemmed from the discussions on art and the dance Isadora was having with many artists and writers, who gathered at her weekly receptions.

In Berlin she rented an apartment in Charlottenburg and spent her free time in deep thought and study. With disarming sincerity she told the German people: "I come to Berlin to learn—I come as an eager and thirsty Pilgrim to drink the great fountainhead of German knowledge and science—I come as a wistful weakling to be made strong—by contact with men and women who have been cradled in the birthplace of such giants as von Humboldt, Goethe and Kant—I come as a western barbarian—to the home of Winckleman, Schlegel, and Ernst Haeckel . . . my entire consciousness is trembling . . . before these great shrines . . . . At present you should leave me in my library—with the help of my big German dictionary, I am just learning the verb—to know."

Although she had never mastered the German language, she was so passionately interested in Nietzsche's works that, as she had done in Munich prior to her visit to Greece, she found a young writer, Karl Federn, who spent hours explaining to her words and phrases in *Also Sprach Zarathustra*. On her own, she even ventured into Kant's *Critique of Pure Reason*, but later she herself was puzzled that she had sought inspiration "for the movement of pure beauty" in this work.

Whether or not she was actually capable of understanding, digesting, and using these newly discovered ideas, this was the period in her life in which she rededicated herself to the passionate study of German philosophic works, as well as German literature, which she had begun two years earlier in Munich. She acquired a large collection of these works as permanent additions to her library. It represented a staggering list of authors for the library of a beautiful young woman in her early twenties, who was a dancer. Having in my possession a part of her library, I can attest to the thoroughness of her studies on the evidence of the volumes annotated in her own hand.

At this time, she received a visit from Cosima Wagner, who again asked her to participate in the Bayreuth Festival. The invitation was timely, moreover, since under the influence of her readings, she was ready as never before to interpret Wagner's music. Frau Wagner had requested that she take part in the Bacchanale in *Tannhäuser*. It meant an absurd combination of Isadora's dance with that of the regular ballet, "whose every movement shocked [her] sense of beauty, and whose expression seemed to [her] mechanical and vulgar." When, many years later, I asked her why she had compromised and accepted Cosima Wagner's engagement, she told me that it was very simple— she was young, passionately involved in her studies, and eager to meet the great musicians, artists, and scholars who congregated in Bayreuth. But to Frau Wagner she had said; "I will come and I will try to give at least an indication of the lovely, soft, voluptuous movements, which I already see for the 'Three Graces.' "

And so in May 1904 she arrived in Bayreuth, accompanied by Mary Sturges, whom she had met in Paris in 1901. Many years later, through Isadora, I met Mrs. Sturges and learned to know her quite well. Originally from Chicago, by the time we met she had already disposed of four husbands, including one Turk—she never missed the occasion to place special emphasis on the Turk—and was called Mary Desti. Under this name, two years after Isadora's death, she was moved to publish *The Untold Story: The Life of Isadora Duncan, 1921–1927*, which unfortunately gave a better portrait of the author than of her heroine.

She was about Isadora's age, a robust woman with a liberal amount of unspent energy, bringing with her wherever she went more noise and disorder than harmony and peace. In her approach to life, she thought everything "terribly funny," except, perhaps, for one thing—she seriously believed that she was Isadora. This could be seen in the aplomb with which she intruded into serious discussions on art, music, and literature, of which she was utterly ignorant, and from the arrogance and extravagance of her behavior in general; such conduct, she thought, was being like Isadora, but indeed it surprised and shocked Isadora. While her intentions were sincere, their being carried out usually meant trouble and confusion. Nevertheless, although occasionally in desperation Isadora had to cut Mary down to her proper size, they always remained good friends.

Since, when she had first met Isadora, Mary claimed to have come to Paris to cultivate her "extraordinary voice," she felt entitled to be among the prominent performers and visitors in Bayreuth, and behaved as if it were one big, gay party where, as she liked to say, royalty and commoners called one another by their first names, She dressed herself in a replica of Isadora's loosely flowing Grecian garments, with white cape and gold sandals, and for the time being seemed content to be merely Isadora's twin.

There are several passages in her book in which she glories in this effect. The first one was fathered upon Cosima Wagner. When Isadora and Mary called on her in Bayreuth, she said, according to Mary, "I thought you were one, but you are two."

Later, during one of the rehearsals, somehow Mary managed to get on the stage and, she reported, "danced Isadora's part in the 'Three Graces' with the two young German ballet dancers, when Frau Wagner who with Isadora was watching from the hall most enthusiastically remarked so all could hear her, "*Wie schön*, but how she resembles you, Isadora." Mary Desti then continues in her book:

"Isadora flew on the stage, shaking me by the two shoulders; 'Don't ever do it again,' she cried. 'Never, never.' I was so astonished I could scarcely breathe. All the way home she kept repeating. 'It's awful, even the very expression of my eyes. No, I will never teach anyone again. They only succeed in making an imitation of me.' That ended my dancing, and it also ended my stage career. The next day all was forgotten." Mary Desti added, when concluding her recital of the incident, "I asked Isadora a few days before her death whether she remembered the scene, and she said she didn't remember it at all." Isadora was always too kind to Mary.

In Bayreuth, Isadora at first stayed at the hotel Der Schwarzer Adler (the Black Eagle), but as the opening festival was approaching and the hotel was getting crowded, Cosima Wagner, at Isadora's request, assigned Christian Ebersberger, the young major domo of the Villa Wahnfried, the Wagners' own home, to help Isadora find more pleasant living quarters.

Eventually, after spending days in looking for a suitable place, Isadora came upon an old stone house in the garden of the Hermitage, which had been built for Ludwig II of Bavaria, Richard Wagner's friend and patron. To take possession of Phillip's Ruhe, the old hunting lodge, Isadora had to pay a large sum to the peasant tenants and, since it was in a dilapidated state, it had to be completely renovated. This was expertly done upon Ebersberger's instructions in accordance with Isadora's taste, while Isadora "flew," as she said, back to Berlin to order the furniture.

In her memoirs, Isadora said that she was alone in Bayreuth, but she was so only in her intimate contact with Wagner's music. In addition to Mary, who stayed with her in Phillip's Ruhe, were her mother, Isadora's niece, Temple (Augustin's daughter), Mary's four-year-old son, Preston (later famed as a Hollywood director and writer, Preston Sturges), and Oscar Beregi, who had come from Budapest—all living at the Hermitage Gardens not far away from Phillip's Ruhe. Mary managed a series of elaborate parties for the royalty and notables attending the festival. Always a provincial woman at heart, Mary collected as many titled men and women as she could to satisfy her ego, while Isadora much preferred to be impressed by men such as the famous conductors, Hans Richter and Karl Muck, Humperdinck, the composer of the charming children's opera *Hänsel und Gretel*, and Heinrich Thode, the art historian, who were constant guests at Frau Wagner's lunches and dinners, to which Isadora was always invited.

Heinrich Thode fell in love with Isadora. But he was married to Cosima Wagner's daughter, and, while remaining physically faithful to his wife, he carried on a cerebral love affair with Isadora. Each night he would come to the lodge to recite poetry, or chapters from the manuscript of *The Life of Saint Francis*, which he was writing at the time. Or he would come in the evening and read to her the *Divine Comedy* until daybreak. These intellectual sessions inevitably led to a closer contact. Although Thode stammered, "*Ja ja, du bist mein Traum, Du bist meine Santa Clara,*" caressing and kissing Isadora, his kisses and caresses were not inspired by an earthly passion, and they left Isadora utterly frustrated. She was not very successful in trying to explain her feelings. On the one hand she said: "Always that luminous gaze, until, looking into his eyes, all faded around me and my spirit took wings on those astral flights with him. Nor did I wish for an earthly expression from him. My senses, which had slept for two years, were completely transformed into an ethereal ecstasy." And yet further on in the same passage of her book, as she continued to analyze the emotions evoked by Thode, she seems almost to contradict her first statement. "He never caressed me as a lover, never tried even to undo my tunic, or touch my breasts or my body in any way, although he knew that every pulse of it belonged only to him. Emotions I had not known to exist awoke under the gaze of his eyes. Sensations so ecstatic and terrible that I often felt the pleasure was killing me, and fainted away, to awaken again to the light of those wonderful eyes. He so completely possessed my soul that it seemed it was only possible to gaze into his eyes and long for death. For there was not, as in earthly love, any satisfaction or rest, but always this delirious thirst for a point that I required."

This was a problem which could have been solved by Oscar Beregi, who was staying at the hotel within walking distance and who could never have been accused of coming to Bayreuth solely to attend the festival. And yet Isadora does not mention his presence in Bayreuth at this time.

Far less sensual was her relationship with Professor Ernst H. Haeckel, the famous German biologist. While Isadora was in London, she had read in an English translation some of his works, including *The Riddle of the Universe,* and so, when in February 1904 the

Berlin press noted Haeckel's seventieth birthday, Isadora congratulated him in a letter. She wrote, "Your works had brought me also
religion and understanding, which count for more than life." And
she closed her short note flamboyantly with, "Greetings and all my
love. Isadora Duncan."

Haeckel replied, thus starting a correspondence with his young
admirer. Very much touched by the warmth of his letter, Isadora
asked him for his photograph and his books. These he sent her from
Jena, where he was the director of the Zoological Institute, and so
on July 6, 1904, Isadora wrote to him from Bayreuth: "Dear Master,
your dear letter, as well as your beautiful photograph gave me great
pleasure. I am sending you a photograph of myself sitting at my
writing desk in Phillip's Ruhe with your picture in my hand and all
your works before me on the table. When I come to Jena, I am not
coming to dance, only for you. . . . Perhaps you will come to the
Festspiele? If you do, you are always welcome at Phillip's Ruhe. In
any case, I must see you this summer. . . ."

A month later, Haeckel arrived in Bayreuth for a visit. Isadora
proudly announced to Frau Wagner the presence of her distinguished
guest, only to find a cool response from the old lady, who was a
devout Catholic. It never occurred to Isadora that Haeckel, whom
she admired as "the greatest iconoclast since Charles Darwin," would
be denied an invitation to Villa Wahnfried, and that Frau Wagner
would reserve a place for Haeckel in the Wagner family loge for
the performance of *Parsifal* only because she could not do otherwise,
on account of her friendship with Isadora. With heroic stoicism
Haeckel sat through the six-hour performance, which Isadora tried to
excuse by saying that "the mystic passion did not appeal to him—
his mind was too purely scientific to admit the fascination of a
legend." And because of Frau Wagner's inhospitable attitude toward
Haeckel, which no doubt did not bother the old scientist in the least,
Isadora gave a dinner party in his honor to which she invited many
prominent men then in Bayreuth.

After more than a month of rehearsals, Isadora finally made
her appearance as the leading Grace in the *Tannhäuser* Bacchanale.
Her performance received the press and audience reaction that
Isadora had anticipated. The general comment was that she danced
"delightfully," but that her dancing was badly framed by the regular
ballet dancers, thus making it an unpleasing spectacle. And yet there

were some critics with more daring views, who thought that Isadora's performance was an indication of what would be the future character of the Bacchanale.

When the festival closed at the end of August, Bayreuth suddenly became deserted. Isadora arranged for a tour in Germany, and for a short vacation in which she would be joined by Mary and her son, and Temple; she also invited Beregi to go to Heligoland. But their visit there was more of an excursion, because the raging storms sweeping over the small island off Heligoland, where they had hoped to vacation, frightened them and they returned to Bayreuth.

Beregi went back to Budapest, but this time Isadora did not shed as many tears as she had two years before, on leaving Hungary. It was the last time she ever saw Beregi.

Mary was going back to the United States, and Isadora insisted on first showing her the beauties of Italy. They went to Florence and then to Venice, where later Mary's husband came to fetch his wife and son. The Sturgeses boarded a train for Paris, and Isadora took a train back to Berlin.

Thus ended the Bayreuth chapter in her life, her first and last appearance on the stage as part of a regular ballet. Henceforth she was to dance alone on the stage, or if she had to have an ensemble for the sake of interpreting the music she chose, then she must create her own school from which she would select a group of dancers worthy of accompanying her. These were her thoughts as the train raced the restless Isadora back to Berlin.

PART TWO

Chapter IX

To understand Isadora's restlessness, it would be sufficient to read the short paragraphs in her memoirs in which she refers to her emotional state at that time. One does not doubt the sincerity of her analysis and her conclusions with regard to her feelings since her love affair with Oscar Beregi. It is quite clear that, through the initial, although physically painful, introduction to lovemaking, she had at last learned, as she said, "what heaven was on earth," but that, much too soon afterward, she had suffered mentally from the separation from her lover, and physically, as we have seen, from the consequences of her affair. It is also quite believable that, during the following two years, she was actually convinced that her experience in Budapest had caused such a revolution in her emotional reactions that she was convinced that she had "finished with that phase, and in the future would only give herself to Art."

In fact, she claimed that, while she was in Vienna, she did not even think of Beregi, who was in Budapest only a short distance away, and did not hold against him his not joining her in Vienna. She was happily preoccupied with her art and did not expect her relationships with men to be anything more than friendly. But, while her friendship with Herman Bahr, the young art critic of the Vienna *Neue Presse*, the leading newspaper, was purely platonic, her romance with Heinrich Thode drove her to a quite natural despair.

She was irresistibly drawn to Thode. In Heidelberg, her first stop on her tour through Germany, she heard him lecture on art, and on that occasion he spoke of Isadora's introducing a new esthetic form. Frau Thode gave a reception in Isadora's honor. Isadora thought, of course, that Frau Thode was not worthy of her husband, that she was "quite incapable of the high exaltation in which Heinrich lived. She was too thoroughly practical to be a soul-mate for him." But Isadora had to admit that she was a "kindly woman," certainly kind enough to overlook her husband's behavior in Bayreuth, and its continuation in Heidelberg.

But now the long nights spent with Heinrich Thode, and his abnormal treatment of a thoroughly normal woman, began to affect Isadora both physically and mentally. She lost her appetite, and "was attacked by a queer faintness which gave her dancing a more and more vaporous quality." What was far more serious, while she was on tour she began hearing his voice calling her at night, and constantly saw his eyes in front of her. In anguish, she would leave her bed and rush by train, "traveling over half Germany only to be near him for an hour, and to return again alone on [her] tour to even greater torments."

In her memoirs, Isadora mentioned her fears that her readers would doubt the truthfulness of her descriptions of her platonic love affairs. But while there is no question of the honesty of her confessions about her emotional state, Heinrich Thode's behavior remains puzzling. Unless he felt that by not consummating his love for Isadora he was being faithful to his wife, or unless he was suffering from some incapacitating illness, his treatment of the young woman who passionately desired him was cruel to the point of sadism.

Fortunately, Isadora received an engagement to give performances in Russia. It had a sobering effect upon her, just as the plans for her school demanded that she keep her mind on practical issues. She had to find a suitable home for her future pupils, and had to furnish and completely equip it to house them. She was devoting as much time and energy to these tasks as she could, while still fulfilling her final engagements in Berlin, when shortly before Christmas of 1904, an event of major importance occurred in her life.

However, before going into what is thus far the most important event in her life, I must say something about her memoirs that has been apparent to me ever since *My Life* was published in 1927.

Despite the assurances of those who say they know better, I am fully convinced that her manuscript was not only freely edited, but that some passages were completely rewritten. Because of her death, Isadora never saw the galleys, nor had she had a chance to go over the manuscript, correcting, adding or deleting, prior to its publication. Thus many errors, especially in dates, remained uncorrected, and at this particular moment in her life story, three chapters in *My Life* are not in proper chronological sequence.

The major event—her meeting Gordon Craig, the famous English stage designer—did not take place in 1905, but in 1904. She met him before she went to fulfill her engagement in Russia, and not after she returned. And some of her stories about her life in Russia do not belong to her first visit there in 1905, but to her second in 1908.

Gordon Craig was a stage designer and director already famed for his revolutionary productions. He was a strong advocate of a greater use of movement, color, and a freer use of the designer's imagination. He was a great theatrical pioneer and his influence has been enormous. Isadora was twenty-six, Craig was thirty-two years old, but he looked very much younger. Unaware of that fact, however, when someone spoke of a "young man," Craig himself turned around to see who was the young man in the room. Isadora described him as tall and willowy, with a face recalling that of his mother Ellen Terry: "his eyes, very near-sighted, flashing a steely fire behind his glasses."

There are three different versions of Isadora's meeting Gordon Craig: her own, as given in her memoirs; Gordon Craig's, as included in his *Index to the Story of My Days*, published in 1957; and in *Gordon Craig, The Story of His Life*, written by his son Edward and published in 1968.

According to Isadora's memoirs, at one of her performances she noticed a man in the audience. After the performance, he came into her dressing room. "You are marvelous," were supposed to have been his first words to Isadora. "You are wonderful! But why have you stolen my ideas? Where did you get my scenery?" Then, after Isadora had learned who he was, she and her mother took him to supper at their home.

This description differs from that given by Gordon Craig in his book. Under the date of December 1904, Berlin, he wrote, "I

had heard there was a sort of governess who had taken to dancing in
an artistic manner—at whom some people laughed, while others
crowded in thousands to see her dance—the name Isadora Duncan.
It was chiefly in Weimar that the laughter was to be heard." Then
he explained that, at that time, Weimar was a cultural center in Germany, ". . . and as I went to Weimar *before* seeing her dance and
before speaking with her, the notion of a heavy-footed American
who pranced was conveyed to me.

"Nothing screamingly funny about a governess from America
taking off her boots (she wore none) or sandals (she had some)
and dancing nicely on her bare feet . . . but here came the trouble,
here was the true reason for the laughter. She didn't dance nicely—
she danced 'artistically,' said the Weimar group, who were critical
of Isadora's dancing. But Munich, Berlin, Dresden and Vienna added,
'with genius.' "

About his meeting Isadora, Craig wrote: "Some of you will
have read a book on this lady, in which it is stated that the first time
I saw her dance I was bereft of the artist's heart, which all artists
possess and which, when it is touched by beauty in anything, is
greatly moved. It prompts us all to silence, to be reverent. Now that
book states that, after seeing this lady dance, I went to speak with
her in her rooms. I did. No one else was there, and I went in and
found her lying down tired after her dancing, and I sat facing her.
I did not say a word. I looked at her. We shared in this silence. And
some fool in a book asks the world to believe that I grew angry and
said all sorts of stupid, rude things to her. No one being present but
we two, the writer of that paragraph tries to assert that Isadora
herself wrote it. That can only be a lie. She died before that book
came out: had she seen that lie, how she would have grieved." Apparently, Gordon Craig felt as I do about the rewritten parts of
Isadora's manuscript.

But the most authentic account of this first meeting is given by
Edward Craig, who had access to his father's notes, which were
apparently not consulted by Craig himself when he was writing
his own account of his meeting Isadora.

It actually happened on December 14, 1904. During a lunch
with his friend Elise de Brouckers (in *My Life* spelled Elsie de
Brugaire), Craig talked so much about "his forthcoming exhibition,
and his school where 'Movement' would be one of the main courses

of study," that Miss de Brouckers asked him whether he had seen Isadora Duncan dance, and then suggested taking him immediately to the Duncans, who lived not far away. They arrived there as a certain Mrs. Madison was playing a piece by Gabriel Fauré, and Craig took a place behind the piano next to Isadora. "We became friends and lovers from the moment we stood there at the piano," he wrote in his notebook.

He was the son of Ellen Terry, though it was hardly for this reason alone that he interested Isadora but rather because of his work, of which he spoke to her—as he did to everyone—stimulating her in fact to visit, the very next day, his exhibition of sketches and drawings for the stage at Friedmann and Weber's gallery. Again he talked to her about his ideas of "movement," as he pointed to his various designs—"static pictures," which were conceived in motion, "the movement of light—color—form." It sounded familiar to Isadora, and, as if to show him how well she understood his ideas, she invited him to her next performance.

Describing his first impressions of her dance, Gordon Craig wrote:

I shall never forget the first time I saw her come on to an empty platform to dance. It was in Berlin—the year 1904, the month December. Not on the theatre stage was this performance given, but in a concert-hall, and you may know what the platforms of concert-halls were like in 1904.

She came through some small curtains which were not much taller than she herself—she came through them and walked down to where a musician, his back turned to us, was seated at a grand piano—he had just finished playing a short prelude by Chopin when in she came, and in some five or six steps was standing by the piano, quite still and, as it were, listening to the hum of the last notes . . . quite still—you might have counted five or even eight, and then there sounded the voice of Chopin again in a second prelude or étude—it was played through gently and came to an end and she had not moved at all. Then one step back or sideways, and the music began again as she went moving on before or after it. Only just moving—not pirouetting or doing any of those things which we expect to see, and which a Taglioni, or a Fanny Elssler, would have certainly done. She was speaking in her own language, not echoing any ballet master, and so she came to move as no one had ever seen anyone move before.

((75))

The dance ended, she again stood quite still. No bowing, no smiling —nothing at all. Then again the music is off, and she runs from it— it runs after her then, for she has gone ahead of it.

How is it that we know she is speaking her own language? We know it, for we see her head, her hands, gently active, as are her feet, her whole person.

And if she is speaking, what is it she is saying? No one would ever be able to report truly, yet no one present had a moment's doubt. Only this can we say—that she was telling to the air the very things we longed to hear and till she came we had never dreamed we should hear; and now we heard them, and this sent us all into an unusual state of joy, and I—I sat still and was speechless.

I remember that when it was over I went rapidly round to her dressing-room to see her—and there too I sat still and speechless in front of her for a while. She understood my silence very well—all talk being unnecessary. No one else came to see her. Far, far off we heard applause going on. . . .

What happened after their first meeting has also been recounted in different versions. In Isadora's memoirs, after the supper with the Duncans at their flat, where he is supposed to have gone with Isadora and her mother, he talked incessantly about his ideas on art and the theater. When left alone with Isadora, "suddenly in the midst of all this, he said: 'But what are you doing here? You, the great artist, living in the midst of this family? Why, it's absurd! I was the one who saw and invented you. You belong to my scenery.' "

Needless to say, nothing of the kind ever happened, and all those purported quotations only show that the person who freely rewrote those pages did not know Gordon Craig.

The passage goes on: "I, [Isadora,] like one hypnotized, allowed him to put my cape over my little white tunic. He took my hand, we flew down the stairs to the street. Then he hailed a taxi and said, in his best German, '*Meine Frau und mich, wir wollen nach Potsdam gehen.*' Several taxis refused us, but finally we found one, and off we went to Potsdam."

Gordon Craig himself offered two versions of this escapade, and apologized for forgetting the details. According to one of the versions, after they had sat silently in her dressing room, Isadora put on her cloak and shoes and they went down to the street, "where the snow looked friendly and the shops still lighted up, the Christmas trees all spangled and lighted—and we walked and talked of the shops. The shops—the Christmas trees—the crowd—no one heeded us." But he also wrote a more fanciful account of that trip to Potsdam:

She and I met in December 1904—in Berlin. She took quite a liking to me, and I thought she wasn't such a bad sort of governess after all. She was dancing in the city, but I hadn't seen her dance yet. She didn't impress me as anything especially learned: a governess generally says "Hic, haec, hoc" before half an hour has gone by, but Isadora said none of these things. So I took it that Weimar was just a bit stupid, and I asked Isadora how she did.

She said "I'm all right—how are you?" "I'm fine," I said. She then asserted that I was her *lieber Mann*—her dear husband. She began singing this to all and sundry—the room was full of the sundry. She then called for her coach, like poor Ophelia, and said to me, "Hi! you come along—you, *mein lieber Mann*." And down we went, down the spacious staircase leading to the vast hall which conducted to the street.

A coach awaited us. We got in: and after saying "To Potsdam," we leant back in the spacious coach and began to sing. We were not drunk; we had not touched wine or any stuff out of bottles—we were, I grieve to say, only happy.

If I do not make a great mistake, the happiness of Genius is an intense and awful delusion, born of the imagination. Both this girl and I were held to possess genius and we agreed we would not be party to any silly delusion like that—"no, no—*nothing serious*—look at all the serious faces!"

We were galloping past hundreds of them, all really serious people —grave, grieved, some tied hand and foot, others clothed in gloomy dark raiment. "*Schnell—schnell nach Potsdam*," and she began to sing an ancient German ballad which begins '*Hochzeit machen, dass ist wunderschön*'; and she translated the strange song to me, for at that time I knew but a few words. In American the voice spoke . . . "*es war ein Traum*" (Heine has something rather like this, ending also in "*Es war ein Traum*"; scholars can look it up if they want to).

So this governess and I were off to Potsdam—and almost got there, too. We started late and said to the coachman "Don't hurry," and so it was quite early as we neared the Palace where Voltaire and Frederick had talked. But Frederick and Voltaire never talked as much as we did, we talked sort of three-ply, if you can guess what I mean. We said a lot of words and looked a thousand more. When we looked at a big tree which passed us, we knew its whole history and told it to each other. When one of the horses neighed, we cried, "Let him neigh again!" The horses were but two when we started, yet there were four when we got to the lake which is beyond Grünewald, and six by the time we had gone three times round the lake. Once we stopped the flight of these graceful animals and got out and walked—and then the chariot and the six horses vanished. They had certainly gone; nothing but a breeze blowing through the fir trees could be heard—and a night-owl came around and was not afraid. There came, too, a couple of field mice, and we sat on a bank . . . no, that was six months later. We were in our carriage again when the owl and the field mice came around. It is said they don't get on well together, these creatures, but they seemed to get on well that night. A second owl came along, stayed with us all the way to Potsdam and back to the Grünewald.

The journey to Potsdam took quite a time—about forty-eight hours, and most of the hours were dark. We began to count the hours after twelve had struck. Every hour, it seems, counted in Germany differently from hours in Holland or the Azores. In Prussia in 1904 an hour had 700 minutes if it was a *good hour*. By five o'clock in the morning, the horses were hungry for their breakfast; so we stopped a mile or three from Potsdam and went into a roadside inn and there had some coffee and cake, and the horses had their meal; and after a few words about the weather and the distance to Charlottenburg, we got into the coach and a fresh relay of steeds galloped us back to town.

All these details maybe dazzle you. Yes? But I forget some. There was the cake of Swiss chocolate we bought at the inn. It was never eaten—and its remains were found in two boxes, one in Nice and one in Florence, some time around 1920.

This poetic description demonstrates chiefly that Craig's memories were still dear to him after more than fifty years had passed since Isadora and he took that journey to Potsdam. The actual trip was not that romantic. According to Edward Craig, who understood his father's character very well and who based his information on Craig's notes, Gordon Craig's immediate reaction, after seeing Isadora dance, was of "overwhelming admiration and furious resentment—admiration for what had been to him the greatest artistic experience in his life, resentment that this revelation should come from a woman. Unknown to him, she had been traveling the same path as himself, and it was her unique genius that made it possible for her to show him something about abstract movement, which he was still struggling to understand."

Disturbed by this revelation, Craig went again to see Isadora dance, and later, after the performance, he called at the Duncans' apartment. As usual, there were many guests, but Isadora and Craig wanted to be alone, "somewhere away from the family." They managed to escape Augustin's watchful eye and join two guests who were leaving the party. Dr. Karl Federn always had long discussions of Nietzsche's works with Isadora, and had translated into German a little book on the *Future of Dance* Isadora had recently written. He owned a car, and he and his sister were easily persuaded by Isadora and Craig to drive all four of them to Potsdam. As we have seen, in Isadora's imaginative reconstruction, the car turned into a taxi, and in Craig's description into a carriage drawn by two, four, and six horses, although in his original notes he referred only to Dr. Federn's car.

They returned to Berlin next morning and Isadora did not dare face her family. Both she and Craig thought it would be wise to find out first what sort of reception was awaiting Isadora at home. They chose Elise de Brouckers as their emissary. The news she brought back to them made Isadora prefer to remain at Elsie's until her family's wrath had subsided.

On the following day, however, Isadora went to Craig's studio for tea, a call that lasted longer than such visits usually do. Craig's establishment was a traditional artist's studio with a high ceiling, a skylight, and a little alcove balcony reached by a flight of stairs. Since Craig did not live there, but in a room down the street, he had never bothered to install a stove, or to put a bed in the alcove. The next day Isadora had to return home because a reception was to be held at the Duncans' apartment.

After the reception, Isadora disappeared again to Craig's studio, this time for so long—two weeks, according to the account given in her memoirs—that the family notified the police, and her manager had to inform the press about Isadora's "illness," as well as cancel a number of scheduled performances.

Their honeymoon arrangements lacked the most essential comforts, their nuptial bed was made from two old rugs and Isadora's fur coat, and instead of champagne dinners with lobster and filet mignon, they were lucky to be able to get food from a nearby delicatessen, paid for by the generous porter of the house where Craig had his room. "From their first moment of meeting Craig has recorded all that they said and did in one of his secret little books of confessions," Edward Craig wrote about his father. "He even remembered telling her that he was expecting to marry in a few months' time—she said she did not believe in marriage."

In his notebook Craig wrote: "She tells me about her life and whom she has loved before—then laughs, and laughs, and laughs . . .

"Do I love her?

"Does she love me?

"I do not know or want to know."

Both of them needed time to analyze their feelings and to answer these questions adequately. Two months later, Craig tried to confess his answer, but he did more arguing with himself than coming to a definite conclusion. He insisted that he loved only Elena Meo, a violinist, whom he was going to marry, and yet he admitted to the irresistible attraction Isadora held for him—Isadora, "who may be a witch or a pretty child (and it really doesn't matter which)." He said that he was either delighted or bored with her, but his pro and con impressions were simply professional jealousy. He resented both Isadora's talking "about herself incessantly for a quarter of an hour," and her appreciative listeners; he wanted to be in her place, talking incessantly about himself and his art. He says further that he hated to admit that he had a feeling of contempt for her, because he found her "so dear and delightful." And though he told her and himself that he did love her, he tried to explain the meaning of the word "love," in his own philosophical way. "Love regards no other thing or person except through the eyes of the loved one. . . . Love which torments is not love. Love is all which is dear and beautiful, without fluster or excitement, without excess of laughter or tears, something at ease and gravely sweet—And where love is there is no room for any other thing."

Since Isadora never kept a diary, nor wrote confessions in notebooks or in letters to friends, one has to accept her analysis of her feelings toward Craig and their relationship as written in retrospect in her memoirs a little over twenty years later. From many conversations with her about Gordon Craig, I have the very strong impression that despite their old habit of continually subjecting their feelings to analysis, and although she clearly saw his failings, she admired, respected, and loved him more than any other man in her life. Twenty-odd years later, she still spoke about him with the same enthusiasm as if their affair had happened only yesterday: "His love was young, fresh and strong, and he had neither the nerves nor nature of a voluptuary, but preferred to turn from love-making before satiety set in, and to translate the fiery energy of his youth to the magic of his Art." Isadora said in her reminiscences: "Craig was a brilliant companion. He was one of the few people I have ever met who was in a state of exaltation from morning till night. Even with the first cup of coffee, his imagination caught fire and was sparkling. An ordinary walk through the streets with him was like a promenade in Thebes of Ancient Egypt with a superior High Priest."

Had these two strong-willed personalities not been possessed by identical ideas of their own respective art, their union would not have suffered from stormy arguments. Isadora was well aware that Craig appreciated her art as "no one else has ever appreciated it," and yet, when trying to explain their incompatibility, she was supposed to have quoted him as saying, during one of their verbal skirmishes about the singular significance of their discovery in art, "Why don't you stop this? Why do you want to go on the stage and wave your arms about? Why don't you stay at home and sharpen my lead pencils?"

Neither this representation of his attitude nor the words attributed to him were authentic, but merely showed the influence of some women in her entourage at that time, who hated men, upon what Isadora wrote in her memoirs. Nor was Craig ever so rude as to shout at her: "All women are damned nuisances, and you are a damned nuisance, interfering with my work. My work! My work!" At the time Isadora was writing her book, "My work! My work!" was constantly used by the women I have mentioned, who claimed that their attempts to contribute to art had been thwarted by the rude interference of a male who would not admit that a woman can be an artist. Nothing had been further from Craig's mind. To begin with, Craig loved women—his life proved it—though he *was* prejudiced against women in his own branch of Art. "Women," he said, "ruin the theatre. They take a bad advantage of the power and influence they exercise over men. They use these evilly and bring intrigues, favoritism, and flirtation into the realm of art."

Isadora did better when, in a less emotional and fanciful statement, she explained their difficulties in this way: "It was my fate to inspire the great love of this genius, and it was my fate to endeavor to reconcile the continuing of my career with his love. Impossible combination! After the first two weeks of wild, impassioned love-making, there began the waging of the fiercest battle that was ever known, between the genius of Gordon Craig and the inspiration of my Art."

Fortunately for both of them, the first skirmishes were put to an end by Isadora's departure for Russia.

Chapter X

Isadora arrived in St. Petersburg at the end of January 1905. Her train was twelve hours late because of snowdrifts; instead of arriving at 4:00 P.M., as scheduled, it arrived at dawn the following morning. No one was at the station to meet her. It was a bitterly cold day. As she drove to her hotel, her carriage was blocked by a long funeral procession of men, women, and children. Not knowing a word of Russian, Isadora could not have understood her coachman's explanation of this unusual sight, and so she was completely unaware of the tragic event known in Russian history as "Bloody Sunday."

The funeral had come about through the activities of Gregory Gapon, a thirty-year-old priest who was a combination of hysterical enthusiast, adventurer, and imposter. Having won their confidence as a reformer, this agent of the Tsarist police led thousands of workers, carrying ikons, crosses, and large photographs of Nicholas II, to the Winter Palace to present their petition to their Tsar. They expected him to come out on the balcony of the palace, but instead they were met by shots from the guns of Uhlans and Cossacks, which killed or wounded hundreds of workers.

Isadora witnessed the mass funeral that followed. It was permitted to take place only at dawn, for in the daytime it might have led to serious repercussions. In her memoirs she said, "If I had never seen it, all my life would have been different. There, before this seemingly endless procession, this tragedy, I vowed myself and my forces to the service of the people and the downtrodden." But this passage was written in retrospect, over twenty years later, and represents an attitude that she arrived at only later. For, from the moment her carriage brought her to the Hotel Europa, where she "mounted to [her] palatial rooms and slipped into the quiet bed," she joined the world of those who enjoyed their lives to the fullest—those against whom the "downtrodden" were someday to rise.

Isadora was totally ignorant of the political situation in Russia. Among her new acquaintances, the upper class of Russian society and the aristocrats, she did not have the slightest chance of meeting a single revolutionary. In those circles, if she heard any reference at all to "Bloody Sunday," it would have been as interpreted by the staunch supporters of absolute monarchy, who regarded as strictly necessary the measures taken in dealing with the petitioning workers. As for the "downtrodden," that was an epithet Isadora did not learn until the Russian Revolution of 1917.

Accordingly, her attempt to connect what she thought of as her revolutionary spirit with the funeral of the hundreds of victims of the massacre before the Tsar's palace was a work of the imagination—as might be concluded from a neighboring passage in her recollections: "Two nights later, I appeared before the elite of St. Petersburg society in the *Salle des Nobles*." Indeed, given the nature of her art and the social situation in Russia at that time, it goes without saying that her performances were for the aristocratic stratum of Russian society and not for the working classes.

Dancing, like singing, is a part of Russian life, but the ballet had been developed into a cult by the court, and the Tsars often paid out of their private fortunes for the most extravagant productions. Isadora arrived in St. Petersburg at a time when the ballet was at its zenith—there had never before been such a roster of brilliant performers: Anna Pavlova, Mathylda Kschessinska, Tamara Karsavina, and later Vazlav Nijinsky, as well as painters intimately connected with the spectacles, such as Leon Bakst and Alexander Benois, and the impresario Sergei Diaghilev, who later founded the Ballets Russes.

On the day following her debut in St. Petersburg, Isadora received "a visit from a most charming little lady, wrapped in sables, with diamonds hanging from her ears, and her neck encircled with pearls. To my astonishment," Isadora said, "she announced that she was the great dancer Kschinsky." Isadora meant Mathylda Kschessinska, known in Russia by her Russified name Kschessinskaya, who in addition to having been a member of the Imperial Ballet since 1890, had also been the mistress of Tsar Nicholas II before he married Princess Alix of Hesse-Darmstadt, the future Tsarina, in 1894.

This was Kschessinska's first meeting with Isadora, although she was no stranger to Isadora's art. Three years previously, she had seen Isadora's performance in Vienna, and was so carried away by her Viennese waltz, danced in a red costume, that she had climbed upon a chair and cheered her at the top of her voice.

Kschessinska came to welcome Isadora in the name of the ballet and to invite her to a gala performance that night at the Opera. Three elegant members of the *"jeunesse dorée* of St. Petersburg," as Isadora referred to them, called for her that evening and took her to the Maryinsky Theater in a luxurious carriage, supplied with beautiful furs to keep her warm. There, from a specially reserved seat in a loge filled with flowers and bonbons, she watched the audience, which dazzled her with its splendor: "The most beautiful women in the world, in marvelous décolleté gowns, covered with jewels, escorted by men in distinguished uniforms."

Whenever Isadora was free from her own engagements, she was constantly invited to ballet performances, followed by late suppers, either at Kschessinska's home, known as Kschessinska's Palace, or at the more modest, "but equally beautiful," home of Anna Pavlova. There, in addition to the aristocrats and balletomanes from the Tsar's court, she met Bakst, Benois, and Diaghilev, the three men who had contributed most to the glamor of the Imperial Ballet performances, and with whom she had long discussions on the art of the dance.

Although she was fundamentally opposed to the ballet as an art form, she could not fail to be enthusiastic about Kschessinska's and Pavlova's performances—the former, a "fairy-like figure, as she flitted across the stage, more like a lovely bird or butterfly than a human being," and the latter "an exquisite apparition which floated over the stage in the ravishing performance of Giselle."

She was amazed at Pavlova's energy and discipline. After her performance, Pavlova was not only capable of dancing for her guests after supper, but also of doing her exercises at eight o'clock the following morning. Having left Pavlova's at five one morning, Isadora overslept and was three hours late when she came to Pavlova's studio, where the indefatigable dancer was going through the most rigorous gymnastics, while Marius Petipa, the famous ballet master, was spurring her on to still greater efforts. For three hours Isadora watched her exercises with admiration, but also with bewilderment, for "the whole tendency of this training seems to be to separate the gymnastic movements of the body completely from the mind." "The mind can only suffer . . . from this rigorous muscular discipline," Isadora maintained when speaking of the theories on which she founded her own school. She urged that the body become transparent and, as it were, a medium for the mind and spirit. In fact, Isadora was ready to apply her theories against rigorous exercises not only to dancers but also to musicians. Many years later, at her studio in Nice, she pointed out to me a young pianist, who was showing to his admirers his well-developed muscles and especially his biceps. Isadora shook her head, and whispered to me, "an artist?" And then she added "a pianist should have no muscles at all. He should be *porous*. Music should freely flow through his arms and fingers."

Her theories of dance technique were always disputed by the admirers of ballet schools. But, after attending a class at the Imperial Ballet School where, she said, she saw little pupils "stand on their toes for hours, like so many victims of a cruel and unnecessary Inquisition," she became "even more than ever convinced that the Imperial Ballet School was an enemy to nature and to Art." One such day was so exhausting for Isadora that, after Pavlova left her at her hotel on her way to a rehearsal, she fell onto her bed and "slept soundly, praising [her] stars that no unkind fate had ever given [her] the career of a ballet dancer!"

"The school of ballet today, vainly striving against the natural laws of gravitation of the natural will of the individual, and working in discord in its form and movement with the form and movement of nature, produces a sterile movement which gives no birth to future movements, but dies as it is made.

"The expression of the modern school of ballet, wherein each action is an end, and no movement, pose or rhythm is successive or can be made to evolve succeeding action, is an expression of degeneration, of living death."

And, addressing those who "nevertheless still enjoy the movements, for historical or choreographic or whatever reasons," she said, "they see no further than the skirts and tricots. But look," she advised, "under the skirts . . . underneath the muscles and deformed bones. A deformed skeleton is dancing before you. The deformation through incorrect dress and incorrect movement is the result of the training necessary for the ballet. The ballet condemns itself by enforcing the deformation of the beautiful woman's body. No historical or choreographic reasons can prevail against this. It is the mission of all art to express the highest and most beautiful ideas of man. What ideas does the ballet express?"

Although her rather short visit to St. Petersburg could not have torn down such a mighty institution as the Imperial Ballet, Isadora was fully entitled to feel that she "had left a considerable impression." Diaghilev admitted that "Isadora gave an irreparable jolt to the classic ballet of Imperial Russia."

Diaghilev was with Michel Fokine at Isadora's first performances in St. Petersburg. Then a young dancer, and a future choreographer, Fokine was so impressed by Isadora "and so mad about her," as Diaghilev said, "that the influence of Duncan on him was the foundation of all his creation": *Les Sylphides, Carnéval, Cléopâtre, Acis et Galatée.*

Mathylda Kschessinska, whom Fokine had chosen for the main role in *Eunice,* first given in December 1906, in which his new choreographic ideas were revealed, was even in a better position than Diaghilev to speak of Isadora's influence. "Fokine at once began to cut new paths for classical ballet. He rebelled against fixed poses, against arms raised like a crown around the head. . . . He wanted a free expression of emotion. For his ballet *Eunice* whose theme was drawn from Henryk Sienkiewicz' *Quo Vadis,* he went to the Hermitage Museum in order to study classical dances on vase paintings, and made a close inspection of everything which could reveal Greek and Roman art to him."

"*Eunice* had great success," Kschessinska recalled later. "But most important of all were Fokine's new ideas, embodied in the remarkable production, which took the public by storm. *Eunice* caused a great stir and provided heated arguments. There was a violent clash between the upholders of tradition and the supporters of the new. Fokine had to wage a real war, both in the theater and out, against certain critics and balletomanes; but the conflict merely gave him more energy and strengthened his convictions. The older balletomanes reproached him with having a tint of 'Duncanism.' Young people, on the other hand, gave an enthusiastic welcome to this breath of fresh air, which had come to give new life to the unalterable canons of classical ballet, which Fokine certainly had never intended to demolish."

Restating the arguments for Isadora's principles, Fokine later said: "Duncan was the greatest American gift to the art of dance. She reminded us of the beauty of simple movements. She proved that all the primitive, plain, natural movements—a simple step, run, turn on both feet, small jump on one foot—are far better than all the richness of the ballet technique, if to this technique must be sacrificed grace, expressiveness, and beauty . . . . She reminded us: 'Never forget that beauty and expressiveness are of the greatest importance.' "

Nevertheless, in defending traditional ballet, Fokine speaks of the artistic resources it affords the dancer.

"The technique of the ballet dance offers an innumerable variety of movements, develops the sense of rhythm and of the plastic line, and adds charm to movements. The dancer not only advances on her two feet, she glides on her toes, moves on one foot, or flies through the air in a high leap. She turns not only on her two feet, but also on one foot, or on her toes."

Isadora, however, made clear her own views of a dancer's technique in the following words:

. . . I enthusiastically believed that only upon awakening the will for beauty could one obtain beauty.

Also, in order to attain to that harmony I desired, they [the pupils] must go through certain exercises chosen with this aim in view. But these exercises were conceived in a way to coincide with their own intimate will, so that they accomplished them with good humor and eagerness. Each one was not only to be a means to an end, but an end in itself, and that end was to render each day of life complete and happy.

Gymnastics must be the basis of all physical education; it is necessary to give a body plenty of air and light; it is essential to direct its development methodically. It is necessary to draw out all the vital forces of the body towards its fullest development. That is the duty of the professor of gymnastics. After that comes the dance. Into the body, harmoniously developed and carried to its highest degree of energy, enters the spirit of the dance. For the gymnast, the movement and the culture of the body are an end in themselves, but for the dance they are only the means. The body itself must then be forgotten; it is only an instrument, harmonized and well appropriated, and its movements do not express, as in gymnastics, only the movements of the body, but, through that body, they express also the sentiments and thoughts of the soul.

The nature of these daily exercises is to make the body, in each state of its development, an instrument as perfect as possible, an instrument for the expression of that harmony which, evolving and changing through all things, is ready to flow into the being prepared for it.

The exercises commenced with a simple gymnastic preparation of the muscles, for their suppleness and their force; it is only after these gymnastic exercises that the first steps of the dance come. The first steps are to learn a simple, rhythmic walk or march, moving slowly to simple rhythm, then to walk or march quickly to rhythms more complex; then to run, slowly at first, then jump slowly, at a certain moment in the rhythm. By such exercises, one learns the notes of the scale of sounds, and thus my pupils learned the notes of the scale of movement. These notes, in consequence, are able to be agents in the most varied and most subtle harmonies of structure.

These exercises are only a part of their studies. The children were always clothed, too, in free and graceful draperies in their sports; in their playground, in their walks, in the woods; jumping, running naturally, until they should have learned to express themselves by movement as easily as others express themselves through speech or through song. Their studies and their observations were not to be limited to the forms in art, but were, above all, to spring from the movements in Nature. The movements of the clouds in the wind, the swaying trees, the flight of a bird, and the leaves which turn, all were to have a special significance to them. They were to learn to observe the quality peculiar to each movement. They were to feel in their souls a secret attachment, unknowable to others, to initiate them too into Nature's secrets; for all the parts of their supple bodies, trained as they would be, would respond to the melody of nature and sing with her.

Fokine had said that Isadora's rejection of ballet technique was not so much a mistake on her part as the result of her lack of advanced schooling and of being far removed from the evolution of artistic dance. He was convinced that Isadora "fully realized that the art of simple movements must develop and grow to enrich and perfect the forms of dance," for four years later (in 1909), after the first performances of the Ballets Russes in Paris, she asked him to become an instructor of dance technique in her school. Despite his admiration for Isadora, Fokine had to decline her offer because of his position at the Imperial Theater in St. Petersburg.

But Isadora defined her contribution to the art of dance in Russia as her influence on the ballet's new use of the music of Chopin and Schumann and even Greek costumes—"some ballet dancers going so far as to discard their shoes and stockings."

After a brief visit to Kiev and Moscow, where her performances were especially acclaimed by throngs of students, Isadora hastened back to Berlin to fulfill her engagements there, and, above all, to establish her own school. For no matter how eloquent her arguments were, she realized that they could best be proved by the example afforded by her pupils.

Chapter XI

Since Isadora's school and her pupils were to prove her theories about the art of the dance, the best taste must prevail in arranging and furnishing the large villa on the Traudenstrasse in Grünewald. Shortly before going to Russia, she had bought this three-story yellow stucco house, with its large garden framed by a high picket fence, in a suburb of Berlin. She planned to take as pupils no fewer than forty little girls, for whom forty little beds, each covered in satin with silk bedspreads and white muslin curtains drawn back with blue ribbons, were installed by one of the large department stores in Berlin. To complete the children's illusion of *Himmelbett*, heavenly bed, Isadora ordered that a small picture of an angel playing a musical instrument be at the head of each bed, and everyone was to have an angel playing a different musical instrument.

To create an ambiance in which the children would learn to appreciate beauty, which would in turn influence their feelings toward the dance, Isadora had the spacious, high-ceilinged hall and the dancing room adorned with statues, bas-reliefs, and statuettes representing young girls dancing, running, or jumping, while the air was made fragrant by dried laurel wreaths hanging on the walls.

But mere ambiance is not sufficient for any school, and especially not for "a real children's Paradise," such as the one Isadora envisioned. It required a large staff of cooks, maids, nurses, a doctor and a dentist, in addition to a gardener and gatekeeper. Fortunately, at first, Isadora had ample funds from her earnings and could indulge in such an extravagant scheme, for the children between the ages of four and eight were to be treated as if they had been adopted by her —that is, they were to be boarded, educated, and provided with all necessities, free of charge. There was one condition attached to this arrangement—the girls were to remain at the school with Isadora until they reached the age of seventeen; but this, of course, as the future was to prove, could scarcely be enforced.

No wonder, then, that the announcement of her school in the papers brought a favorable response. Once, as she was returning home from a matinee, her carriage was blocked by a crowd of parents and their children. "A crazy American woman who lives over there," Isadora's coachman explained, "has announced in the papers that she would love to have a lot of children, and so—here they are."

Soon, however, Isadora realized that she would have to cut in half the number of pupils originally planned—twenty instead of forty —especially since she had to admit that she was not well equipped to make the selection and could only choose on a basis of "a sweet smile or pretty eyes." The children had to be supervised from morning until night, and Isadora devised a program for their day's activities to which they had to adhere just as in any other well-disciplined school.

They were to rise at six-thirty in the morning, and, after some limbering-up exercises, either in the fresh air or holding onto bars along the walls in the dancing room, they were to have their breakfast, consisting of milk and bread. After breakfast, they were taught to do acrobatic stunts, such as turning somersaults or leaping over chairs, as part of their physical exercises. This was followed by classes in general education, as in the first grades of any other school, but with more emphasis on lessons in music, speech, singing, painting, and ceramics. They had their dancing lessons twice a week, from four to six in the afternoon. In the periods between these classes, the children were either taken for walks or left to play by themselves in the garden.

All these activities required a far larger staff than Isadora had anticipated, and continually increasing funds. At that time, Isadora was at the height of her popularity in Germany but even her large earnings were not sufficient to cover the rising expenses. Therefore, Elizabeth organized a committee from among the wealthy and prominent members of Berlin society. It was called an *Association for the Support and Maintenance of the Dance School of Isadora Duncan*. Despite the highly promising title, the association did not live up to Isadora's expectations.

To help the subscription, Isadora wrote a foreword for the illustrated brochure that was to be circulated among the prospective patrons of the association. Here, Isadora stated again in concise form the ideas and aims of her school: "To rediscover in its ideal form the beautiful rhythmic movements of the human body, in harmony with the highest beauty of physical form, and to resuscitate an art that lay dormant for two thousand years—that is the serious purpose of my school."

And to illustrate her ideas, Isadora gave a matinee performance at the Royal Opera House in Berlin in July 1905. Unannounced in the program, a small group of her pupils came on the stage toward the end of the performance and danced two numbers of Humperdinck: the Ringelreigen from his opera *Königs-Kinder,* and the waltz from his *Hänsel und Gretel.* Gordon Craig witnessed the first results of her school and he noted his impressions in his book:

> . . . after dancing her own dances she called her little pupils to come with her and please the public with their little leapings and runnings. As they did—and with her leading them the whole troupe became irresistibly lovely. I suppose some people even then and there began reasoning about it all, trying to pluck out the heart of the mystery, but I and hundreds of others, who saw this first revelation, did not stop to reason . . . for we, too, had read what the poets had written of life and love and nature, and we had not reasoned—we had read, and wept, and laughed with joy; and so was it at Kroll's Opera House that day—we wept and laughed with joy.

> And to see her chaperoning her little flock, keeping them together and especially looking after the one very small one of four years old, Erika was the name, I believe, was a sight no one there had ever seen before or would ever see again.

But not every one among the spectators at this performance was as favorably impressed as Craig. No less a personage than the Kaiserin Auguste Victoria was appalled by the shocking sight of "children's bare limbs." The Kaiserin was known for her Victorian views and for inspiring the Kaiser's (Wilhelm I) famous statement—*Kinder, Küche, Kirche* as the sole duties of a woman. Her negative reaction was widely publicized and had an immediate influence on the members of the newly created association. It was not long before the patronesses of the association discovered Isadora's relations with Gordon Craig and chose Frau Franz Mendelssohn, the wife of the banker, to deliver their note of resignation to Isadora, "couched in majestic terms of reproach," as Isadora remarked, because they "could no longer be patronesses of a school where the leader had such loose ideas of morals." Embarrassed by her ungrateful mission, Frau Mendelssohn told Isadora that the patronesses had nothing against Elizabeth, thus suggesting that the subsidy could be saved if Isadora would relinquish her role at the school to Elizabeth. Isadora was willing to have Elizabeth take up permanent residence at the school while she herself continued to live in her apartment in Berlin. But what Isadora would not let go unanswered was the reference to her loose morals.

At the Berlin Philharmonic Hall, which she hired for this special occasion, although she started with a lecture on "the dance as an art of liberation," she became so carried away by her enthusiasm and the eloquence of her delivery that she ventured into her theories about "the rights of a woman to love and bear children as she pleased," meaning that she should choose the father for her children regardless of whether she was married to the man or not.

This was Isadora's first public declaration of her credo and it provoked a scandal rather than an appreciative reaction. Some of the audience hissed, others threw onto the stage whatever they could lay their hands on in the theater, and half of those present left the hall. But Isadora had her say, and even a short debate with those who remained in the hall.

Since Isadora had returned from Russia, she and Gordon Craig were inseparable—not a day or night passed without their being together. "We could see little else. We were indeed full of admiration for each other," Craig wrote in his book. "Astonished, too,—but I would say to her 'It is not, of course, *real*'—and yet . . . No, not *real* . . . no, not real, echoed in rings on and on."

Since Craig had recently acquired a manager to take care of the business part of his various projects, such as his experimental school, the exhibitions of his drawings, his magazine, *The Mask*, and his book of theories on the art of theater, Craig suggested adding to Maurice Magnus' activities the management of Isadora's performances as well. Until then Isadora's business had been managed by her brother Augustin, who was "a lovable person, but hardly a business man."

Now Maurice Magnus was to organize everything on a truly businesslike basis—at a rented office with a secretary and a typewriter. The management was given the glamorous name of "United Arts," which in German had the even more impressive title of *Direktion Vereinigter Künste*. Although of German parentage, Magnus was an American who had returned to Germany as a correspondent for various American magazines, but who had high hopes of making a more brilliant career by following his firm belief that "all things are possible—one only has to know the right people."

Isadora liked Maurice Magnus and his suggestions. She opened a joint bank account with Gordon Craig at the National Bank of Germany and agreed to pay 10 per cent of her receipts to the management. But somehow, two of the three partners in this enterprise behaved more like irresponsible artists than businessmen—continually borrowing from the business account—and Isadora charging to it some of her extravagant bills, so that there was often no money to pay the rent, the secretary, or Magnus's salary.

But, since Isadora was the only one who was constantly earning money, Craig undertook first to see that all her activities were carried on in a professional manner rather than in the casual way they had been conducted thus far. He began by redesigning her programs and all her publicity material. Six drawings of Isadora dancing were to accompany her on her tours and to be exhibited in the foyers of the theaters where she gave her performances, as well as on the posters displayed in the streets of the cities. Thus Isadora's association with Craig was not merely emotional. Craig accompanied her on her tours through Germany, Belgium, and Holland.

"*In January to Dresden, Hotel Bellevue, with Topsy (my name for Isadora)*," Craig wrote in his notebook, "and a week later to Hamburg with Topsy, where Isadora invited people to bring her their girl children and she would make dancers of them." She made speeches about it at the end of her performance, and Craig sat as her consultant at the Hotel Hamburger Hof, while Isadora chose her future pupils. They would return to Berlin, Isadora to her school, Craig to prepare the exhibition of his drawings in Düsseldorf, and then again to Frankfurt-am-Main, or to Breslau where Craig, watching from the wings of the stage, made a drawing of his Topsy, later reproduced in the Insel Verlag portfolio. "To the friendship and inspiration of Isadora, I owe some of my best designs of these two years (1905–1907)," Craig said later.

> Good God, had you seen her dance (she danced *alone*, remember,— no ballet comrades—*always* alone, till a few pupils came along later to ruin things)—had you seen the crammed house and heard the glorious cries of pleasure the public gave—and then seen her utter exhaustion after it was over—you, too, would have run in and taken her up with me and said, "Off you go—run, run and rest and be happy." It is this which all great public performers on the stage have to be assured of and given—*their freedom after work hours.*

Isadora needed rest, which she found whenever she could spare the time for her school, for being in that atmosphere was rest to her. This was not too often because of the heavy tour schedule. She left the school in the hands of Elizabeth, who, unfortunately, was lame, and who, perhaps by way of compensation for not being able to dance like her sister, had become a strict disciplinarian. That, at any rate, was the outward impression she liked to give, for she felt that it was an integral part of her authority in administering the school. Actually, like the rest of her family, she was a kind-hearted woman with a good sense of humor, which she betrayed by a twinkle in her eyes, even when she meant to appear severe in giving orders.

Through Isadora I met Elizabeth in Paris. Four years after Isadora's death, while I lived in the Schloss Klessheim in Salzburg, we became very good friends; the Duncan school, which she conducted, was on the Schloss Klessheim estate, and I saw her almost every day. By then, the inmates of the school were the third generation of Duncan dancers, who had come to the school from different countries in Europe and from the United States. Paying guests in Elizabeth's pension, the girls of fourteen to seventeen years old enjoyed their long summer vacation, which included some not too strenuous instruction in dancing, presumably according to Isadora's precepts. Elizabeth was called *tante*, as she had been nicknamed in the Grünewald school, and was both loved and a little feared by the girls.

But at Grünewald, where the children were afraid of her and obeyed her, they learned some simple steps of ballroom dances, which

Elizabeth had successfully taught in San Francisco and New York; however, they longed for Isadora—Isadora was everything to them: "their beloved mother, their *Good Fairy*, their inspiration, and they knew no greater happiness than to dance during Isadora's lessons." But these occasions were rare because of Isadora's constant touring, and they had to be consoled by little presents that Isadora never forgot to send them from her travels.

One day, while Isadora was at the school, she went into the classroom and quietly listened to a lesson in arithmetic being given to them by their stern teacher. On receiving a surprise visit from Isadora, the teacher suggested changing the dry subject of their lesson to reading poetry. "Yes, reading poetry would be very nice," Isadora agreed. But, though while dancing for or with Isadora, the children never felt self-conscious, the reading of poetry suddenly became an unsurmountable ordeal—they stammered and had constant lapses of memory. Isadora realized this and interrupted their efforts by asking them a question which had been on her mind for some time.

"Tell me children," she asked, "what is the greatest thing in life?" "To dance," the children shouted in reply. "No, dancing is not the greatest thing in life," Isadora said, as she shook her head. The children were stunned to hear this admission from Isadora. What could it be? Music, painting, sculpting? "None of those," Isadora continued and, lifting her forefinger she announced: "The greatest thing in life is—love!" Then, turning to the confused teacher, she added "Is it not true?"

"Delighted with the dramatic effect she had created, Isadora waved a graceful farewell, said 'Adieu,' and disappeared." Irma Duncan, one of the six girls at Isadora's school who was later given the Duncan name, then among the children at the school, thus described this scene in her autobiography, published almost sixty years later. Not until almost a year afterward did the children realize the meaning of Isadora's words, and the reason for her saying them at that time. Isadora was pregnant.

Because of the loss of her patrons' backing for the school, Isadora had to rely almost entirely on her own resources for its support, and that involved continuous touring. But after the performances in Munich, Augsburg, Amsterdam, Copenhagen, Stockholm, and Gothenburg, she was too uncomfortable to dance and so, accompanied by Craig, she returned to Holland, where she rented a small house, the Villa Maria, perched on the dunes of the North Sea. The house could be reached only after climbing a flight of almost a hundred steps in the little village of Nordwyjk. Craig loved the sea as much as Isadora, but he was restless and his inactivity only aggravated his state of mind. He traveled, first to England for a few days, then back to Rotterdam, where he was organizing an exhibition, and thence to Amsterdam, where he was hoping to interest the State Theater in his work. His various trips were varied with sporadic visits to Isadora.

Writing in retrospect about that period, Isadora said that she was so inexperienced that having a child seemed to her a perfectly natural process, so that she was perfectly satisfied with having a local country doctor attend her. Living alone most of the time, she occupied herself corresponding with Elizabeth, giving her advice about administering the school. She also composed a "series of five hundred exercises, which would take the pupils from the simplest movements to the most complex, a regular compendium of the dance."

This, and her daily walks along the seashore, Nordwyjk to Kadwyjk and back, six kilometers in all, did not suffice to dissipate the excitement Isadora felt because of the approaching event. Since motherhood was even more sacred to Isadora than all her theories of the dance, I think it is proper to quote at some length her feelings, observations, and self-analysis, as she expressed them in her memoirs.

> . . . But I no longer was alone. The child asserted itself now, more and more. It was strange to see my beautiful marble body softened and broken and stretched and deformed. It is the uncanny revenge of Nature, that the more refined the nerves, the more sensitive the brain, the more all this tends to suffering. Sleepless nights, painful hours. But Joy, too, boundless, unlimited joy, when I strode every day over the sands between Nordwyjk and Kadwyjk, with the sea, the great waves, looming on one side, and the swelling dunes on the other, along the deserted beach. . . . Occasionally the storms grew terrific, and the Villa Maria was rocked and buffeted all night like a ship at sea.

> I grew to dread any society. People said such banalities. How little is appreciated the sanctity of the pregnant mother. I once saw a woman walking alone along the street, carrying the child within her. The passers-by did not regard her with reverence, but smiled at one

another derisively, as though this woman, carrying the burden of coming life, was an excellent joke.

. . . As I walked beside the sea, I sometimes felt an excess of strength and prowess, and I thought this creature would be mine, mine alone, but on other days, when the sky was grey and the cold North Sea waves were angry, I felt myself some poor animal in a mighty trap, and struggled with an overwhelming desire to escape. Where? Perhaps even into the midst of the sullen waves. I struggled against such moods and bravely overcame them. . . .

And Isadora was convinced that she had managed to conceal her fears from everybody she saw at that time. She wanted to be alone, and yet she felt deserted. She felt abandoned by her mother, who had gone back to the United States. Besides, her mother would have never approved of her having a child by a man to whom she was not married. Dwelling on her mother's own situation, Isadora questioned her attitude toward marriage; she herself had been unhappily married and had divorced her husband. And Isadora reviewed in her mind instances that supported her conclusion about marriage "leading—especially among artists—inevitably to divorce courts, and preposterous and vulgar law suits."

What Isadora overlooked, or preferred not to admit, was that, in her case, brave as she had been in lecturing on disregarding the accepted moral code and bearing illegitimate children, when she herself was faced with the problem she was overcome by such fear that she contemplated suicide. For Isadora knew only too well that Gordon Craig had no intention of marrying her, and that the illegitimacy of his children did not bother him in the least. Himself an illegitimate child, during his lifetime he sired ten illegitimate children of his own. At that time he was planning to marry Elena Meo, with whom he already had two illegitimate children.

"Craig was strangely remote," Isadora recalled later, "and was always immersed in his art, whereas I could think less and less of my art, and was only absorbed in this fearful, monstrous task which had fallen to me; this maddening, joy-giving, pain-giving mystery."

And, since it was inevitable, it was far wiser to use her own example to validate her theories against marriage, and in support of her assertion that women should choose at will the fathers of their children. Thus the myth, which has ever since been connected with

Isadora's name, was partly a product of an expediency forced upon her by her particular situation.

This was attested to by Kathleen Bruce, the Scottish sculptress with whom she had become friends after their meeting in Rodin's studio in Paris in 1903. When Miss Bruce received Isadora's letter, "a queer cry, childish and pathetic," she rushed to Nordwyjk to be at Isadora's side.

" 'Can't you see?' cried the dancer, spreading high her lovely arms," Kathleen Bruce related later. "Slowly, and with many a lie, the story came out at last . . . and her baby was due . . . . She had dared tell nobody, not her mother or her sister. She had danced as long as she dared. She was lonely and miserable. In after years . . . she said and probably believed that she had done this deliberately and was proud of her courage and independence. But at that time she was still nothing more than a frightened girl, frightened and pitiful."

Nor was Isadora entirely alone in her retreat. This was an exaggerated statement. All her life Isadora felt deserted when another person might not have minded being temporarily alone, and perhaps might have desired solitude. Although in her reminiscences she wrote that she closed her doors to every visitor, she also said that a good and faithful friend (she did not give his name), who came from the Hague on his bicycle rain or shine, used to bring her newspapers and magazines and entertain her with discussions on art, music, and literature.

She asked Elizabeth to send Temple, her niece, Irma, and little Erika for a visit, but Elizabeth allowed only Temple to go. Isadora enjoyed having her for a few weeks, enjoyed especially seeing what progress she was making at the school as Temple danced for her on the dunes by the sea.

Hoping that it would please Isadora to have him near her, Craig came to stay with her in August. In addition to Kathleen Bruce, Marie Klist, a nurse and Isadora's friend, was now living at the villa. Craig got on very well with Kathleen Bruce, but not so well with Miss Klist. When Craig and Kathleen Bruce spent one hot night sleeping on the beach, prodded by Miss Klist's insinuations, Isadora had a fit of jealousy.

Craig, who was always "terrified of emotional display," soon went back to Rotterdam, leaving Isadora in a more depressed state of mind than ever. She now often spoke of suicide to Kathleen, who always laughed it off, and would not take Isadora's threats seriously because she was convinced that no one actually commits suicide as long as he talks about it. However, she was fated to see Isadora's attempt to carry out her threat.

One night Kathleen Bruce awoke and discovered that Isadora was not in her bed. She rushed to the sea and there she found her standing in the water. The sea was calm. As she reached Isadora, "she turned around with a gentle, rather childish smile and said, 'The tide is low, I couldn't do it, and I'm so cold.' "

Finally, on September 24, 1906, Isadora gave birth to a little girl. Craig was in Rotterdam, but he hastened to be with Isadora. She was radiant. She told him that now she knew "the tremendous love surpassing the love of man." And later she wrote, "Oh, women, what is the good of us learning to become lawyers, painters or sculptors, when this miracle exists? . . . Oh, where is my Art? My Art or any Art? What do I care for Art? I felt I was a God, superior to any artist."

They decided to call the child Deirdre, "beloved of Ireland," because Craig always loved the "Irishness" in his Topsy, and perhaps because Deirdre was the heroine of a play by Craig's friend, William Butler Yeats.

Chapter XII

Shortly upon their return to Berlin, Isadora and Craig were invited to Frau Mendelssohn's palatial villa to meet Eleonora Duse, who was visiting the banker's family. Duse was already Isadora's admirer.

In 1890, as a young man of eighteen, Craig had seen many of Duse's performances in London, and he had admired her acting even more than Sarah Bernhardt's. But, as the years went by, he became more absorbed by his own ideas of stage directing and thought less and less about the talents of individual performers. By the time he was taken by Isadora to meet Duse, he could claim that he had completely forgotten her and Sarah Bernhardt both.

Craig's name was not unfamiliar to Duse, however, for in the previous year he had done the designs for Hugo Von Hofmannsthal's *Elektra*, in which Duse had been engaged to play the leading role. Although nothing came of the production, Duse was very much impressed by Craig's work, and now she proposed that he do something "similarly beautiful" for a production of Ibsen's *Rosmersholm*, in which she planned to appear in Florence at the end of the year.

One of the greatest actresses in the history of the theater, Duse was a complex personality. A very beautiful woman, she seemed to be living in two worlds—the land of her dreams, and the land of reality to which she descended only as long as was necessary in order to conduct her business. Speaking of herself, she said; "I gave my love to Camille when I was young—*now* it is past love. It is the same with plays and people—one does not love the same person and one cannot love the same play *always*: but to *renew* love—that is the secret."

Duse always knew what she wanted, and always declared it in her famous clear voice. Craig also knew what he wanted, and was never self-conscious about his language nor the tone of *his* voice. Craig knew neither French nor Italian, and Duse knew no English. And so it was up to Isadora not merely to act as their translator, but to use the most astute diplomacy in "interpreting" what these two strong-willed artists were bargaining about. "Tell her I'll design the whole production, or nothing," Craig would say. In Isadora's translation, this was transmitted to Duse as, "He will comply with all your wishes."

Craig felt that for Isadora's sake he should accept Duse's proposition. Craig's work with Duse, whom he knew Isadora revered, would make her happy, while Isadora was convinced that at last Craig was going to be closely associated with someone worthy of his genius.

Thus, in November, Craig, Isadora, Deirdre, and Miss Klist, the nurse, went to Florence to join Duse. Isadora had difficulty in nursing her child, and her milk had to be supplemented with prepared food in bottles. Despite her discomfort, Isadora was extremely happy, especially when she saw Craig's growing enthusiasm for Italy, which she herself loved, as the beauty of the countryside unfolded before them in the train. They raced through the Brenner Pass into Lombardy, and on to Florence with its magnificent architecture.

They chose a small hotel, modest by comparison to the nearby Grand, where Duse lived in a royal suite. With Isadora resuming her role of translator-interpreter, the Duse-Craig discussions about the stage settings began almost immediately, since there was no time to be wasted.

"I see the window into the courtyard as a small window. It cannot possibly be a large one!" Duse would direct Isadora to tell Craig. But Craig had entirely different ideas for the set. Where Ibsen intended the sitting room to look comfortably furnished in old-fashioned style, Craig wished it to resemble the interior of a great Egyptian temple, with the unlikely addition of a great square window somewhere at the far end of the stage. Isadora quickly realized that, if she were to convey Craig's fantastic vision to Duse, she would end by giving Duse an erroneous impression. "Tell her to keep out of it," Craig instructed Isadora, and she assured him that Duse would "make no more suggestions for his sketches, but would pass them as they were." And to avoid any further arguments which would have ended the Duse-Craig collaboration at once, Isadora succeeded in convincing Duse to withhold judgment until Craig had completed his work.

Craig was feverishly going ahead with his sets in the theatre, either cursing the Italian workers who could not understand his orders, or in desperation trying to do everything himself. He subsisted on meager lunches and dinners, brought to him in a basket by Isadora. In order to keep Duse away, she took her on long walks through the luxurious gardens of Florence. During those anxious weeks of collaboration between Duse and Craig, Isadora grew to love and appreciate the great actress even more.

"She did not look like a woman of this world, but rather like some divine image of Petrarch or Dante, who found herself upon the terrestrial sphere by some mischance," Isadora wrote of her later. According to Isadora's recollections of their long walks together, as soon as they were alone, "Duse would pull off her hat and let her raven locks, just turning grey, free to the breeze. Her marvelous eyes—sorrowful eyes, yet, when this face lit up in enthusiasm, I have never seen a more beatific expression of joy in any human face or in any work of art!"

At last the day arrived when Craig was ready to let Duse see his work. Never letting Duse's hands out of her own icy grip, Isadora brought her to the theatre and sat with her in a loge not daring to utter a word while Craig's irritated last-minute orders and sounds of hammering were clearly heard from the stage behind the curtain. Minutes passed, which seemed like hours of torture to Isadora, because Duse kept asking her about the "small window," which she wanted to be of the right size and in the right place.

But when the curtain was finally raised, Craig's set was so overwhelming that the two women, clasped in each other's arms, wept with joy. "Never have I seen such a vision of loveliness," Isadora recalled years later. "Through vast blue spaces, celestial harmonies, mounting lines, colossal heights, one's soul was drawn toward the light of this great window which showed beyond, no little avenue, but the infinite universe. Within these blue spaces was all the thought, the meditation, the earthly sorrow of man. Beyond the window was all the ecstasy, the joy, the miracle of his imagination. Was this the living-room of Rosmersholm? I do not know what Ibsen would have thought. Probably he would have been as we were—speechless, carried away."

Still clasping Isadora's hand, Duse rushed to the stage and called for Gordon Craig, who came out of the wings, looking, according to Isadora, like a shy boy. Having assembled the whole company on the stage, Duse embraced Craig and in her rapid Italian poured on him so much adulation that Isadora was unable to keep up in her attempts to translate it to him. But she did manage to convey to Craig what was most important in Duse's speech, and what made Isadora herself sublimely happy: "It is my destiny to have found this great genius, Gordon Craig," she said in that voice which was Duse. "I now intend to spend the rest of my career [*sempre, sempre,*] devoting myself to showing the world his great work."

On December 5, 1906, the day following the first performance of *Rosmersholm* at the Teatro alla Pergola, in Florence, Duse wrote to Craig:

Merci—
C'est ma première parole ce matin.
J'ai travaillé hier soir dans le rêve—et lointaine—
Vous avez travaillé dans des conditions très pénibles, et d'autant
plus je vous dis MERCI.
J'ai compris hier soir votre aide—et
votre force—
Encore:
MERCI
J'espère que nous travaillerons encore, et avec liberté et joie—E.*

* Thank you—
These are my first words this morning.
Last night I worked as if in a dream—far, far away—
You have been working under very difficult conditions and
therefore I say again—Thank you.
Last night I realized your great help—and your strength—
Once more:
Thank you.
I hope that we will again work together and with freedom and
joy—E.

It was a great triumph for Craig. "The pleasure I got from seeing Miss Duncan watching my work with Duse was *infinite*," he wrote to a friend.

And it was a great triumph for Isadora to see the fulfillment of her cherished dream—to have Craig and Duse work together. But her happiness was short lived. Her finances were becoming straitened once more. The responsibility of her school weighed heavily upon her. And so they all went back to Berlin.

Alone, Isadora went to Amsterdam to fulfill an engagement. But just after a performance she became so ill that she fell on the stage and had to be carried to her hotel. Her condition was caused by the nervous strain she had been under during those hectic days in Florence; the doctors diagnosed it as "neuritis." As a cure she had to remain in bed for weeks, with doses of milk and opium to sustain her.

Craig rushed to her side but soon had to return to Berlin. There was a telegram from Duse awaiting him. She wanted him for another play that she planned to give in Nice, in addition to further performance of *Rosmersholm*. From her sickbed, Isadora urged him to accept Duse's proposal "Look toward your star and be your own sweet joyous self. Don't be impatient with D, but *go* to Nice and you will see all will turn out as you wish. Not allowed to write any more than this . . . be wise and take the hint of your most loving Topsy."

Two days before the opening night of *Rosmersholm*, Craig arrived in Nice to find that because the stage was smaller than the one in Florence, the set had been cut, thus altering all the proportions. Craig flew into a rage, cursed everybody, including Duse; though she could not understand the words, there was no mistaking the wrath behind them.

Ill as she was, Isadora journeyed to Nice. But she came too late to intervene successfully. True to his uncontrollable temper, Craig severed his relationship with Duse. The rupture further aggravated Isadora's illness. Her convalescence progressed very slowly; her relationship with Craig was tormented by her indecision. She thought she could not live without him, and yet she could no longer endure living with him, witnessing his violent outbursts. Besides, she was suffering terribly from fits of jealousy.

Chapter XIII

There are various approved methods for healing the wounds caused by unhappy love. Some people devote themselves entirely to their work, some believe in changing their environment, others seek forgetfulness in drinking, and still others seek recovery of their emotional balance in sensations, the denial of which, they believe, was the origin of their unhappiness. Far from being completely recovered from the aftermath of childbirth, Isadora complicated her convalescence by constant mental anxiety over the success of the Duse-Craig collaboration; its sudden collapse plunged her from the heights of happiness into utter misery. Craig's sudden declaration of independence in all his artistic concerns had implications, in her mind, for their personal relationship as well. Hence, just as her passionate love for him had absorbed her whole being, now a most irrational but equally passionate jealousy beclouded her mind.

Jealousy was, astonishingly, one of the most pronounced traits in Isadora's character. She could be jealous of everything and everybody, and that trait sometimes led her to the most exaggerated behavior. With her vivid imagination, she worked herself up into fits in which she seemed to revel, but which on more than one occasion led to a catastrophe in her life. These fits were, I always felt, unworthy of her otherwise reasonable and charming personality. She could not be appeased by common sense or logic. She behaved like a wounded animal or a sulking child.

In the case of Craig, she exhausted herself with her own manufactured doubts about him. "Visions of Craig in all his beauty in the arms of another woman haunted me at night, until I could no longer sleep. Visions of Craig explaining his art to women who gazed at him with adoring eyes—visions of Craig being pleased with other women—looking at them with that winning smile of his—the smile of Ellen Terry—taking an interest in them, caressing them—saying to himself, 'This woman pleases me. After all Isadora is impossible.' "

Her jealousy almost destroyed her willpower and her self-control. As she freely admitted, in these cases she herself closed off the various ways of regaining her emotional balance. She lost interest in her art. However, she still felt financial responsibility toward her family and her school, which she could only sustain by earnings from her performances. These usually entailed traveling, which might be beneficial in other ways as well. But this time the mere physical escape from the scene of her unhappiness was unavailing. Always admired as a woman and desired by men, she even began to doubt her physical attraction for them. Hence "Pim."

"I must find a remedy," she kept saying to herself. The remedy in this case was a young man whose friends called him "Pim." He was pretty, blond, blue-eyed, homosexual, the possessor of eighteen trunks containing suits, shoes, neckties, linen, and extra fur-trimmed waistcoats, all of which he took with him as he accompanied Isadora on her 1907 trip to Russia. Once in that country, Pim disappeared and left no trace in her life.

This irrational episode put an end to her two-year-old passionate affair with Gordon Craig. After their parting in Nice, they were never lovers again. Craig wrote in his notebook many years later: ". . . All's past . . . all's said . . . all's done. What now? It seems that all has not been said. I loved her—I do still—but she, the complex she, might have wrecked me, as she wrecked many—and finally herself."

Her Russian tour was frequently marred by embarrassing manifestations of her still uncured illness. After a week in St. Petersburg, she went to Moscow and would have cut her tour short had she not met Konstantin Stanislavsky, the famous director of the Moscow Art Theater. His discussions with her on art completely revived her.

Although during her previous visit to Russia she had enjoyed the performances of the Imperial Russian Ballet, and even more her personal contact with the stars of the company and the prominent men connected with it, nothing in Russia had thrilled her as had the Moscow Art Theater. Not knowing the language did not prevent her from attending the performances, for in the theater's repertory there were Western classics with which Isadora was thoroughly familiar, and which she could easily follow in the Russian translation.

Stanislavsky, who according to his recollections had missed her first appearances in Russia in 1905, this time attended one of her first performances in Moscow, purely by chance. Neither her audiences in Moscow, more conservative than in St. Petersburg, in 1905, nor those in 1907, were particularly enthusiastic, and "the first appearance of Duncan on the stage did not make a very big impression. Unaccustomed to seeing an almost naked body on the stage, I could hardly notice and understand the art of the dancer," Stanislavsky noted in *My Life in Art*. "The first number on the program was met with tepid applause and timid attempts at hissing. But after a few succeeding numbers, I could no longer remain indifferent to the protest of the general public and began to applaud demonstratively. . . . From that time on I never missed a single Duncan performance. The necessity to see her often was dictated from within me by an artistic feeling that was closely related to her art."

When they finally met, Isadora talked to him about Gordon Craig, whose name was not unfamiliar to Stanislavsky. Isadora tried to introduce to him as best she could Craig's ideas on modern art and the theater. What astonished Stanislavsky—and his discovery has been quoted ever since—was that when he learned of Isadora's aims and methods, as well as Craig's, he realized "that in different corners of the world [California and England], due to conditions unknown to us, various people in various spheres sought in art the same naturally creative principles. Upon their meeting [i.e., that of Isadora and Craig] they were amazed at the similarity of their ideas. This is exactly what happened to us. We understood each other almost before we had said a word to each other."

And speaking of his first meeting with Isadora, he said: "Duncan did not know how to speak of her art logically and systematically. Her ideas came to her by accident, as a result of the most unexpected everyday facts. For instance, when she was asked who taught her to dance, she answered: 'Terpsichore.' "

"A very beautiful answer," Michel Fokine remarked in his memoirs. And in the same vein, Gordon Craig, who was better able to analyze Isadora's art than anybody else, and made valuable contributions toward resolving some questions raised by her actual practice as an artist, has said of her: "How did she do it? Ask a poet how he rhymes his verse—he answers: 'I must do it out of a mouthful of air.' You may find that an unpractical answer, but do you get any further if he tells you, like Baudelaire, '. . . by reading the dictionary'? Words, words, words—it's about all the poet has to work with. . . . But do you think that by sending your girl to a ballet school you will help her to dance? You won't—you will hinder her. What must she do, then? Why, what Isadora did—learn what it is to *move*: to step, to walk, to run; few people can do these things. First the thought—then the head—then the hands and feet a little—just move, and *look around, watch, watch all which moves*. For dance comes with movement—but there are no 1st, 2nd, and 3rd positions unless you are drilling for a soldier, though after all each dancer will make his 1st, 2nd, and 3rd position if he wants to—but his *own*."

Isadora herself said always that she had danced all her life, and that she believed dancing was a natural gift bestowed by nature.

But on one occasion she complained to Stanislavsky about the visitors who came to see her in her dressing room during intermission. "I cannot dance that way," she said to him. "Before I go out on the stage, I must place a *motor* in my soul. When that begins to work, my legs and arms and my whole body will move independently of my own will. But if I do not get time to put the *motor* in my soul, I cannot dance."

"At that time, I was in search of that very creative motor, which the actor must learn to put in his soul before he comes on stage," Stanislavsky reported in his book.

Through discussions with Isadora, I learned that her idea of the "motor" was far wider in scope than a mere physical instrument to facilitate her actions. Two years before her death we attended a piano recital in Paris by Irakly Orbeliani, at one time her accompanist, and an old friend of mine. During the intermission, we saw him chatting gaily with a few giggling young girls. "How can his performance be artistic," Isadora asked, "if instead of meditating on the interpretation of his next compositions all by himself in the green room, he can distract himself in such a frivolous manner?"

Any performance, whether in public or not, was to Isadora a product of concentrated inspiration, which should not be interfered with by any external matter. Isadora herself always avoided even speaking to anybody before her performances.

For Isadora, it was this absolute communion of the performer with his subject—be it as actor, dancer, or musician—that was the indispensable basis for true and authentic expression. "In remembering all our impromptu discussions of art, and comparing what she did with what I was doing," Stanislavsky said, "it became clear to me that we were looking for one and the same thing in different branches of art." And it was then that Isadora spoke to Stanislavsky about Gordon Craig: "He belongs not only to his country, but to the whole world, and he must live where his genius will have the best chance to display itself, where working conditions and the general atmosphere will be best fitted to his needs. His place is in your Art Theatre."

Stanislavsky knew of Isadora's enthusiastic reports to Craig about himself and the Moscow Art Theatre, and he himself set everything in motion "to persuade the Direction of the Theatre to invite the great stage director to come to us."

Feeling that she had accomplished her mission as far as Craig was concerned, Isadora also spoke to Stanislavsky about establishing her own school in Moscow. Assured of Stanislavsky's cooperation in this project, she promised to return the following season. She left Russia in a far better state of mind than when she had first arrived there.

In the true Duncan spirit she was again prepared to envisage the brightest of futures: the Craig-Duse collaboration had failed, but now she hoped for an even greater future for Craig in his work with Stanislavsky and the Moscow Art Theater. And as for herself, she was becoming more and more convinced that her personal resources were not sufficient to support her school, that it should be placed in the hands of some large organization, or better still, have government support. Although she did not lack admirers and close friends among the wealthy and aristocratic families in Germany, she somehow felt that she would have a better chance of interesting the Russian government, which subsidized the Imperial Ballet, in her projected school of the dance.

Since she planned to illustrate her theories on the art of the dance by showing her pupils in performance, upon her return to Berlin she immediately began working with the children on several choruses from Gluck's *Iphigenia in Aulis*, which were to form the main numbers of their program. The performance was to close with Joseph Lanner's *Werber-Walzer*, which she had taught them a year before. Choosing twelve girls, and taking along Elizabeth, a pianist, and a governess, Isadora guided her "caravan" to Russia at the end of January 1908. Their first appearance in St. Petersburg was a gala performance under the patronage of the Tsar's sister, the Grand Duchess Olga Alexandrovna, and created a sensation with the elite public at the Maryinsky Theater.

The children were admired, applauded, feted and pampered, and Isadora now renewed her contacts with Pavlova and Kschessinska as an old friend. Isadora hoped to gain Kschessinska's powerful support in approaching the government for a financial subsidy and spent many evenings arguing with her about her own art of the dance. But Kschessinska was not converted to Isadora's ideas in general, and she was particularly unwilling to accept Isadora's belief that the art of the dance need not necessarily be based on a ballet technique. Isadora's girls improvised dances at a party given for them at the Kschessinska Palace and, although she had to admit that as a rule ballerinas were incapable of such improvisation, Kschessinska remained adamant in her arguments with Isadora, who still predicted that the classical ballet "was bound to give way to her new school."

Kschessinska was willing to admit Isadora's influence on the productions of the Russian Ballet, but she insisted that this was not so much due to Isadora's theories as it was to her unique personality, and that her theories, when advanced by her imitators, would leave no impression whatsoever.

Writing about Isadora in her memoirs, Kschessinska said, "Her imitators, who lacked her gifts, and were prepared only for a narrow and very specialized form of dancing, lacking any solid foundation, were condemned to a speedy disappearance." And so saying, she foretold the fate of those whom she called the "imitators of Isadora," a prediction which has been confirmed by time.

Isadora's very originality in some ways prevented her exerting an immediate influence on other dancers, as did the improvisational nature of her art, which avoided set movements and a formalized system. And because she was not the only nor even the main influence on the many schools that used her name, her direct teachings more or less died with her. But there can be no doubt that she did affect the theater in her own time, and later on, through new generations of dancers who never knew her, she at last affected the main stream of dance itself. If her own career in the dance was a personal phenomenon, by the 1930s her artistic ambitions and achievements were more in tune with the emerging period of new forms, of experimentation, of questioning, of liberating movements in all the theatrical media. The famous Dance Project, for instance, a part of the New Deal's Federal Theatre Project, subsidized dance employment in the period of the Depression and gave many imaginative choreographers government sponsorship for interesting, sometimes revolutionary, work, of a kind for which Isadora had so long pleaded. Though this particular project lasted only a few years, it did give impetus and encouragement to many new dancers. Most of these artists, and later generations as well, gave credit to Isadora as an inspiration for freedom in the dance and as a propagandist for popular support—and even government support—of the arts. For all these reasons—spirit, style, costume, free dance, devotion to music, and to literature—few of the great contemporary dancers and few of the pioneers in modern dancing such as Martha Graham, Hanya Holm, Doris Humphrey, Charles Weidman, Sophie Maslow, and Robert Joffrey would fail to acknowledge Isadora's own pioneer challenge.

Though as a result of these theoretical discussions Isadora did not feel particularly close to her hostess, Isadora may have found an affinity in their position as women. Like Isadora, Kschessinska had had an illegitimate child, Vova, by the Grand Duke Andrei Vladimirovich, the Tsar's cousin, whom she did not marry until some twenty years later, when in exile in France after the Russian Revolution.

In Moscow, Isadora was received as an honored guest by Stanislavsky and the Moscow Art Theater. Always vague about dates in her recollections, Isadora nevertheless speaks of an episode in her personal relationship with Stanislavsky which can be attributed to her visit to Moscow in 1908. Again there are several extant versions of the story. If Isadora recounted one or the other, it was simply because she felt it added an amusing and revealing touch to Stanislavsky's portrait.

Isadora describes in detail her unsuccessful attempt to seduce Stanislavsky in her hotel room, a program that was frustrated by Stanislavsky's utter surprise and his exclamation, "But what should we do with a child?" "What child?" Isadora asked him. "Why our child, of course. . . . You see I would never approve of any child of mine being raised outside my jurisdiction, and that would be difficult in my present household." His ponderous manner "was too much for my sense of humor, and I burst out laughing," Isadora commented. And by way of further explaining Stanislavsky's character, she quoted his wife, to whom many years later she herself related the anecdote. "Oh, but that is just like him. He takes life so seriously," Madame Stanislavsky was supposed to have responded.

Isadora gave a different version of the incident to Ilya Schneider, who was the director of her school in Moscow, which was founded after the Russian Revolution. Then a young man, Schneider happened to be in the courtyard of the Moscow Art Theater when he saw a man and woman arriving in a sleigh. "They were holding hands, looking into one another's eyes, and smiling: he with embarrassment, she excitedly and as though surprised. Her smiling lips seemed about to burst into laughter," Schneider recalled in his book, *Moi Vstretchi s Esseninym*, translated as *Isadora Duncan, The Russian Years*.

Years later Isadora explained to Schneider the scene he had witnessed that day: "When, forgetting everything in the world, we were ready to fall into each other's arms," Isadora said, "he startled me by asking a question with such charming seriousness and such big, bright eyes: 'And what will happen to our child?' "

And to me she gave still another version of Stanislavsky's remark, which was, after all, the main point of this anecdote. We were discussing the puritanical attitude of Russian men toward sexual relationships, of women tormented by guilt and the fear of losing a man's "respect"—all as depicted in the works of the great Russian novelists. She told me that she had once discussed a similar subject with Stanislavsky. On that occasion she had told him that she believed affection was one thing, true love another, and the latter could only be proved by complete consummation. Thereupon, she told me, Stanislavsky had made his remark.

One way or another, this passage was supposed to have been the end of their romance. But in his letters to Isadora, Stanislavsky certainly left no doubt of his deep affection for her. In one instance, perhaps, he even betrayed regret for his timidity. A few letters in the Stanislavsky archives at the Moscow Art Theater shed some light on their personal relationship, as well as on Stanislavsky's concern with helping Isadora to establish her school in Moscow. Above all, the letters document Isadora's complete release from her depression and her revived enthusiasm for her art.

On February 4, 1908, Isadora wrote to Stanislavsky from St. Petersburg and included her photograph signed "With love—Isadora":

Dear Friend:
I have just come back from Madame Duse. [Duse was then on tour in Russia.] She is so beautiful. We spoke about you. She said she would be delighted to see you in Moscow, and that you did not need any letter of introduction. She is very fond of you.

I danced last night. I thought of you and danced well.

I received your cards and today received your telegram. Thank you. How good and thoughtful of you! And how I love you!

I feel a surge of new, extraordinary energy. Today, I worked all morning and put many new ideas into my work. Rhythms again.

It is you who have given me these ideas. I am so glad I feel like flying to the stars and dancing round the moon. This will be a new dance, which I will dedicate to you.

I have written to Gordon Craig. I told him about your theatre and about your own great art. But couldn't you write to him yourself? If he could work with you, it would be *ideal* for him. I hope with all my heart that this can be arranged. I will soon write you again. Thank you once more. I love you. I still work with joy.

Isadora

P.S. My tender love to your wife and children.

To this letter Stanislavsky replied:

((115))

Dear Friend:

I am so happy! I am so proud! I have helped a great artist to find the atmosphere she so badly needed. And all this happened during a delightful talk, and in a cabaret where vice reigns. How beautiful it is at times! Oh, yes, you are good, you are pure, you are noble, and in the greatest rapturous feeling and artistic admiration I have felt up until now, I feel the birth of a deep and true friendship.

Do you know what you did to me? I haven't yet told you about it.

In spite of the great success of our theatre and the great number of admirers who surround it, I have always been lonely. (My wife alone supported me in moments of doubt and disappointment.) You are the first who has told me in a few simple and convincing words the chief and fundamental thing about the art I wanted to create. That gave me strength at a moment when I was about to give up my artistic career.

Thank you sincerely, thank you with all my heart.

Oh, I was waiting impatiently for your letter and danced with joy when I read it. I was afraid that you would put a wrong interpretation on my restraint and mistake my pure feeling for indifference. I was afraid that your feeling of happiness, strength, and energy, with which you had left to create a new dance, would desert you before you reached Petersburg.

Now you are dancing the Moon Dance, while I am dancing my own dance, which has as yet no name. I am satisfied. I have been rewarded. . . .

Every free moment, in the midst of our work, we speak of the divine nymph who descended from Olympus to make us happy. We kiss your beautiful hands, and we never forget you. I would like to see this dance. When shall I see it? Alas, I don't even know your itinerary! ! ! !

Having promised to help Isadora with her project of establishing a school in Russia, Stanislavsky spoke about her success in St. Petersburg and Moscow to Vladimir Telyakovsky, the director of the

Imperial theaters, trying to win his support for creating an Isadora Duncan School. He arranged a meeting for her with Telyakovsky, and Isadora promised to give Telyakovsky and the members of the ballet a demonstration of her system of dancing.

While advising Isadora to describe her theories thoroughly to Telyakovsky, Stanislavsky also cautioned her "not to ask him at first for more than 15,000 roubles a year as subsidy for the school, and not to abuse the old Ballet too much."

> . . . Here they are saying that your delightful children will be coming to St. Petersburg. Does it mean . . . that your school is about to be founded? My dream is being realized and your great art will not disappear with you. Do you know that I admire you much more than the beautiful Duse? Your dances have said more to me than her beautiful performance I saw tonight.
>
> You have shattered my principles. After your departure, I kept looking in my art for the thing you have created in yours. It is beauty, as simple as nature. Today the beautiful Duse repeated to me what I already knew and what I have seen hundreds of times. Duse will not make me forget Duncan!
>
> I implore you; work for art and, believe me, your work will bring you joy, the best joy of your life.
>
> I love you, I admire you, and I respect you (forgive me!)— great artist.
>
> Write to me even a short note, so that I may know your plans.
>
> Perhaps I shall manage to come and be enraptured with you. I implore you to let me know beforehand the day you will give a performance with your school. I should not want to miss that incomparable spectacle for anything in the world, and I must arrange to be free. I kiss your classical hands a thousand times and
>
> > *au revoir,*
> > Your devoted friend K.S.

But the project failed, not for lack of enthusiasm on Telyakovsky's part, and not because of the challenge it would have presented to the Imperial Ballet—for that institution perfectly satisfied the taste of the court and the elite of Russian society—but because leading Russian musicians, then at the peak of their fame and influence in artistic matters, were not as unanimously enthusiastic about Isadora's theories of the art of dance and its connection to music as were Stanislavsky and the members of the Moscow Art Theater.

What puzzled them was Isadora's using well-known compositions, and even classical masterpieces, as mere vehicles for her performances. What exactly was her function in those performances? On this subject, Nikolai Rimsky-Korsakov clearly expressed not only his personal views, but those of most of his confreres in the musical field: "Concerning Duncan, I shall tell you that I have never seen her. Presumably she is very graceful, a splendid mime, etc; but what repels me in her is that she foists her art upon and tacks it onto musical compositions, which are dear to my heart and whose authors do not at all need her company, and had not reckoned with it. How chagrined I should be if I learned that Miss Duncan dances and mimetically explains, for instance, my *Scheherezade, Antar,* or *Easter Overture!* Musical works intended for dancing and miming must really be accompanied by the latter, and, moreover, in certain decorative surroundings, but works not intended for it do not require any mimic interpretation, and, in truth, it is powerless to interpret them. All in all, miming is not an independent kind of art and can merely accompany words or singing, but when it foists itself unbidden upon music, it only harms the latter by diverting attention from it."

Rimsky-Korsakov's opinion was based on the accepted routine of specially composed music for each number of the Russian Ballet, regardless of the intrinsic qualities of the compositions. It was later admitted that one of the paramount influences of Isadora's first performances in Russia in 1905 was the gradual introduction of classical compositions into the ballet performances, in place of music especially written for the dances. This practice was further developed by Diaghilev's Ballets Russes, and even included some of Rimsky-Korsakov's own works. But the question of Isadora's role in her own performances, in which she made use of musical masterpieces, remained unresolved at least in theory.

As a musician myself, and having come to be well acquainted with Isadora's theories on the art of dance from discussions with her, I endeavored to get directly from her a clear answer to these puzzling questions: Was she trying to enhance the listener's capacity to follow the music? Was there not a danger, as Rimsky-Korsakov said, of distracting the listener by the visual spectacle of her dancing on the stage? Did she mean to create an art similar to that of the opera, where the action on the stage is an integral part of the music? Or was she deliberately imposing her own personal interpretation upon the music? If so, on what was that interpretation based—musical authority?

Although her mother must have been quite musical, having taught piano and played constantly for her children, so that Isadora had had the privilege of always being close to music, she never actually received a musical education. She never learned to play the piano. She remarks in her autobiography that her "studies of the theory of orchestral composition, as a child, must have remained in my subconscious." But those studies were pure fantasy.

What she did have was an uncannily good musical ear and musical memory. These gifts allowed her to learn music by ear. She heard many excellent performances in England and Germany, especially in Bayreuth, where she frequently attended the rehearsals of great conductors. For a person not thoroughly trained as a musician, she had an extraordinary intuitive feeling for a musical phrase. She felt its dynamics, as well as tempi, with all its integral parts—the beginning of the phrase, its climax, and its end, accompanied by crescendos, diminuendos, accelerandos, ritardandos, and accentuated as well as almost muted notes.

Still, her judgment of the content of a musical work could not always be infallible; it might actually have been in contradiction with that of the performer of the musical score, be it a pianist or the conductor of an orchestra. Were these performers to act merely as her accompanists, following her interpretation, or was she to follow theirs?

Although she sincerely believed in complete union of interpretation with that of the man who provided the music, she nevertheless accepted the general term of "accompanist" for the role of her musical partner in her performances. But, since she insisted on being assisted by great performers—whether pianists or conductors—the question raised by Rimsky-Korsakov was again apposite. Did these artists need her collaboration to project to an audience their interpretation of the music?

Actually, Isadora could never give a clear answer to questions of this kind. In fact, she was puzzled when I insisted on further analyzing the whole problem by comparing her solo performances with that of a pianist or violinist playing a concerto with an orchestra. Before his public performance, a soloist consults with the conductor during rehearsals concerning the interpretation of each part of the composition. He leaves nothing to improvisation during the course of the public performance itself. And yet Isadora's interpretations could never have been anything but "improvisations."

What was it then, I asked her, that she meant to present to her audience in the performance of these symphonic works that was not already clearly delivered in the conductor's interpretation? *"Der Geist der Musik"* (the spirit of the music), Isadora said emphatically. This was the best and the clearest definition I ever heard her give, and in fact an excellent answer.

In her performances, through her powerful personality and musical intuition, she not only did present visually the spirit of a composition, but actually compelled her audience to feel and see with her this spirit of music.

I have seen, of course on a much smaller scale than a two-hour-long performance, a similar manifestation of such a power of suggestion by a performer to his audience. I saw Feodor Chaliapin, the famous Russian bass, project the Tsar's hallucinations, in the well-known "Hallucination Scene" from Moussorgsky's opera *Boris Godunov*, so vividly that many in the audience leaned forward in their seats, and some even got up to see for themselves what Boris Godunov was supposed to be seeing in the dark far corner of his bedroom.

I also saw similar feats performed by Emma Grammatika in *Medea* and Alexander Moissi in Ibsen's *Ghosts*. Vasily Katchalov, of the Moscow Art Theater, while delivering Mark Antony's funeral speech in concert form—and dressed, therefore, in a plain business suit—suddenly conveyed the illusion that he was wearing a toga.

Isadora could successfully accomplish such projections when interpreting the spirit or even the content of what, in musical terms, is called "program music," compositions illustrating a definite idea or situation. It was quite another thing to try to convey the spirit of what is called "pure music"—and even in this she occasionally succeeded.

Although Gordon Craig was not a musician, his reactions can be accepted as those of an average intelligent man. Referring to a performance of Bach's *Passion According to Saint John,* to which Isadora never thought of dancing, he remarked, "The thought came stealing into my mind, 'What is this music to her?' To me it was something very much greater than myself, and if I may speak of this music as a voice, there are commanding messages in that voice. She and I are what are called two artists: I wonder whether each is an artist? As a being, I should certainly place her in a much higher category than myself or most people I have come across. But there again, when I see the way she handled music in her own perform-ances, I am brought to a full stop. I know very well I would not have done such a thing: I think I probably have more fear of God in me than she! Perhaps that was it . . . I would not make use of it to ex-ploit a fancy which would fill a theater."

But, to the best of my knowledge, Isadora never tried to dance to similar monumental works. In fact, from among many Bach com-positions of lesser magnitude, two airs—one, the so-called *Air on the G string,* and the other, *Air in D*—were her favorites, particularly the latter. But to neither of these did she ever make a single gesture; she simply listened, utterly absorbed by the pure sound, just as she was when she heard a melody from Gluck's *Orfeo ed Euridice,* played solo by a flutist. "I often found myself remaining immobile on the stage with tears flowing from my eyes, just from the ecstacy of lis-tening to him," Isadora remarked in her memoirs, and it was quite in keeping with her usual response to music.

One of the main characteristics of Isadora's nature was her innate good taste. She often told me that, if dancers realized how closely their gestures are related to words, they would be ashamed of the indecency of some of them. But, in the presence of vulgarity, unless she were most seriously provoked, she kept her observations and opinions to herself. On such occasions, she was generally content to smile and remark to a friend, "But I am too polite to mention it."

She also had a well-exercised sense of measure in her perform-ances, maintaining that even a slight exaggeration would diminish the effect of her message, and perhaps even distort her intentions.

Whether or not she was conscious of the power of her spirit and temperament upon an audience, her choice of the costumes in which she performed was directed solely by a desire to give the true image that was in her imagination. She had no desire to draw the audience's attention to her personality. "She puts on some bits of stuff which, when hung upon a peg, looked more like torn rags than anything else; when she put them on, they became transformed," Gordon Craig commented. "Stage dress usually transforms the performers—but in her case it was these bits that became transformed by her putting them on. She transformed them into marvels of beauty and at every step she took, they spoke. I do not exaggerate."

Constantly analyzing Isadora's artistry in his mind, Craig asked himself: "Was it art? No, I should not call it that. It was something which inspired those men who labor in the narrow fields of the arts, hard and more lasting. It releases the minds of hundreds of such men: one had but to see her dance for one's thoughts to wing their way, as it were, with the fresh air. It rid us of all the nonsense that we had been pondering for so long. How's that?—she said nothing. On the contrary, she said everything that was worth hearing—and everything that everyone else but the poets had forgotten to say."

Taking into consideration all these extraordinary gifts, I questioned Isadora about the necessity of having any music at all as a partner in her performances. I have seen her—at short range in a hotel room, as well as at a fair distance in her large studio—creating a dance without any music at all. After thinking it over carefully, she said that for a two-hour performance she needed continuous inspiration that only music could give her. I asked her whether she used the music written by the great composers *faute de mieux*, because none had been especially written for her performances. She laughed and said it was a cynical question.

As for the performing artists, it is probably because of the feeling about her interpretations then prevailing among the Russian musicians, as expressed in the remarks I have quoted from Rimsky-Korsakov, that neither the Russian orchestra conductors nor the pianists had offered her their collaboration, which would have helped her cause.

Isadora's hope of having her school as a part of the Moscow Art Theater also failed, but merely for financial reasons.

Chapter XIV

Disappointed in her efforts to establish her school in Russia, Isadora returned to Berlin. But despite the dim probabilities for success with that *idée fixe*, she never abandoned the search for fertile soil for her project in one of the European countries. Germany, where she had enjoyed her greatest popularity, was no longer a possibility because of the attitude of the Kaiserin, who, according to Isadora, was so puritanical that "whenever she visited a sculptor's studio, she sent her Major Domo in first to cover all the nude statues with sheets."

It was clear that, without a substantial subsidy, Isadora could no longer meet the growing expenses of the Grünewald school out of her own earnings. The school, which had held out so much promise, had to be closed. After choosing twelve of the twenty girls, she took her reduced flock to Paris to try her luck there. But she arrived in Paris at a most inopportune time to present her original artistic conceptions. What she did not realize was that she was going to have to face formidable competition with all the odds against her.

Sergei Diaghilev had just come to Paris hoping to popularize Russian art beyond Russia's borders. Isadora had met him during her first visit to St. Petersburg in 1905. She had admired his extraordinary talents as an impresario and his genius in choosing remarkable performers for his remarkable projects. Once in France, Diaghilev caught the enthusiasm of the art-loving Parisians by exhibiting, during May 1907, a large assortment of Russian paintings and sculptures lent from Imperial palaces, museums, and private collections. He now followed his initial success in 1908 with what was called his "Russian Season," when he presented "Five Historical Concerts" at the Opéra.

The festive nights at the Opéra, called "Russian Music Through the Ages," included Rimsky-Korsakov conducting his symphonic suite from *Tsar Saltan* and the submarine kingdom scene from *Sadko*. Rachmaninoff played his Second Piano Concerto and conducted his cantata *The Spring*. Felix Blumenfeld of the Imperial Opera of St. Petersburg, and Arthur Nikisch, the great exponent of Tchaikovsky, were to share the conductor's desk in the programs, which included Glinka's overture and the first act from *Russlan and Ludmilla* and his *Kamarinskaya;* Tchaikovsky's Second and Fourth symphonies, excerpts from Borodin's *Prince Igor*, the second act from Moussorgsky's *Boris Godunov*, as well as other masterpieces in Russian musical literature.

These spectacles drew thousands of music lovers from all over Europe. Diaghilev's description of the audiences at the Opéra has been quoted ever since: "If the theater were to burn down tonight, the best artists and the most elegant women in Europe would perish."

This overwhelming conglomeration of stars in the musical and artistic world, entirely enlisted by Diaghilev's Russian spring, was too great a rival for Isadora's modest performances at the small Gaieté-Lyrique Theater. After giving nightly performances during the whole month of May 1908, with no apparent hope of even approaching anyone with her problem of financial support for her school, Isadora moved on to London.

It was Isadora's first return to England, and her first public appearances there, since she had danced at Charles Hallé's New Gallery seven years earlier. Charles Frohman, Isadora's manager, arranged performances for her and her pupils during the month of July at the Duke of York Theater, beginning on July 6. Isadora's girls charmed the London audiences, but her own solo performances caused a regular polemic among the spectators, as well as in the press.

Now, for the first time in her career as a dancer, Isadora was faced with a direct competitor. This was not competition such as she had met with in the Russian Imperial Ballet, or with some performer who offered his own original ideas on the art of the dance, worthy of serious consideration. The challenge came, instead, from an imitator of Isadora's individual art. A young Californian woman, Maud Allan, who had studied music in Germany, had closely observed Isadora's dancing in Berlin, and had somewhat superficially acquired an insight into Isadora's aims. She apparently decided that she could do just as well if she discarded her shoes and dressed herself "à la Duncan" for her stage performances. She had only one advantage over Isadora—she had introduced herself to the London public long before Isadora's return to England. She thus posed the question: Which of these two American dancers was imitating the other? But while managing to place herself in a competitive position with a famous artist, Maud Allan had not succeeded in rising above her own inferior tastes. Her programs were designed to appeal to music hall audiences rather than to the kind of public that had applauded Isadora on the continent and at the Duke of York Theater.

Isadora seems to have been perfectly satisfied with the choice eventually made by the public between herself and Maud Allan. She certainly had reason to be pleased with the final pronouncements of the London press, in an article in the literary weekly, *The Academy:*

> The difference between the dancing of these two ladies is the difference between the real thing and a not very successful imitation. It is quite ridiculous for Miss Allan and her representatives to pretend that her dancing is not a deliberate imitation of Miss Isadora Duncan's. In some dances she is moderately successful, but the overwhelming superiority of Miss Duncan's dance must be at once evident to anybody possessing the smallest knowledge of the technique of dancing. With regard to the *Salomé* dance, Miss Maud Allan is entitled to what credit she may achieve for having invented it. In our opinion it is a repulsive performance, and one which we should not consent on any account to witness a second time.

Undaunted, Maud Allan commissioned no less than Claude Debussy to compose ballet music for her on a scenario by W. I. Courtney.

Had Debussy not been at the time in strained financial circumstances, he would most probably have turned down her request, but because of "domestic economy," as Debussy put it, and despite his characteristic contempt for the "artistic" presentation of his work, he agreed to compose music for what he called "this weird concoction of music-hall attractions," which was to present some sort of legend about a high priest and a crowd of worshippers of the god

Amon-Ra. The finished work was to be a ballet, entitled *Khamma*. It was "to be in Egyptian style, and to have trumpet calls, suggesting riots or an outbreak of fire, and to give shivers to the audience."

But after writing a few pages, Debussy abandoned the project.

Isadora was always tolerant of her innumerable imitators. But years later, I remember her amusing friends with a rendition of Maud Allan, "wiggling" through her version of the "Dance of the Seven Veils," which Allan did not even bother to set to Richard Strauss's operatic music.

Perhaps at any other time, under different circumstances, the lively discussion in the press could have meant effective publicity for Isadora's cause. But, after a whole month of a most flattering reception on the part of the British beau monde, who showered Isadora with praise and her little pupils with presents and entertainments, the upshot was "words, words, words"—promises on which Isadora could not depend for the establishment of her school in England. Indeed, she could not even afford to remain in London and wait for something to happen.

Isadora was faced with the most serious problems. Not only had she been forced to abandon the Grünewald School, but all her attempts at finding another home for the twelve children still in her care had failed. With no hope of a subsidy for her school, she could count only on her own resources, which in turn, were wholly dependent upon her performances. Next in her plans was the United States, where her manager offered her a contract at the Criterion Theater in New York.

But what about her pupils, who were not included in the contract? Fortunately, one of Isadora's admirers came to her rescue. A former musical comedy performer, Mabel Gilman, had married W. E. Corey, a steel magnate, and become a patroness of the arts. On hearing of Isadora's plight, she had generously invited the children to her estate, Château Villegenis, about twenty miles from Paris. Since she herself was living in New York, and the chateau was "available," she saw no reason why the children should not live there, especially since "there was a farm there, too, which could supply them with all they could wish to eat, and servants with nothing to do but wait upon them."

The chateau, which at one time had been occupied by Napoleon's brother Jerome Bonaparte, was indeed situated on a magnificent estate, and beautifully appointed as befits a royal residence, but because Mrs. Corey's old mother, who lived there in solitary splendor, would not have the children "scuff up the parquet floors and scratch the nice furniture," Isadora's pupils were relegated to a barn, next to the stables, with the emphatic instructions that the children "never set foot in the manor house."

Their apartment of four small rooms, which must have been meant to be occupied by grooms, was devoid of all comforts, including sanitation, electricity, and furniture—except for one large table and a few chairs. For the girls, who had slept in *Himmelbetten* in their immaculately kept home in Grünewald, it was a real shock to be quartered in mice-infested rooms, where they had to sleep on pallets spread on the floor.

Elizabeth brought them there, left them in charge of their French governess, and promising to visit them again, she returned to Isadora's apartment in Paris to take care of Deirdre. Isadora, who by then was already in New York, was apparently unaware of the children's sad banishment. But Mary Sturges, Isadora's companion in Bayreuth in 1903, suddenly appeared at the chateau, saying that she would like to report to Isadora how happy the children were in their lovely new environment. Irma Duncan, one of the children in question, recalled that visit in her autobiography.

"A gay, rather frivolous woman, [she was by then divorced from Mr. Sturges, and as an expatriate lived in Paris]. . . . who liked to laugh at everything and was constitutionally unable to take anything seriously, she conceived the idea of posing us festooned all over her automobile."

Indeed, without any attempt to go into the children's plight, she snapped the picture, which was to accompay her report to Isadora. She also left them all completely bewildered by saying "in mock-seriousness that the Grand Duke of Hesse had offered Elizabeth a piece of property near Darmstadt for the building of a school of her own." Having exploded this piece of dramatic news, "she grinned her last big grin." and departed. The children feared for their future. Did Isadora know anything about it? And would they now be taken away from Isadora and transferred into Elizabeth's "own school"?

In her autobiography, Irma gives a very good picture of the existence these girls (Irma was twelve, three of them were fourteen, and the rest younger) had to endure in the squalor of their manor house residence. It was fortunate for all concerned that the girls were healthy enough to escape the effects of malnutrition—their daily diet consisted of pumpkin soup, or a dish of boiled potatoes—a lack of the most elementary hygiene, and inadequate clothing; for, by the time the winter months came, they had worn out their summer dresses and their sandals.

Abandoned by Elizabeth, who went back to Germany to attend to the project of her "own school," and then by their English governess, the girls were left to their own devices. Their life was thoroughly demoralizing. They were literally penniless. As for writing directly to Isadora, they knew nothing of her whereabouts, except that she was in America. Thus, as the winter months passed, they lived on hope, expecting that some day Isadora would come to their rescue.

(Their tragic situation was later confirmed to me by Anna and Therese Duncan—these two girls, like Irma, were later given the Duncan name—who with Irma were among the girls at the chateau.)

There was no excuse for Isadora's irresponsibility toward the girls entrusted to her care, except for her belief in Mary Sturges's report that all was well with them. Although Mary Sturges spoke to everybody only in secret about the promised school at Darmstadt, she no doubt also took Isadora into her confidence. This news overshadowed anything she had to report about the girls at the chateau.

The beginning of Isadora's own appearances in the United States was far from satisfactory. This was her first return to her native country since she had left it on a cattle boat in 1899. During those years she had made a name in Europe, she had created an art of her own and her first school, and, as she said, she had created a baby. "Not so bad," she reasoned, but apparently she did not take into account the fact that in order to discharge the responsibilities that went with these creations, she required money which she simply did not have.

She thought that Charles Frohman was a great manager, but it was not long before she realized that he was the last man to present her art because of his complete ignorance of it. As a result of the arrangements he had made for her, Isadora was forced to dance, as a Broadway attraction, Beethoven's *Seventh Symphony* and Gluck's *Iphigenia in Aulis* to the accompaniment of a small orchestra inadequate for the musical execution of her programs.

During her absence from the United States there had been only occasional reports in the press about her European activities, and most of them were rather derogatory. Now, lacking any advance publicity, her performances were either ignored or unfavorably criticized. Utterly discouraged, she started on a tour through the small towns, but the tour had to be cancelled, because it was even more of a failure than her appearances on Broadway. "America doesn't understand your art," Frohman told her. "You had better return to Europe." And while he was counting his losses from his six-month contract with her, which had made him responsible for success or failure, Isadora magnanimously tore up the agreement.

But she did not return to Europe immediately. Her hurt pride was somewhat assuaged by George Grey Barnhardt's admiration of her art. At that time the well-known sculptor advised her to remain in New York to wait for a more appropriate opportunity for introducing it, despite Frohman's claim that it was "considerably over the heads of Americans, who will never understand it."Barnhardt also asked Isadora to pose for his large statue, "America Dancing." Echoing Walt Whitman's "I hear America Singing," Isadora announced "I see America dancing," as the sculptor progressed in his work, which unfortunately had first to be interrupted and later completely abandoned on account of his wife's illness.

Meanwhile, Isadora settled herself in one of the large studios of the Beaux Arts Building facing Bryant Park. There, almost every evening, she played the charming hostess to all the young poets, artists, and literati brought to her by Barnhardt, danced for them, and discoursed upon her ideas to this newly acquired, sincere, and enthusiastic audience. But this was too reminiscent of the similar "private performances" she had been giving ever since she had begun her career many years before, and which seldom led to anything beyond enlarging the number of her admirers; certainly it did not suffice to put her art on a solid professional basis. She had failed in England, France, and Russia, and she had even left Germany, where she had been more popular than anywhere else. In the United States she had lost her manager; he had held out no hope to her for her future attempts to win American audiences with an art incomprehensible to them. But, at the time when her spirit was sinking to its lowest ebb, "a miracle," which Barnhardt had predicted would happen sooner or later, actually did happen. Walter Damrosch, conductor of the New York Symphony Orchestra, not only became a regular guest at Isadora's evenings in her studio, but also offered her his collaboration in her future performances.

Damrosch, better than any other musican, could fully appreciate Isadora's art, for he was to become one of the foremost pioneers of "musical appreciation," on which he lectured himself, and which later developed into regular courses in music schools and universities.

Isadora could not have dreamed of anything better. In Bayreuth she had appeared to the accompaniment of an excellent orchestra led by eminent conductors, but she had been part of the ensemble of dancers. In Budapest, where she had made her debut in a solo performance on the stage, neither the orchestra nor its leader could have claimed special qualities. Now she was to appear with one of the major orchestras of the world, and under the most popular conductor in the United States. But that was not all. Her performance with Walter Damrosch and the New York Symphony Orchestra would not be given in some Broadway theater, but at the Metropolitan Opera House. That fact in itself lent an entirely different aspect to the presentation of Isadora and her art; it made her seem worthy of the most serious artistic consideration.

Presented under such favorable auspices, Isadora danced in a sold-out Metropolitan, as well as in full houses on the subsequent tour with Walter Damrosch and the orchestra, which followed their New York matinee debut on November 16, 1908.

Her programs included numbers taken from Gluck's *Iphigenia in Aulis*, two movements from Beethoven's Seventh Symphony, the Bacchanale from Wagner's *Tannhäuser*, as well as excerpts from the Flower Maidens' music from *Parsifal*.

Any musician who has experienced the exhilarating feeling of performing for the first time in his life as a soloist with an orchestra composed of some eighty men or more can easily understand Isadora's emotional state during her debut. As a rule, in time the oft-repeated experience is taken in stride by the performing soloist, but this was not true in Isadora's case because, in addition to the excitement of performing with a large ensemble, which she relived each time anew, she always lost herself in it, as if she were in a trance. She wrote in her autobiography:

> . . . At the first sound of the orchestra, there surges within me the combined symphonic chord of all the instruments in one. . . . The mighty reverberations rush over me and I become the Medium to condense in unified expression the joy of Brünnhilde awakened by Siegfried, or the soul of Isolde seeking in Death her realization. Voluminous, vast, swelling like sails in the wind, the movements of my dance carry me onward—onward and upward, and I feel the presence of a mighty power within me which listens to the music and reaches out through all my body, trying to find an outlet for this listening. Sometimes this power grew furious, sometimes it raged and shook me until my heart nearly burst from its passion, and I thought my last moments on earth had surely arrived. At other times it brooded heavily, and I would suddenly feel such anguish that, through my arms stretched to the Heavens, I implored help from where no help came. Often I thought to myself, what a mistake to call me a dancer—I am the magnetic centre to convey the emotional expression of the orchestra. From my soul sprang fiery rays to connect me with my trembling vibrating orchestra.

This, in my opinion, is the clearest exposition of the nature of Isadora's emotions during her performances.

There are two schools of thought concerning the dramatic portrayal of a character by an actor: One advocates "acting" the role, which requires of the performer a high degree of personal detachment from the part, which he nevertheless has to convey in an authentic way that depends entirely on the technique he has acquired through his acting career. The other—living the role, so to speak—advocated by Stanislavsky, expects the performer to be completely identified with the character he is portraying. The former approach to the solution of this problem "would not require using up so much of one's self," as many actors maintain, but Isadora was definitely an exponent, and in its most extreme form, of the second school of thought.

No wonder, then, that even the most primitive audiences in the United States, whose taste was perfectly satisfied by music hall divertissements, and for whom, according to Charles Frohman, Isadora's art was above their heads, were now so overwhelmed by Isadora's magical personality that they sat spellbound in the packed halls, not knowing whether to cheer or to remain reverently silent.

PART THREE

Chapter XV

Most probably it would have been wiser for Isadora to remain in New York, and try to further the initial success she had at last achieved in the United States. She even toyed with the idea of having some of her pupils brought over to join in her future performances. But she was homesick for Paris, where she did not yet have a house, except for the one she had been dreaming she was going to buy; she was longing for Deirdre, whom she had not seen for more than six months; she was anxious about her pupils, of whom she had heard practically nothing, except in one of Mary Sturges's flippant letters; and she was also disturbed by the mysterious gossip about Elizabeth establishing her own school in Darmstadt. Therefore, made confident by the new turn of her fortunes, and with her "coffers replenished with gold," as she liked to say, she sailed back to France early in January 1909.

Upon her arrival in Paris, she wept with joy on taking Deirdre in her arms again. She proceeded to rent two large apartments at 5 rue Danton—one for herself and the other for her pupils, whom she rescued from the "magnificence" of the Château Villegenis. Full of energy, she decided to give a series of performances in Paris almost immediately.

From her previous experiences, as well as her most recent one in the United States, Isadora was convinced that "no matter how great the artist, without the proper setting even the greatest art can be lost." Therefore, she was extremely pleased when Lugné-Poe, the director of the Théâtre de L'Oeuvre, offered to manage her performances at the Gaieté-Lyrique Theater. Isadora had perfect confidence in him because of his successful record in introducing Eleanora Duse to the Parisian public, as well as Henrik Ibsen's plays. He was convinced that Isadora should be presented in the best possible light, and he engaged Edouard Colonne, the eminent French conductor (the Colonne Orchestra was one of the major ensembles in France), to complete the programs as Isadora's partner.

But even with the success of these performances during the month of March, Isadora's financial resources were far from sufficient to allow her to organize and maintain another school in France, as she had been planning ever since her appearances with Walter Damrosch had considerably improved her situation. And now that "Paris had turned a smiling countenance" upon her during her engagement at the Gaieté-Lyrique under the Lugné-Poe management, she was more than ever stimulated to pursue her design. But she simply did not have the money, nor could she ever hope to earn enough by herself to subsidize such a project. "I must find a millionaire!" she kept saying. As she reported later, that prayer was repeated "first in a joke and then, finally, according to the Coué system, in earnest."

I am no judge of Emile Coué's system of autosuggestion and its immediate effect on millionaires, but while Isadora was resting in her dressing room after one of the matinee performances, Isadora's maid brought her the visiting card of a man who had come to pay homage to her—Paris Eugene Singer.

With this meeting, the second part of Isadora's personal and artistic life began. About this period, we have relatively little reliable information, especially with regard to the intimate relationship between Isadora and Paris Singer. The chief reason is that while Isadora was writing her memoirs, in which she naively professed to tell "nothing but the truth," Paris Singer was himself living in Paris. He was aware that she was working on an account of her life, and as her publishers and she herself feared, he could easily stop publication if he chose. Thus, despite the vital importance of this stage of Isadora's life, neither the chapters dealing with this period in her reminiscences nor information supplied later by those who wrote about Isadora, provide an adequate picture of the problems raised by their union, albeit it endured for several years, and included the most tragic event of Isadora's entire life.

Actually, the version given in Isadora's memoirs of her relationship with Paris Singer was so belabored, so rewritten, included so many insinuations or so-called frank disclosures, and exaggerations and misquotations, that it leaves the reader with a picture that is not merely inaccurate but necessarily one-sided as well. Paris Singer never publicly disclosed his own views on the subject, and to the best of my knowledge he left nothing in writing that might contribute to a fair portrayal of this episode in Isadora's life.

I myself saw more than one of Isadora's "provisional" drafts, which were intended to keep "the sheep alive, and the wolves satisfied." Each of these was rewritten over and over again to conform to every new bit of advice from well-wishing friends and those who claimed to be competent in literary matters. Accordingly, the final published version bears no resemblance whatsoever to some of the facts.

"My first thought was: Lohengrin." Or so Isadora reports in describing their meeting. But this formula was actually adopted after long deliberation on how best to disguise Singer's identity, for, as Isadora herself told me, when she first read his visiting card, she did not have the vaguest idea who Paris Singer was. Fortunately for her, in describing their first meeting, she did not follow her own thought: *Wer Will mein Ritter sein?* with *La ci darem la mano.* Nor did Singer behave like the rich merchant Semyon Rogozhin in Dostoevsky's novel *The Idiot,* who comes to buy Nastasya Filipovna by throwing a large package of roubles on the table.

After being ushered into Isadora's dressing room, and having bent down to kiss Isadora's hand, according to her recollections, Singer said in a shy and charming voice: "You do not know me, but I have often applauded your wonderful art."

We can be sure, however, that he was not so blunt as to say to Isadora, as soon as he introduced himself, "I have come to help you. What can I do? Would you like, for instance, to go with all the dancing children to a little villa by the sea, on the Riviera, and there compose new dances? You don't need to worry about the expense, I will bear it all. You have done a great work; you must be tired. Now let it rest on my shoulders." At that meeting, despite Isadora's testimony, he clearly said nothing of the kind, but he did ask her if at some future time he could call on her at her home and bring his daughter, who had just returned from school in Germany, to meet Isadora's pupils. Only much later, when he learned that after Isadora completed her Paris appearances at the Gaieté-Lyrique she was going to Nice to fulfill her engagements there, did he graciously invite her to stay at a small villa near the sea in Beaulieu.

This man over six feet tall, with copper blond hair and a small beard—as was then customary for men of distinction—was *the millionaire* apparently selected and guided to Isadora by Coué's system. Singer's attitudes and actions were such as befitted a member of the family to which he belonged. He was one of the youngest sons among the twenty-three children of Isaac Merrit Singer (1811-1875), the American magnate of the Singer Sewing Machine Company. Contrary to the supposition that he was named for Priam's legendary son, who by abducting the beautiful Helen ignited the Trojan War, his name was really given him because he had been born in Paris, just as one of his brothers was named Washington because he first saw the light in the capital of the United States.

Not at their first meeting, but much later, Isadora remembered that some eight years before she had seen him at the funeral of Prince Edmond de Polignac. During those years at the turn of the century, when Isadora went to Paris for the first time, the prince was a great admirer of her dancing, and he and the princess were always among the most generous patrons of her art. Now she learned that the princess was Paris Singer's eldest sister. She also learned that his youngest sister, Isabella, "had married and regilded the *blason* of the Duc de Decazes, another member of the French aristocracy," and that Paris himself was on an intimate footing with many members of the French and British aristocracies.

He had been educated in England, where he had married. He had five children, four sons and a daughter. At the time he met Isadora he was forty-two years old, a handsome prince with impeccable manners. His generous schemes were ministered to by his large fortune.

Although the name "Lohengrin" was invented simply to serve as a disguise in Isadora's book, and she never thought of calling him by that name, she did regard him at the time of their first meeting as a Prince Charming "to be worshipped at a distance, in an almost spiritual fashion." However, in a very short while they became lovers. Leaving Isadora's pupils in care of a governess, but taking Deirdre along with them, they sailed to Italy on Singer's magnificent yacht the *Lady Alicia,* which he now rechristened *Isis* after the Egyptian goddess of fertility. Later he always used this name as an endearing term for Isadora.

But when Isadora was writing her reminiscences, she was so bewildered about her feelings toward Paris Singer—ranging from the memories of true happiness to hurt pride, resentment, and even antipathy—that she was incapable of giving a rational account of their union. One thing was certain: Her love affair with Paris Singer could not be compared to the one she had had with Gordon Craig. The solid basis of mutual artistic interests that had provided a stimulus in her relationship with Craig was lacking in her new liaison. Paris Singer, unlike his sister, was neither musical nor particularly interested in music or the other arts. I am inclined to trust the verity of the occasional recollections of her life with Paris Singer in which she tried to explain to me aspects of her feelings toward him. She said, "You see, he was a man who, after we had shown ourselves for everybody to admire during the intermission of a play or the opera, could barely wait for the end of the performance to take me to a sumptuous dinner. Sometimes, even worse, we would go to a noisy nightclub, wiping out the sublime enjoyment I had had while watching the performance. I used to grow so nervous in anticipation of this almost inevitable finale that I, too, would become fidgety and miss what I otherwise would have enjoyed to the last word."

In her recollections, Isadora wrote: "If I had only realized that the man I was with had the psychology of a spoilt child, that every word and every action of mine should have been carefully prepared to please, all might have been well.

"But I was too young and too naive to know this, and I prattled on, explaining to him my ideas of life, Plato's *Republic,* Karl Marx, and a general reform of the world, without the least notion of the havoc I was creating. This man, who had declared that he loved me for my courage and generosity, became more and more alarmed when he found what sort of red-hot revolutionary he had taken aboard his yacht."

Writing this in retrospect over fifteen years later, Isadora underestimated Paris Singer's intelligence, which was in fact superior. Having myself seen Isadora pose as a hot revolutionary on many uncalled-for occasions, and having heard her "prattle" on political and revolutionary themes after her sojourn in Soviet Russia, where she had picked up some names connected with world history, I can easily imagine how her superficial attitudes on such questions could finally have persuaded Singer that he could not reconcile her ideas with his own peace of mind. It was one thing for her to allude in her speeches from the stage to vague revolutionary theories, thus producing on the less informed in her audience the effect of the red-hot revolutionary she so much desired to appear. It was quite another to discuss those notions with someone who would have to have his questions answered, if he was ever to be convinced.

Among the political speeches she delivered, one remained almost classical. After the Russian Revolution, and after her return from Russia, when she apparently felt well versed in political matters, she started her speech after her performance with an account of her private version of the Soviets. Fortunately, she was interrupted by Charles Rappaport, at the time a distinguished member of the French Chamber of Deputies and an adherent of the Communist Party, who got up from his front row seat and, gesticulating wildly, threatened: "If Isadora Duncan continues to talk on communism, I will do a Greek dance." Even Isadora had to laugh with the audience and stop her speech.

Charles Rappaport was Isadora's devoted friend, and during the last years of her life, he often spent whole evenings reading poetry to her, or discussing the arts in general. But, while with such men as Rappaport, Isadora was careful not to bring up the names of Marx and Lenin, she did not always succeed in keeping off the subject of communism and her own ideas about it. Rappaport would listen quietly to her, and nodding his head, would say to me in Russian, "Isadora is like a child, but she has a great soul."

If Stanislavsky was justified in saying that she "did not know how to speak of her art logically and systematically," she certainly was utterly incoherent in her attempts at political discourse. I venture to say that at the time she was lecturing Paris Singer on "a general reform of the world," as she recounts in her memoirs, if she had been shown a photograph of Karl Marx, she would most probably have taken it for that of Giuseppe Verdi.

As it happened, Paris Singer was passionately in love with her and took all her "prattle" seriously, and what was even more disturbing to him, personally. The poor man suddenly found himself in the unfortunate position of being rich and therefore responsible for the social injustice in the world. "And, in the meantime, the magnificent yacht sailed on through the blue Mediterranean," Isadora wrote later. "I can see it all as if it were yesterday; the broad deck of the yacht, the table set with crystal and silver for lunch, and Deirdre, in her white tunic, dancing about. Certainly I was in love and happy. And yet, all the time I was unpleasantly aware of the stokers, stoking in the engine-room, and fifty sailors on the yacht; the Captain and the Mate—all this immense expenditure for the pleasure of two people."

Paris Singer, who most probably never gave a thought to his right to his fortune, now was made conscious of the intrinsic values in human endeavors from an economic point of view. One evening Isadora read to him Walt Whitman's "Song of the Open Road," her favorite poem. Singer exclaimed "What rot! That man could never have earned his living."

"Can't you see," Isadora protested, "he had the vision of Free America?"

"Vision be damned!" Singer exclaimed.

Apparently Isadora did not realize that she was reaping an unexpectedly rich harvest from virgin soil, which it would have been wiser to leave uncultivated. Thus, when she finally approached the subject of financial support for her school, to Paris Singer it merely meant another investment. But, since he regarded all arts as "pleasure and leisure," he saw no particular enticement for capital here, except as a personal present to his beloved, which he could easily afford.

But, as for Isadora's vision of having hundreds of thousands of children all over the world prancing in tunics because, according to her, Greek art had developed from just such youthful exercises, Paris Singer would have been more interested to hear of some practical aim for the girls, instead of having them spend their seventeen years merely "worshiping beauty."

But as far as Isadora was concerned, Singer was not entirely lacking in some romantic vision of his own. When they reached Pompeii, he conceived the idea of having Isadora dance for him in the Temple of Paestum by moonlight. That temple stands near the Bay of Salerno. A small Neapolitan orchestra was to provide the necessary music, but the performance was "rained out," so to speak. He should have stopped right then and there his first experiment in theater management, but as became a generous host, he "had ordered dozens of bottles of wine and lamb . . . which they all ate Arab fashion with their fingers. The famished orchestra ate and drank so much and were so fatigued from . . . waiting . . . that they were quite unable to play." A drizzling rain and the rolling of the yacht sent the musicians back to their cabins, thus ending Singer's romantic scheme of Isadora's "dancing for him."

While Singer expected to continue their voyage in the Mediterranean, Isadora became subconsciously, as she said, "uneasy of mind at the passing of the days." Remembering that she had to fulfill her engagements in Russia, she insisted on an immediate return to Paris. Whether while writing her memoirs she forgot or intentionally omitted mentioning her performances at the Gaieté-Lyrique in June before going to Russia, they do not figure in her book. And yet, as far as Paris Singer was concerned in sharing her "great idea" of using practically the whole world as a playground for dancing youth, and carrying its financial responsibility, it was in connection with those very performances that he was given a vivid example of the problems arising from such an enterprise.

Upon their return to Paris, Singer was given the most realistic example of the promotion of an artistic project on the scale that Isadora envisioned for her own appearances: They found themselves in the midst of the Parisians' entire absorption in Sergei Diaghilev's forthcoming presentation of his third Russian season. Having learned from experience during the previous year that it was useless to try to divert audiences from their enthusiasm for the Diaghilev productions, Isadora should have refrained from competing, but her confidence in Lugné-Poe and his seemingly reasonable arguments overruled her indecision. She agreed to fulfill her contracts with him for her return performances in June.

Still, no amount of ingenuity in Lugné-Poe's publicity for the finesse and superior qualities of Isadora's art compared to anything Parisian audiences had ever been offered could stand up against Diaghilev's genius for promoting his product, the Ballets Russes, as the glamorous attraction of the season. Even before the spectators ever witnessed the sensational feats of the Ballets Russes, led by Anna Pavlova, Ekaterina Geltzer, Tamara Karsavina, Michel Mordkin, and Nijinsky, Diaghilev saw to it that enthusiasm for the forthcoming productions engulfed the whole artistic world of Paris. "The very air should be intoxicated," was Diaghilev's own prescription. And neither Isadora nor Paris Singer could fail to be aware of it.

The Russians, as might have been expected, arrived in Paris at the end of April, a little late to prepare for the opening night in May, especially since they discovered that the floor at the Châtelet Theater, where their performances were to take place, was uneven, that the orchestra pit was too large and had to have loges built there, that the theater looked like a barn, and that no masterpiece could be adequately appreciated in such an ambiance.

Practically everything had to be renovated and redecorated. Carpenters, electricians, and workers of every trade were required. But watching the feverish preoccupation with every detail of these "barbarians," as the French affectionately referred to them, and all of whom were a little mad, everyone was willing to help. In the midst of all the hammering that went on throughout the theater, including the stage, where the carpenters were at work, while half-unpacked trunks were in everybody's way, the dancers kept rehearsing their *entrechats* and pirouettes to the accompaniment of an invisible upright piano; in haste they snatched their lunches, which were delivered from the most elegant restaurants and placed near them on chairs, tables, and even on the floor of the stage. "What do you expect? They are savages," the French smiled and shrugged, and Diaghilev, who valued above all the publicity of "human interest," saw to it that the whole of Paris heard about his troupe, read of it in the press, and talked about it.

"Something akin to a miracle, the stage and audience trembled in a unison of emotion," Tamara Karsavina, the famous ballerina, later remarked about the first night performance on May 19, 1909.

Innumerable flattering reports, covering whole pages in the Paris newspapers, described in detail every manifestation of the remarkable artistry of the Russian performers. But none could ever credibly explain Nijinsky's leap into the air during the performance of *Pavillon d'Armide*, the first ballet on the program which, like an opening gong, ignited the enthusiasm of the audience—never to abate until the end of the Russian Season. After completing his *pas de trois* with Tamara Karsavina and his sister Bronislava, Nijinsky was supposed to leave the stage and later return for his solo number, but when he was a few yards from the wings, he leaped into the air, describing a parabola, floated on high, and vanished from sight.

The audience gasped at this impromptu virtuoso stunt, and cheered so loudly that the orchestra had to stop. From that moment on, with each following ballet on the evening's program, the enthusiasm of the audience grew in a steady crescendo, until it reached its climax when the curtain rose for the final dance on the program— the Polovetsian Dances from Alexander Borodin's opera *Prince Igor*. As if to show to the civilized Europeans what the true Asia can look like, the Russian painters produced a stage setting of such fantastic colors that no splendor of the Orient, familiar through fables, could surpass the picture that was offered to the audience. And when, in addition to this background and Borodin's exotic and powerful music, a horde of wild Tartars were seen on the stage dancing, leaping over each other with their unsheathed curved sabers slicing the air, it is not surprising that the audience rushed forward at the end of the dancing and actually tore down the orchestra rail to clasp the performers in their arms.

But there was more than one reason for Diaghilev's productions overshadowing Isadora's performances at the Gaieté-Lyrique. She no doubt saw with satisfaction that her choice of masterpieces from musical literature as partners in her performances, which she had introduced in Russia during her first visit there in 1905, not only had borne fruit, but had been further developed by the Russians, who chose music of the most fabulous coloring. And she must have been equally pleased to see that the Russian ballet masters and choreographers no longer adhered strictly to the old routine ballet precepts, according to which each technical "stunt" was sufficient unto itself and independent of the movements that preceded and which followed, but was now treated as a part of the meaning of the whole composition. Nevertheless, while the Russians had chosen the most exciting, colorful, and glamorous music for their repertory, Isadora's program was more select, refined, and even sublime, though perhaps less exciting visually. To the audiences that had witnessed the Polovetsian Dances at the Châtelet, Isadora's Bacchanale from *Tannhäuser* might have seemed like a dignified minuet.

But, fortunately, astute manager that he was, Lugné-Poe had assembled a different kind of audience for Isadora's performances, composed mostly of eminent painters, sculptors, poets, and literati, as well as a large number of students from the École des Beaux Arts.

Isadora's performances also resulted in drawings by Jean-Paul Laffite in four sections: *The Religious Dances, The Vases, The Bacchantes,* and *The Return of the Warriors,* published a year later (1910) by Mercure de France: designs by André de Segonzac in a limited edition of *La Belle Édition;* Grandjuan's series of twenty-five colored pastel facsimiles, and the famous sculptor Émile-Antoine Bourdelle's *Isadora Duncan, Fille de Prométhée,* as well as many watercolor and line drawings. In addition to his drawings, Bourdelle was responsible for immortalizing Isadora in the marble bas-relief of the façade in the interior of the auditorium of the Théâtre des Champs Élysées.

But all this was merely another succès d'estime. Isadora's admirers showered her with praise and assured her that she had taken Paris by storm—and in her memoirs she gives the impression that she really believed it. Yet deep in her heart she must have known that it was not so, and not being a novice in theatrical matters, she saw that she was getting no closer to her cherished goal—her school and the eventual choice of an ensemble for her performances.

But what was most discouraging was that Paris Singer was not as good an organizer as Diaghilev, and so far her millionaire showed more interest in her as a woman than in her ideas, her school, or her pupils. Perhaps at his suggestion that she be more practical, she decided to put on a more seemingly realistic basis her future arrangements with those pupils she already had and those she hoped to acquire in a future school. In a letter dated June 9, 1909, addressed to the parents of the girls who were still with her, she stipulated again that their children should remain at the school until they were seventeen, but this time she added that after their graduation they should repay the expenses of their education from half of the fees they earned from teaching in other schools.

This, however, was purely academic, for she well knew that she could never enforce such conditions. Meanwhile, since her "replenished coffers" were not as overflowing as she made them out to be on her return to France, she suggested that her pupils vacation with their families while she went on her tour to Russia.

Two remarks in her memoirs reveal the nature of her initial relationship with Paris Singer: "He would have come to Russia with me, but feared passport difficulties." If, indeed, she was given that impression by Singer himself, the story is wholly unlikely, for if only a few years before, the so-called Pim, a gigolo kept by a rich old woman, and whose avocation was to collect snuff boxes, was allowed to accompany Isadora to Russia, it is inconceivable that in Tsarist Russia Paris Singer would have met with anything but the most cordial welcome. Obviously Paris Singer did not wish to go to Russia with Isadora.

"He filled my compartment with flowers, and we said a tender good-bye," Isadora continues the description of her departure for Russia: "It is a strange fact that, when parting from a loved one, although we may be torn by the most terrible grief, we experience at the same time a curious sensation of liberation."

Chapter XVI

Besides having a "warm spot in her heart for Russia," this time
Isadora looked forward to a tour there because of the enthusiasm
always shown her by her audiences, and because her old cherished
desire to have Gordon Craig work at the Moscow Art Theater,
which despite the passing years had never left her mind, now seemed
to be nearing fulfillment. At least she had received that impression
when Stanislavsky had visited her in Paris and had told her of the
progress made in negotiations with Craig.

During that afternoon, Isadora had proudly showed him Deirdre, perhaps facetiously reminding him of his remark, "What will
we do with a child?"

"I saw Craig's and Isadora's little girl," Stanislavsky wrote to
his friends in Moscow, "a most charming child. Craig's temperament
and Duncan's grace. I liked her so much that Duncan promised to
let me have her if she [Isadora] should die. So here I am already
in a new role of grandfather or daddy. If she leaves me all her
future children, too, I can rest assured that I shall spend my old
age surrounded by a numerous family."

And, upon his return to Moscow, he wrote to Isadora: "It
was you who recommended Gordon Craig to us. You told us to
trust him and to create a second country for him in our theatre.
Come and find out how well we have carried out your wish." In
another letter he said: "Our whole company swears by the new

system and for that reason, as far as our work is concerned, this year promises to be interesting and important. In this work you have played a great part without knowing it. You have suggested to me many things which we have now discovered in our art. I thank you and your genius for that."

Craig arrived in Moscow in the middle of October "on a day of crackling frost, dressed in a spring coat, wearing a felt hat with large brim, with a long scarf around his neck, and without a cent in his pocket," according to Stanislavsky's recollections. The Russian director found him in one of the most expensive hotels in the city, where Craig received his distinguished visitor while splashing about in icy water in his bathtub. To save him from pneumonia, Stanislavsky saw to it that Craig was immediately supplied with a fur coat, a fur hat, and felt boots from the Moscow Art Theater wardrobe.

"When I made the acquaintance of Craig in his Adamic costume, I felt as if I had known him for a long time," Stanislavsky wrote in his memoirs. "The discussion of art that began between us seemed to be the continuation of a discussion that we might have been having the very day before. In his bathrobe, with his long wet hair, he heatedly explained to me his beloved fundamental principles, his original researches in the quest of a new art of movement." All this exposé Craig carried on in his Anglo-German jargon, while Stanislavsky could only converse in German or French. As might have been expected, the members of the Moscow Art Theater never left Craig in peace. He was taken to see Maeterlinck's *Blue Bird*, Ibsen's *An Enemy of the People*, Griboyedov's *Woe from Wit*, and Chekhov's *Cherry Orchard* and *Uncle Vanya*. All the productions, despite his not understanding a word of Russian, delighted him.

Craig proposed doing *Hamlet*.

"When I saw the sketches of scenery that Craig brought with him, I knew that Isadora Duncan had been right when she told me that her friend Craig was great not when he philosophized about art, but when he took brush in hand and painted," Stanislavsky said in his memoirs. "His sketches explained his artistic dreams and problems better than any words. The secret of Craig, however, was not in painting, but in his wonderful knowledge of the stage and of scenic nature. Craig was first of all a genius as a stage director."

At first Craig wanted Stanislavsky to play Hamlet, but eventually agreed to play the title role himself; as it happened, Stanislavsky admired him as an actor as much as he did as a stage director. The two men devoted Craig's three-week stay in Moscow to preparing the production of the play, scheduled for the following season. Craig insisted on analyzing every character in the play in the minutest detail, and on arriving at interpretations of the meaning of practically every sentence in the drama. It is interesting to note that when they were discussing the various ways of realizing Craig's conception of the "To be or not to be" soliloquy, they finally had to abandon Craig's way of interpreting it, because they agreed that no one except Isadora "could have realized the image of bright death, finding no scenic means for the showing of the dark shadows of life as they were drawn in Craig's sketches."

Isadora was not present at their meetings, nor did she witness Craig's work, but she heard that "all the actresses of the Stanislavsky company were in love with him, that they were delighted with his beauty, gentility, and extraordinary vitality, and that he would harangue them by the hour on the art of the theatre and that they did their best to follow all his fantasies and imaginings."

According to Isadora's recollections, Craig came to see her in Moscow, and Isadora "felt again all his old charm and fascination," in fact so much so that for "a short moment," she said, "I was on the verge of believing that nothing mattered—neither the School, nor Paris Singer, nor anything—but just the joy of seeing him again." About this point of her final meeting with Craig, there are two stories. Isadora's account is that, a few days later, during dinner on the eve of her departure for Kiev, Craig asked Isadora if she "meant to remain with him," and she hesitated with her answer: Craig "flew into one of his old-time rages, lifted my pretty secretary from her chair, carried her into the other room and locked the door."

According to Craig's "Collected Notes on Isadora Duncan," there was a rather tragic scene; she sought to rekindle his affection by making him jealous. In the process, she drank too much champagne, and Craig and Stanislavsky, who was also present, abandoned her rather than see her make a fool of herself.

Which of the two versions is authentic is unimportant, since the really significant fact is that they never met again. But, later, whenever she was forced for the sake of her memoirs to review her love life, she always maintained that she had never deserted a man, that it was the men who had left her, and she claimed that the dominant trait in her character was fidelity—in Craig's case her fidelity to Paris Singer.

The tragic end of their unresolved love was due to their incapacity to follow Duse's prescription: "To renew love—that is the secret."

After completing her tour in Russia, which this time was very brief, she returned to Paris, where Paris Singer received her in his apartment on the Place des Vosges.

At this point, her own record of her life suffers especially from the attempt to compromise between her sincere desire to write a good book about her ideas on art and her publishers' request for "love chapters—make it spicy." She succeeded in fulfilling neither one ideal nor the other.

To make things worse, in addition to the numerous suggestions from everybody who dropped in at her apartment and inquired about the progress of her memoirs, Mary Sturges, who then, after four marriages, had become Mary Desti, took an especially active part in helping Isadora to present the chapters concerning her relationship with Paris Singer in the "right light." She claimed wide personal experience in male psychology and considered the sexual domain to be her own. She took pains in assisting Isadora to describe her experiences and even interpolated some of her own emotional sensations gained through her various love affairs. Fortunately, in their primitive form these never reached the printed pages of Isadora's book.

One day, when Mary Desti came to continue her work on the "controversial chapter," I happened to be in Isadora's studio, and could easily see Mary's reaction to a recently written page, which she picked up from the manuscript lying on the piano. She settled herself on a couch and, after reading a few lines, came to a paragraph which apparently was familiar to her from her collaboration on it, but which she now proudly read aloud in its final form:

He took me there [Paris Singer's apartment in the Place des Vosges] into a Louis XIV bed, where he fairly smothered me with caresses. There, for the first time, I knew what the nerves and sensations can be transformed to. It seemed to me that I came to life in a new and exhilarating manner which I had never before known. . . .

Like Zeus, he transformed himself into many shapes and forms, and I knew him now as a Bull, now as a Swan, and again as a Golden Shower, and I was by this love carried over the waves, caressed with white wings delicately, and strangely seduced and hallowed in a Golden Cloud.

Obviously puzzled by the lines of the last paragraph, Mary Desti reread them; for she would have put in plainer language what she guessed was Isadora's description of her experiment in love making. But then she burst into loud laughter. Rereading the whole quotation aloud once more, she shouted to Isadora, who was getting dressed in the adjoining room: "This is marvelous! Terrific! Now this should get any man! My, oh, my! Now you needn't worry, he won't stop your book from being published. Men lap up that kind of stuff."

And, indeed, the paragraph was published. I am sure Isadora would herself have censored these uncalled-for intimate revelations had she not died before the manuscript went to press.

It is interesting that she, who only a few months before, according to a previous chapter in her memoirs, professed that "all money brings a curse with it, and the people who possess it cannot be happy for twenty-four hours," and that "sometimes [she] contrasted unfavorably the ease of this life of luxury, the continuing feasting, the nonchalant giving up of one's being to pleasure, with the bitter struggle of [her] youth," now seemed to have turned her back on the purely intellectual and artistic experiences with Stanislavsky and on the discussions of Craig's forthcoming production of *Hamlet*, and taken with ease to the life of a millionaire's mistress in Paris.

In his novel *The Life of Klim Samgin*, Maxim Gorky says, "Ah, but there are no 'simple people.' Some pretend to be simple, but actually they are like algebra problems with three or many unknowns."

No one in his right mind would ever have considered Isadora a "simple person"; that is, no one except herself, who was sincerely convinced of it. Isadora's was a most complex nature, full of contradictions, all of which were reflected in her beliefs, and in her actions.

Having gained a most glamourous consort, Paris Singer immediately introduced her to a luxurious life, in which first of all she had to sacrifice her simple attire for fashionable gowns designed by Paul Poiret, the leading Parisian designer at that time. Isadora, who cherished almost with reverence her little white tunics and her golden sandals, now "fell to the fatal lure of stuffs, colors, form—even hats." She dressed in beautiful gowns, her elegant escort led her proudly into fashionable restaurants and night clubs, and they seemed an admirably happy and distinguished couple.

Isadora quickly learned to appreciate French cooking, and to distinguish among the great vintages. She no longer worried over the fate of the downtrodden and enjoyed seeing the headwaiters bow and scrape before Singer as he lavishly tipped them. Isadora told me of the rather shrewd way Singer went about dispensing gratuities for good service—he distributed his generous tips to the waiters and chefs not after the meal had been served but before it began, to assure himself special attention.

But although she may not have been reminded of any ideas of social injustice, now perhaps she felt that she herself had become, as Paris Singer's consort, almost his accomplice in social injustice toward the world. There is no doubt that she felt very self-conscious about her position. She showed little sympathy for Singer's wealthy friends, referred to his women friends as "women with feathers in their heads," and, whenever she could, displayed an obvious preference for her own friends from the artistic world. She tried to impose upon Singer her belief in their personal superiority and the superiority of their values. Such attempts at preserving her independence of thought led to inevitable conflicts between the two. Stanislavsky, who was on a short visit to Paris in 1909, gives more than a glimpse of the developing situation in the following letter:

> I went to Duncan's for lunch. I was greeted by a very handsome man, taller than I. That was Singer. With exaggerated courtesy he takes me upstairs to D. and then he leaves. She is finishing dressing in her bedroom. I am awaiting her in the dining room. About twenty minutes pass without a word. It seems that they don't have lunches at home and so we drive to a restaurant.

> I am taken to a restaurant filled with cocottes and gigolos. We had exquisitely prepared dishes and talk of superficial banalities, slightly off-color.

D. is not to be recognized. She is trying to appear as a Parisian woman. He [Singer] is magnificent, business-like, and with excellent manners. I felt like a fool and didn't know how to escape. We finished our lunch. I wanted to pay, they would not let me. I wanted to leave but D. begged me to go with her to her studio. However, it turned out that we were driving back to Paris and, when we passed my hotel, I bid them good-by, and left.

The car begins to move, and D. bashfully, and almost secretly throws me a kiss. All this nonsense drove me into a depression.

No such sudden transformation could have happened without leaving more than mere traces, and especially in the eyes of such a close friend and admirer as Stanislavsky. Where previously there had been an intimate relationship, now suddenly there was a barrier, almost indicating the necessity for distance in the presence of Singer. And yet Stanislavsky could not miss her embarrassment in her attempts at acting a secondary role in a play unworthy of the Isadora Duncan he loved and admired.

Summarizing his first impression of the Isadora-Singer situation, he asked, "Is it possible that she has sold herself, or perhaps still worse that she actually needs this sort of thing?"

Obviously not wishing to be a witness to a similar occasion, he decided to go to her next performance and then to bid her good-bye in her dressing room.

". . . Last night I saw the performance," Stanislavsky continued. "D. danced Beethoven, and this time exceptionally well. The program was very difficult. I did not go to see her during the intermission, but after the performance her maid ran after me and begged me to come to see D. It seems that during the day she had telephoned three times to my hotel, but they know me there only as Alekseyev [Stanislavsky was his stage name] and, therefore, assured her that there was no Mon. Stanislavsky staying at the hotel."

While he was in her dressing room, Isadora was resting, but from their conversation Stanislavsky gathered that "there had been some kind of stupid scene of jealousy between Singer and D. and that Singer had left." The jealous scene with Singer obviously was caused by Isadora's exceptional interest in Stanislavsky. "Therefore D. suggested that the two of us should have supper together. She was again very simple and witty. We were still in her dressing room, when Singer suddenly reappeared. We drove to supper at an elegant restaurant.

"D. was very charming and simple—dressed herself up in a white décolleté gown. Very effective. The supper was less *tortuous*. Singer was more simple and aimable, but I felt myself out of place. D. somehow makes everything confusing and Singer (speaking in English) laughed off her explanation for being dressed in a ball gown. [Stanislavsky did not know English.] After supper, I bid them good-by, this time for good, explaining that I was leaving Paris on the following day. Then D. begins to insist that I should come on the following day at about 4:30 for tea, because she had promised Charetie (the director of the Comédie Française) and somebody else that I will come to her. She was going to have a conference and a demonstration of her school. Many people were supposed to come. Singer also advised me to come.

"I became interested and decided to go by postponing my departure by one more day." And Stanislavsky closes his letter, saying, "Thus, all my sojourn in Paris brought nothing interesting. Perhaps today [his visit to Isadora] will compensate for the wasted time."

In September, taking Deirdre with her, Isadora went to Venice where, while watching her little girl play in the sands of the Lido, she spent hours contemplating her new mode of life, which seldom left her time for sober analysis. "I loved," she later wrote in her memoirs, "but I now knew something of the fickleness and selfish caprice of what men call love, and this sacrifice coming for my Art —perhaps fatal for my Art—my work—and suddenly I began to suffer an intense nostalgia for my Art—my work—my School. This human life seemed so heavy besides my dreams of Art."

Actually, Isadora's disquietude was caused by a problem to which she felt she had to attend without delay. She had discovered that she was pregnant. By comparison with her previous experience, this time her problem was two-fold: First, was she ready to have a child by a man who, though she loved him, indicated through his "selfish caprices" uncertainty in their future relationship? Secondly, was she ready to make the sacrifice, for the sake of her personal life, that would take her away from her art for a considerable length of time? Her physician, an old friend, was summoned to

Milan for a consultation on her problem, but apparently his advice was unsatisfactory, for despite his arguments, Isadora remained undecided.

Like some others who knew Isadora well, I was always skeptical about her "visions," which she attributed to being psychic. "We Irish are psychic," she liked to say. All her revelations on this subject given in her memoirs were, in my opinion, products of her desire to add color to her post factum narrative—products of an imagination that could and did, indeed, carry her into the most fantastic spheres of mental experience.

But considering her strong maternal feelings, far surpassing her passions, I am inclined to believe that at this time her mind was disturbed by indecision to a point that could easily have led to a vision such as she describes in her recollections. After asking her physician to give her an hour in which to make up her mind, she returned to her hotel:

I remember the bedroom of the hotel—a rather gloomy room—and facing me I suddenly saw a picture, a strange woman in an eighteenth-century gown, whose lovely but cruel eyes looked straight into mine. I stared at her eyes and they seemed to say, "it is the same. Look at my loveliness, that shone so many years ago. Death swallows all—all—why should you suffer and bring life into the world, only to be swallowed up by death?"

Her eyes became more cruel, more sinister, my anguish more terrible. I hid my eyes from hers with my hands. I tried to think, to decide. I implored those eyes, through the mist of my troubled tears, but they seemed to show no pity: relentless they mocked me. Life or Death, poor creature, you are in the relentless trap.

Finally I rose and spoke to the eyes. "No, you shall not trouble me. I believe in Life, in Love, in the sanctity of Nature's Law."

Was it imagination, or did there suddenly shine in those hard eyes a gleam of terrible, mocking laughter?

Isadora had made up her mind. She telegraphed Paris Singer, and after returning to Venice, took Deirdre into her arms and whispered: "You will have a little brother."

Chapter XVII

A month later, in October, accompanied by Paris Singer, Isadora sailed for the United States to fulfill her engagements with Walter Damrosch and the New York Symphony. Traveling to and in America, the life of luxury she led with Paris Singer at her side was no different from the one they had led in Europe, whether in sumptuous suites on ocean liners, or hotels in New York and other cities.

As had happened before, and will always happen to an artist of high caliber, there were reviews of her performances that sounded like odes to her art, and there were those that cried anathema, but the galleries of the sold-out houses clamored for more and more performances. Unfortunately, Isadora could not satisfy *vox populi*, because her pregnancy was becoming obvious to her audiences, especially to that portion seated in the front rows.

To a lady who remarked about Isadora's apparent physical condition, Isadora tried to explain that that "was just what she meant by dancing to express Love—Woman—Formation—Springtime. Botticelli's picture, you know," she said, "the fruitful Earth—the three dancing Graces *enceinte*—the Madonna—the Zephyrs *enceinte* also. Everything rustling, promising New Life. That is what my Dance means. . . ."

Isadora had to cancel her tour and return to France.

Now a happy expectant father, Paris Singer was no longer

suffering from his neurasthenia (according to Isadora "a typical rich people's disease") and he took Isadora and Deirdre on a long journey to Egypt.

First they sailed in his yacht to Alexandria, and then they boarded a *dahabeah,* a sort of Egyptian houseboat, which Singer equipped with civilized conveniences. It was manned by thirty native sailors and several excellent cooks, and was bound up the Nile to Thebes and Denderah. To complete Isadora's pleasure, he had even engaged Hener Skene, a young and talented British pianist, to play Beethoven and Bach on a beautiful Steinway grand.

Thus the battle between love and art, which, Isadora claimed, was always raging in her own case, had now gone decisively in favor of love. She no longer asked, "What is going to happen to my performances?" and "What is going to happen to my school?" Besides, Paris Singer, apparently not too well informed, assured Isadora that her school was well taken care of by her sister Elizabeth.

The school, which had been Isadora's *idée fixe,* the main topic of her private and public discourses, was slowly progressing but in no way resembled Isadora's original ideas in its aim and functions, nor was it much affected by her sister Elizabeth's cooperation and mild influence. It had now been reconceived, and was being administered by a certain Max Merz, who would have called the school by his own name had he not been shrewd enough to know that Isadora Duncan's name would bring more prestige and financial profit than the unremarkable one of Max Merz.

He was an Austrian, born in Vienna of Czech parents—or so he said, because at that time it was fashionable and almost mandatory for a musician to be Czech. He did study music, had learned to play the piano, and called himself a composer when he went to Berlin in 1906. After seeing Isadora dance, he applied for a job at the Grünewald School. It seems that at this time his "Viennese charm of Küss-die-Hand type of flattery" (as Irma Duncan puts it in her book) had won him favors from the Berlin ladies, but he failed to attract Isadora. He consoled himself with the second choice, Elizabeth, with whom he soon had a love affair; she bore a stillborn child. Though they did not marry, their participation in the school provided a bond from that time on.

Because of the circumstances of Isadora's personal life, as well as because of her tours, she was too far away to exert effective influence on the school. While Elizabeth still retained her confidence, Isadora nevertheless lost all real control of the institution. Merz wasted no time in transforming the school according to his own precepts and, unbelievable as it may appear today, his ideas were forerunners of what almost a quarter of a century later were to be the themes of Adolf Hitler's *Kraft durch Freude*—Strength through Joy—movement and the *Hitler Jugend*.

Merz possessed the qualities and characteristics that in Hitler's Germany made a noble Nazi. That is, he was fanatically devoted to everything Germanic, accepted as an axiom the superiority of the German race, insisted on the importance of "race culture"—all of which were to be the basis for creating an image of perfect German womanhood. Merz found that, with his eloquence on these subjects, he could divert those Germans at whose financial assistance he aimed from Isadora's principles of the dance to his own. These were confined to purely gymnastic exercises, no different from those practiced at Swedish schools. As Ernest Louis, the Grand Duke of Hesse, Merz's benefactor and the donor of the large property for the school at Darmstadt, once remarked, "These gymnastics can be taught by any corporal in my regiment."

Thus, except for the furniture and some of Isadora's possessions at the Grünewald School, which Merz found useful enough to transport to Darmstadt, there was practically nothing left of "Isadora Duncan" in Merz's own enterprise.

When Merz learned of Isadora's intentions of eventually moving her school to France, he prevailed on Elizabeth to remain in Germany and keep all the furnishings appropriated from Grünewald. He had sufficient power over Elizabeth to induce her to have the following statement published in the German press:

With reference to the sojourn of my sister Isadora Duncan and her school in Paris, [then nonexistent except in Isadora's plans but already feared by Merz] I beg to state that I have been associated with this school since its foundation in the capacity of both teacher and director. My own activities have been widely recognized in Germany. I, therefore, declare that I am not taking any part in the reestablishing of a new school in Paris, France. As repeatedly stated, I shall continue my activities in Germany, especially at Darmstadt, where my own school is now in the progress of being built. I beg you not to construe this as turning against my sister. I merely will

I *Mary Dora Gray Duncan, Isadora's mother, a music teacher who supported her family of four by herself, imbuing them with an interest in music and dance. She named her younger daughter Dora Angela but an early manager changed it to Isadora.*

Joseph Charles Duncan, Isadora's father, a Californian whose newspaper ventures went sour, provoking him to abandon his family. The parents were later divorced.

II *Isadora, with the*
Augustin Daly troupe,
traveled across the U. S.
and to London, 1895.
Unhappy because she
could not dance in her
own style, she left to
make her own way.

III *Munich, about 1902.*
Called "the goddess-like,"
Isadora was more
popular in Germany
than anywhere else at the
time. Students harnessed
themselves as horses
to her carriage to drive
her home from the
theater, serenading her
most of the night.

IV *One of a series in this dress, given by Isadora to friends as a New Year's greeting, January, 1903.*

V *Isadora with Oskar Beregi, Budapest, 1903. The handsome Hungarian actor, whom she called "Romeo" in her memoirs, was her first lover. The formal portrait belies the emotional and physical stress this affair caused, making it impossible for Isadora to dance for some time.*

VI   *Isadora and Gordon Craig photographed in 1904 by Elise de Brouck-*
ers. Craig, famed pioneer stage designer, was to be father of Isadora's first
child.

VII   *Gordon Craig,*
photographed by Isadora,
Berlin, 1905. Their affair
was poignant and stormy,
on Isadora's part full of
jealousy.

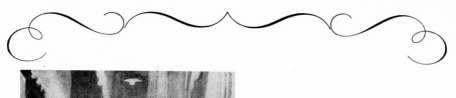

VIII *Drawing of Isadora by
Gordon Craig, 1905.*

IX *Water color and
pencil drawing by Auguste
Rodin who said of Isadora
that she perfectly unified
life and the dance.*

X *With Deirdre and Patrick (whose father was Paris Singer), her beautiful children killed in an accident. Isadora told the author, "They were the best of my life."*

XI *Paris Singer, the millionaire Isadora called "Lohengrin" in her memoirs. His affair with her lasted on and off for many years. His card, borne on a tray by a servant, arrived at her dressing room just as Isadora, a great believer in the occult when it worked, had wished for a "millionaire" to solve her problems.*

XII *Eleonora Duse, the great Italian actress who was so good a friend to Isadora, so great a comfort upon the tragic death of her children, that this miniature she gave Isadora was always kept at her bedside.*

XIII *Isadora at her school in Grunewald, Germany, 1905.*
Among the students are Irma, Anna, Therese, Lisl, Margot, and
Erica Duncan.

XIV *Duncan Dancers, the six "Isadorables" photographed by Arnold*
Genthe at a later age.

XV *Rare dance programs of Isadora's influential performances in Moscow before the Revolution, 1908, 1912, 1913, 1914. The revolutionary dances,* Marseillaise *and* Marche Slav, *would not be seen in Russia till her later visit.*

БОЛЬШОЙ ЗАЛЪ КОНСЕРВАТОРІИ.

Въ Четвергъ, 22-го Мая.

≡ ВЕЧЕРЪ ТАНЦЕВЪ ≡

УЧЕНИЦЪ

Айседоры ДУНКАНЪ.

Начало въ 8 час. вечера.

ТЕЛЕФОНЪ № 35-23

ОПЕРА
С. И. ЗИМИНА.

Сезонъ 1912—1913 гг.

Драматическій театръ.
(Городской)

Въ среду, 6 февраля 1913 года
ВЕЧЕРЪ
А. ДУНКАНЪ
Chopin-abend

Отдѣленіе 1-е.

1. Nocturne	. . . . . .	Hener Skene.
2. Deux Nocturnes	. . . .	Miss Duncan.
3. Etude	. . . .	Miss Duncan.
4. Etude	. . . . . .	Hener Skene.
5. Mazurka	. . . . . .	Hener Skene.
6. a) Mazurka b) Mazurka	. . . . .	Miss Duncan.
7. Valse	. . . . . .	Hener Skene.
8. a) Valse b) Valse	. . . . .	Miss Duncan.

Отдѣленіе 2-е.

9. Ballade	. . . . .	Hener Skene.
10. Quatre Preludes	. . . .	Miss Duncan.
11. Valse	. . . . .	Hener Skene.
12. Deux Valses	. . . .	Miss Duncan.

Рояль фабрики К. М. Шредеръ.

Начало въ 8½ час. вечера.

Дирекція В. Д. Рѣзникова.

Печатать разрѣшено—за Полиціймейстера Шостенко.
Харьковъ, Тип. М. Брейтшутъ и С-вья, Павловск, 14.

Театръ „МУЗЫКАЛЬНОЙ ДРАМЫ"
(КОНСЕРВАТОРІЯ).

Въ Понедѣльникъ, 18-го Февраля,

ПРОГРАММА
ПРОЩАЛЬНАГО ВЕЧЕРА
Айседоры
ДУНКАНЪ,

съ участіемъ солистовъ, хора и оркестра «Музыкальной драмы» подъ управленіемъ М. А. Бихтера.

Цѣна 5 коп.

XVI *Isadora on her terrace
at Bellevue, St. Cloud,
France, about 1914. On this
beautiful estate purchased
for her by Singer, Isadora
lived, taught and had some
of her most optimistic years,
her hopes still high for a
permanent school.*

XVII *Isadora, wearing
ermine, about 1915.*

XVIII *The so-called Isadora Duncan School, Darmstadt, Germany, run by her sister Elizabeth and Max Merz, at far right.*

XIX *A posed photo about 1915. Ellen Tells, the dancer, told the author that when Isadora made a gesture, it seemed to leave a ripple in the air.*

XX *With Allan Ross Macdougall, Palm Beach, about 1917; the secretary hired for her by Paris Singer, "Dougie" was to remain her good friend.*

XXI *Isadora on the Caryatid Porch of Erectheum, Acropolis, photographed by her friend, Edward Steichen, about 1920. Anna Duncan is on the left, Therese on the right.*

XXII *Isadora with her school in Moscow, 1921. Irma is standing at her left.*

XXIII *Konstantin Stanislavsky, left, founder of the Moscow Art Thea-*
tre. He and Isadora were good friends; though rumors of their affair were
false, they did influence each other theatrically. Commissar Anatoly Luna-
charsky, right, in charge of cultural matters in the Soviet Union, made
possible Isadora's work, her school there, and her later departure, too.

XXIV *Isadora and the Russian poet, Sergei Essenin, Moscow, 1922. She had had several lovers and two children, had talked against marriage, yet in 1923, she was to marry this man 15 years her junior who spoke not a word of English. Their life together, in Russia, in Europe, touring the U. S., was a tragi-comedy of tears, poignance, and absurdity.*

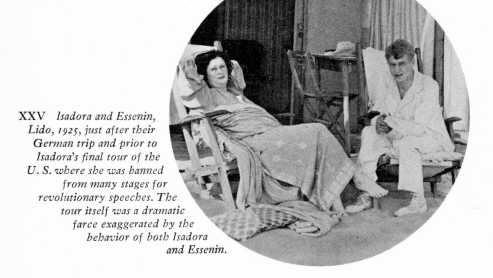

XXV *Isadora and Essenin, Lido, 1925, just after their German trip and prior to Isadora's final tour of the U. S. where she was banned from many stages for revolutionary speeches. The tour itself was a dramatic farce exaggerated by the behavior of both Isadora and Essenin.*

XXVI *Raymond Duncan,
an early self-styled Bohemian,
in the garden of the author's
studio, Paris, 1925.*

XXVII *Augustin
Duncan, Isadora's eldest
brother, who was to
become a successful actor
and director in the U.S.*

XXVIII *Elizabeth Duncan,
Isadora's elder sister, in a
photo given the author in
Klessheim in 1934.*

XXIX   *Isadora's funeral, Paris. Raymond in his toga escorts Elizabeth;
behind, the author escorts Mary Desti and Christine Dalies, one-time
Duncan secretary.*

Nice, September 16, 1927

Tonight Isadora Duncan's remains will be sent to Paris. Her Soviet
passport was found in her bag and it was therefore necessary to get
permission from the Soviet representative in Marseilles but these
formalities were quickly handled and the casket taken to Paris. It is
accompanied by Raymond Duncan and the Russian pianist, Victor
Seroff.

—*Translated from the Russian-language paper,* Poslenye Novosty, *Paris*

continue to pursue my long and successful—if at times difficult—activities in Germany. I shall proceed on my chosen path with the guarantee of the fine support I have received so far for my undertaking.

This declaration was beyond Elizabeth's powers of invention, and was most probably dictated by Merz to Elizabeth and sent to the parents of all Isadora's girls, whom Merz was anxious to have in his own school. And it did have an immediate effect. Since all the girls were German except Anna, who was Swiss, the parents were in favor of having their girls in a school in their own country.

But Merz needed at least a few dancers to illustrate his main topic—*Körperkultur* (physical culture) and there were none advanced enough to be exhibited except the pupils from Isadora's school. According to Irma Duncan, Elizabeth, following Merz's directives, tried to kidnap a few of Isadora's girls at the time when they were uncertain about their future at the Château Villegenis. And later, when on leaving for a tour in Russia, Isadora suggested the girls have their vacations with their families, Merz went about collecting Isadora's best pupils who willy-nilly joined his school for they were dancers, and where else could they go? At least while still connected with a so-called Isadora school, they could hold on to the hope that sooner or later Isadora would call them to her.

And, indeed, after learning from the girls what had been happening and exclaiming, "what do you mean by saying my sister has stolen my girls? . . . This is an outrage! How could my own sister do a thing like that to me? It is utterly incredible!" Isadora did promise the girls, "Very soon I'll have a beautiful new school in France—just have a little patience." But at that time, she did nothing about it and let the girls remain at Elizabeth's school.

While waiting for the buildings to be completed at Darmstadt, the Elizabeth Duncan—Merz school was located in Frankfurt-am-Main. There the six girls (Anna, Irma, Therese, Lisa, Margot, and Erica) the nucleus of the future school, were living in an old "musty-smelling house, filled with books, for the owner, Dr. Kling, an elderly bachelor, had been the founder of the German Museum in Nürnberg. To rapidly indoctrinate the girls into *Körperkultur* and racism, and the theories of the purity of German blood, and to erase even from their physical appearance the Isadora Duncan stamp, Merz devised for them uncomfortable uniforms of "scratchy gray woolen cloth, with similar scratchy woolen underwear, and gray woolen stockings shaped like long opera gloves."

Although posing as a great idealist, Merz was actually a shrewd businessman. To recruit an even larger number of pupils, he periodically arranged dance performances with Isadora's girls as the main performers and also took them on tours. He never missed an opportunity to lecture the audiences on his favorite theme—the perfect image of German womanhood, as a result of *Körperkultur,* as provided by his school. In his enthusiastic presentation of this overwhelming idea, he evoked the Germanic Gods: "Baldur! Oh, mighty sun god! I implore thee to cast thy golden rays upon our work!" Irma Duncan quotes the following remarks by a Hamburg critic:

> The Elizabeth Dancing School for young girls of the privileged class purports to be an institution devoted to physical culture—and not to the art of the dance. Then why, for heaven's sake, do they distort the picture of their intentions by giving dance performances?

> I am convinced that the majority of the public, despite the explanations of director Max Merz, left the theatre with the impression that this physical-culture institution represents a dancing school. This is probably due to the name of Isadora Duncan, whose spirit presides over the whole show.

And indeed Isadora's girls had managed to retain in their dance what they had learned from her. What was even more fortunate, they were completely immune to Merz's lofty ideals, which they did not understand, but which later on, with Hitler's appearance, succeeded in evoking the contempt of the rest of the world. Of the various propaganda exhibition tours through German provincial towns, one, devised by Merz and given as a climax to the girls' gymnastic performances, was particularly noteworthy. It took place during the Hygienic Exhibition in Dresden in 1911. According to Merz's appraisal of the individual beauty of the different parts of each girl's body, special plaster casts had been made which, when exhibited in a large hall, were to show the onlookers the success Merz had achieved in creating the perfect body of German womanhood. The girls' torsos, legs, arms, feet, and hands were displayed, each separately placed on a stand, while "a giant replica of a transparent heart pumping red blood greeted the visitors."

Speaking of this extraordinary "propaganda" scheme for Merz's national ideas, as well as his methods of recruiting pupils for the school, Anna Duncan recently told me that when Isadora was passing through Dresden on a pleasure trip with Paris Singer, she saw the Hygienic Exhibition. She was so horrified that all she could exclaim was, "But this is a morgue!"

No wonder that Isadora was even more shocked when she saw the girls dance. But this happened later, after her return from her latest tour of Russia, when she had asked Elizabeth to bring to her the six girls who were to participate in her performances at the Châtelet Theater. "They are terrible, so stiff, simply terrible!" she cried to Hener Skene, "They dance like automatons!"

I later saw enough of Max Merz to know the man, when the so-called Duncan School, which for commercial reasons always either insinuated or directly carried Isadora's name, was quartered in the Winter Palace at the Schloss Klessheim in Salzburg. As I have mentioned, I was living in the Summer Palace on the same estate and saw Elizabeth and Merz almost daily. Although it was in the early 1930s, when hordes of Hitler's *Jugend* were marching all over Germany, I failed to recognize the true reasons for Merz's "racial discrimination" toward the girls of the by then—so to speak—third generation of "pupils" at the school, who were *en pension* there, just as his ranting about "racial hygiene ideology" was more bewildering than illuminating to me, as it used to be to Isadora's girls in Darmstadt.

Still preaching high morals, the sanctity of matrimonial ties, and the "German family," nevertheless he did not seem to feel out of step with his own preachings while living openly in a *ménage à trois*, for he had brought a third person into the by now merely friendly relationship with Elizabeth, Gertrude Drück, a young woman from Stuttgart, who in addition to being his mistress, was elevated by him to the position of principal teacher at the school. And yet, while advocating the superiority of the aims and ideas of "his" school over those of Isadora, he did not flinch at criticizing Isadora as a woman. To gain favors from the mothers of prospective new pupils in Darmstadt, he confidentially whispered to them that Isadora actually used to rouge her lips in front of the girls.

Never suspecting that Merz could be among the fanatic adherents of the Nazi ideals, I saw him as merely a frail old man and a poor pianist. His ideas of German domination over the world should have been slightly dampened by the German debacle of World War I, but when given a chance, he spoke quite openly of *Der Tag,* when Hitler's Reich would set everything in sublime order for "a thousand years to come."

But while Isadora was enjoying the luxury of her trips to New York and Egypt, she was completely unaware of the transformation of her school under Merz's administration.

After their long voyage in Egypt, Paris Singer brought Isadora and Deidre to a palatial villa in Beaulieu Sur Mer, on the French Riviera, where, as Isadora recalled it, "On the first day of May, a morning when the sea was blue, and the sun was burning, and all Nature bursting into blossom and joy, my son was born."

Chapter XVIII

The blond, blue-eyed, healthy little boy was called Patrick. Having been provided by Paris Singer with the very best care, and with her private physician, Dr. Bosson, attending her at the child's birth, Isadora quickly recuperated and returned to Paris. Singer had an apartment awaiting her, at the Trianon Palace Hotel in Versailles, with one of his cars in the garage for her trips to Paris during the fashionable summer season.

"That same summer L. took it into his head that we should be married, although I protested to him that I was against marriage." That is the way Isadora put it when describing Paris Singer's proposal, which followed his separation from his first wife. Since her principles about marriage have been accorded so much public discussion, I feel I should quote verbatim her conversation with Paris Singer as she recollected it in her memoirs.

"How stupid for an artist to be married," I said, "and as I must spend my life making tours round the world, how could you spend your life in the stage-box admiring me?"

"You would not have to make tours if we were married," he answered.

"Then what should we do?"

"We should spend our time in my house in London, or at my place in the country."

L. proposed that we should try this life for three months.
"If you don't like it, I shall be much astonished."

Isadora agreed and they went to Devonshire, where Singer had
"a wonderful chateau which he had built after Versailles and the
Petit Trianon, with many bedrooms and bathrooms, and suites, all to
be at my disposition, with fourteen automobiles in the garage and a
yacht in the harbor."

"But after this experiment you still didn't marry him, and yet you
did marry later," I said to Isadora, many years after she had broken
her vows against marriage by marrying Sergei Essenin, the Russian
poet. We were on the beach in Nice, at the time when she was
writing her memoirs, and when she was especially confused and
concerned about her chapter dealing with her relationship with
Paris Singer, a subject that otherwise she rarely brought up. And,
perhaps because she was not feeling happy about the various drafts
of that chapter, she hoped that by merely expressing her thoughts
aloud to somebody like me, who was a more or less impartial listener,
she would find a better solution to the problem, She spoke slowly
in her low, warm, melodious voice, sometimes pausing between
sentences and looking at the wide horizon, as if trying to remember
an important detail in her story, or to find answers to my questions.

"I married Essenin for an entirely different reason," she said.
"There could never be any comparison between the two cases.
Marrying or not marrying Paris Singer had nothing to do with his
money. At that time I could have had all the money I needed and
all the luxury, at least for myself. All I had to do was to give my
performances and the money would flow like water into my bank
account." What Isadora failed to consider here was that the money
would flow out of her account with equal facility. "Nor did it have
anything to do with my love for him, or I wouldn't have had a
child with him. Even today I simply cannot comprehend how little
he understood me and my work. But, you see," Isadora looked at
me seriously, and then, smiling, added, "you have never lived with
a rich man and, unless you had, you wouldn't understand it."

I must have said that nothing could be easier to imagine than
a life where everything is accomplished as by waving a magic wand.

"That is the trouble, that is the core of it," Isadora said. "Can
you imagine a worse curse—I didn't have to imagine it, I have

witnessed it and am sorry to say even have lived through it. Just imagine how degrading it must be to be identified, not with yourself as a person, with what you have done or are doing, but with your signature on a check—the magic wand you just mentioned . . . . It is certainly more difficult for a rich man to accomplish anything serious in life— always that yacht in the harbor inviting one to sail these blue waters. And what can you say when a man says to you, 'I could never possibly earn as much money as I can sign for by simply writing out a check'?"

"But some rich men do work. Didn't Singer ever do any work at all?"

"Why, he was the busiest man you ever heard of," Isadora said. "At one time he was going to build an Italian castle on Cap Ferrat and on Mondays he would be rushing to Paris, and then rushing back to Cap Ferrat on Wednesdays."

"Didn't he have an office for his business?" I asked.

"Probably more than one, I don't remember, but he worked at home."

"What kind of business did he do at home?"

Isadora gave me a pitying look. "What does a rich man work at? He telephoned for hours, sitting at his huge desk—I wish I had one like that for writing my book—with two telephones—one wouldn't be enough—and he telephoned to his friends, making dates for lunches, parties, God knows what. That is hard work. You wouldn't understand it because you are not a rich man. Don't you see that when I asked him, 'What will we do when we get married?' he didn't have the faintest idea what I meant, and he never seemed to understand that for a creative person, 'doing something' was living, was breathing. He was neither creative nor 'interpretive' I mean in his schemes—none of them were ever carried out to the end, because they were products of momentary caprice. The building of that Italian castle was never finished," Isadora said pointing in the direction of Cap Ferrat. "All those schemes, and always on the grandiose scale, were his diversions, and he thought the same way about my Art. Why should I want to do anything if everything would be served up to me by the magic wand?"

I asked Isadora if he were not really interested in literature, history, or the arts.

"He had magnificent libraries, I mean *libraries*, in England and in France. They were so beautifully taken care of by his librarian, that I doubt if anybody ever dared touch a single book."

· "But he was a well-educated man, wasn't he?" I asked. "Was he?" Isadora repeated my question, and, after thinking about it, said, "I guess for his kind of society and friends . . . . Oh I must tell you, from all those years I remember only one story that he told me. I guess it was in exchange for all my erudite discourses on every possible subject. It was about the invention of the sewing machine."

"Did he invent it?" I asked. "Of course not, I wish he had. It was not even old Isaac, his father, but his grandfather who invented it. It seems that he struggled with it for years, because he could not solve the most important problem. Since a person sews with a needle, he first pierces the cloth with it and then, letting go of the needle, catches it again with his hand on the other side of the cloth. But the machine did not have such a hand."

I was fascinated by the dexterity of her fingers, and their ability, in imitating the action of sewing, to produce an effect of reality similar to the one she had achieved when she had imitated the performance of two ballet dancers. I never did know whether the romantic solution of the problem which she told me then was a product of Isadora's or Paris Singer's imagination, but according to Isadora the old man had a dream in which "a rider on a horse was rushing at him with a spear in his hand. The spear had a hole at its point, threaded with a yellow ribbon, which waved in the wind. The problem was solved: the hole for the thread had to be changed to the point-end of the needle."

Although Isadora appeared to be fully satisfied with this solution, for my part I do not see that it quite answers the problem. At any rate, although Isadora ridiculed this anecdote as poor compensation for her lectures to Singer about Nietzsche, Heine, and Walt Whitman, she really enjoyed repeating the story, perhaps as a prelude to her story illustrating that a rich man does not know how to enjoy life, mainly because he lacks a sense of humor.

But first she told me about a party suggested by Singer to which she was not only to invite all her friends, but for which he gave her carte blanche, regardless of expense, to choose her own program for the entertainment of their guests. As she remembered it, it was one of the most resplendent private fetes ever given. It took place in the park of Versailles, and began with a program of

Wagner's works performed by the Colonne Orchestra under the direction of Gabriel Pierné, at that time one of the most distinguished musicians in France. This was followed by a banquet, which lasted until midnight.

However, she was much disappointed, because an hour before the beginning of the party, she received a telegram from Singer saying that he would be unable to attend the fete because he was ill, and she should receive the guests without him.

She did not tell me what caused Singer's sudden illness, but instead followed her party story with another one, which she thought would bolster her argument that the rich do not know how to enjoy life.

Without saying exactly when it took place, she told me that Paris Singer again proposed that she organize a party, name the guests, and choose the entertainment.

This time Isadora decided to invite a group of about twenty artists to whom the party would be a unique experience. She asked Singer to take them all on a trip to Egypt. Nothing could have pleased him more, especially when Isadora gave him the list of the guests she had selected for the party: prominent men in music, painting, sculpture, poetry and writing, as well as acting, whom Singer recognized either from his personal acquaintance with them, or from their having been mentioned in the newspapers. In fact, he suggested putting his yacht entirely at the disposal of her friends, while Isadora and he would accompany them on another, smaller yacht, keeping in close touch with them.

After two days of sailing during the most beautiful weather, Isadora thought that it would be a good idea to join their guests for lunch. Their small yacht pulled alongside the *Isis*. Isadora was elegantly dressed for the occasion, as was her custom at that time. Paris Singer was in the white uniform of a yachting skipper. When they boarded the *Isis* they were greeted by a sight that Isadora described with tears of laughter streaming down her cheeks.

"As their hosts, we were expecting to be led to the head of the table, which was always glittering with silver and crystal. Instead, we saw many dear friends sprawled all over the deck on blankets and pillows, which they had brought for comfort from their cabins. Dressed in old torn sweaters and patched trousers and dirty slippers, they were sunning themselves, or were absorbed in games of cards, checkers, and chess. Meanwhile the immaculately uniformed stewards were passing trays of food, and refilling their glasses with the choicest wines from the yacht's cellar. Hating to be interrupted, only a few of them paid any attention to our arrival—still munching their food, or throwing overboard the remnants of their lunch."

Seeing Singer's livid face, Isadora quickly got him to return with her to their own yacht, where she tried to explain, as best she could, that these artists considered the voyage to be their vacation, and that was the reason for their informal dress and behavior; they had not shaved for days because they thought this would be a good time to give their faces a rest.

Through Thomas Cook and American Express, Paris Singer had arranged to have guides, with camels and donkeys, waiting in Cairo to take the guests on sightseeing trips. But when Isadora's friends heard about it they declined to leave the yacht, which they said was much cooler than the desert. They claimed to have learned from books and illustrated magazines all that they cared to know about the pyramids and the mummies, and said that they would much rather be excused.

But the final touch to this party was given in Monte Carlo on their return from Egypt, where every night Paris Singer gave each guest twenty-five dollars with which to gamble at the casino. Isadora's friends did go once, but after they had lost, they decided that it was wiser to keep the money and stay aboard the yacht, doing their gambling there.

I do not know the reason, but of these two stories the first one was included in Isadora's memoirs, while the second was either never written by Isadora, or was omitted by her publishers.

Had she treated the whole escapade at that time with the same sense of humor with which she described it later to me, she might have succeeded in getting Singer himself to enjoy it, or at least make less of a drama of it. But Isadora took delight in flaunting in his face the difference between their sets of friends, the superiority of hers, and, of course, his incapacity to appreciate the chance she offered him to gain a better understanding of the true aristocrats of society—the artists.

So much was plain from the way she told me the story, and I have always believed that this and many similar episodes contributed to his general neurasthenia. Certainly it showed the abyss in their relationship—they simply failed to understand each other. With the best intentions, Singer tried over and over again to be helpful with financial assistance—with the conspicuous exception of subsidizing Isadora's school. After all, what else could he offer her? But Isadora, often out of pure devilment, and hurting only herself, would let his offers fall on barren ground.

Isadora summarized these episodes in her memoirs, with, "No wonder that I felt inclined to become a Communist when I so often had exemplified for me the fact that for a rich man to find happiness was like Sisyphus trying to roll his stone uphill from Hell." But these are empty words. At that time, 1910, and even for almost a decade later, the word "communist" was not in common usage, and Isadora could have had only the vaguest idea of its meaning. No ideology of any kind had to be called upon to explain a simple case of incompatibility between a person with a definite aim in life and one devoted simply to enjoying it.

In any case, on that occasion in Nice, as Isadora came to the end of her account of her relationship with Singer, she repeated to me what she had often said before: "Even today I simply cannot comprehend how little he understood me and my work," and then turning to me, she added: "You see . . . can you imagine me no longer being Isadora Duncan, but Madame Singer—well, I couldn't."

She said this very seriously, as if giving the key to one of the most important decisions in her life, and in doing so pronounced Singer's name, not in English but in the French way. Intentionally or not, she added a humorous touch to it as if the name were derived from *singe*, the French word for monkey.

Thus their attempt at just "living and enjoying life" at Singer's chateau in Paignton in Devonshire, was doomed to failure. For any woman as full of vitality as Isadora, and as accustomed to constant activity, to suddenly become a mere *châtelaine* would be disastrous. So it proved to be for Isadora. To entertain and to be entertained by "society," to keep changing the topics of conversation artificially contrived for each occasion, and her dresses, and her moods, bored her so much that she grew desperate. Now she realized that she lived fully only while she was engaged in artistic creation; she was still alive when she felt that she had even a small part in the Duse-Craig project, or took part in long discussions on art with Craig and with Stanislavsky. But she was not made to be a mere spectator of the

Ballets Russes performances, ending with superficial appraisal of the art dear to her during a supper at some restaurant or nightclub, interspersed with remarks about the qualities of the wines and dishes served for her pleasure. She wanted to dance, she had to dance, she told Singer. For his part, he saw no reason why she should not use the large ballroom in the chateau. That this was not at all what she meant did not discourage his characteristic enthusiasm and his readiness to play his part in any undertaking.

What could be simpler than to cover the waxed floor with her own carpet, to replace the Gobelin tapestries and a picture of the coronation of Napoleon by David with the blue curtains which always formed the background for Isadora's performances? All this could be imported in no time from Paris. And as for her music—an orchestra or a pianist? She could have her choice. She asked for a pianist and cabled Édouard Colonne to send her one.

Isadora's old friend and admirer immediately dispatched his choice from among the available French musicians, the thirty-two-year-old André Caplet. The pianist had been Colonne's assistant conductor at eighteen, and at twenty-one the music director at the Théâtre de l'Odéon. As recently as April 20, 1910, he had been acclaimed for his septet, when it was performed at the inauguration of the *Société Musicale Indépendante*, with Maurice Ravel heading the list of founders.

In Isadora's published reminiscences the much belabored version of her short relationship with Caplet disproportionately stresses the physical aspects of the ensuing episode, rather than the spiritual ones. In this way it opens an even wider field for speculation about Isadora's private life with Paris Singer.

According to this version, from the first time Isadora had seen him in the Colonne Orchestra, where Caplet happened to be playing the first violin, she was so affected by the man's unattractive physical appearance that he gave her a "sense of absolute physical revulsion." Because of this, the story goes on, when Edouard Colonne was too indisposed to conduct one of her performances at the Gaîeté-Lyrique and suggested Caplet to take his place, Isadora refused to appear under those conditions, and Lugné-Poe succeeded in having Gabriel Pierné conduct that evening. And now, whom did she meet upon his arrival at the station, but André Caplet—whose name Colonne had failed to mention.

It is doubtful that the tactless greeting she was supposed to have accorded him, emphasizing his ugliness, was really uttered. Whatever else could have been criticized in her character, charming and gracious behavior as a hostess was her special quality. However, she reports that she consented to work with him only if he were concealed behind a screen while playing the piano for her. At least, that is what she recounts in her memoirs. But I do know that the climax of the episode as she tells it was derived from a love scene Isadora saw in a motion picture which amused her at the time she was writing the story.

Supposedly accused by a certain Countess A, Paris Singer's friend, who was a guest at the chateau, of treating her pianist badly, Isadora invited him to join her on an automobile ride. Where the car swerved at a sharp turn in the road, Isadora was thrown into the arms of the pianist, who was sitting next to her, and she felt her "whole being going up in flames like a pile of lighted straw. . . . I have never felt anything so violent."

The entire story, as she told it to me, was very different. First of all, she did not need to disguise André Caplet under the initial X. He was well known for his friendship with Debussy, for his orchestration of Debussy's *Children's Corner*, and for his assistance in producing the composer's *Martyrdom of St. Sebastian* in 1911. Besides, at the time when Isadora was writing her autobiography, he was already dead of a lung disease caused by gas poisoning during World War I. She never mentioned to me their activities in the car, nor the presence of the alleged countess.

Isadora brought up the name of Caplet when she was explaining to me her firm conviction that music has such a direct and powerful influence on the performer that it can transform an ugly man into a most beautiful one. And she used Caplet to illustrate her theory because in her eyes he was a striking example of it.

The business about his playing for her behind a screen had been a pure invention. No sudden jolt in a speeding car, but the transformation of which Isadora spoke to me, had made her ask herself, how have I not seen it before?

According to Isadora, the direct sequence of events leading from a supposedly violent antipathy to violent love did not take place behind the screen, in the conservatory, in the garden, nor even on the long walks in muddy country lanes, but—and Isadora laughed as she told me the story— "on the floor under the grand piano." "Not very comfortable," I said, realizing that Isadora was merely making up this part of the story—her own device for suppressing personal information, which in her opinion it would have been bad taste to mention, and substituting for it an obviously absurd detail, remarking only that it was a *"façon de parler."* "Certainly not, especially for what happened, anyway," she said. And yet she had to admit that it had unpleasant consequences.

Paris Singer, who had been sick for weeks after his attack in Paris —with what illness no one has since revealed—and who was now constantly attended by nurses and a doctor, had suggested that Isadora stay in another wing of the chateau for fear that she might disturb him. One day, she told me, he walked into the ballroom unannounced and found Isadora and Caplet at closer range than he had expected.

As it happened, Isadora was the last person to mention some physical defect or even a blemish in anybody's appearance, and especially in a performer or a talented person. She would be the first to encourage any artist, and I have seen her many times go backstage to congratulate a performer—a perfect stranger to her— and with tears in her eyes lavish praise *first* on his appearance and then on his or her performance.

A few years after her death, Moritz Rosenthal, a pupil of Franz Liszt, and who was at the time of our conversation at the zenith of his pianistic career, told me that, after one of his concerts in Paris, Isadora had come backstage and congratulated him by saying, "But Meister, you are so beautiful." André Caplet was an Apollo compared to Rosenthal, who was just over five feet tall with grotesquely long arms, bowlegs, and with a head that reminded one of a circus ringmaster—his grey hair was dyed red, his moustache jet-black, and he squinted his left eye as if suspicious of his interlocutor.

I record this anecdote as one of the many that served to create for Isadora a reputation as a female Casanova, whose generous flattery of a performer's appearance was to be construed as an invitation to her bed.

When Paris Singer had first learned whom Édouard Colonne was sending her, and knowing Isadora's prejudice against the young pianist's looks, Singer had remarked, "At least I'll have no cause for jealousy." But now he was enraged. Despite Isadora's pleading with him, Singer had Caplet practically thrown out of the house bodily.

Singer's jealousies, some utterly baseless, resulted in violent fits of rage that left Isadora depressed and disheartened. Speaking again of Singer's behavior toward her in connection with Caplet, she said in her memoirs: "This episode proved to me that I certainly was not suited to domestic life, and so, in the autumn, somewhat wiser and sadder, I sailed for America to fulfill a third contract. Then, for the hundredth time, I made a firm decision that hereafter I would give my entire life to Art, which though a hard task-master, is a hundred per-cent more grateful than human beings."

Chapter XIX

During her United States tour, Isadora, having realized that her millionaire had thus far shown little interest in furnishing financial support for her school, went on with her own appeals for funds in the speeches she addressed to her audiences after each performance. Although she herself was convinced that she was a good speaker—in fact, she claimed, an even better speaker than she was a dancer—Isadora always delivered her speeches extemporaneously, was usually driven by the emotions of the moment, and was one of the least gifted orators I have ever heard. Incapable of presenting the main theme of her address clearly, logically, and concisely, she rambled on, often contradicting herself, and yet somehow managing to coax her listeners to join in a discussion. As they shouted their queries from all over the house, the occasion would turn into a kind of commedia dell'arte show.

Her own detailed recollections of these appeals, even though edited to make them more coherent, show how mistakenly optimistic she was in delivering them at all. Her audiences certainly admired *her* dancing, but so far had seen no examples of the products of her school. It was naïve of her to expect them to be carried away by her purely abstract discourses on music, the arts, and poetry, which she complicated by introducing the theories of German philosophers and poets of whom her listeners had never heard.

She was extremely confident of her expertise in "handling the rich"—unjustifiably, for she had not learned enough about their psychology from her close contact with them during the past year or so, not even from living with one of them. Instead of flattering their egos and making them believe that she was merely echoing their original ideas, she would lose herself in her enthusiasm and take the opposite tack, thus arousing the antagonism of those whose sympathy and help she was seeking. She never said a truer word than when she quoted the reaction of the newspapers to these speeches: "I harangued the audience in their boxes of the Metropolitan Opera House, and the newspapers brought it out as a headline scandal: 'Isadora Insults the Rich.'"

As I have said, I saw most of the original chapters of Isadora's memoirs, and it is surprising to find in the published version an extra, uncalled-for discourse on what she calls "Pagan Love." Apparently, she came to feel that this was as good a place as any to portray herself as a female Casanova, and thus comply with her publisher's previously cited cable: "Enough of your hifalutin ideas, send love chapters, make it spicy." She did what she could in that regard, but this passage, like all those concerning sex, bears the editorial imprint of Mercedes de Acosta, of whom I shall speak later.

"Now that I had discovered that Love might be a pastime, as well as a tragedy, I gave myself to it with pagan innocence." Did she now consider her love for Paris Singer a "pastime," no longer worthy of her fidelity, that dominant trait in her character, as she had proudly said, and which only a year before had been the sole obstacle in her resuming her relationship with Gordon Craig, when she met him again in Moscow?

"Men seemed to be so hungry for Beauty, hungry for that love which refreshes and inspires without fear of responsibility. After a performance, in my tunic, with my hair crowned with roses, I was lovely. . . . Why should not this loveliness be enjoyed?"

For anyone who knew Isadora, this passage is clearly spurious. As for "I was lovely," that is a phrase Isadora was incapable of writing.

"Gone were the days of a glass of hot milk and Kant's *Critique of Pure Reason*. Now it seemed to me more natural to sip champagne and have some charming person tell me how beautiful I was. The divine pagan body, the passionate lips, the clinging arms, the sweet refreshing sleep on the shoulder of some loved one—these were joys which seemed to me both innocent and delightful. . . ." These, again, surely could not have been her words.

After completing her tour in the United States, she returned to Versailles, where she had left her children with a governess. Although she resumed her relationship with Paris Singer, their "try-out" in Devonshire had proved that instead of strengthening their union, it could only relegate Paris Singer to the role of master of ceremonies at parties, while confirming Isadora's conviction that her art must come first, and that no matter what sacrifice and painful experience she might have to suffer, she would have to have her independence and follow the aim to which she had dedicated herself.

Even before she had met Paris Singer, after her return from her successful tour with Walter Damrosch in 1908, she had bought Henri Gervex's studio at 68 rue Chauveau in Neuilly, near Paris. It was as large as a chapel—almost three stories high, because Gervex had it built with the intention of painting there the murals commissioned by the Russian royal family. Isadora had the place entirely redecorated by Paul Poiret. While leaving Isadora's blue curtains, which covered the high walls of the studio, Poiret transformed the small apartment on the balcony into "a veritable domaine of Circe," as Isadora called it in her memoirs. "Sable black velvet curtains were reflected on the walls in golden mirrors; a black carpet, and a divan with cushions of Oriental textures, completed this apartment, the windows of which had been sealed up and the doors of which were strange, Etruscan tomb-like apertures. As Poiret himself said upon its completion, '*Voilà des lieux où on ferait bien d'autres actes et on dirait bien d'autres choses que dans des lieux ordinaires.*' (Here are rooms where one says and does other things than in the usual places.)"

Little did Poiret know that romantic dramas and later a great tragedy were to take place in Isadora's new home.

Thus, to these seemingly ideal quarters Isadora came to live with her children, for whom she had furnished a little house in the garden. It was far enough removed so that the piano playing of Hener Skene, with whom she sometimes worked late into the night hours, would not disturb them. Skene, because of his warm temperament and gentle manners, had become not only her partner in her work but also a comforting friend when she needed one. This was often enough, for as might have been expected, the lavish parties given by Paris Singer at Isadora's new home were seldom without some dramatic finale. Singer's jealousy, sometimes disproportionate because of his neurotic tendencies, led to violent scenes, after which he would leave in a huff and go to Egypt, where he would stay for weeks.

This evidence of his passionate love for Isadora, which in its initial stage was endearing and even further stimulated her love for him, now through too many repetitions of his uncontrolled fits of rage gradually lost its charm for Isadora, and she devoted herself more and more to the preparations for her next tour in Russia, and the enjoyment of her children.

Isadora quite seriously maintained that she was "not only allied to these two adorable children by the poignant tie of flesh and blood, but also had with them a higher bond to an almost superhuman degree, the tie of Art."

Patrick was also beginning to dance, to a weird music of his own. Only he would never allow Isadora to teach him. "No," he would solemnly say, "Patrick will dance Patrick's own dance alone."

In later years, Isadora was inclined to speak more about Deirdre because she was older and offered more varied material for reminiscences. Isadora could repeat verbatim everything the little girl had said as she was composing her own dances in the garden of their house. "Watching her exquisite grace and beauty, I dreamed that she, perhaps, would carry on my School as I had imagined it. She was my best pupil."

Whenever Isadora mentioned her children in conversation, she invariably left me with an impression of her almost uncanny physical, animal love for them. Perhaps because of the simplicity of her manner in referring to them, the expression of that love excited in her listener a tide of painful sympathy. She not only remembered every meeting with them upon her return from her tours, their looks, their gestures, and their every word, but the scarcely perceptible details in the development of their bodies and speech, as they were brought to her "breakfast in bed" every morning.

Isadora seldom spoke to me about her children but, if and when she did, it was somehow prompted by her convictions about the right of women to choose the fathers of their children without regard to the conventional marriage laws. "I know, I know," Isadora said. " 'You don't seem to care,' people have remarked to me, 'that the children would be considered illegitimate,' and they used that ugly word 'bastards.' In such arguments I have always been much too polite to mention many cases of persons whom millions worship as saints. Instead I would call for the governess and ask her to bring in my children. 'Now, here they are,' I would say, 'just tell me, aren't they lovely . . . or what is wrong with them?' "

She told me about an afternoon in her studio when Raoul Pugno, at that time considered one of the greatest French pianists, was playing Mozart; she gives this account of the same incident in her memoirs: "The children entered on tiptoe and stood on either side of the piano as he played. When he had finished, they each, with one accord, put their blond heads under his arms and gazed at him with such admiration, that he was startled and exclaimed: 'From whence come these angels?—Mozart's angels?—' at which they laughed and climbed on his knees and hid their faces in his beard."

Once on this subject, she would keep on reminiscing about the children. She admitted that she grew so close to them that she dreaded any separation from them, especially for long periods of time, as some of her tours required. Therefore, she insisted on rather tightly scheduled dates for performances during her next Russian tour. She left in January 1913, accompanied by Skene.

To the best of my knowledge, only a few programs of her appearances in Russia have survived. I have a program of February 9, 1908; three from 1913—February 4, February 11, and February 18; and one of May 22, 1914.

Judging from these programs, all of them indicating performances over two hours long, Isadora's selections for her numbers were of markedly contrasting character. She devoted whole evenings to excerpts from Gluck's *Iphigenia in Aulis* or his *Orfeo*, or from Wagner's *Tannhäuser, Lohengrin,* and *Tristan und Isolde.*

When it was not necessary to have the participation of an orchestra in her "concerts," as her appearances were called in Russia, Hener Skene shared the program with her, both as her accompanist and in his solo numbers.

I believe it is noteworthy that, not only as an artist and a dancer, but as a woman, Isadora, who cherished every manifestation of joy in life and endeavored to infuse her audiences with her own happy feelings, actually was drawn almost irresistibly to anything that was morbidly dramatic in its nature. I have seen her over and over again enjoying dramatic or tragic situations in the theater, rather than comedy, the former leaving a lasting impression on her, while the latter merely gave her superficial amusement, soon to be forgotten. It also had always influenced her choice of dramatic music and, of course, her interpretation. Therefore, I, who otherwise have always been skeptical of her "visions," and her Irish sense of the psychic, was inclined to look for the origin of any of her super-natural experiences in her rich imagination, which was capable of taking her into a sphere where fantasy and reality were inter-mingled—always with death as a major element in the situation. According to her, during the tour in Russia, while driving in a carriage from the railway station to her hotel in Kiev, barely awake, she saw "two rows of children's coffins" in the snow, while Skene, who sat next to her, saw nothing but "the snow heaped up on either side of the road." Later, when, because she had caught a cold, had a high fever, and was not fit for a performance that night, she still insisted on not disappointing her audience, she sud-denly asked Skene to play Chopin's Funeral March, to which she improvised her previous hallucination so vividly that, according to her, even Skene could now visualize the coffins of children.

The Kiev experience seemed to pursue her even upon her re-turn to Paris in April, keeping her awake at night, while her imagination created all kinds of phantoms, transforming doorknobs or similar objects into apparitions.

I feel I should tell my personal experience with Isadora in regard to predictions, which were to her not a mere fascination, but an actual belief. The masters of this craft were usually old women who lived in gloomy, ill-ventilated rooms, overcrowded with bric-a-brac.

Knowing my indifference to such pastimes, even as a simple diversion, Isadora had never brought up the subject in all the years I had known her except once, about a year before her death, when her well-wishing friends, instead of helping her in some construc-tive way, suggested that she consult a soothsayer. Without ever admitting it, she was always a little afraid to go to see such people by herself. Though well aware of my attitude, Isadora asked me to take her to the address of a woman somewhere in Neuilly. Not to be a destructive spirit during the "séance," I agreed to pick her up within an hour. (Since this was the only experience I had with her in matters to which, in her memoirs, she attached such significance, I remember the occasion in detail.)

When Isadora finally rejoined me in my car, she was visibly moved and was still wiping her tears. She told me that the woman was simply miraculous. It seemed that she revealed to Isadora some long-forgotten incidents in her past. But, just as I was going to drive away from the woman's house, she suddenly noticed that she had forgotten her little silk scarf and asked me to fetch it for her. Thus I had an opportunity of seeing, not only the room, which looked exactly as I had anticipated, but also the old woman. As I picked up Isadora's scarf, I thanked her for the "séance," and told her how much Isadora was impressed by her capacity and extraordinary knowledge. "Oh, monsieur," the woman said to me, "why wouldn't I know everything about Madame Duncan, about her life, about her past, her children? For years, my husband and I were the concierges practically next door to Madame's property in Neuilly . . . and you can imagine yourself how we concierges. . . ." and she gave me a knowing look, which required no further explanation.

For a while as we drove, Isadora was so lost in her thoughts that, realizing that her depression might get the upper hand, I suggested getting some fresh air by driving for lunch to one of her favorite restaurants in St. Germain-en-Laye, near Paris, and later, *pour changer les idées*, to hear Ignaz Friedman, the famous exponent of Chopin, at his concert that night. When nothing else would influence Isadora's state of mind, anything *pour changer les idées*, her favorite expression, never failed to do wonders. And, hoping, perhaps, to appeal to her sense of humor, I facetiously remarked that Friedman was not going to play Chopin's sonata with a funeral march, and that I expected his program would give her far more pleasure than wasting time in silly chatter with an old concierge who used to live next door to her in Neuilly. "You're just being mean," was Isadora's reply.

After the concert, purely by chance, we saw Friedman having his after-concert supper at Pruniers, and Isadora resolved to join him. We spent a delightful evening, Isadora's remarks sparkling with wit; she had definitely forgotten her morning's discomfiture.

Thus it is very understandable that, when she had begun to complain to a friend in Paris about her latest hallucinations brought about by her experience in Kiev, her friend, instead of getting "icy hands," as Skene had after her performance in Kiev, simply called in a physician. The doctor, who diagnosed Isadora's depressions, "visions," "phantoms dressed in black," and her Irish imaginings as the result of overwork and strained nerves, was a "young and handsome man," a circumstance that seldom failed to *changer les idées* for Isadora. She still had a long list of engagements to fulfill in Paris and could not go away for a long vacation, but she could go to Versailles, at least to have a temporary rest there.

Chapter XX

If Isadora let her imagination play such havoc with her nerves that she began having hallucinations, and long sleepless nights in which she was subject to mysterious and sinister premonitions, nothing could have been more beneficial than staying at Versailles and being seriously concerned with her six favorite pupils, whom Elizabeth had agreed to send for the forthcoming performances at the Trocadero and Châtelet theaters.

Even her initial disappointment in the dancing of "her girls"— due partly to their long separation from her, but even more to the years spent under tutelage to Merz's directives entirely alien to her own principles—kept her mind on the realistic problem of bringing the girls up to their earlier form. In that way she was encouraged not to brood over the fantasies created by her tired nervous system. "They are impossible, they are stiff, they are like automatons!" she kept saying. And she asked herself repeatedly what was she to do with them. But because of the scheduled performances there was no time to be wasted, and she had to concentrate on working with the girls. Yet now, for the first time in her life, she arrived at the depressing conclusion that she did not know how to teach. She, Isadora Duncan, who was given to promising what amounted to a new life for the generations to come if only she were given the opportunity to "teach thousands and thousands" of children before they had been crippled by the conditions of the modern world, had to admit to herself that she did not know how to teach.

What this revelation amounted to, of course, was that Isadora was incapable of giving a pupil exact instructions as to how, when, and to what extent she was to move her hand, arm, leg, or body—thus "teaching" the technical production of a dance. But, fortunately, the example of her own performance of a dance was so inspiring to her pupils that it often made up for her lack of ability to teach the mechanical sequence of movements.

This difference between purely technical, analytic instruction and the spiritual-inspirational method of teaching by example always has been and always will be encountered in the teaching of all the arts. In fact, it is not uncommon that a teacher capable of detailed technical analysis follows that instruction by his own performance—and thoroughly bewilders the student by an unexpected discrepancy between his theory and his practice.

Of course, this was not Isadora's case. But, according to Irma Duncan who speaks in her book for the rest of the girls as well:

> Her method consisted in demonstrating the sequence of a dance perfectly executed by herself. Then, without demonstrating it step by step, she expected her pupils to understand immediately and repeat it. . . . She danced the sequence again and again without obtaining any result and then gave up in disgust. When her pianist politely suggested she repeat the fast dance movement at a slower tempo, so we could get the steps, she readily consented.

> . . . She floundered and found herself incapable of demonstrating the movement step by step. She looked surprised and then annoyed at several unsuccessful attempts to come to grips with the situation. Wearily, she leaned against the piano and said to Skene: "How perfectly extraordinary! This is a great revelation to me. I am apparently unable to dissect my own dance in order to teach it to others. I had no idea how difficult this would be for me. I can dance my own choreography, but am unable to analyse any part of it for the benefit of the others."

> She continued to train us in this "catch as catch can" fashion, repeating the dance movement until at last one of us caught on. Then she would say, "You have got the movement correctly. Now teach the others and I expect everybody to have it right by tomorrow." And that was that.

Perhaps the results of such methods would have been disastrous had the six girls not been so talented and so anxious to shed the last vestiges of the traces left upon them, like scars, by the years spent at Merz's school.

When they finally appeared with Isadora in a performance at the Châtelet Theater, the poet Ferdinand Divoire wrote:

> Six slender young girls appeared on the scene attired in rose-colored scarves and crowned with flowers. Bare-limbed and light-footed they threw themselves joyfully into the dance. They are the little *Isadorables* [Divoire had coined this nickname for them when he first saw them years before] we used to see dance when they were children. They are grown up now. Tall, supple, and graceful, they combine their erstwhile naive gaiety with all the charm of young girls. No painting of Botticelli or [Fra] Angelico, no Greek fresco depicting the vernal season, expresses as much beauty, chastity, and artlessness as these youthful dancers.
>
> Isadora dances with them and is part of them. And the delighted audience applauds and applauds, freed of all everyday worries and care, left with no other thoughts but those of grace and youth eternal.
>
> It rarely happens at an artistic performance that, with the orchestra gone, the lights extinguished, the ushers waiting to close the doors, so many of the audience remain to applaud frantically in a manner amounting to worship. They insist on recalling the Isadorable one again and again, unable to part from her. After masses of flowers have been presented, she gives the enthusiastic audience one last dance.
>
> Joining hands with her six young girls, they dance silently, without music, around the flowers heaped in the center of the stage—a ring around the roses—such as children play. This charming improvisation, as we watch it unfold, is unforgettable. Oh, garden of happy spirits!

Such triumphs were not the only manifestation of the zenith of her artistic career but were an additional crowning to the happiness of her personal life. Paris Singer had planned for some time to buy a large property right in the heart of Paris, in the vicinity of the Champs Élysées, to build a theater for Isadora, but because of their frequent emotional scenes, resulting in his leaving Isadora for weeks at a time, their relationship remained strained, and Isadora's hope for the theater was left in suspense. But at this time, when after several months of absence, Singer telephoned her, Isadora sincerely believed that it would lead to their reconciliation, perhaps even to a revival of their former love. She thought again of the great artistic center that would arise from Paris Singer's plans. "I thought that Duse would find there a fitting frame for her divine art, and that here Mounet-Sully would be able to realize his long-cherished ambition to play the trilogy of *Oedipus Rex, Antigone,* and *Oedipus at Colonnus* in sequence." And, of course, at last she would have a home for her school.

Singer had returned from Egypt only two days before. He wanted to see their children, whom he had not seen for almost four months, and he invited everybody, including Isadora's pupils, to lunch. "I whispered the news to Deirdre," Isadora relates, and she quotes Deirdre as saying to her little brother, "Oh, Patrick, where do you think we are going today?"

During their lunch at an Italian restaurant, Singer spoke of his plans again. "It will be Isadora's theater," he said. "No, Isadora replied, "it will be Patrick's theater, for Patrick is the great composer who will create the Dance to the Music of the Future."

Singer felt so happy that he suggested that all of them go somewhere for a ride, but Isadora's pupils had to return to their pension near the studio in Neuilly for their daily music lesson, and Isadora herself had an already scheduled rehearsal.

I prefer to quote Isadora's own description of the following events.

I returned to my studio. It was not yet time for the rehearsal. I thought to rest awhile and mounted to my apartment, where I threw myself down on the couch. There were flowers and a box of bonbons that someone had sent me. I took one in my hand and ate it lazily, thinking—Surely, after all, I am very happy—perhaps the happiest woman in the world. My Art, my success, fortune, love, but above all, my beautiful children!

I was thus lazily eating sweets and smiling to myself, thinking, "L. [Singer] has returned, all will be well," when there came to my ears a strange, unearthly cry.

I turned my head. L. was there staggering like a drunken man. His knees gave way—he fell before me—and from his lips came these words: "The children—the children—are dead!"

At that moment, Isadora knew nothing more. She learned later what had happened while she had been thinking of her life with such satisfaction. When, after lunch, Isadora had returned with her children to her studio in Neuilly, she had suggested to their nurse that they wait until the end of her rehearsal so they could go back home to Versailles together. But the nurse thought that the children were tired and needed a rest. So, kissing the children, Isadora left them in the hired limousine, which drove off.

According to Raymond Duncan, who told me the following details, the car was still not far away from the studio, when it was suddenly faced with a taxi coming toward it. To avoid a collision, the driver stopped the car, and while doing so, stalled his engine. Since the car was going uphill, the driver, for better safety, meant to leave the car in gear; unfortunately, he put it into reverse. Then he got out of the car, closing the door after him. In those days starting the motor had to be done by cranking a handle in front of the car. But, as he cranked the handle and started the motor, to his horror he saw the limousine backing away, and, since there was no parapet at that point of the embankment on the Seine, the car plunged into deep water.

Several attempts by persons who had witnessed the accident and who dove into the river were unsuccessful in even locating the car. Finally, with the assistance of the police, the car was raised. Deirdre and the nurse were dead, but the boy still showed some signs of life and he was rushed to the nearby American Hospital. However, all efforts to save his life were fruitless.

When Singer pronounced the horrifying words, "The children are dead," Isadora, as she wrote later, "felt a strange stillness, and only in my throat I felt a burning, as if I had swallowed some live coals. But I could not understand. I spoke to him very softly; I tried to calm him; I told him it could not be true."

Then other people came, but I could not conceive what had happened. Then entered a man with a dark beard. I was told he was a doctor. "It is not true," he said, "I will save them."

I believed him. I wanted to go with him, but people held me back. I know now that this was because they did not wish me to know that there was indeed no hope. They feared the shock would make me insane, but I was, at that time, lifted to a state of exaltation. I saw everyone about me weeping, but I did not weep. On the contrary, I felt an immense desire to console everyone. Looking back, it is difficult for me to understand my state of mind. Was it that I was really in a state of clairvoyance, and that I knew that death does not exist—that those two little cold images of wax were not my children, but merely their cast-off garments? That the souls of my children lived in radiance, but lived forever?

Only twice comes that cry of the mother which one hears as without one's self—at birth and at death. For when I felt those little cold hands that would never again press mine in return, I heard my cries —the same cries I had heard at their births. Why the same? Since one is the cry of supreme joy and the other of sorrow. I do not know why, but I do know they are the same. Is it not that in all the Universe there is but one great continuing Sorrow, Joy, Ecstasy, Agony —the Mother Cry of Creation?

According to one version, Augustin went to the pension where Isadora's six pupils were living, and gave them news about the accident. They were told to be ready to return on the following day to the Elizabeth-Merz school in Darmstadt. But Anna (Duncan), one of the six, recently told me that, upon hearing of the death of her children, Isadora had remained sitting on the couch so erect and still, as if her whole being were petrified, that her doctor feared she would go insane unless some other shock would bring her some release from her tension. This, on his advice, was accomplished on the following morning. By prearrangement, the six girls burst in upon her, thus breaking her away from the spell that had kept her for hours in its grip. "Now you must be my children," Isadora was supposed to have said, as she enfolded them in her arms.

Isadora's tragedy struck at the heart of mothers all over the world. Innumerable letters, telegrams, messages, and every imaginable token of condolence were sent to her, and, although at the time she could not bear to see them all, she kept one to the last days of her life. It was a letter from Gordon Craig, who was in Florence:

Isadora dear—I never shall be able to say anything to you. It is a mysterious thing but when I begin to think of you or speak to you, I feel as though it was as unnecessary as if I should speak with myself. This feeling grows. And, as I seem to be a man mad about something outside myself—I no longer seem to count. A glimpse of myself—if I dared to lift a veil—might kill me. I have left myself (as it seems to me who dare not look) and what is me is a bag of sawdust with a head on one end and two leaden feet at the other end—and so on—I seem to be outside myself. Supporting myself by one arm or by the hair—like a bunch of furies—and with some strength too for I have serious things to attend to, get done, and then go. My life as yours has been strange—you are *strong*—but not to me. And, my darling, I know how you can suffer and not show more than a smile—I know your weakness which is that of a little, dear dear little fool—for I, a big fool, have looked at you. I know your strength too—for I who can taste strength have seen all yours—never was there one weaker or so strong as you—and all for Hecuba. My heart has often broken to see your weakness. Large chips (you couldn't have noticed them, for I as you, will never show them). My heart has often shaken with *terror* to see your strength. For my heart and your heart are one heart and an utterly incomprehensible thing it is. *I want to be with you*—and it was only to say that that I write too much—And as I am with you, being you, what more is there to be said. Let us not be sorry for anything—or where shall we begin. You and I are lonely—only that. And no matter how many came—or shall come—you and I must be lonely—that is our secret. I kiss your heart.

Gordon Craig's letter, addressed to Isadora from Florence, reached her much later when she was staying in Corfu. In the letter was enclosed a small, square envelope containing a few dried flowers and a note: "Isadora, There is much to do."

"My friends have helped me to realize what alone could comfort me—that all men are my brothers, all women my sisters, and all children on earth my children." This statement, however, she was able to make only years later, when she had finally more or less regained her composure; at the time of the accident, the witnessing of preparations for the funeral, or any slight allusion to her loss, only forced deeper into her consciousness the significance of the tragedy.

By the following morning, men and women, old and young, led by students from the Beaux Arts School, had covered the trees and bushes near Isadora's home with roses and fresh branches of white lilac, and the path to the house with masses of marguerites. And there people remained for hours, silently weeping.

None of the Duncan family were religious—Isadora even less so than her sister and brothers: She had an almost physical revulsion to the conventional funeral rituals. Shuddering at the thought that her beloved children's bodies would be eaten by worms, she insisted on their cremation. Their ashes, with those of Miss Sim, their nurse, were placed in a vault in the Père Lachaise cemetery in Paris.

"If this sorrow had come to me much earlier in life, I might have overcome it; if much later, it would not have been so terrible, but at that moment, in the full power and energy of life [Isadora was thirty-five] it completely shattered my forces and powers. . . . If a great love had then enveloped me and carried me away—but L. did not respond to my call."

Immediately after the accident, Singer was taken so ill that he had to be removed to a hospital. It was Isadora who had to visit and comfort him.

"When I heard of the horrible tragedy, I ran to Isadora's home," Cécile Sorel wrote in her memoirs* in much the same words she had used in telling me the incident.

> I saw before me a woman immobile, rigid as a statue. "Is it real? Is this monstrous torture a nightmare," she murmured, "will I wake up? Will it last a long time?' How could one rescue her from this terrible dream? She had not yet realized what had happened. She seemed to be both spectator and victim of this tragedy. She recalled the fresh young lives that were her pride and joy. She spoke of them with tragic calm. . . .

> A silent crowd invaded her home on the day of the funeral. In the large studio her blue curtains, which served Isadora as a background to her dancing, now threw tender light as if to soften the vision of death. A pyramid of roses covered the beloved bodies. The musicians of the Colonne orchestra softly played the most beautiful classical pieces that had inspired Isadora's divine dances. The mourning mother, in her frozen suffering for all eternity, remained in her room. She seemed to belong to that other world to which her children had gone.

> Later, she passed before us like a shadow on the way to the room that held the coffins. Then she seemed suddenly stricken with the reality of what had happened. Her knees gave way, she reeled, collapsing into the folds of a gray curtain. Then, slowly, as if the slightest sudden movement would cause her to fall again, she raised herself. The funeral march with its rhythm alternating between love and death, carried her toward her beloved children.

* Cécile Sorel: *Les Belles Heures De Ma Vie*. Monaco: Éditions du Rocher, 1946.

Never was there a more moving ceremony. All Paris accompanied those two young flowers that had been cut down. Alone, Isadora walked at the head of the endless cortege. She resembled a mourner of the ancient times. The people were crossing themselves as they followed the folds of her dress.

I wanted to kiss her naked feet in their sandals.

PART FOUR

Chapter XXI

All this happened at a time when the war in the Balkans had come to an end—1913. The Turkish Army had left Greece in a devastated condition. Raymond and his Greek wife, Penelope, were going there to help take care of the refugees. Supported by Elizabeth and Augustin, they suggested to Isadora that some preoccupation would be beneficial for her state of mind and that she should accompany them to Greece. Isadora agreed, and Elizabeth took the six girls back to Darmstadt.

Leaving Isadora with Augustin on the island of Corfu, Raymond and Penelope went to Epirus, the most devastated province. They were to let Isadora know within a week the true conditions there before she joined them in helping the thousands of homeless and starving inhabitants and refugees.

Her bedroom window at the Villa Stephanie faced the wide expanse of the sea. "I can see right to the mountains on the opposite side, which seem to float in the azure between earth and heaven—like a vision of a promised land," she wrote to Louis Sue, the architect whom she had met when, with Paris Singer, they had been discussing plans for the building of the theater near the Champs Élysées. "Sometimes looking out on it, I think that maybe I'm dead with my children and have entered Paradise—I feel them close to me—and then comes again the cruel physical suffering—my eyes will never see them, my hands never touch them again, and I see once more the poor little things waving their little hands—in the automobile driving off—and I want to scream."

She tried to wear herself out by long walks in the country, but at night when she could no longer read, she was helpless before her torment. "What is surprising," she said, "is that the body still lives—in spite of the fact that I drink nothing but milk—it agrees with me perfectly and I'm merely getting stronger; if I could get ill it might be a great relief."

But getting ill would not have helped. She needed to have someone with her who was neither a member of her family nor a friend trying to cheer her up with distractions. She needed someone to share her pain. Perhaps she should have called for Craig, who was living in Florence with his family. But Isadora thought that he was happily married at last, and she did not want to disturb him. Instead, she used all her powers of telepathy in calling Singer, who was in London: "Come to me—Come to me—I need you—I am dying. If you do not come, I will die."

And Paris Singer did go to Corfu. Isadora hoped that "by spontaneous love gestures, the unhappiness of the past might be redeemed. . . . But it was not to be."

In her naïve way, Isadora apparently did not realize that a millionaire is likely to find it more congenial to write out a check and to give advice rather than get mixed up personally in depressing sights and squalor. In an emergency, Singer might be called upon to give a helping hand to the sick or the dying and that simply would not work with his delicate nervous system. So all her efforts to persuade Singer to join her in helping the stranded and hungry families in Epirus only convinced him that she too should not get involved in it. Or, she thought, perhaps her sorrow, her intense yearning, were too much for him. One morning she saw a small boat leaving the Corfu harbor, and she felt that Singer was aboard. She was not mistaken. Without a word of warning he had left her and gone back to Paris, or perhaps to London—she did not know where.

Once again she was alone. Putting on her old Greek tunic and sandals, she went with Raymond to Albania, where her inventive brother in no time organized quite a successful business. Instead of merely distributing relief supplies, for which he would have had to beg, Raymond bought raw wool in the marketplace in Corfu and brought it back with him to Albania, where he had the women weave the wool into fabrics. These he sold in London—at such a profit that he was not only able to open a bakery, but managed to sell the bread at a cheaper price than the Greek government charged for the yellow corn offered to the refugees.

And, although Raymond even taught the women to sing in unison while weaving, as well as infecting his "new villagers" with his cheerful mood and enthusiasm, nevertheless the dismal, often tragic, scenes in the refugee camps could not fail to affect Isadora. Unlike Raymond, she felt helpless not only "to stop the flood of misery, but even to comfort a mother sitting under a tree with her baby in her arms and three or four small children clinging to her —all hungry and without a home; their house burnt, the husband and father killed by the Turks, the flock stolen, the crop destroyed."

At times she felt her own strength returning to her and she thought that "there is a great difference between the life of the artist and that of the Saint," that she no longer could look at this human disaster, that she had had enough of the mountains, great rocks and stones, and instead "longed for the feeling of a carpet under her feet." She begged Penelope to accompany her on a trip to Constantinople, where in the solemn quietness of a mosque, she could meditate about her future life and her art.

Isadora's effort to get away from other people's troubles was completely thwarted. During the first night on the ship she made the mistake of listening to the woes of a young man. He claimed that his sorrow was as great as hers, and told her that he was returning home to Constantinople because two of his brothers had committed suicide, and, though his fervent wish was to console his mother, he had little hope of succeeding—for he, too, was determined to commit suicide. It seemed that Isadora's grief was destined to be nurtured by the misfortunes of others. However, in the case of this particular young man, she was at least a little relieved when she learned that, while his desperate state was caused by an unhappy love affair, the object of his passion was not a young woman, but a pretty boy.

Being a woman, Isadora was less revolted by male homosexuality than she had been by Loie Fuller's entourage of young females. Now, indeed, Isadora not only tried to comfort the young Turk's mother, who did not seem to understand what it was all about, but she attempted over and over again to reconcile the two lovers. Her efforts were in vain—the younger partner of the love affair insisted that he just could not love Isadora's protégé—too deep a mystery for her understanding. Isadora had little comprehension of homosexual love and affection. Indeed, the long quotation from Jowett about Zeus when he was in love with Ganymede, which appears in her reminiscences, was inserted at the suggestion of her so-called intimate friends—homosexuals of both sexes who sponged on both her sympathy and her rapidly dwindling financial resources.

Having myself witnessed many neurotic scenes on the part of her homosexual and Lesbian friends, in which Isadora was called upon, not in the role of psychiatrist, but of a loving mother, I feel that, instead of the poetic, but misplaced, quotation from Jowett, she would have done better to summarize her tolerance of the so-called human frailties, as she learned to do in later years, by simply saying who but "they" could better understand "To be or not to be."

Fortunately, the dreary monotony of her useless preoccupation was sidetracked by her favorite diversion of going with Penelope to an old Armenian fortune-teller.

"She greets you as the daughter of the Sun," Penelope translated the Armenian's solemn pronouncement to Isadora. "You have been sent on earth to give great joy to all people. From the joy will be founded a religion. After many wanderings, at the end of your life, you will build temples all over the world. In the course of time, you will return to this city where, too, you will build a temple. All these temples will be dedicated to Beauty and Joy because you are the daughter of the Sun."

But the old woman's prediction of Penelope's future was less comforting. In fact, she told her that she was not long for this world and that both her husband and her son were near death. Upon their return to their hotel, Penelope indeed found a telegram from Raymond asking her to return because he and their son Menalka were ill, thus giving support to Isadora's fluctuating faith in the verity of predictions, but at the same time cutting short her sojourn in Constantinople.

Although Raymond was ill, Isadora failed to persuade him to leave Albania, and she herself could no longer bear staying there. She telegraphed for her car to meet her at Trieste, and from there drove aimlessly to Switzerland, until, "following an irresistible impulse," she went back to Paris.

There, working again with Hener Skene, she hoped to revive her spirits, but the empty studio, the little house in the garden where the children's clothes and toys were still scattered about, and above all the sound of the familiar music played by Skene, brought on her final collapse. For the first time, Isadora wept. The sight of her blue curtains, the silent witnesses of her triumphs and of past happy days, and the somber witnesses of her tragedy, the nightly hallucinations, and the remembered echoes of her children's voices, soon set her to packing her small traveling suitcase and getting into her car, to escape the nightmare that was threatening to envelope her whole being, to drive at top speed. Where? Anywhere.

Endlessly restless, she found herself traveling aimlessly all over Italy—spending one night in a gondola rowing back and forth on the Grand Canal in Venice, the next at Rimini, and the next in Florence. She knew that Craig was still living there at the time, but again she did not want to disturb him. Toward the middle of September, Isadora found a telegram in her hotel in a little town by the sea: "Isadora, I know you are wandering through Italy. I pray you come to me. I will do my best to comfort you." The telegram was signed Eleonora Duse.

"It is not true," Isadora wrote in her memoirs, "that Duse's long retirement from the stage in the fullness and ripeness of her Art was due, as some people prefer to think, to an unhappy love or some other sentimental reason, nor even to ill-health, but she had no help or the capital necessary to carry out her ideas of Art as she wished—that is the simple, shameful truth. The world that 'loves Art' left this greatest actress of the world to eat her heart out in solitude and poverty. . . ."

To the best of my knowledge, no two other great women artists have ever met in their sorrows.

Though she drove at top speed, Isadora arrived late at night at Viareggio, where nearby, in the country, Duse lived in a small villa.

At the hotel, the manager handed Isadora a letter from Duse dated September 13, 1913:

Chère, my heart has been awaiting you for a long time—am here within two steps of you and shall come to you as soon as you desire—yours with all my heart.

This morning at the Grand Hotel I left a letter and some flowers for you. Chère Isadora, *des roses de la campagne*, flowers from my garden. Tell me that you are not too sad to be in a hotel room. My dear, all day I hoped to be with you and tomorrow morning early I shall come and fetch you. But forgive me for not coming this evening. It is raining too hard and I am not feeling well. I embrace you and thank you . . . for having come so close to me at this moment which is without life, without art for you.

My dear, I have called four times today at the Grand Hotel to see you. The last time they told me you had moved to the Regina [Duse wrote in another note]. I would have liked to see you this evening but a headache and the thunderstorm prevented me from going out again. I hope the sojourn at the seashore, so lonesome for you, will not be too painful. Shelley will speak to you there. Dream, work, and be valiant in your beautiful strength.

When next morning Isadora arrived at Duse's little rose villa behind a vineyard at Fossa dell' Abata, Duse came down a vine-covered walk, took her into her arms, and looked at her with infinite gentleness. "I felt," Isadora wrote of this scene, "just as Dante must have felt when in the *Paradiso*, he encounters the Divine Beatrice."

". . . From then on I lived at Viareggio, finding courage from the radiance of Eleonora's eyes. She used to rock me in her arms, consoling my pain, but not only consoling, for she seemed to take my sorrow to her own breast, and I realized that if I had not been able to bear the society of other people, it was because they all played the comedy of trying to cheer me with forgetfulness."

Duse did not advise Isadora to forget her sorrows, she did not even attempt to distract her, but on the contrary, she begged Isadora to tell her everything about Deirdre and Patrick, to repeat over and over again their words, tell her about their dances and their childish games, when every morning they were brought to Isadora while she was having her breakfast in bed. To have an even more vivid picture of the children, she asked Isadora to show her all their photographs she had with her, and with tears in her eyes, she pressed them to her heart. Duse never told the distraught mother that she should not weep; Duse wept with Isadora, and for the first time since the death of the children, Isadora no longer felt alone in her pain.

Isadora never wavered in her admiration for the great actress. Indeed, she wrote in her memoirs, "Eleonora Duse was a super-being. Her art was so great it could receive the tragedy of the world, her spirit the most radiant that had ever shown through the dark sorrows of this earth."

Duse, Isadora told me, was a poor correspondent—during the years Isadora knew her, Duse would from time to time send her a long telegram; but now when they lived in close proximity, she was capable of sending two or even three charming short letters each day, to be delivered directly into Isadora's hands.

"Forgive my fatigue the other night," she wrote in one of these letters. "I could not speak to you, my heart pains me when I see you suffer. Be of good cheer tomorrow! I hope the view of the sea and the mountains will bring you peace. My thoughts watch over you and wish you courage, *chère loyale amie*. To regain my own strength, I must rest a little while longer on my doctor's advice. But I shall see you soon and we will talk more about the children—and art."

They took long walks by the sea, walks to which Duse referred as "The Tragic Dance promenades with the Tragic Muse." "When Duse walked along the beach," Isadora said, "she took long strides, walking unlike any other woman I have ever seen." With unbounded admiration and love, Isadora watched Duse's every movement, every gesture, just as she watched the expression of her face when Duse spoke, and listened to every shade in Duse's remarkable voice. "Often when I walked with her by the sea . . . it seemed to me that her head was among the stars, her hands reached the mountain tops. . . ."

"Look at the rough sides of the Croce, how somber and forbidding they seem beside the tree-covered slopes of the Ghilardone, the sunny vines and lovely flowering trees," and Duse would point to the mountains. "But if you look to the top of the dark rough Croce, you will perceive a gleam of white marble waiting for the sculptor to give it immortality, while the Ghilardone gives only the wherewithal for man's earthly needs—the other his dream. Such is the Artist's life—dark, somber, tragic, but giving the white marble from which spring the aspirations of man."

Or, "sometimes at the end of September, in the frequent storms, when a flash of lightning broke over the sullen waves," Isadora would say as she recalled her walks with Duse, "she would point to the sea, saying: 'Look, the ashes of Shelley flash—he is there, walking over the waves.' "

A great admirer of Isadora's art, Duse kept saying to her that only in her art, in her work would she find solace and peace. But, she advised her: *"Ne perdez pas la belle douleur* (never lose the beauty of pain)."

". . . Duse was a magnificent woman, then in the full power of her life and intelligence. . . . Everything about her was the expression of her great and tortured soul," Isadora said later.

One day during their "promenade" by the sea, when "the setting sun made a fiery halo about her head, she gazed at me long and curiously," and Isadora never forgot Duse saying in a choking voice: "Isadora, don't, don't seek happiness again. You have on your brow the mark of the great unhappy ones of the earth. What has happened to you is but a Prologue. Do not tempt Fate again."

And Isadora, moved by Duse's admonition and inspired by the magnificent view, seen from a terrace on the roof of a large red brick villa in a regular forest of pine trees, with the sea on one side and the mountains on the other, rented a grand piano and telegraphed to Skene to come immediately to work with her. But as if she were destined to be pursued by a morbid atmosphere, Isadora soon discovered that, according to local legend, the villa had at one time been occupied by the young mistress of a member of the Austrian Court, that her son had become insane there; a small room with barred windows, where the young man was kept because he was considered dangerous, had an opening cut into the door for supplying him with his daily ration of food.

It was in this house of almost sixty rooms, one more gloomy than the next, that one day at dusk Isadora danced for Duse the adagio from Beethoven's Pathétique Sonata. "It was the first gesture I had made since the 19th of April, and Duse thanked me by taking me in her arms and kissing me. 'Isadora,' she said, 'What are you doing here? You must return to your art. It is your only salvation.' "

Although Isadora for the first time in her life was afraid to face an audience—it was different, she said, to make some gestures before Eleonora—her friend urged her most emphatically to resume her public performances at once. "If you knew how short life is and how there can be long years of *ennui, ennui*—nothing but *ennui!* Escape from the sorrow and *ennui*—escape!"

"You, who can flee reality, chère généreuse!" Duse pleaded with Isadora. "So courageous in life and gentle and submissive before death, how I wish I, too, could escape from tragedy! Without work, without risk, life is nothing—a dream empty of dreams. What joy to see you take up a new flight, far, far away from here. *Mon coeur et mon âme sont remplis de votre grandeur.* For all the beauty I perceive in you, I thank you."

As long as Isadora was immersed in her work with Skene or was in the company of Duse, she did not feel oppressed by the gloomy atmosphere of the villa. When left alone at night, however, she was sleepless, seeing strange forms and hearing strange sounds in the empty rooms. Her weary nerves were wrought to such a pitch that on one gray, autumn afternoon, while she was walking by herself along the sea, she suddenly had a vision of her children, hand in hand before her. She called to them, ran after them, but could not catch up with them; they ran away laughing, and "suddenly disappeared in the mist of the sea-spray."

It frightened Isadora. Not the vision, but the sudden thought that she might be losing her mind.

She told me that, if there was anything that she ever doubted in a man's or a woman's confession, it was their saying that they did not remember the exact words they had heard or had said themselves during incidents that were important in their own lives. Therefore, I do not doubt her description in her memoirs of the following scene.

"I fell upon my face and cried aloud. I don't know how long I had lain there when I felt a pitying hand on my head. I looked up and saw what I thought to be one of the beautiful contemplation figures of the Sistine Chapel." Considering her state of mind at that moment, her obviously romanticized vision should not be questioned.

"He stood there, just come from the sea, and said: 'Why are you always weeping? Is there nothing I can do for you—to help you?'

"I looked up.

" 'Yes,' I replied. 'Save me—save more than my life—my reason. Give me a child.'

"That night we stood together on the roof of my villa. The

sun was setting beyond the sea, the moon rising and flooding with sparkling light the marble side of the mountain, and when I felt his strong youthful arms about me and his lips on mine, when all his Italian passion descended on me, I felt that I had been rescued from grief and death and brought back to light—to love again."

Isadora told all this to Eleonora Duse. Isadora later said that Duse knew the "changeable ways of life, but she herself did not know how to forget deep sorrow, the gnawing pain." Isadora's story both surprised and impressed her, but it also frightened her, because Isadora spoke of a new intense mysticism that had taken possession of her. She believed that her children's spirits "hovered near her and that they would return to console her on earth."

Duse concealed her feelings and went with Isadora to her young lover's studio—he was a sculptor. "You really think he is a genius?" Duse asked Isadora later. Isadora had no doubt about it. Indeed, she assured Duse that he would probably be a second Michelangelo.

She was more reasonable when she remarked in her memoirs, "Youth is wonderfully elastic. Youth believes in everything, and I almost believed that my new love would conquer sorrow. Then I was so tired of the constant horrible pain."

Later, Isadora learned that the young man was already engaged to be married, but it did not disturb her. Had Craig not said in his letter, which she always kept with her: "You and I are lonely—only that. And no matter how many came—or shall come—you and I must be lonely—our secret"? She still believed that the young sculptor had saved her reason. What was even more important, she knew that she was no longer alone—she knew that she was pregnant.

When Isadora told Duse that she and Skene were leaving for Rome, where she intended to spend the winter, Duse did not express her disapproval. But later Duse wrote to Lugné-Poe, their manager and mutual friend:

. . . I do not understand, my friend, that this woman dares to will the *remaking* of her life!

Nothing of that which is irreparable is understood by this magnificent and dangerous creature! Her generosity is quite as great as her error of judgment.

The irreparable, which, nevertheless, exalts the tone of life— no—she does not even see it and wishes to throw herself back into life, bleeding life . . . and see again . . . what? The smile of the dead child, *in another* smile of another child that will be hers!

Be sorry, my friend, for my pettiness, for I understand nothing of *that will*, of that folly, of that supreme wisdom.

Isadora Duncan has on her side the Supreme Strength—greater than life itself. . . .

Eleonora

"Unfortunately," as Duse had said so many times, "in this short life nobody ever helps anybody and words are nothing but words. . . ."

But to Isadora, Duse had written earlier:

Dear Isadora,

Since we must say farewell, I beg you not to say it tonight, but rather tomorrow in the full light of the day at noon. *Chère* Isadora, how sad to see you leave! But you must find your wings again all by yourself, then you will re-enter a state of grace which is your art, your strength, your nobility—for sorrow is everywhere in this world . . . My thoughts are with you, recuperate, have a good rest, do not despair. Your graciousness and all the illusions of your heart will never be lost.

Adieu, et au revoir,
Eleonora Duse

Chapter XXII

Neither Skene nor Isadora could have predicted how long they would remain in Rome. Isadora wandered aimlessly by herself through the streets of the city, grateful for the soothing effect it had on her—its monuments and ruins, somber witnesses of a great past.

Skene was her constant companion, her dear friend, silent, and sympathetic in her grief. He played her favorite compositions, and at times she tried to work with him, but she had almost developed a habit, entirely new to her, of vacillating. "It is one thing to make a few gestures, perhaps even dance for Eleonora, a dear friend, but it is quite another thing to give a public performance before a large audience." Would she ever regain her confidence, she questioned herself. And what was to become of her school, her pupils?

Often she thought of the "Seminary of Dancing Priests of Rome," which some one hundred years after Christ was housed on one of the hills overlooking Rome. Chosen from the old aristocratic families, the pupils, in addition to their studies in the arts in general and in philosophy, were especially trained in dancing. Four times a year—spring, summer, autumn, and winter—they gave public performances. "The boys danced with such happy ardor and purity that their dance influenced and elevated their spectators as medicine for sick souls," Isadora maintained. It was such a school, capable of developing such dancers, that she had always dreamed of creating.

But now, she felt herself to be merely a ghost, wandering on the Appian Way, "a tragic figure between the rows of tombs."

It was when her sense of desolation was at its worst that she received a long telegram from Paris Singer suggesting her immediate return to Paris. He offered to fulfill her long-cherished dream—her school.

She was enchanted when Singer showed her the large estate he had bought at Bellevue on the outskirts of Paris, which had formerly housed a luxurious restaurant and hotel, Le Pavillon Pavilliard. Isadora could not have imagined a more beautiful place and, at the same time, one so perfectly suitable for her school; perhaps it would eventually have the same significance to Paris and its artists as the seminary of the dancing priests had had for the city of Rome. Situated on a hill, the spacious terrace had a sweeping view of the Bois de Boulogne and the city below, and of the gardens all the way down to the Seine. The large mansion, with its two hundred rooms and eighty bathrooms, could easily accommodate a large number of children, in addition to having sufficient quarters for a large staff to take care of them and the school.

Moreover, Isadora already visualized not only a Temple of the Dance of the Future, but an art center, where Eleonora Duse or Mounet-Sully would give dramatic performances, and where all the prominent artists would meet to discuss their works and their plans. "Here, too, I hoped to celebrate the Centenary of Beethoven with the Ninth Symphony and a thousand of my pupils. I pictured a day when the children would wend their way down the hill like Pan Athene, would embark on the river and, landing at the Invalides, continue their sacred Procession to the Panthéon and there celebrate the memory of some great statesman or hero."

No other good fortune than this gift of Paris Singer could have revived Isadora so much. She attended the many necessary conferences with Singer and Louis Sue, the architect, who was to execute at Bellevue the same plans he had made originally for the theater that had never been built near the Champs Elysées. And Isadora had abundant energy for supervising the actual transforming and redecorating of the building.

As far as the personal relationship between Isadora and Singer was concerned, matters appeared to be still very much as before, so that when Isadora told him about expecting a child by a man she had met on a beach in Viareggio, and her "mystic dream of the children's reincarnation and return to earth, he [Singer] hid his face in his hands. . . ."

"I came to you first in 1908 to help you, but our love led us to tragedy," Singer had said to her, according to Isadora, when, in response to his message, she had returned to Paris. "If you are willing to leave all personal feeling and, for the time being, to exist only for an idea, let us create your School, as you always had wished it, and some beauty on this earth for others."

So, as once before, when Isadora had lived in Versailles, and Singer had given sumptuous parties, now, as soon as the school began to function, he resumed his role as master of ceremonies par excellence, especially on Saturdays—artists' day—when luncheon was served in the garden, followed by music, poetry, and dancing.

To start on her plans for the school, Isadora first of all telegraphed to Elizabeth to send her the six girls who had taken part in her performances before the death of the children. Apparently aware that this request might not find favor with Merz, Isadora sent Augustin to Germany as her ambassador. And, indeed, this final breaking away of the best pupils in the Isadora tradition from Merz's ideas caused a night-long stormy scene, to which Anna, the eldest of the six, was a witness. Recently Anna herself told me about this episode. She said, "For the first time I was permitted to voice an opinion during a conference between Elizabeth and Merz.

"Elizabeth made a remarkable statement when Merz objected to our leaving their school: 'If these girls are to become artists,' she said, 'there is only one person who can do it and that is my sister. I cannot lead them any farther in their art. If they are to be dancers, only Isadora can accomplish that.' But Merz protested that she would be betraying her faith in herself and in the school. Elizabeth tried to reason with him, saying that, after all, the main thing was that Isadora was taking renewed interest in life, and we must do everything we could to help her. But Merz was adamant: 'This is absurd, Elizabeth, utterly senseless. Why must we send all the girls at the same time? Can't we simply send one or two, and keep the rest? You know very well that we have a command performance to give for the Crown Prince and his wife in Potsdam in a few weeks. And what about our plans for appearing at the Salzburg Festival this summer? Have you thought of that? You don't know what you are doing! This is ruin for us!'" And, Anna added, he became red in the face with fury and threatened to throw himself out the window. He opened the window, but he did not provide a dramatic finale to the scene.

The six girls were happily reunited with Isadora in the middle of January 1914. She had already selected almost fifty new pupils from among French children. She said that in the mornings, when she entered the dancing room and heard them shout "Good morning, Isadora," it sounded so joyful that she could not be sad among them.

She left the teaching of the beginners to the six older girls, for working with them became too strenuous for her in her condition; she could not risk doing strenuous things but confined herself to demonstrating slow movements and to explaining her concept of dancing and music. "Some of us derived much from this way of conveying her ideas to us," Anna said, in summarizing her memories of that period at the Bellevue School. But they were talented girls, and they were deeply imbued with Isadora's inspiration.

Three months later, in April, Isadora sent Anna and Irma accompanied by Augustin, his second wife, and Skene, to Russia to select some pupils from among Russian children and bring them to Bellevue.

Upon their arrival in St. Petersburg, Anna and Irma gave a short program in the ballroom of the hotel where they were staying. Isadora's old friend Konstantin Stanislavsky added importance to the event by introducing the girls to the audience and delivering an impromptu lecture on Isadora's art. This small dance recital was followed by a regular performance, "'An Evening of Dances,' given by Isadora Duncan's pupils at the Grand Hall of the Conservatory," on May 22, 1914.

I have the program of that performance. The following is the text (in my translation) of the announcement in the program:

> Isadora Duncan has founded a dance school at Bellevue, near Paris, with an aim of rearing about fifty children, girls and boys, in the spirit of the art created by her. Children between the ages of six and nine are accepted in the school, after a preliminary examination especially planned for this purpose.
>
> The accepted children will receive a general education at the Bellevue School and will be kept there at the expense of the school. In

turn, the children will devote themselves to the study of Isadora Duncan's art until they reach the age of twenty-one, when they can decide whether or not they are interested in remaining with the other pupils to pursue their artistic activities under Isadora Duncan's direction.

Isadora Duncan has sent four of her pupils, who were educated at her former school in Grünewald, near Berlin, in 1904, to choose ten Russian children. The preliminary examinations began on April 20, on which day work started with the children who are participating in the present performance. This evening's program will open with exercises performed by Isadora Duncan's pupils to show the possibility of teaching the "Isadora Duncan dances."

The girls remained in Russia for two months and, after giving a few more performances, which included the newly recruited Russian children, all departed for Bellevue.

Once again, as in the old days at Grünewald, the rooms and halls of the school resounded with children's joy and laughter. Always hoping that "this time" at last she was going to achieve her main aim, Isadora was already making plans for their future performances. In the evenings, Augustin had been reading to them from Shakespeare's plays, or Byron's *Manfred*, and Isadora thought he could play the part of Dionysus in a performance of the *Bacchae* of Euripides. Since D'Annunzio was an old friend, and a great enthusiast for Isadora's school, she succeeded in making him promise to participate in some of her planned programs.

But, as the time for the birth of her child approached, she found it more and more exhausting to stand while teaching; instead, she tried to direct her pupils by movements of her hands and arms while she reclined on a couch in the studio.

Isadora was indeed exhausted from the effort she had made "to change grief and mourning into new life." Paris Singer arranged for the whole school to take a vacation on his estate in Paignton in Devonshire. Again Isadora was left alone in a huge establishment, whose empty rooms and echoing hallways provided a morbid atmosphere that was conducive to a recurrence of her depression.

Toward the end of July 1914 the political situation in Europe was steadily growing more alarming. Isadora read the headlines in the newspapers, or listened to the warnings of forthcoming disaster brought to her by an occasional dinner guest. She tried deliberately to keep her mind on the child she was expecting at any time, on the pupils who would return in September to continue the joy of their work together, and on the apotheosis of all her artistic endeavors in her future performances.

But, when in the first days of August she began to notice the first signs of childbirth, she heard the servants, the gardeners, the workers on the Bellevue premises, the whole of France—the whole of Europe, she thought—cry: *"C'est la guerre! C'est la guerre!"* The nurse who was attending her spoke to her only of the mobilization and of her own husband, who had already left for his regiment. Isadora's old friend Dr. Bosson was ordered into the army and was replaced by another doctor, a stranger to Isadora, who kept saying to her *"Courage, Madame, courage, Madame,"* though Isadora never knew whether he referred to her suffering or the repeated cry heard all over a France suddenly faced with crisis.

And then one day, Isadora gave birth to a boy and her happiness was so great that for once she did not mind being so egotistical as to think: "What do I care if there is War? My baby is safe in my arms. Let them have their War. What do I care?"

In the evening, after all those who had come to congratulate her and wish her happiness had left, Isadora, holding the child in her arms, whispered: "Who are you, Deirdre or Patrick? You have returned to me."

"Suddenly the little creature stared at me and gasped, as if choking for breath, and a long whistling sigh came from his icy lips."

She called for the nurse, who came and hurriedly carried the child away. She heard orders for oxygen and hot water. Almost an hour passed before Augustin came in and told Isadora that the child had died.

Isadora wrote later: "I believe that in that moment I reached the height of my suffering that can come to me on earth, for in that death it was as if the others died again—it was like a repetition of the first agony—with something added."

She saw the cradle being taken away, and she heard hammer taps closing the little box—her child's only cradle now.

Chapter XXIII

"But what is one's personal sorrow when war—the disaster of
either killing or maiming thousands—is mentioned," Isadora's friends
told her when they called on her and tried to comfort her. What
about art? What about the treasures that have been preserved and
guarded as sacred which the catastrophe will render unto dust?
Is art greater than life? This is not the time to pose or discuss such
questions, Isadora heard. Thousands are wounded, and even dying
men are being sent back to the front—"So take Bellevue, I am giving
it to France," Isadora said from her sickbed. Thus Isadora's Acropolis was transformed by *Les Dames de France* into a hospital for
war casualties.

Before Isadora left Bellevue, she had herself carried on a
stretcher from room to room, each already emptied of its furniture,
to see for herself how quickly her temple of art had been turned
into what Isadora called a Calvary. Her blue curtains, as well as the
bas-reliefs of bacchantes and dancing fauns and nymphs and satyrs,
had been taken down from the walls and replaced, as Isadora said,
by "cheap effigies of Christ on a golden cross, supplied by one of
the Catholic stores, which turned out thousands of them during
the war."

Isadora was depressed at the thought that the wounded would
awaken in such drab surroundings rather than in the cheerful rooms
carefully designed for her pupils. When she began to hear the

groans of the maimed soldiers being brought in, and the heavy steps of the stretcher bearers resounding through the empty halls, she got up from her bed and left Bellevue.

Whenever she was alone, Isadora somehow had the urge to be near the sea. Now, although it meant driving through the restricted war zone, she insisted on going to Deauville. Later she said that she was treated everywhere with the greatest courtesy. "When I gave my name, the sentry on duty would say: 'It is Isadora, let her pass.' I felt that was the greatest honor I had ever received." It was again *vox populi—vox Dei*. Only on this occasion the recognition was not accorded to Isadora the great artist, but to Isadora the mother, who had suffered the ultimate grief.

This time, however, her hopes for speedy recuperation were thwarted by her melancholy state of mind. Her Bellevue dream had vanished, and the whole world seemed as if it were suffering the agony that precedes the final collapse. Isadora felt utterly alone, abandoned, and physically so weak that, only rarely could she take walks along the seashore to breathe the sea air and watch the vast span of water, which she believed would always bring peace to her spirit—so that she could scarcely profit by what had been the main reason for her escape to Deauville. At first she stayed at the luxurious Hotel Normandie, but the nightly entertainment in the large ballroom of the hotel, improvised by prominent actors, poets, and musicians, depressed rather than encouraged her to "keep up an optimistic spirit in the face of the daily sad news from the fighting-front."

Restless, Isadora moved to a small furnished villa called Black and White which indeed was furnished and decorated to conform with its name. The gloomy atmosphere of the villa only further discouraged her—she felt ill and needed to consult a doctor. But when the doctor did not come to see her, she went to the military hospital where he served to learn the reason for his refusal to respond to her call. "The short man with a black beard," at that time a famous surgeon, stammered some excuses but promised to come on the following day. And he did come, patiently listened to Isadora's answers to the usual medical questions, and to Isadora's account of her losing her child and her home at Bellevue. Then he declared that there was nothing wrong with her except that she needed "love, love, and more love."

This prescription he administered himself, and to such effect that Isadora rapidly improved physically, as well as mentally. There is no way of knowing what the future of this love affair might have been had the doctor not made the fatal mistake of telling Isadora the reason for the "hallucinated manner," with which he always stared at her.

He was the same doctor "with a black beard" who, when Isadora was stricken dumb by the death of her children had said: "It is not true, I will save them."

André (Isadora did not give his last name in her memoirs) may have been a good doctor and the lover that Isadora needed at the time, but he was a poor psychiatrist. In explaining the "hallucinated manner," he told her how he had tried to blow life into Deirdre from his own mouth, and how much Isadora, when asleep, looked like Deirdre.

"I realized that I loved this man with a passion I had myself ignored, but as our love and desire for each other increased, so also increased his hallucinations, until one night I awoke and found those terrible eyes of sorrow gazing at me, and I knew that the obsession that possessed him might lead us both to insanity."

Distraught, Isadora was determined to escape from the black-and-white villa, from this deathlike love, and put an end "forever to the intolerable grief from which she could find no relief in Art, in the rebirth of a child, or in love." She attempted to drown herself by walking into the sea. Fortunately, André, who missed her at the villa, found the hat which she had dropped on the beach and came up in time to rescue her. But one more gruesome portent was added when a trunk presumed to contain Isadora's winter clothes arrived. Upon opening it, Isadora discovered that it was the wrong trunk—it contained Deirdre's and Patrick's clothes—"the little dresses they had last worn—the coats and shoes, and little caps." And she heard again the cry that she had heard when she saw them lying dead—a strange, long, wailing cry, which she did not recognize as her own voice—but as if some cruelly hurt animal called its death cry from her throat.

André found her unconscious.

As soon as England entered the war, Paris Singer turned his estate in Devonshire into a hospital. In September, he sent seventeen of the girls to New York. Isadora herself left Deauville and at the end of October arrived in New York. She was met by Elizabeth and Augustin and her girls, who after a harassing experience at Ellis Island, were now, thanks to Singer, comfortably installed in a brownstone on Gramercy Park. Augustin and Margherita, his second wife, were taking care of them. Augustin had become a well-known actor on Broadway, and was soon to become a theatrical director.

Isadora was welcomed by the whole entourage of her former friends and admirers, and a large studio was found for her on the northeast corner of Twenty-third Street and Fourth Avenue. By the time Isadora's blue curtains covered the walls and low couches with soft cushions were in place in the studio, her new residence resembled Bellevue more than it did the Polytechnic Institute, which had formerly occupied the building. There she worked with her pupils, gave private performances with them, and entertained her steadily growing number of followers, who she believed would be valiant supporters of her aim to have a school in the United States.

But before she had even begun her campaign to find sponsors for her school, she discovered that she already had competition. Max Merz, not being one of those audacious Germans who believed that the war would be over in a few months, but being a shrewd man, arrived in London with Elizabeth and a dozen pupils from their school in Darmstadt shortly before England entered the war. Keeping himself well in the background, he directed Elizabeth to go to Paris Singer's estate with their pupils, so that they could all be sent to the United States. All this occurred even before Isadora's girls were sent to New York.

At this time the United States was not yet involved in the European war and Merz successfully posed as a "Viennese *Küss die Hand*" musician rather than a Teutonic hero. But Elizabeth kept him and his solicitations for funds for the school they planned to open—this time for obvious commercial reasons to be called the Isadora Duncan School—close to the German colony in New York rather than to her own old acquaintances in New York society.

The fact that, by the time Isadora arrived in New York, Merz and Elizabeth had already established a school in Ossining did not bother her in the least.

Shortly after her arrival, Isadora gave a performance at the

Metropolitan Opera House. It was an important event for her, for this was her first public appearance since the death of her children, and also her first test of whether she would be able to overcome the stage fright which had been worrying her ever since she thought that "it is one thing to dance for a sympathetic friend like Eleonora Duse, and quite another for a large group of strangers in a theatre."

"The program had a religious character," Irma, who was one of the six girls in this performance, reports in her memoirs. "It opened with a requiem march and Isadora's . . . presentation of Schubert's 'Ave Maria.'" According to Irma, "Isadora's magnetism had not diminished with the years." But Irma also adds that "her older pupils did most of the dancing."

This performance remained memorable, not only because it was a triumph, but because of what followed. Paris Singer, who, in the opinion of some of his intimate friends, was the long-suffering but always devoted friend of Isadora—driven away occasionally by her tempestuous behavior, but always ready to patch up their quarrels—had financed this matinee performance at the Metropolitan, to present under the best auspices her first public appearance since the death of her children. To further celebrate the occasion, he invited about twenty of their friends to dinner at Sherry's restaurant, and another hundred to dance after dinner.

According to Arnold Genthe, the famous photographer and a friend of Singer and Isadora, who was present at the party, Singer told him that he had placed him at the table next to Isadora because, since she never ate anything before a performance, and actually on that day had had nothing since her cup of coffee at breakfast, he wished Genthe to see to it that she did not drink anything before she got some solid food.

Extremely happy about the success of her performance, as soon as she sat down Isadora said, "I'm dying of thirst. I just have to have a sip of champagne." But apparently the "sip of champagne" did not have the fatal effect Singer had feared, for she had never been in better form than she was during dinner. It seemed that to please Singer, Isadora, who had dressed fashionably and worn jewelry only at the beginning of their liaison, on this occasion wore an exquisite white chiffon frock and a diamond necklace that Singer had just presented to her.

According to Genthe, "All went well until the dancing began."

Then, after noticing a young man dancing a tango, Isadora told Genthe that he was one of the most famous Argentine tango dancers, and that she would like to dance with him. Their tango performance seemed to have astonished "the guests by something more than mere grace and rhythm," and Paris Singer, a furious giant, "strode into the middle of the floor, took the Argentine by the scruff of the neck and slithered him out of the room."

"If this is how you treat my friends," Isadora was supposed to have said, "I won't wear your diamonds." Tearing off the necklace, and letting the diamonds scatter on the floor, she swept out of the room. But either because the happiness brought her by her successful matinee could not be marred by anything, or because by the time she reached the door of the dining room, she had regained her sense of humor, she whispered to Genthe, who happened to be at the door: "Pick them up." (There is another version of this incident with the necklace which, according to Isadora's memoirs, happened much later. Of this, I shall speak in due course.)

However, once having regained her confidence, Isadora could not refrain from making speeches to her public after each performance. "If I were only a dancer, I would not speak. But I am a teacher with a mission. . . ." Invariably carried away by her own enthusiasm, she would enlarge her "mission" to take in economics, politics, and the war in Europe.

After one of her performances, she enveloped herself in a red shawl and danced the "Marseillaise." Her interpretation of the "Marseillaise" had become one of the masterpieces of her repertoire, and was immortalized by Genthe's photographs. "It was a call to the boys of America to rise and protect the highest civilization of our epoch," she explained, "that culture which has come to the world through France." And for once she was gratified by seeing her message well represented in the press on the following day.

"Miss Isadora Duncan earned a remarkable ovation at the close of her program with an impassionate rendition of 'the Marseillaise,' when the audience stood and cheered her for several minutes. . . . Her exalted poses were imitative of the classic figures on the Arc de Triomphe in Paris. Her shoulders were bare, and also one side, to the waist line, in one pose, as she thrilled the spectators with a representation of the beautiful figure of Rude on the famous arch.

The audience burst into cheers and bravos at the living representation of noble art."

Carl Van Vechten, the writer and critic, wrote as follows about her interpretation of the "Marseillaise": "Part of the effect is gained by gesture, part by the massing of her body, but the greater part by facial expression, thereby arousing as vehement and excited an expression of enthusiasm as it would be possible for an artist to awaken in our theatre today. . . . In the anguished appeal she does not make a sound . . . but the hideous din of a hundred raucous voices seems to ring in our ears. We see Felicien Rop's 'Vengeance' come to life . . . and finally we see the superb calm, the majestic, flowing strength of the Victory of Samothrace. . . . At times, legs, arms, a leg or arm, the throat, or the exposed breast assume an importance above that of the rest of the mass, suggesting the unfinished sculpture of Michelangelo."

Having thus reintroduced herself to New York, Isadora was ready to start her campaign for her school by following the advice of her friends, in whose powerful influence she had perfect confidence. To fulfill their latest suggestion of inducing John Mitchell, the Mayor of New York, to let her use one of the abandoned armories for her school, Mabel Dodge, who had a literary salon in New York, the journalist Walter Lippmann, then twenty-five years old, and the poet John Collier, had arranged a reception at Isadora's studio to which many prominent people were invited. They pinned their hopes on Isadora's charm for winning the mayor's approval for their scheme.

But on that day, apparently, Isadora was in the wrong mood. She greeted the mayor with: "You, the Mayor of New York? You certainly don't look like a Mayor of this big city. You look like a very intelligent and handsome young man." She refused to dance for him, and instead, sitting down beside him on a couch, she had her girls simply parade before him in their school uniforms. She tried to convince the mayor of the health-giving properties of that costume, and suggested that he order all the New York school children clad in the same attire. Also, instead of talking to him about the main reason for his visit—her school—she started a long discussion of a criminal case then making headlines in the newspapers. Often there was a complete and embarrassing silence in the studio and only Isadora's voice could be heard: "Who are these people? What do they know about art, or what can they understand of my work? Who are these women? Wives with feathers!" Her observations did not impress the mayor in her favor, and she had to abandon her project.

Walter Lippmann wrote to Mabel Dodge:

I'm utterly disgusted. If this is Greece and Joy and the Aegean Islands and the influence of Music, I don't want anything to do with it. It's a nasty, absurd mess, and she is obviously the last person who ought to be running a school. . . .

I went into this because, like a damn fool, I deluded myself with thinking that we could have one spot of freedom and beauty. I should have known better. These spots exist only in the imagination we weave about performers like Miss Duncan. I should have known better than to be dazzled into a short cut to perfection—there are none, and Isadora is not the person to show the way.

Isadora did a little better when, again at the suggestion of her well-wishing friends, an evening program was arranged—the girls were to dance and Isadora to talk about her school and its aims. This time her friends did not fail to advise her to be in a "more receptive state of mind." "As nine o'clock approached, she appeared in her draperies and assumed a graceful and fetching pose on one of the low couches," Arnold Genthe, who was among the guests, recalls in his book, *As I Remember*. "Now," she said to the girls, "I hope you understand the importance of the occasion. We must do everything we can to make a hit with Mr. Kahn." The reference was to Otto Kahn, the well-known financier and patron of the arts.

Mr. Kahn came attired in full evening dress. Isadora, in the most innocent manner, asked him to be seated. He looked around for a chair. There was none. Isadora, with a graceful gesture, invited him to sit beside her. For a moment the only sound to be heard was the creaking of his stiff shirt as he negotiated the distance between them. Isadora turned the full spell of her radiance upon him. Before the evening was over, he had placed the Century Theatre, of which he was a patron and a subsidizer, at her disposal. She was to give a performance there and he further arranged for the girls to live in some of its upper rooms, and she could also have her school there.

But Kahn held his breath when he walked into the theater during Isadora's first performance and saw the transformation she had made of its interior. "The snobbish shape of the theatre angered me," she said. "The Greek was essentially a democratic theatre." She had had the first ten rows of seats taken out so that the orchestra would not be too close to the stage, and a blue carpet covered the rest of the orchestra space. Under her direction the ugly loges were draped with blue curtains, and the elaborate gold of the founder's loge with unbleached muslin.

Kahn's wrath melted, however, as he watched Isadora and her school as the chorus in a performance of *Oedipus Rex*, with Augustin in the title role, and some eighty musicians and one hundred singers.

The Century seemed so ideal, especially since it had many rooms and even a kitchen, that Isadora was happy to move the girls from the brownstone on Gramercy Park and have them take up residence in the theater. It seemed to her a logical thing to do, because the girls were spending practically all their time at the theater in any case—either rehearsing or giving matinees and evening performances. All was well until April 23, 1915, when, on orders from the New York Fire Department, the little children and the older girls were awakened in the middle of the night and evicted from their improvised dormitories.

Isadora, who lived at the Majestic Hotel on Central Park West, had received the Fire Department's order during the afternoon, but she had not taken it seriously. That evening she had put on the scheduled performance of *Oedipus Rex*. But, when she witnessed the ousting of her little dancers from their cots, she became ill with shock and distress. She vowed to leave the country, "to leave New York to Philistine Darkness!" as one newspaper announced in its headlines.

It was, however, not so simple to act on that announcement. She had barely enough money for her own trip to Europe, and certainly none with which to meet the travel expenses of the seventeen girls. But the mere suggestion that, if worse came to worst, the girls would have to be sent to Elizabeth's school, brought an uproar of protest, especially from the older girls. They refused to be thrown back to what to them was Merz and Darmstadt all over again. Accordingly Isadora reserved berths for herself and all the girls on the *Dante Alighieri* sailing to Italy. Three hours before the scheduled departure of the ship, Isadora, surrounded by the girls dressed in their traveling cloaks, but with no money to pay for their trip, sat quietly meditating in her studio. After her rupture with Singer at Sherry's, she could hardly expect any assistance from him. It was then that a young woman "quietly dressed," as Isadora described her first impression of the unexpected caller, walked into the studio and asked Isadora when she was leaving.

The following description of the scene as given by Isadora in her memoirs can be taken as authentic, for she never forgot a single detail of it and told it to me many times, illustrating most vividly every gesture of her unexpected caller, and even imitating her voice.

" 'You see,' I said, pointing to the children in their traveling cloaks, 'we are all ready but we have not yet found the money to complete payment for the tickets.'

" 'How much do you need?' she asked.

" 'About two thousand dollars,' I replied, at which this extraordinary young woman took out a pocketbook, counted out two notes of a thousand dollars each, and placed them on the table, saying:

" 'I am delighted to help you in this small matter.'

"I looked in amazement at this stranger, whom I had never seen before, and who without asking for any acknowledgment even, placed this large sum of money at my disposal."

And, indeed, as Isadora goes on to say in her memoirs, she imagined that the young woman must be an heiress. "I am delighted to help you in this small matter," was enough to make Isadora come to that conclusion, though it was merely her new benefactress's way of expressing herself. Actually, Isadora learned years later that in order to make this generous gesture, the young woman had sold her very modest securities the day before, having heard of Isadora's predicament.

About ten years later I met this young woman, Ruth Mitchell, through Isadora. (For some reason Isadora failed to give her last name in her memoirs.) I saw her nearly every day whenever she went to Paris to see Isadora. I saw her again a few years after Isadora's death when I came to New York City. On the basis of my knowledge of her, I feel entitled to speak of her as the most sincere, unselfish, and generously devoted friend Isadora had during the last years of her life. Isadora said of her, "Her name was Ruth—Ruth who said: 'Thy people shall be my people; thy ways as my ways.'

And such a Ruth she has been to me ever since." This somewhat perfunctory acknowledgment of Miss Mitchell's benefactions I can ascribe only to the influence of the constantly intriguing females who surrounded Isadora during the writing of her memoirs. And the noble quotation was the least suited to Ruth Mitchell's relationship with Isadora. "Thy ways as my ways," could only have given an entirely false picture of Ruth Mitchell, who was neither an artist, nor a dancer, nor a musician, but a very simple young Californian of middle-class family who at one time had been a Sunday school teacher. In all the years I knew Ruth, she never seemed to change in the slightest. At the time of her first meeting with Isadora, she must have been a very pretty girl. She was of medium height, blue-eyed, with white teeth, chestnut hair, rosy cheeks, and a perfect complexion. Very reserved in her manner and speech, she was nevertheless pleasant, polite, and attentive.

As for "Thy people shall be my people"—this is not accurate either, especially if it is applied to Ruth Mitchell's attitude toward Isadora's entourage. Actually she would have been able to do even more for Isadora if the boldly demanding homosexuals and the more subtle Lesbian parasites, who sponged on Isadora during her last years—a sect not easily assimilated by one of Miss Mitchell's puritanical views—had not drained the funds that she used to bring with her, and which were intended entirely and solely for Isadora's personal use.

But when, on May 9, 1915, among many other of Isadora's friends, Ruth Mitchell waved bon voyage to Isadora, and saw Mary Desti climbing aboard without luggage, passport, or ticket, bellowing, "I am coming with you, I am coming with you," she was merely a novice, and did not realize that she was already paying for Mary Desti's voyage to Europe.

Extraordinarily, Isadora had been forbidden by the police to dance the "Marseillaise" again in New York; instead Isadora, as her final gesture of defiance to a neutral United States, had equipped all her girls with small French flags, which, as soon as the ship began to move, they flipped from their sleeves as they sang a loud chorus of the immortal anthem.

Actually to Isadora the "Marseillaise" was not merely the French national hymn, a call to arms to defend the fatherland, nor a musical signal to her compatriots to defend civilization, as she repeated in her speeches referring to the war. It was the expression of a guiding spirit which was to free the world from the shackles of outmoded conventions. The embodiment of her ideas in the creation of her dance made Isadora's "Marseillaise" a masterpiece which, as Genthe remarked, "was something that no painter could do with colors and no sculptor in bronze or marble."

Thus, the police order forbidding her to dance the "Marseillaise" in New York, the complete failure of her journey to the United States, her homeland, where she always hoped to find support for her ideas, and the final exilelike departure to an unknown future in Europe, led her to many reflections, of which only a few were included in her memoirs.

To begin with, she thought her art was completely misunderstood—she had never wanted nor professed to be a Greek dancer. Her own conception was that she was making use of "the Greek dancing legend handed down in statues, friezes, and painted vases as an inspiration for a play of rhythmic motion and gesture that would have grace and beauty and freedom, synchronizing the body and spirit of the modern woman and making it the implement of a great plastic art."

"America is a free land," Isadora repeated over and over again, when, as yet undaunted by constant failure, she still firmly believed in her final success. "America is as free as Greece was in her Golden Age." She actually believed that "the bodies of American youth were close to the Greek ideal, and should be used for beauty and with the same lightness and grace as those of the young in that fabulous era when the creative arts came to their finest blooming."

Isadora loved the United States and was very proud of being an American. "It has often made me smile—but somewhat ironically—" Isadora wrote in her memoirs, "when people have called my dancing Greek, for I myself count its origin in the stories which my Irish grandmother often told us children of crossing the plains with grandfather in '49 in a covered wagon—she eighteen, he twenty-one—and how her child was born in such a wagon during a famous battle with the redskins, and how, when the Indians were finally defeated, my grandfather put his head in the door of the wagon, with a smoking gun still in his hand, to greet his newborn child." Isadora traced the origins of some of her dances to her grandmother's Irish songs and jigs, "reflecting the heroic spirit of the pioneers, as well as the gestures of the redskins themselves, and perhaps even an addition of a bit of Yankee Doodle."

"And that was the origin of the so-called Greek dance with which I had fooled the world," Isadora declared. "That was the origin—the root—but afterwards, coming to Europe, I had the great Masters, the three great precursors of the Dance of our century—Beethoven, Nietzsche, and Wagner."

In later years Isadora often spoke of Duse's disappointment with America, in the wealth wasted in Hollywood on mediocre productions, in the primitive taste of the American public, in the utter lack of any desire for beauty on the part of the average American. And Isadora often quoted Sarah Bernhardt's remark when, upon her return to France from the United States, she was asked about her impressions of America: *"Les fleurs sans odeur, les fruits sans saveur, les femmes sans pudeur et les hommes sans honneur."*

Even though Isadora's experience tended to justify the verdicts of her sisters in the arts, and though she had been disappointed in her deepest ambitions in her own country, she was never bitter toward America. Reflecting seriously on the future of her country, she left a legacy which today, almost half a century later, has as much validity as it had when she wrote it in 1926.

> In a moment of prophetic love for America, Walt Whitman said: "I hear America singing," and I can imagine the mighty song that Walt heard, from the surge of the Pacific, over the plains, the voices rising of the vast Chorale of children, youths, men and women, singing Democracy.
>
> When I read that poem of Whitman's, I, too, had a vision—the Vision of America dancing a dance that would be the worthy expression of the song Walt heard when he heard America singing. This music would have rhythm as great as the exhilaration, the swing of or curves of the Rocky Mountains. It would have nothing to do with the sensual life of the jazz rhythm: it would be like the vibration of the American soul striving upward, through labor, to harmonious life. Nor had this dance that I visioned any vestige of the Fox Trot or the Charleston—rather was it the living leap of the child springing toward the heights, towards its future accomplishment, towards a new great vision of life that would express America.

. . . I often wonder where is the American composer who will hear Walt Whitman's America singing, and who will compose the true music for the American Dance which will contain no Jazz rhythm—no rhythm from the waist down, but from the Solar Plexus, the temporal home of the soul, upwards to the Star-Spangled Banner of the great sky which arches over that stretch of land from the Pacific, over the Plains, over the Sierra Nevadas, over the Rocky Mountains to the Atlantic. I pray you, young American composer, create the music for the dance that shall express the America of Walt Whitman —the America of Abraham Lincoln.

It seems to me monstrous that one should believe that the Jazz rhythm expresses America. Jazz rhythms express the primitive savage. America's music would be something different. It has yet to be written. No composer has yet caught this rhythm of America— it is too mighty for the ears of most. But some day it will gush forth from the great stretches of Earth, rain down from the vast sky spaces, and America will be expressed in some Titanic music that will shape its chaos to harmony, and long-legged shining boys and girls will dance to this music, not the tottering, ape-like convulsions of the Charleston, but a strong, tremendous upward movement, mounting high above the Pyramids of Egypt, beyond the Parthenon of Greece, an expression of beauty and strength such as no civilization has ever known.

I see America dancing, standing with one foot posed on the highest point of the Rockies, her two hands stretched out from the Atlantic to the Pacific, her fine head tossed to the sky, her forehead shining with a Crown of a million stars.

How grotesque that they have encouraged in American schools of so-called bodily culture, Swedish gymnastics, and the ballet. The real American type can never be a ballet dancer. The legs are too long, the body too supple and the spirit too free for this school of affected grace and toe-walking. It is notorious that all great ballet dancers have been short women with small frames. A tall, finely made woman could never dance the ballet. The type that expresses America at its best could never dance the ballet. By the wildest trick of the imagination you could not picture the Goddess of Liberty dancing the ballet. Then why accept this school in America?

Henry Ford has expressed the wish that all the children of Ford's City should dance. He does not approve of the modern dances and says, let them dance the old-fashioned Waltz and Mazurka and

Minuet. But the old-fashioned Waltz and Mazurka are an expression of the unctuous servility of courtiers of the time of Louis XVI and hooped skirts. What have these movements to do with the free youth of America? Does not Mr. Ford know that movements are as eloquent as words?

Why should our children bend the knee in that fastidious and servile dance, the Minuet, or twirl in the mazes of the false sentimentality of the Waltz? Rather let them come forth with great strides, leaps and bounds, with lifted forehead and far-spread arms, to dance the language of our Pioneers, the Fortitude of our heroes, the justice, kindness, purity of our statesmen and all the inspired love and tenderness of our Mothers. When the American children dance in this way, it will make them beautiful beings worthy of the name of the Greatest Democracy.

That will be America dancing.

Chapter XXIV

Upon their arrival in Naples, Isadora learned that Italy was on the verge of joining the Allies in the war against Germany and Austria, and since most of her pupils traveled on German passports and would have been immediately detained as enemy aliens, Isadora proposed going to Greece, which was still neutral. But again, because Greece too was expected to be involved in the war, the girls begged Isadora to take them to Switzerland, always the safest country during European conflicts, and that is where they finally landed: Isadora at the luxurious Hotel Bar du Lac in Zurich, and the girls in a *pensionnat des jeunes filles*. But Isadora was determined to sit out the war in Greece and not in Switzerland, perhaps even camping in their temple at Kopanos which Raymond in vain still tried to complete, while he, also hoping to sit out the war, was living in the vicinity of Kopanos and weaving clothes. This was the origin of his later famous rug-weaving business in Paris. Tourists from all over the world would become familiar with his handmade rugs, togas, and sandals. In her memoirs, Isadora tells of the adventure that finally fulfilled her wish to see Greece again.

During the summer, after she moved from the Bar du Lac to the Hotel Beau Rivage in Ouchy, Isadora seemed to have acquired a large number of admirers—a whole band of young homosexuals, pretty boys in shining silk kimonos, who formed the entourage of an older man, but who apparently believed that flirtations at suppers to which they invited Isadora, or during motorboat rides on romantic Lake Leman, would be as satisfactory to her as they obviously were for them.

"The amusing society of these charming youths diverted me in my otherwise sad and lonely state, but their evident indifference to feminine charms rather piqued my pride," Isadora said. And she "proceeded to put her powers to the test." It seems she succeeded so well that, as she abducted the leader of the band, speeding at night in a Mercedes car along the shores of Lake Leman, she couldn't help chuckling to herself about the "young beauties when they discovered that their Sultan was gone, and with one of the abhorred sex." Isadora loved fast driving—"farther, farther," she directed the driver, until they had passed Montreux, Viege, St. Gotthard Pass, Rome, Naples, and, after taking an Italian steamer, arrived in Athens. It was one of those escapes that Isadora never could resist.

Many years had passed since Isadora had climbed the marble steps toward the Temple of Athens. And, in reviewing her life, she could not help, as she admitted to herself, "feeling ashamed when she thought how terribly she had lapsed in wisdom and harmony in the interval, and alack with what a price of suffering she had paid for the passion that had entranced her."

In 1915, however, Athens was not the peaceful town where the Duncans had dreamed of having their temple of art in 1904. Since Greece was still a neutral country, the capital was now a veritable hell, teeming with men and women of the most dubious professions, which camouflaged their true activities as spies and counterspies, double-dealing agents and informers—all working for the belligerent countries. Isadora soon found that the very atmosphere was as warped as the consciences of the men and women she was constantly meeting. It was neither the time nor the place to "sit out the war," nor were there people there with whom she could discuss her art. She decided to return immediately to Ouchy, but, of course, she could not restrain herself from making at least one gesture of defiance in favor of her Franco-British sympathies. In the large dining room of the Hotel d'Angleterre, where she was staying, she gave a dinner party accompanied by the frequent playing of the "Marseillaise" on her portable phonograph, whenever the German officials called for toasting the Kaiser. After dinner, Isadora led her guests to the Syntagma Square where, standing in the middle of a large crowd of curious Athenians who had been following her procession from the hotel, she sang the "Marseillaise" and delivered a speech in favor of the Greek sympathizers with the Allies, a speech which, although not understood because she spoke in English, was most enthusiastically acclaimed by her audience.

And then, with her newly acquired escort, she raced in his powerful Mercedes back to Ouchy. Once there, she went by train to Paris to find some way of raising funds to keep her girls alive; left to themselves all this time in the *pensionnat des jeunes filles* in Zurich, they were completely ignorant of what was going to happen to them.

The whole frivolous adventure of going to Greece with a homosexual sultan, whose name Isadora could later never correctly remember, who bored her, and whom she could extricate only with difficulty from the web of young adherents he had acquired immediately upon their arrival in Athens, was one of Isadora's many efforts to "escape" both the gnawing pain in her heart and the threatening signs of insanity. "The sight of any little child who entered the room suddenly, calling 'Mother,' stabbed my heart, twisted my whole being with such anguish that the brain could only cry out for Life, for Oblivion, in one form or another. . . ." Intelligent enough to know that she was not a "leader," and that, no matter how inflammatory, the speeches of even a famous dancer could not possibly change the course of political events, Isadora nevertheless kept on calling the citizens to arms, to destruction, death, and the sorrows of mothers.

Like a ship without sail or rudder, she let herself be tossed wherever she still believed she would find support for her aspirations of creating new life, creating art. Borrowing money from money lenders at 50 per cent to keep the stranded girls in Zurich, she went to Paris. There, at first, she was stricken with typhoid fever, but upon her recovery she installed herself in an apartment on the avenue Messine, which with her uniquely gracious hospitality she made into a rendezvous, not only for her friends and artists, but also for soldiers on leave from the fighting fronts. She was, of course, accused by the more practical of being too extravagant in keeping open house in that manner. But when the size of her bills for food and wine were pointed out to her, she simply said, "Oh, the poor things, they are artists, and they were so hungry! It was the least I could do. Who can tell? Perhaps among them is a future Carrière or a Rodin." Cécile Sorel, the famous actress of the Comédie Française, said to me of these gatherings: "Such regal gestures conceal the sacrifice they entail. That is the privilege of great artists."

But Isadora did not devote herself solely to "entertaining." She donated her services as an artist and the prestige of her name to a fund-raising performance at the Trocadero for *L'Armoire de Lorraine*, one of the many charitable organizations in France during the war. It was again an important event for her because it was to be her first public appearance in Paris since the death of her children. She composed a special program: César Franck's "Redemption"; Tchaikovsky's Sixth Symphony (Pathétique), and the *Marseillaise* as the closing number.

Men and women of all ranks and classes in the audience wept shamelessly during her rendition of the first two numbers on the program, which were connected with her personal tragedy, and indeed had been selected deliberately by her for that reason. Her interpretation of Franck's "Redemption" was the beginning of what was later called her monumental period, and was at first not even understood by those who expected her "to dance it." While the orchestra performed the score, Isadora at first simply lay on the stage, as if stricken down by a terrible blow; then she slowly rose from that position to her full height, and with her outstretched arms toward "Heaven and God, hands filled with goodness and charity," she remained motionless to the end of the composition.

While in her rendition of Tchaikovsky's Sixth Symphony, there was more "movement," more "actual dancing," she never failed to emphasize its subtitle, the Pathétique. But with the closing number of the program—the *Marseillaise*—which she performed dressed in her blood-red tunic and red shawl, her audience rose to their feet, and with such frenzied enthusiasm that they sang their national hymn as one immense chorus accompanying Isadora's entire performance. It was as if Isadora were justifying Thomas Carlyle's prophecy: "And whole armies and assemblies shall sing it with eyes weeping and burning, with hearts defiant of death, despot, and devil."

Although upon an invitation immediately following her success at the Trocadero, she gave two similar performances in Geneva and Lausanne, and once more repeated her program at the Trocadero at the end of April 1916, she simply did not earn enough to support the girls in Zurich, and certainly not enough to establish a school. For that reason, she decided upon a tour in South America.

With Maurice Dumesnil, the young French pianist whom Isadora chose as her accompanist and musical director, she sailed for New York in the middle of May 1916. There Augustin joined them, for he was to act as Isadora's business manager during those financially promising performances in South America.

They arrived in Buenos Aires in July and almost immediately were plunged into typically South American conditions, which had disastrous effects on the appearances scheduled for Isadora in Argentina. Nothing even in the vaguest way resembling business had been done in preparation for her performances, and nothing except promises, which were never kept, were given to Isadora when, upon her arrival, she was informed that the stage materials—Isadora's blue curtains and carpet, as well as musical scores for the orchestra— had not arrived. Isadora and her two companions were reduced to enjoying the sightseeing of Buenos Aires, especially its nightclubs. All their expenses were charged to the elegant hotel where they were staying, to be paid eventually by Isadora from her earnings in Buenos Aires.

During one of their nightclub outings, Isadora was so fascinated by the authentic dancing of the Argentinian tango that she not only joined the enthusiastic dancers but later, wrapping herself in the Argentinian national flag, improvised to the strains of the national hymn of Argentina. It delighted her nightclub audience but enraged her Argentinian manager, who used her improvised act as a pretext for breaking her contract, according to which she had no right to dance in public except at her performances. Also, her nightclub performances shocked Buenos Aires society, the main subscribers to Isadora's concerts, who canceled their reservations and thus created a devastating effect on the box office receipts for Isadora's three scheduled performances.

Discouraged and unable to help, Augustin went back to New York, and Isadora and Dumesnil, leaving practically all their belongings as collateral for their unpaid hotel bills, went to Montevideo in August.

Isadora fared better in Uruguay. In fact, her performances were so enthusiastically received that she could not refrain from flattering her audience in their traditional rivalry with Argentina with the following sentences in her farewell speech:

"My friends, I am happy that I came here. When I arrived, my heart was sick. I had visited a place [Buenos Aires] where Art is a dead issue. There I went through great humiliation—they did not even respect Beethoven or Wagner. It was like casting pearls before swine. . . ." And when Isadora closed her remarks with, "They are savages!" her audience rose to its feet and roared its approval.

In Rio de Janeiro and São Paulo, during the months of August and September, her performances incited an enthusiasm among the young members of her audiences that could only have been compared to that of the German students in Berlin and Munich at the beginning of Isadora's career, when she was called the *Göttliche*, the Divine One. And yet her South American tour was a dismal failure. She started the tour with great hopes of earning plenty of money to keep her school going, but already in Buenos Aires Augustin had realized the hopelessness of the situation and left her. Although Maurice Dumesnil remained with her through all her misfortunes in Buenos Aires, he preferred to stay in Rio de Janeiro while Isadora returned alone and penniless to New York.

Chapter XXV

It was at the end of September 1916 that Isadora arrived in New York. There was nobody at the pier to meet her. Wondering what to do next, she took the chance of reaching Arnold Genthe by telephone. To her surprise, it was Paris Singer who answered her call. Hearing that she had arrived alone, he came to the pier to fetch her.

At this point in her memoirs, Isadora made the following statement: "When I saw his tall, commanding figure again, I had a curious feeling of confidence and safety, and I was as delighted to see him as he was to see me.

"As a parenthesis, you may notice in this biography that I have always been faithful to my loves, and in fact would probably never have left any of them if they had been faithful to me. For just as I once loved them, I love them still and for ever. If I have parted from so many, I can only blame the fickleness of men and the cruelty of Fate."

Many times I heard Isadora proclaiming this final analysis of her personal life, with such naïveté that she always left me with the impression that she firmly believed what she was saying. However, while no one would be so gauche as to question her statement, there was a purely technical side to her claim of faithfulness to which she was indeed entitled—Isadora never did carry on two separate love affairs at the same time, as some of her lovers did.

Once again, although no longer on the terms of their former relationship, they resumed their friendship. As in the old days of his generous assistance in Isadora's plans and affairs, Singer immediately took care of the unpaid Zurich bills for Isadora's girls. Eleven of them went back to their families, and Augustin brought Isadora's six favorite pupils to New York. Singer engaged the Metropolitan Opera House for Isadora's performance in November and a studio for her to work in on top of Madison Square Garden.

The Metropolitan performance was a brilliant gala, to which no tickets were sold, the entire audience consisting of Singer's friends and Isadora's admirers. The loges were occupied by the elite of New York society and prominent members of the artistic world, while the gallery was filled with enthusiastic students—all cheering Isadora's every appearance on stage.

But Isadora was too tired and her health not robust enough to permit further strenuous work. As the cold winter approached, Paris Singer suggested that she go to Havana for a short vacation. To keep her company and to "take care of her needs," Singer sent along his private secretary, Allan Ross Macdougall.

I knew Dougy, as everybody called him, very well. He was one of Isadora's most devoted friends and, in fact, I would venture to say that he was as much in love with her as a man could be, except for the important reservation implied by the fact that he was a homosexual. In his youth—he was in his twenties on that trip to Havana—he was a handsome young man with the most engaging smile and a contagious laugh, which burst out at almost any of Isadora's frivolous or humorous remarks.

"Why do you think Singer chose Dougy to go with me to Havana?" Isadora interrupted her recollections of that trip as she was telling them to me. "Why should Singer send a man with me— there were plenty of females around, who would have been delighted to have been my *dame de compagnie* plus such a marvelous vacation? It was simply that with Dougy he did not have to be jealous."

Falling in with the tone of Isadora's narrative, I asked her, "Didn't you try to convert him?"

"Oh, indeed I tried—but I simply failed to seduce him. I got as far as getting his head close to my breast, but when I thought he might go to sleep in that comfortable position, I gave it up. But we did have fun, and I have always enjoyed Dougy."

According to Macdougall, one of the incidents of that trip had been transformed by Isadora in her memoirs into "a grade B movie scene with no relation to reality." Isadora's version is this:

> On a festival night, when all the carbarets and cafés were teeming with life, after our usual tour by the sea and the pampas land, we arrived at a typical Havana café, somewhere about three o'clock in the morning. Here we found the usual assortment of morphomaniacs, cocainists, opium smokers, alcoholics, and other derelicts of life. Taking our places at a small table in the low-ceilinged, dimly-lit, smoky room, my attention was drawn to a white-faced, hallucinated-looking man, with cadaverous cheeks and ferocious eyes. With his long thin fingers, he touched the keys of a piano and to my astonishment, there came forth Chopin's Preludes, played with marvelous insight and genius. I listened for some time, then approached him, but he could say only a few incoherent words. My movement had riveted the attention of the café upon me, and realizing that I was absolutely incognito, there came over me a fantastic desire to dance for this strange audience. Wrapping my cape about me, and directing the pianist, I danced to the music of several of the Preludes. Gradually, the drinkers of the little café lapsed into silence, and, as I continued to dance, not only did I gain their attention, but many of them were weeping. The pianist also awoke from his morphia trance and played as though inspired.
>
> I continued to dance until the morning and when I left, they all embraced me, and I felt prouder than in any theatre, for this I knew to be the proof of my talent, without the help of any impresario, or fore-notices engaging public attention.

Macdougall's version is different:

> On New Year's Eve, she gave a small dinner party on the dining-room roof—which, when it had trailed along into boredom, was left in charge of the secretary [Macdougall himself] as a substitute host. Later, in the early hours of the morning, when he had seen the last guests go, he went pub-crawling, hoping to find her [Isadora].
>
> "Sometime later he found her at the Hotel Telegraphic about to leave in company with a young Cuban journalist, correspondent of a New York musical magazine, his Senator brother, and their followers. Asked by one of the accompanying group to dance for them, the dancer took off her Poiret toque, which she tossed aside. The small group made a circle about her and the Senator's girl went to the small upright piano near by to thump out an incongruous

tango. Standing there in the deserted room, the dancer began, as she invariably did, with her two hands crossed before her breasts. Slowly they opened out in a rounded gesture, making a lovely sight with her arms stretched out and her black silk shawl falling down in a semi-circle over the long scarlet skirt of her Lucille dress. At that moment, one of the onlookers, no doubt expecting her to do some high-kicking to the dance music being played, laughed nervously. The dancer stood transfixed with her arms outstreched, her smiling face suddenly transformed into a mask of agony, her body quivering. For a few moments she remained thus and then her arms slowly dropped and the smile returned to her flushed face. "My God, Isadora," said her companion, "what were you doing?" "Didn't you see?" she answered. "I was about to dance the tango that creature was playing when I heard somebody laugh. I immediately thought of the jeering crowd on Calvary and I danced Christ on the Cross. Now," she went on, pulling the back of her black shawl over her head so that her face became almost invisible, "now I'm going to dance the *Mater Dolorosa.*" The girl thumped on with her incredible dance music and the dancer grimly moved a few steps forward. Then changing her mind, she said: "No, I'll do the *Dance of Death.* They're like the Gaderene swine! I'll lead them to drown in the sea." With these words she walked towards the door, looking back over her right shoulder and beckoning the sheepish crowd to follow her with the ineffable gesture she used as she danced Orpheus and called upon Eurydice to follow her from the Elysian Fields.

Once outside in the plaza with the "Swine" standing astonished about her, the Senator piloted her towards his open car. By the time she was seated there and laughing with her companion, the pianist—having suddenly found herself playing to the empty room—rushed out to the car. Isadora, in answer to her, "Did you like my playing, Miss Duncan?" looked at the heavily made-up chorus girl and said softly: "Get thee to a nunnery. Why wouldst thou be a breeder of sinners? . . . I have heard of your painting too . . . God hath given you one face and you make yourself another . . . To a nunnery go. . . ." And with that the car started off to make the rounds of the outlying cafés of Havana, leaving the mute piano player standing astonished on the sidewalk.

Personally, I do not see any reason why both incidents could not have taken place at different times, in different locales, among different people.

Isadora's friendship with Dougy lasted until practically the end of her life, but with small interruptions caused by Dougy's occasional lapses into what Isadora preferred to call "Lesbian" rather than feminine ways (she had much too high a respect for the word feminine), gossip, lies, and—especially futile and trivial in themselves—treacheries. In her latter days, after spending an evening with her so-called friends, each of them claiming to have been her most intimate confidant, Isadora would simply shake her head as if trying to get rid of everything she had heard. But Paris Singer was apparently less charitable in his attitude toward Dougy; whatever the precipitating circumstances, Macdougall lost the most luxurious living and the highest salary he ever had in his life.

"I don't know how much Paris knew about Dougy when he engaged him as his private secretary," Isadora told me—"all he knew was that Dougy was a Scotsman and a poet—but he must have loved him like his own son, for believe it or not, every morning he used to turn on his bath for him, and he gave him one thousand dollars pocket money a month. Do you wonder that Dougy went to pieces when, shortly after our return from Havana, he lost his job with Paris and had to fall back on some hundred or so dollars a month which he received from his family somewhere in Scotland?"

Paris Singer refused to see Dougy ever again. But Dougy, who followed Isadora's life not only by frequent visits with her, but by collecting all printed material about her, shortly after her death even went to Russia to collaborate with Irma on *Isadora Duncan's Russian Days*. Later, in the nineteen fifties, he embarked by himself on the most thorough research into Isadora's early days in California, and especially studied the background of her parents.

After Isadora's death, I gave, as mementoes to her admirers, books from Isadora's library, which had been given to me. But aware of Dougy's deep grief, I let him choose as many as he wished. Shortly before he went to San Francisco to do his research, he consulted me in New York on the authenticity of many of the stories and legends of Isadora's life, and, upon his return to New York, told me in detail about some of his discoveries. Unfortunately, these are missing from his book, as is the appropriate documentation —perhaps because of his sudden death in July 1956.

Isadora was generally restless when on a prescribed vacation. After several weeks in Havana she had had enough of Cuba and, escorted by Macdougall, returned to the United States, stopping in Palm Beach. Meanwhile, Paris Singer was working on a plan he had wished to carry out for a long time—that is, during the harmonious periods that occurred from time to time in their relationship. Singer was anxious to immortalize Isadora and her art. At the suggestion of George Barnard, the sculptor, he planned to endow an art center where artists, poets, writers, and dancers could carry on their work without financial problems.

For a large sum of money he had obtained an option on Madison Square Garden, but as he wanted it to be a surprise for Isadora, he said nothing about it until he joined her in Palm Beach. Again there are various versions, each claiming authenticity, of the dramatic scene between Isadora and Singer, which not only made Singer scrap his plans, but finally brought an end to their relationship.

According to Macdougall, Singer brought Percy MacKaye, the dramatist and poet, with him to Palm Beach, and as they were describing to Isadora their ideas for the future art center, Isadora suddenly turned from enthusiasm to suspicion. Since at that time MacKaye was anxious to stage the masques he was writing, Isadora thought that the project was simply MacKaye's idea, and that she would be relegated to the role of trainer of hundreds of girls "from Wanamaker's Department Store" who would perform in MacKaye's shows. Isadora's irrational attitude put an end to Singer's scheme.

According to the version of Arnold Genthe, who had the embarrassment of being present during the final break between Singer and Isadora, it had happened upon Singer's return from a short visit to Florida, where he had endowed a hospital for war casualties.

At a dinner party at the Hotel Plaza in New York, to which Singer also invited Augustin and Margherita, Elizabeth, and George Barnard, Singer began by telling Isadora of all the things he was doing for the wounded soldiers at the hospital and convalescent center in Florida.

"Is that what you brought me here for?" Isadora said, according to Genthe. "I'm sick and tired of hearing about the war and the sick soldiers. Can't you think of anything else?"

Obviously embarrassed, it was then that Singer told her of his project for the art center, and of his negotiating for the purchase of Madison Square Garden, with which he had planned to surprise her at the end of the dinner. Apparently the timing of the announcement was wrong, for Isadora, still in a belligerent mood, is supposed to have said to him: "Do you mean to tell me that you expect me to direct a school in Madison Square Garden? I suppose you want me to advertise prize fights with my dancing."

"Singer turned absolutely livid," Genthe recalls. "His lips were quivering and his hands were shaking. He got up from the table without saying a word and left the room.

" 'Do you realize what you have done?' we asked in a chorus of dismay. 'You could have had the school that was your life's dream, and now you have ruined everything.'

" 'He'll come back,' she said serenely. 'He always does.'

"He never did. She sent her brother, her sister-in-law, and finally the pupils to plead with him. He was adamant. Her letters to him went unanswered. All funds were stopped."

But in her own version, as given in her memoirs, the final break happened early in 1917.

Ever since the United States had entered the war on the side of the Allies, Isadora had danced the "Marseillaise" in nearly all of her performances; but in February 1917, on the night the news of the Russian Revolution reached the United States, Isadora, so she said, danced the "Marseillaise" with especial enthusiasm. Whether her statement that Singer was "somewhat perturbed, [and might] have asked himself whether the School of Grace and Beauty, of which he was a patron, might not become a dangerous thing that would lead him and his millions to annihilation," had any valid basis, or was purely a figment of her imagination, belongs to the field of conjecture—as well as the closing phrase of her statement: "But my Art impulse was too strong for me, and I could not arrest it even to please one I loved."

Then, according to her account, "L. [Singer] gave a fête at Sherry's in my honor."

It began with a dinner, and went on through dancing to an elaborate supper. Upon this occasion he presented me with a wonderful diamond necklace. I had never wanted jewels, and had never worn any, but he seemed so delighted that I allowed him to place the diamonds round my neck. Towards morning, after gallons of champagne had continually refreshed the guests, and my own head was more or less light with the pleasures of the moment and the intoxication of the wine, I had the unhappy idea of teaching the Apache tango—I had seen it danced in Buenos Aires—to a beautiful young boy who was present. [Billy Hamilton, Anna Duncan's beau, so Anna later told me, "and in a fashion one does not exhibit in public," Anna was told at the time.] Suddenly, I felt my arm wrenched in an iron grasp, and looked around to find L. storming with rage.

This was the only occasion upon which I ever wore this unlucky necklace, for shortly after this incident, in another rage, L. [Singer] disappeared. I was left with an enormous hotel bill and all the expenses of my School on my hands. After appealing to him in vain for help, the famous diamond necklace was taken to the pawnshop and I never saw it again.

Fortunately, Isadora managed to sell some other valuables Singer had given to her, including an ermine coat and an emerald, originally "from the head of a famous idol," which Singer had bought from a son of a maharajah who had lost all his money at Monte Carlo. The theatrical season came to an end and Isadora moved with her six girls to a small beach cottage at Long Beach, Long Island.

Although Isadora had just about enough money to pay the rent of the cottage and a car, and for their daily needs, her new "residence" soon became a rendezvous for artists and other persons of distinction, who came from New York especially on weekends. (Marcel Duchamp, Francis Picabia, Edgard Varèse, Elsa Maxwell, Count Florinsky and Baron Ungern-Sternberg, the Russian diplomats, and one of the most frequent and most welcome of guests, Eugène Ysaÿe, the famed Belgian violinist.)

They were enjoying their summer with daily bathing, dancing on the beach, drives to Montauk Point "*à grande vitesse*" (in those days, forty-five miles an hour was very fast, as Irma relates), and impromptu performances for their guests with Isadora's parodies "of the Ziegfield Follies that would have done credit to Mr. Minsky."

Having spent my life among artists, and having many friends among them, I think that I can say with some authority that Isadora was one of the few who did not take delight in criticizing or ridiculing individual artists. In fact she had the most astonishing respect for any achievements, even for those that did not really deserve her attention. Therefore, I doubt that she had ever favored her friends with her imitation of one of the self-appointed instructors of the so-called Isadora Duncan school—an imitation that illustrated the story she later told me about her visit to a dance school.

"Undulate, girls, undulate!" this teacher is supposed to have said, "Isadora says: 'undulate!'" And standing in the middle of the room, Isadora imitated the dancing instructor's gestures. However, I must say in parenthesis that, try as she might, Isadora's own lovely arms and delicate hands simply did not lend themselves to any kind of distortion.

It was during one of his frequent walks with Isadora on the boardwalk in Long Beach that Arnold Genthe witnessed for himself Isadora's humility toward those whom she considered truly great. Although Isadora knew that Sarah Bernhardt was recuperating from an operation in Long Beach, she was reluctant to call on her whenever Genthe suggested introducing her. "How do I know she wants to meet me? What have I to give to one of her divine genius?" Isadora asked Genthe. But, when Bernhardt's wheelchair appeared almost directly in front of Isadora, "Now," Genthe said, "you speak to her. Her doctor has recognized us and Sarah will be hurt if we don't go up to her." And Genthe recorded the short scene of their meeting.

When the introduction was made, Sarah, pointing to the place beside her in the chair, said: "Sit down here beside me." "Ah," replied Isadora, with a moving sweetness, "that would be too great an honor. I ought to be at your feet." In the excitement of the meeting, she had forgotten that Sarah had had one of her legs amputated. For, while playing Victorien Sardou's *Tosca* in Buenos Aires, Sarah became the victim of the professional jealousy of one of the actresses, who removed the mattresses backstage on which Tosca should land after her jump over the parapet in the last act. Sarah hurt her knee badly, and eventually her leg had to be amputated.

Although it does sound strange, according to Irma's recollections, Isadora had never seen a motion picture before she lived in Long Beach. At first, she protested, "What? Me set foot in there?" But, after the show was over, Isadora laughed "It was more fun than I imagined—but what an awful picture!" Not long afterward, Isadora was offered contracts by the motion picture companies, but she always refused to sell her art to the "flicks," as she called the pictures. She said that in those jumpy pictures her dance would resemble a St. Vitus dance. "I would rather not be remembered like that by posterity."

Since those days the technique of motion pictures has greatly improved, but the minds of the producers and directors of films have deteriorated to such a vulgar level that forty years after her death, her life and her art were presented "to be remembered by posterity" in the most ignominious way.

Chapter XXVI

Once the pleasant, outwardly carefree days of summer came to an end, Isadora found herself again in the same old predicament—without funds, and with the responsibility for her six girls, the only living illustration of her school, which was always on her mind. At this point she had no hope of finding financial support for that great project in New York. Isadora left the girls on their own, so to speak, in a large studio on the top floor of the newly built Hotel des Artistes, signed a contract for a tour of the West Coast, and departed for California.

During the twenty-two years since Isadora had left San Francisco, so much had happened to her native city that she could barely recognize it. Most of the familiar sights of her childhood had been destroyed by the fire of 1906, and the reconstructed buildings and homes held no sentimental memories for her. She gave a performance at the Columbia Theater, to what Isadora later termed a "select and expensive audience, kind and appreciative, as were the reviewers," but which did not bring her the satisfaction she had hoped for—to dance for the "people on a grand scale."

Nor was her meeting with her aging mother a particularly happy event. In her memoirs, Isadora blamed her mother's return to the United States at about the time of Deirdre's birth on homesickness for American ways and American food. But from the few times Isadora spoke to me about her mother, I got the impression that their estrangement was caused by the old lady's disapproval of Isadora's personal life.

To add to her depression, Isadora received news that her six girls were about to give performances as a group of Isadora Duncan Dancers. She telegraphed to Augustin, "I forbid it. The girls are not yet ready for performances on their own in New York." This was, of course, unreasonable. The girls had given performances without Isadora at the Duke of York Theater in London as early as 1908, in Russia before the beginning of the war, and at the Trocadero in Paris. They were no longer children, but young women in their twenties, and they could not miss an opportunity to contribute to their own support. Whether unconsciously or not, Isadora still treated them as children, disregarding their personal desires. In point of fact, they were handsome and talented young women who were ready to follow her example in more than artistic matters alone. Isadora's dictatorial attitude was resented by the girls and this incident marked the beginning of their struggle for a certain amount of independence—something that eventually brought about their final separation from her.

But while she was in San Francisco, Isadora gave relatively little thought to them. For she was finding moments of rare happiness, which speaking generally, she said "do not exist in this world," in her association with Harold Bauer. Forty-five years old at the time, Bauer was then at the height of his popularity as a pianist. A violinist from childhood, at the age of nineteen, on Ignatz Paderewski's advice, he had changed to the piano. In her recollections, Isadora devotes entirely too much space to the "meeting of two musical souls," for their close relationship was not based simply on Bauer's assuring her that she was more of a musician than a dancer, and confiding to her that "her art had taught him the meaning of otherwise inscrutable phrases of Bach, Chopin and Beethoven." They gave joint performances at the Columbia Theater, and Isadora said later, "I had hoped that this might continue and that we might discover an entire new domain of musical expression together."

She showed this sentence to me as she was writing her memoirs, after she had thought for a while of the best way of phrasing something that might possibly cause trouble, since at that time Bauer was still alive. And she added. "But, alas, I had not reckoned on circumstances. Our collaboration ended with a forced and dramatic separation."

Perhaps Isadora did succeed in mystifying some readers, but the simple cause of their "separation" was the fact that, on learning that her husband and Isadora were carrying their ecstatic collaboration beyond the musical field, Mrs. Bauer threatened a scandal.

"Oh, those jealous women," Isadora said to me by way of comment on the incident, "what do they understand about the arts?"

After they had parted, Isadora did not see Bauer again for eight years. At that time she asked that I accompany her to his recital in Paris, and insisted on our visiting him backstage after his concert. Far from showing delight at seeing Isadora, Bauer looked panic-stricken. His eyes shifted from side to side. He was obviously terrified that his wife might hear the few mumbled words he said to us before he hurriedly turned to the next admirer who came to congratulate him on his performance.

"Oh, those jealous wives," Isadora said as we left the green room. I never heard her speak of Harold Bauer again.

But, while she was still in the United States, Isadora could hardly fail to suffer because of the abrupt ending of her emotional relationship with Bauer, feeling it as a further disappointment in her unsuccessful journey. On top of all her misfortunes, her manager had disappeared with the earnings from her California tour. She felt abandoned, penniless, and discouraged. Her appeals to friends in London went unanswered. She decided to return to France. Somehow she believed that for her personal needs she could always mortgage her house in Neuilly, and, despite the war and the strained economic conditions in France, find assistance in raising money for her school. Despite the most vehement protests from the six girls, she left them with Elizabeth in Tarrytown, with the promise to return to fetch them after completing her business in France.

Gordon Selfridge, who once had been kind enough to let her have on credit "a skirt with frills" for her act at the Masonic Temple Roof Garden, when as a young girl she had come for the first time from San Francisco to Chicago, now was willing to pay for her ticket and to take her along to London. In the interim since their first meeting, when he was merely a manager sitting behind a desk at one of the Marshall Field shops in Chicago, Selfridge had become a millionaire.

Isadora enjoyed Selfridge's company during the crossing for, as she said later, "This was my first contact with a man of action. I was amazed how different an outlook on life he had, after the artists and dreamers I had known—he might almost have been of another sex, for I suppose all my lovers had been decidedly feminine. And I had also had the companionship of men who were more or less neurasthenic and either sunk in deepest gloom, or buoyed up to sudden joy by drink, whereas Selfridge had the most extraordinary, even cheerfulness I have ever met, and as he never touched wine, this amazed me, for I had never realized that anyone could find life in itself a pleasant thing. It had always seemed to me the future held only now and then glimpses of ephemeral joy through Art or Love, whereas this man found happiness in actual living." But he was not to become Isadora's second millionaire—he was already the object of Mary Desti's attentions; once Isadora reached London, she was as penniless as she had been when she sailed from New York.

As if she needed extra worries, Isadora was still suffering from a severe fall she had had on board ship, when she fell through an opening in the deck.

Night after night during the air raids in London, Isadora sat in her room in Duke Street and watched the bombing. She almost wished that a bomb might destroy the house and put an end to her life. "The past seems to be but a series of catastrophes, the future a certain calamity, and my school the hallucination emanating from the brain of a lunatic."

From Augustin, she heard that he had arranged some performances for the six girls which, though contrary to her orders, she had to accept as a fait accompli. She learned further that they had engaged George Copeland, one of the many so-called exponents of Debussy's music, and this choice of a new association with a musician alien to Isadora's tastes disturbed her so much that she immediately wrote to the girls:

Please don't let any one persuade you to try to dance to Debussy. It is only the music of the *Senses* and has no message to the Spirit. And then the gesture of Debussy is all *inward*—and has no outward or upward. I want you to dance that music which goes from the soul in mounting circles. Why not study the Suite in D of Bach? Do you remember my dancing it? Please also continue always your studies of the Beethoven Seventh and the Schubert Seventh; and why not dance with Copeland the seven Minuets of Beethoven that we studied in Fourth Avenue? And the Symphony in G of Mozart? There is a whole world of Mozart that you might study.

Plunge your soul in divine unconscious *Giving* deep within it, until it gives to your soul its *Secret*. That is how I have always tried to express music. My soul should become one with it, and the dance born from that embrace. Music has been in all my life the great Inspiration and will be perhaps some day the Consolation, for I have gone through such terrible years. No one has understood since I lost Deirdre and Patrick how pain has caused me at times to live in almost a delirium. In fact my poor brain has more often been crazed than anyone can know. Sometimes quite recently I feel as if I were awakening from a long fever. When you think of these years, think of the Funeral March of Schubert, the *Ave Maria*, the *Redemption*, and forget the times when my poor distracted soul trying to escape from suffering may well give you all the appearance of madness.

I have reached such high peaks flooded with light, but my soul has no strength to live there—and no one has realized the horrible torture from which I have tried to escape. Some day, if you understand sorrow, you will understand too all I have lived through, and then you will only think of the light toward which I have pointed and you will know the *real* Isadora is there. In the meantime, work and create Beauty and Harmony. The poor world has need of it, and with your six spirits going with one will, you can create Beauty and Inspiration for a new life.

I am happy that you are working and that you love it. Nourish your spirit from Plato and Dante, from Goethe and Schiller, Shakespeare and Nietzsche (don't forget the *Birth of Tragedy* and the *Spirit of Music* are my Bible). With these to guide you, and the greatest music, you may go far.

Dear children, I take you in my arms. And here is a kiss for Anna, and here is one for Therese, and one for Irma, and here is a kiss for Gretl [Margot] and one for little Erica—and a kiss for you, dearest Liesel. Let us pray that this separation will only bring us nearer and closer in a higher communion—and soon we will all dance together *Reigen*. All my love.   Isadora

Although she closed her letter on an optimistic note of dancing *Reigen* with them, she was desperately trying to continue her journey to Paris. She wrote for help to her friends in Paris, but received no answers—most probably, she excused them, because of the war. And she even cabled Paris Singer. He did not reply.

But "and this hour too shall pass." With the help of one of the members of the French Embassy, Isadora finally arrived in Paris and settled down in a room at the Hotel Palais d'Orsay, living on money she managed to obtain from mortgaging her house in Neuilly, and funds borrowed at exorbitant interest from money lenders.

In spite of her lecture to the girls, Isadora knew very little about Debussy's music. Perhaps she would have been less harsh in her criticism of it if she had known something about his masterpiece, *Le Martyre de Saint Sebastien*, had known about Gabriele d'Annunzio's collaborating on that composition, and that André Caplet, whose musical collaboration with her at the chateau in Devonshire had been so abruptly terminated by Paris Singer, was indeed the close collaborator of the composer, who entrusted him with the orchestration of some of his works, but also with conducting the first performance of *Le Martyre* at the Châtelet Theater in 1911. Isadora did not know that Debussy had died on March 25, 1918, about the time she finally arrived in Paris, for the Paris newspapers, curtailed because of the war, carried no obituary notice. Thus it was rather ironical that, when she was seeking consolation in music, the thirty-one-year-old pianist Walter Rummel was introduced to her, who, as if presenting his credentials as a musician, proudly declared that he was the foremost exponent of Debussy's music.

This, apparently, was less impressive than Isadora's thinking that "he was the picture of the youthful Liszt, come out of its frame—so tall, slight, with a burnished lock over the high forehead, and eyes like clear wells of shining light." Isadora was no exception to the universal effect of love: perfections of the loved one flowed liberally from her rich and generous imagination.

Isadora loved Wagner's song "The Angel," in which, she said, a spirit sits as she did herself in those dark days, in utter sadness and desolation, and to that spirit comes an angel of light. Such an angel had come to her, and so she dubbed Walter Rummel her "archangel."

Unlike her association with Harold Bauer, which had ended because of Mrs. Bauer's jealousy, in her relationship with Rummel there was no conceivable hurdle for them to overcome to reach a complete "harmony of souls," except for Debussy's music. But this was easily brushed aside by Rummel's adoption of Isadora's preference for Bach, Beethoven, and even the works of Liszt—in the case of the last composer, his nonsensual, more spiritual compositions such as "Thoughts of God in the Wilderness," and "St. Francis Preaching to the Birds."

At a time when Isadora was desolate, penniless, almost abandoned by her friends, who were naturally more concerned about their own world, which was crumbling because of the war, than about Isadora's dreams of her school and of the arts, anybody who could have helped her to find solace would have been welcomed by her. Rummel fitted that role perfectly.

"Each time a new love came to me, in the form of Demon or Angel or Simple Man, I believed that this was the only one for whom I had waited so long, that this love would be the final resurrection of my life."

So with all her passionately romantic nature, Isadora threw herself into the love affair.

However, this relationship was doomed to be on a higher plane than most of her previous "earthy" ones, as she called them. She had quite a problem in trying to be truthful when writing about it, for she was also constrained to be discreet since Rummel was alive at that time. She tried to explain the situation very delicately, but she succeeded only in mystifying her readers.

> He was all gentleness and sweetness, and yet passion burned him. He performed with unconsenting frenzy. His nerves consumed him, his soul rebelled. He did not give way to passion with the spontaneous ardor of youth, but, on the contrary, his loathing was evident as the irresistible feeling which possessed him. He was like a dancing saint on a brazier of live coals. To love such a man is as dangerous as difficult. Loathing of love can easily turn to hatred against the aggressor.

But speaking to me of this love episode in her life, Isadora told me that Rummel "preferred to make love to himself behind the closed doors of his room," rather than to her, lying frustrated in her bedroom.

She said "to love such a man is as dangerous as difficult," and yet in her wornout state and with her shattered nervous system, she apparently had adjusted herself to a relationship that was incomprehensible to her, and offensive to her as a woman.

She actually found happiness in this "most hallowed and ethereal love of her life," as she said, by keeping their relationship on the highest level—the inspiration and the solace she received from the music on which they worked together.

During the summer they went to the south of France, where, near the Port of St. Jean on Cap Ferrat, they turned the old garage of a deserted hotel into a studio and there prepared their programs for a tour of the provincial French towns, which Isadora had always planned. But after three performances on the road, the tour had to be canceled because of the severe epidemic of influenza which closed all the theaters. And then at last came Armistice Day on November 11, 1918. The war was over and Isadora and Rummel returned to Paris.

Chapter XXVII

Once the celebration of the Allied victory was over, like the rest of the world that turned to the old problems of civilian life, Isadora, with Rummel at her side as her consultant in practical matters, visited Bellevue, hoping to pick up her life there where she had left off when the war broke out in 1914. But during those four years Bellevue had been used first as a hospital and later as a school for soldiers, organized by the American army. These two occupations had brought the luxurious establishment created by Isadora and Paris Singer to such a state of dilapidation that the cost of restoring it was prohibitive.

Therefore, after one desperate but unsuccessful effort at raising money "For the Reconstruction of the Isadora Duncan School at Bellevue," as her joint performance with Rummel on July 24, 1919 was called, Isadora accepted the French Government's offer to buy Bellevue at a fraction of its value. She rented and later bought a little house in Passy, which, in addition to a few small rooms, had a large room, called Salle Beethoven, which Isadora turned into her studio. While continuing her "joint recitals"—as they were often called because of Rummel's reputation as a concert pianist—in Switzerland and England, Isadora was again planning to establish her school and have her six girls come to take part in her future performances.

Now, she wrote them, almost immediately after the peace treaty had been signed, they could come to France to be part of her plans if they wished. She promised to solve the problem of their passports —for although the war was over the French Government still refused entry to those who held German passports, and the girls were all German, except for Anna, who was Swiss.

Cécile Sorel, who was influential with members of the French Government, suggested that there was one speedy solution to the problem. That was for Isadora to adopt the girls so they could obtain United States citizenship. With Augustin working on this scheme in the United States, and Isadora doing her part in Paris, the adoption was finally confirmed by the New York State Supreme Court on June 23, 1920, and the girls were officially allowed to use the Duncan name, but only in their professional capacity. This was sufficient to enable them to receive a certificate from the State Department that allowed them to travel to Europe and return to the United States. However, these legal proceedings took time, and it was more than a year before they could join Isadora.

What Isadora seemed to have disregarded was that, ever since the girls had disobeyed her first order forbidding them to perform on their own as a group of Isadora Duncan Dancers, they had given many successful performances in New York, as well as on their transcontinental tours, which took them as far as California. Sol Hurok was their manager and had already booked them for the following season when Isadora's call to join her reached them. Although at first they were delighted at the prospect of being with Isadora again, they were not eager to lose the independence they had won with so much difficulty.

In her cable of April 10, Isadora said that she wanted the girls to come to France to work with her on a new program and take part in performances from June to October. But the girls, and especially Irma, were afraid that at the end of that period Isadora would not let them return to the United States to resume their own engagements. However, after making Isadora sign a contract to that effect, the girls finally sailed for France in the last week of June—minus Ericka, who had decided to give up her dancing career for painting.

Upon their arrival at Isadora's studio, they found her in an exceptionally happy frame of mind. Apparently, she had adjusted to her personal relationship with Rummel, and indeed in the future she was to recall this period in the most glowing terms: "There we spent holy hours, our united souls borne up by the mysterious force which possessed us. Often as I danced and he played, as I lifted my arm and my soul went up from my body in the long flight of the silver strain of the Grail, it seemed as if we had created a spiritual entity quite apart from ourselves, and, as sound and gesture flowed up to the Infinite, another answer echoed from above. I believe that from the psychic force of this musical moment, when our two spirits were so attuned in the holy energy of love, we were on the verge of another world. . . . If my Archangel and I had pursued these studies further, I have no doubt that we might have arrived at the spontaneous creation of movements of such spiritual force as to bring a new revelation to mankind."

There should be no doubt that Isadora was perfectly sincere in making these large claims, for such was the nature of her romanticism.

"Let us all go to Athens and look upon the Acropolis, for we may yet found a School in Greece," she announced to the girls. In less than a month's time they were on their way to Athens. Since Anna had to be operated on for appendicitis, Isadora and Rummel remained behind until Anna could make the journey, and the other four girls went on ahead. They were all reunited in Athens and the first thing Isadora wanted them all to see was Kopanos, the unfinished building where, in 1904, the Duncans had planned to build their temple of art. Although it still had only one room with a roof over it, no water, and traces were left of bivouacking shepherds, Isadora still believed it could be made into a studio. She found an architect who had doors and windows installed and a roof put over one high-ceilinged room. There the green dancing carpet was laid. A large grand piano was brought in, and every afternoon Rummel played to them "magnificent and inspiring music—Bach, Beethoven, Wagner, Liszt." Although the atmosphere in which they lived seemed ideal on the surface, Isadora was restless and showed signs of bad humor that indicated something seriously amiss.

When speaking later of this trip to Greece, Isadora blamed herself for everything that had happened, saying, "How pitiful that earthy passion should have put an end to this holy pursuit of highest beauty. For, just as, in the Legend, one is never content but opens the door for the bad fairy, who introduces all sorts of trouble, so

I, instead of being content to pursue the happiness I had found, felt returning the old will to remake the School, and, to this end, I cabled my pupils in America . . . Alas for me! My pupils arrived, young and pretty and successful. My Archangel looked upon them—and fell—fell to one." The twenty-five-year-old Anna was the "one."

At this point in her memoirs, Isadora runs ahead of the actual events, chronologically speaking, and devotes pages to describing her tormenting feelings of jealousy. Actually, so Anna told me recently, nothing happened in Greece between herself and Rummel to give Isadora cause for jealousy. Worrying over the girls' imminent departure for the United States, as stipulated in her contract with them, Isadora conceived a plan of her own. She had always guarded the girls from any association with men. Now she decided to encourage them in finding beaux, who she hoped would keep them from leaving for the United States.

To this end, she actually encouraged Rummel and Anna. However, though eventually it did develop into a love affair as serious as Isadora describes it, at the time they were in Greece it did not amount to anything more than an innocent flirtation.

August passed in relative peace because most of the time the girls were afflicted with minor physical troubles—fever caused by the heat, infections, and strep throats. But in September, two weeks before Isadora planned to begin work with them on a new program, she announced her refusal to let them return to the United States despite the cable from Hurok, who claimed that they were breaking their contract.

"I did not bring you up to teach you my art, only to have you exploited by theatrical managers!" In this fashion Isadora began her polemic with the girls. And they eventually agreed to remain with her, except for Irma, who took a firm stand against Isadora's curtailing her independence. During their excited argument, Isadora said that, since Irma had acquired "a cheap Broadway spirit," perhaps she had better return to America. Irma "rushed to the steamship office, still smarting from the verbal blows," as she describes the episode in her own autobiography. "Back at the Hotel d'Angleterre, where the girls lived, I sat down and tried to be calm. . . . My anger is soon spent; I seldom harbor grievances for long. I regretted the vehemence of my unguarded utterances. On calmer judgment, I sat down and wrote her a letter, trying to explain my motives and all the things one really can't explain, that remain the secrets of the human heart."

And in her book, Irma published the letter she wrote to Isadora.

Dear Isadora:

I inquired at the steamship office and there is a very good boat sailing for New York on the 10th of October. I think I had better book a passage on it—this will be the most convenient way to get rid of me. I quite understand that a "cheap Broadway spirit" has nothing to do with your art. Because, if that is all you see in me, I should certainly not remain another day with you.

Words are futile. I really cannot explain my true nature to you. It is, at times, even too complicated for me. Your art, which is the highest expression of all that is pure and divine in man, makes those who practice it—if they are pure at heart—purer. And if they are great—greater. But a spirit that is fundamentally not simple and naive cannot so easily be molded. I cannot change my inner self, nor can you.

One thing I am unable to comprehend: How is it that you, with your intelligence and intuition, have not been able correctly to judge my character before? I think it is rather too late now. What a waste and what a crime! For another person might have profited in my stead and been of real help to you. Someone to be proud of, and of real value to you, who could be a fine example to the hundreds who are going to follow.

I don't feel I can thank you for what you have done for me, since it has all been in vain. On the contrary, I would rather curse the day you took my hand and led me to your school. Your hand has always pointed upward. This made us sense there is something beyond—something more important than life. And willingly I wanted to be led. Now, you turn around with a frown on your face and point a finger of scorn at me and say that you see into my soul and what you see is . . . Isadora, do you really think you have the eyes of God?

Maybe only very earthly, petty things are obscuring your vision. Perhaps, if you had tried to peer into my soul with a little more understanding you would truly have been able to see. I am a queer girl, one must take me as I am. If you could have done so, who knows, I might have been of genuine service to you until my death. But I don't believe in sacrifice. You did not sacrifice your life either for the sake of your school. The idea of the school has always been your salvation. In your worst moments of anguish and misery, it has been your only joy and inspiration. *But it has not been everything in your life!* How then can you expect that I should devote mine entirely to the future of the school?

The reader should bear in mind when reading this letter that Isadora had given the best part of herself to her young charges— she poured out unstintingly her artistic insight and put the girls in possession of an artistic instrument that would be theirs to develop. For dancers, what they had experienced was absolutely unique and irreplaceable, intimate contact with a very great artist who was most generous in communicating the secrets of her art. With regard to more mundane matters, if Isadora had sometimes treated her girls in the irresponsible way in which she conducted much of her own life, there is no denying that her feeling for them was maternally loving and tender. But these were not the kind of considerations likely to occur to a young woman like Irma, who was anxious to assert her independence from Isadora's tutelage.

"Two days later I received a message delivered by hand," Irma continues.

Dearest Irma:

I have just received your letter. I can't answer it now but will tomorrow. I think there is a great deal of *misunderstanding*. At any rate, you must confess that the things you say some times would make a saint angry. Whatever you decide and whether you really want to go back to New York, or not, please don't doubt of my great love for you who are to me exactly like my own little girl. And if I become so *furious* it is only that I want your future to be splendid. I am probably stupid to take the small things you say in earnest.

I will answer your letter tomorrow. With a kiss and all my love—

Isadora

"I waited anxiously for her letter, glad that she held no rancor and much comforted by her nice note," Irma continues. "When the messenger appeared next day at my hotel, he handed me an envelope that contained not only her letter of explanation but also a picture. The picture was self-explanatory. It portrayed the Greek goddess Demeter, Mother Earth, handing on a torch to her young daughter Persephone, the new life, bringing light to the world."

Dear Irma:

I answer your letter. In the first place, do not believe the words which were wrung from me in anger by your exasperating attitude. Blot out the "Broadway" phrase, it has nothing to do with you or me. And, as for "getting rid of you," it is *because* you are so precious to me and to my art that I have made such an effort to tell you the *real* future of my work, which is not for *you* or *me* but for the *generations to come*.

As for *sacrifice*—take one example. When in December, 1914, Paris Singer said to me, "If you have the courage to start your school now, I will give you the house in Bellevue and 100,000 francs a year to do it with," I hesitated, for the idea of seeing *little children* at that time meant absolute torture to me. But I answered "yes," for I thought this opportunity might never come again and it would be a crime to deprive these children. No *one* will ever know what it cost me to teach those children at Bellevue. Often, in the midst of a lesson, I went upstairs and cried with agony, "No, I can't look at them!" But the next day I tried again.

I think in fact it was this fearful struggle that killed the little Baby [Isadora referred to her third child] that was my only hope. And you know since then I have not been able to look at a child without bursting into tears. And yet, I am willing to take them again and teach them. Is not that sacrifice?

And such a useless sacrifice, as all Bellevue is gone and the little children that were there have come to nothing.

I have only a few more years to do it. Won't you help me? Before I die, at least one hundred beings must *understand* the work and give it to others.

You irritated me the other day by the stupid things you said until I would have said *anything*. But my expression and tears often when you dance must have proved to you that I found it *beautiful*. I want it to be more so and glorious, especially the Beethoven.

I don't ask any of you to sacrifice all your life for the school. I only want you to give a part of each year to helping me. The rest of the year you may tour as you like. And above all, I want you to learn the Iphigenie, the Orphee, the Beethoven and all to a state of perfection, or as near as possible, before dancing it in a theatre.

Come this morning to work. Forgive anything I have said that wounded you—I did not mean it. You are for me always my little Irma whom I love most dearly. And I am for you—your *friend*

Isadora

Dear, dear Isadora: [Irma replied to Isadora's letter]

I have read your beautiful letter and I think if we don't speak to each other we understand each other better. I also want to ask you a hundred times pardon for everything I have said—it must all have been very insulting to you. For there is nothing in this world too beautiful that I could say or do to compensate you for all that you have given me spiritually and materially. I do want to aid you in *every way* possible so that your wonderful idea shall be realized. And on the day we actually see a hundred children dance, I too will shed tears of joy. You are right; we should all agree to work part of the time together as you suggest. I am willing to wait and not perform till we have perfected our work. We look up to you to guide us and let us know when the time has come.

I want you to know that I love you more than my own mother. I cannot show you my affection but it is all in my heart.

Love,
Irma

October 1, 1920

Dear Irma: [Isadora wrote her]
Your letter has made me *happy*. Now, hand in hand, we will go
forward and conquer the world in *harmony* and *love*.

Isadora

Promising the Greek Government to "create a thousand magnificent dancers" to dance at the Dionysian festivals in Athens in
such a splendid way that "the whole world will come to gaze upon
them with wonder and delight," Isadora gained some financial support and the permission to use a large hall in the Zappeion Museum
for preparing her program. There she taught the girls Beethoven's
Seventh Symphony and the scherzo from Tchaikovsky's Sixth
Symphony. She was about to teach them the Flower Maiden scene
from Wagner's *Parsifal* when news of the death of the young king
of Greece, caused by the bite of a pet monkey, put an end to the
government party that favored Isadora's project. By the same token,
it put an end to Isadora's stay in Athens.

Once again the Greek venture was a complete fiasco—the idea
of a school in Greece had to be abandoned, the scheduled performance in Athens canceled. As for losses, in addition to the money
spent on rebuilding Kopanos and making it into a working studio,
Isadora felt she was losing her archangel, her inspiring musician,
to Anna, her adopted daughter and pupil. So with Erica already
gone, the representatives of her school were reduced from six to
four.

Once they were back in Paris, the girls rented for themselves
a furnished flat that was not far from Isadora's home at 103 rue de la
Pompe in Passy.

"When at length I found myself alone in the house with its
Salle Beethoven all prepared for the music of my Archangel, then
my despair had no words. I could no longer bear the sight of this
house in which I had been so happy, indeed I had a longing to fly
from it and from the world, for, at the time, I believed that the
world and love were dead for me." So Isadora described later her
state of mind after her return to Paris. Since she could not escape
the knowledge of the growing love between her archangel and
Anna, which she now had to accept as a fact, and which afflicted
her with a jealousy more bitter than any she had yet experienced,

she turned in desperation to her art in an attempt to bring some equilibrium to her dangerously disturbed mental state.

She arranged several performances at the Trocadero, starting with an all-Wagner program on November 29, 1920, in which the four girls also took part. But, in her restless torment, Isadora was eager to arrange a tour for herself in the United States; when that project failed, she went to London. Left to themselves again, and with their savings from the United States performances dwindling rapidly, the girls tried to arrange on their own a tour through French provincial towns. However, while giving them her consent to their plan, Isadora cabled them from London the exact program they should perform; the girls' pride as independent artists was hurt and they abandoned the project. The breach in the relationship between Isadora and her girls, which was steadily growing, needed only one more stimulus to make it final. It came in a banal, commonplace form. Mary Desti played the major role in a campaign to influence Isadora's friends in believing that the girls were gossiping about her. Isadora wrote to the girls from London:

My dear children:
This is a message for all of you. Please reflect that all the things you say to my discredit reflect eventually on yourselves. And the people to whom you give your love and confidence have never done for you and will never do for you one percent of what I have done, and am still willing to do for you. But it is discouraging when I hear from all sides that in return you only try to break all my relations in Paris and cut all my friendships. I assure you that this can do you no good and my patience is almost at an end. If you could only learn a bit of discretion. Please work and live simply—read and study—and either be true to me or leave me on your own names and your own responsibility. Please write me. With love,

Isadora

Confronted with such a warning from Isadora, the girls held a council of war, that led to a further exchange of letters between Isadora and themselves. Finally, Isadora wrote that

talking of [her] in the way they were doing was causing [her] great harm and doing harm to themselves. . . . In the meantime

I beg of you to learn not to tell every little stupid idea in your head to strangers. If you wish your tickets to America, or elsewhere, Mr. Harle [Norman Harle, Isadora's secretary] will arrange them, as your present attitude toward me seems to make further relationship very difficult. I am, as Harle says, "fed up."

Isadora

And that was the end of Isadora's school. To be sure, upon her return to Paris in May 1921, she saw the girls and even invited them to join her in her latest project—to go to Soviet Russia to create a school there. Despite their strained relationship, the girls might have remained with Isadora, following her almost anywhere but Russia—a prospect that terrified them because of all they had heard about the Russian Revolution.

Therese decided to return to the United States, and with Lisa and Margot pursue her career as a dancer there. Irma, on the other hand, did not want to join the group and, as she had no other plans, the girl who had offered the most serious opposition to Isadora's wishes in the past, now vowed to go with her to Russia.

PART FIVE

Chapter XXVIII

"In the spring of the year 1921, I received the following telegram from the Soviet Government: 'The Russian Government alone can understand you. Come to us, we will make your School.'" Isadora wrote these words in the last pages of her memoirs. "From where did this message come? From Hell? No—but the nearest place to it. What stood for Hell in Europe—from the Soviet Government of Moscow. And looking round my empty house, void of my Archangel, of Hope and of Love, I answered: 'Yes, I will come to Russia, and I will teach your children, on one condition, that you give me a studio and the wherewithal to work.'

"The answer was 'yes,' so one day I found myself on a boat on the Thames, leaving for Reval, and eventually, Moscow."

Obviously no such actual exchange of "diplomatic notes" between "the Soviet Government of Moscow" (sic) and Isadora ever took place. There can be no doubt that Isadora's dramatic announcement of her intention to go to Russia caused a sensation. But the emphasis was not placed on the fact that for years Isadora had constantly tried and constantly failed to gain support for creating her school in Germany, France, England, Greece, and the United States. What struck people instead was her apparent willingness to risk her life in a country known to be undergoing revolutionary upheaval and widely asumed to have reached a state of cannibalism.

Almost immediately upon Isadora's death in September 1927,

Irma was joined in Moscow by Allan Ross Macdougall, and the two began writing *Isadora Duncan's Russian Days* (published two years later). Mary Desti, who also burst forth as a biographer, made a short visit to Moscow in 1927 to complete Isadora's memoirs and write about Isadora's life in Russia—all of which became a part of her *The Untold Story, The Life of Isadora Duncan, 1921–1927,* which was also published in 1929.

Both Irma and Macdougall subsequently used their material on Isadora's Russian days in their separate books: *Isadora, A Revolutionary in Art and Love,* by Macdougall, published in 1960, after his death, and *Duncan Dancer,* an autobiography by Irma Duncan published in 1966. The information given by these authors suffers from a supercilious and superficial attitude toward conditions in Russia at that time, betraying the natural ignorance of foreign sojourners, handicapped by lack of knowledge of the country, its people, and even its language. Nevertheless, their accounts are more acceptable than the hodgepodge written by Mary Desti. Thus until Ilya Shneider, the Russian who was the director of Isadora's school in Moscow, published *Isadora Duncan: The Russian Years* in 1968, based on his previously published, *Moi Vstretchi s Esseninim* (My Meetings with Essenin), there was no reliable account of Isadora's life in Soviet Russia available.

Mary Desti, who claimed to have played a major role in Isadora's writing of her memoirs, justified her latest contribution as a memorial to Isadora by saying in the introduction of her *Untold Story*: "After Isadora Duncan had finished the story of her life ending in 1921, I begged her to begin at once on her Russian and other experiences from 1921 on. This she put off doing from day to day, in spite of all my entreaties. However, two days before her death, being in a thoughtful mood, she began, declaring all the time she could never write another page. After great effort, she came to me where I was reading and threw into my lap three pages she had started, saying, 'Here, you know the rest of my life as well as I do. Write it yourself. I will not do another line.' And she never did."

I know that only the last sentence in this tale is true.

One more quotation from Mary Desti's introduction should dispose once and for all of her account of Isadora's life, including the purely fictional anecdotes and quotations. Speaking of her own arrival in Moscow to do research for her book, she writes:

When we arrived at the palace now used as Isadora's school, the great doors were thrown wide and pouring down the broad marble staircase came a hundred of Isadora's children, all attractively dressed in red velvet tunics with narrow red velvet bands about their hair. They looked like angels, and the agony that took possession of me, that I and not Isadora had come to them, was beyond endurance. Limp and helpless I leaned against the balustrade as the children gathered about me, almost carrying me up the stairs, making a speech that they had prepared before our arrival. Then they cried, "But, Mary, you look out of your eyes like Isadora. You are like our Isadora."

Only a woman of Mary Desti's near-demented personality, who always imagined herself to be Isadora, could have invented and written such a tale.

"If Isadora could have read what Desti had written in her book, she would have been utterly disgusted," Ilya Schneider says in the introduction to his own memoir. "A novel, serialized by the Yugoslav paper *Borba* in 1958 under the title of *Duncan and Essenin,* is quite obviously based on 'facts' in Desti's book, and in the same year the scenario of an Italian film called *Isadora Duncan* clearly drew on material from Desti's book."

Actually Isadora's decision to go to Russia was not motivated by any such glamorous reason as the creation of a "New World" by the Russian Revolution, but by the timely opportunity for another escape from an intolerable personal situation created by her latest love episode, and by an obvious loss of control over her pupils—her school.

However, once her intention of going to Russia had been publicly announced, the reaction in the press, as well as gossip in both London and Paris by those most concerned about her, provided Isadora with an excellent opportunity to issue a further challenge in the context of the general development of world politics. In the speeches delivered after her performances, Isadora had always blamed the "rich" for their lack of understanding of her art and her aims; now she hailed the Russian Revolution as creating "a New and Beautiful World."

Isadora's desire to go to Soviet Russia was nothing new. She had talked of it to her friends ever since the Revolution. In the United States, when she was discouraged about getting any response to her pleas to establish a school there, she had made a statement that was later reported in the French newspapers: "The school must have a government guarantee. There must be some protection against the pupils of the school leaving and commercializing their knowledge before it has reached the stage of perfection. And this can only be done through the cooperation of a government. You may recall how under the Czar's regime that very thing was accomplished for the Imperial Russian Ballet. It is the only assurance of success. . . ."

When she was asked about the story of her going to Russia to receive help from the "Bolsheviki," although at that time there was no foundation to this, Isadora said: "I did say that it didn't matter to me what the government was and that if Russia offered me a school I would go there and accept it. But of the Bolsheviks and their politics I know nothing. So contradictory are the stories concerning the Bolshevist attitude toward art, that one doesn't have any conception what it really is. I most certainly wouldn't hesitate to accept an offer from Russia. . . ."

During the summer of 1920, at one of her performances at the Champs Elysées Theater, after closing her all-Chopin program with her *Marseillaise*, Isadora said, in her speech which by then had been accepted by her audiences as almost a part of her performances: "France is the only country that understands Liberty, Life, Art and Beauty. . . . But I have great hopes for Russia. At this moment she is passing through the pains of childbirth, but I believe that she is the future for Artists and the life of the spirit."

And once more she appealed to her French audience, "Ask your President to give me one hundred war orphans and in five years I will return to you—this I promise—beauty and riches beyond imagining. . . ." And then she reviewed for her audience all her endeavors to establish a school.

When I was twenty, I loved the German philosophers. I read Kant, Schopenhauer, Haeckel and others. I was an intellectual. When I was twenty-one, I offered my school to Germany. The Kaiserin replied that it was immoral! The Kaiser said it was revolutionary! Then I proposed my school to America, but they said there it stood for the vine . . . and for Dionysus. I then proposed my school to Greece, but the Greeks were too busy fighting the Turks. Today I propose my school to France, but France, in the person of the amiable Minister of Fine Arts, gives me a smile. I cannot nourish the children in

my school on a smile. They must live on fruits and milk and the honey
of Hymettus. . . .

Help me to get my school. If not, I will go to Russia with the
Bolsheviks. I know nothing about their politics. I am not a politician.
But I will say to the leaders: "Give me your children, and I will
teach them to dance like gods, or . . . assassinate me." They will
give me my school or they will assassinate me. For, if I do not have
my school, I would rather be killed. It would be much better . . . .

Actually Isadora's invitation to come to Soviet Russia was far
less dramatic. Certainly no such drastic conditions were attached
to the success or failure of her proposed school.

Leonid Krasin, a music and art lover, who at that time headed
the Soviet Government's Trade Commission in London, attended
one of Isadora's performances at the Prince of Wales Theater. Her
program that evening included her interpretation of Tchaikovsky's
"Marche Slav," an interpretation about which Ellen Terry, who
saw it a month later (June 25, 1921), said that that amazing "Revolutionary" dance was the most magnificent conception of Isadora's
later years, perhaps of her whole life. "I never saw *true* tragedy
before," Ellen Terry commented.

By picturing the "downtrodden serf under the lash of a whip,"
Isadora turned Tchaikovsky's patriotic and obviously monarchistic
hymn into a revolutionary one, which no doubt moved Krasin, a
Russian, even more than it did Ellen Terry. Although he did not
know Isadora personally, Krasin went backstage to congratulate
her and convey his admiration for her art. During their short conversation, Isadora did not fail to mention her desire to establish a
school. To her surprise, the idea caught his interest. And, indeed,
Krasin's enthusiasm was so genuine that he immediately got in touch
with officials in Moscow, and soon afterward called on Isadora
offering her a contract.

"A contract between comrades, what an utterly preposterous
idea!" Isadora was reported to have said to Krasin. But she agreed to
supply an outline of what she proposed to do in Russia, if given the
opportunity, to Anatoly Lunacharsky, the Commissar of Education.

I shall never hear of money in exchange for my work. I want
a studio-workshop, a house for myself and pupils, simple food,

simple tunics, and the opportunity to give our best work. I am sick of bourgeois commercial art. It is sad that I have never been able to give my work to the people for whom it was created. Instead, I have been forced to sell my art for five dollars a seat. I am sick of the modern theatre, which resembles a house of prostitution more than a temple of art, where artists who should occupy the place of high-priests are reduced to the manoeuvres of shopkeepers selling their tears and their very souls for so much a night. I want to dance for the masses, for the working people who need my art and have never had the money to come to see me. And I want to dance for them for nothing, knowing that they have not been brought to me by clever publicity, but because they really want to have what I can give them. If you accept me on these terms, I will come and work for the future of the Russian Republic and its children.

Isadora Duncan

To reassure Isadora further about his government's intentions to provide her with facilities for her work, Krasin told her at the farewell party given in her honor at the Soviet Embassy in London that she would have one thousand children at her disposal, and during the summer months, the use of the former imperial palace in Livadia in the Crimea. And when Isadora returned to Paris, she received a telegram from Lunacharsky: "Come to Moscow. We will give you school and thousand children. You may carry on your idea on a big scale."—"Accept your invitation," Isadora wired to Lunacharsky, "Will be ready to sail from London July first."

The formal negotiations thus completed, Isadora began to prepare for her voyage into the unknown by giving a series of farewell parties—only to discover that her well-wishing friends tried to do their best to discourage her from taking what they represented as a fatal step. One of the most colorful endeavors in this respect was supposed to have been that of Mlle. Tchaikovsky, the daughter of the former Minister of Agriculture under the Czarist regime. According to the story that made the rounds in Paris and London, Mlle. Tchaikovsky, waving a letter from her father, which had been smuggled from Soviet Russia, knelt down before Isadora, imploring her to renounce her decision. "Look what they are doing"—she was quoting from the letter—"food is so scarce that the Bolsheviks are slaughtering four-year-old children and hanging them up by their limbs in butcher shops."

Although it was certainly unintentional on Mlle. Tchaikovsky's part, this insensitive remark about the children naturally touched Isadora's most vulnerable spot. At any other time, it would have made her burst into tears, but it now produced a reaction that was quite unexpected. According to Irma, who was present at this scene, Isadora, looking pale and grim, said, "Well, if that is true, then I *must* go."

And, later, after the guests had departed, leaving Isadora and Irma limp from their gory tales, Isadora, regaining her sense of humor, said, "Don't worry, Irma, they'll eat me first anyway. There is a whole lot more of me than you."

Chapter XXIX

Keyed up with excitement over her imminent departure, Isadora, while making final arrangements for the care of her possessions in Paris during the unpredictable duration of her absence, including the renting of her home in the rue de la Pompe, nevertheless continued to give farewell parties and to attend those given in her honor. At last, however, accompanied by Irma, Therese, and Lisa, she went to Brussels to fulfill a few scheduled performances and then on to London. The word that "Isadora Duncan had sold herself to the Bolsheviks" was quickly spread, and the newspapers had already begun to stir up enmity toward her on account of her "Bolshevism"—thus affecting attendance at some of her appearances. Reviewing her "Grand Festival of Music and Dance," at Queen's Hall, the London *Observer* noted: ". . . It was really in every way a great evening and one is amazed that the hall should be half empty. Will it be full next Sunday, June 25, 1921? This would be the last opportunity of seeing Isadora Duncan before she goes to her work in Russia—to return when?"

And indeed to this, her very last farewell performance, Isadora added an extra personal touch, of which Ellen Terry spoke in her memoirs.

"Isadora made her characteristic speech at the end of the performance—it came naturally to her to wear her heart upon her sleeve—saying that there was one in the audience far greater than she. 'Let us applaud her, let us rejoice in Ellen Terry,' she cried, holding out her arms with one of those primal gestures which seemed to some almost indecent." And Isadora's audience and the orchestra, too, responded, and cheered Ellen Terry for several minutes.

Isadora tried to delay her departure until her mother's arrival from the United States so that she might say good-bye to her. However, Mrs. Duncan's ship was so far behind its schedule that Isadora had to leave before it arrived—she was never to see her mother again. One more farewell parting was to take place in London—this time with Lisa and Therese, who had refused to go to Russia. Her calling them "ingrates" was submerged in their tears and final embraces and kisses, and on the morning of July 13, 1921, Isadora and Irma sailed aboard the *S.S. Baltanic* to Reval in perfect weather, even if the sea was "a bit rough."

Two friends were busy with the last-minute preparations for Isadora's voyage into the unknown. Mary Desti managed to have her friend Gordon Selfridge supply Isadora, Irma, and Jeanne, Isadora's French maid, who always accompanied her, with warm clothing, bedding, and all kinds of canned foods from Selfridge's in London. Ruth Mitchell, who had come from the United States to see Isadora off, attended to such things as passports, tickets, and luggage receipts. However, Mary Desti stayed on the pier, waving bon voyage, while Ruth Mitchell traveled with Isadora as far as Reval.

Six days later, after a short stop in Danzig, the *Baltanic* docked in Reval, where Isadora's party was officially greeted by Ivy Low Litvinov, the English wife of Maxim Litvinov, then assistant secretary for foreign affairs of the Russian government. Maxim Litvinov was to become well known to the American public during World War II, when he served in Washington as the Russian ambassador. Apparently delegated by her husband, Madame Litvinov tried to be as helpful as she could in seeing that Isadora's luggage was sealed for shipment to Moscow, and to make their one-day stay before boarding the train to Russia as pleasant as she could. But Isadora was disappointed—she had expected to be met, not by an Englishwoman, whose manners betrayed her origins in the wealthy class of English society, but, as Irma noted in her diary, by a "red automobile full of black-haired and black-eyed Bolshies." At the time, Isadora could not know how soon and how much she was going to miss Madame Litvinov's courtesy and "European thoughtfulness."

After bidding good-bye to Ruth Mitchell, who sailed back to

England on the *Baltanic*, Isadora's party was finally settled in the second-class compartment of a Russian train that was to take them first to Narva, a small town at the Russian border, and then on to Petrograd. They were to share their accommodations with a young man who was supposed to be a diplomatic courier. It is not clear whether the courier was the young man she later described in the few pages she wrote when she recounted her experiences in Russia.

> We had been told such terrible things that, as the train passed the red flag at the frontier, we would not have been surprised if the pictured Bolshevik with a red flannel shirt, black beard, and a knife between his teeth—*L'homme au couteau entre les dents*—had appeared to violate us all three, and then cut our throats as an evening's amusement. We all confessed to some shiver of excitement and we were perhaps a bit disappointed when there appeared only a very timid young man with gray eyes and spectacles, who said that he was a communist student and spoke six languages and asked if he might help us. He was very shy and not at all our preconceived ideas of a Bolshevik. Only I noticed that when he spoke of Lenin, his gray eyes blazed behind his glasses and his whole slight figure trembled with enthusiastic devotion. He told in shivers of the fantastic sacrifices of the communists and the repulses of the White Armies, which savored of a miracle and holy war.

In my opinion, in Isadora's description of her first day in Narva, on Russian soil, she gave not merely a picture of a pastoral day spent in that "barbarous" country but provided a key to the question of the success and failure of her project in Soviet Russia, and I am willing to accept the accusation of giving a romantic interpretation of it.

Highly excited, Isadora was too restless to remain asleep, and practically at dawn, while her companions were still asleep, she went out to explore the village, where, after finding a market, she managed to get some flowers and raspberries, which she brought back to the train for her party's breakfast.

> Later she again went for a walk in the village with Irma and they paid a visit to the school. On the way back to the station, they were followed, like two Pied Pipers, by a motley juvenile throng. When they arrived at the train, Isadora had Jeanne bring out the portable gramophone and some records. And there on the platform she gave

the astonished and wide-eyed children a concert and a dancing lesson. Then she improvised a little dance for them and ended the party by giving them all the white bread and cake from the lunch basket, which General H—— [sic] had presented to them in Reval. All the candy and sweetstuffs that she could find in her baggage she also gave them, with no thought of the lean days to come.*

I see this devasted village of Narva as the symbol of Soviet Russia, which had arisen after World War I, revolution, civil war, foreign armed interventions, famine, persecutions, and premature death. I see Isadora's visit at dawn in this village as a physical illustration of what she said: "On the way to Russia, I had the detached feeling of a soul after death making its way to another sphere. I thought I had left all forms of European life behind me forever. I actually believed that the ideal State, such as Plato, Karl Marx, and Lenin had dreamed it, had now by some miracle been created on earth. With all the energy of my being, disappointed in the attempts to realize any of my art visions in Europe, I was ready to enter the ideal domain of Communism."

I see Isadora, the apostle of beauty, eager for flowers and raspberries to adorn her breakfast table, and her desire to embody in a school the symbol of progress for millions who had heretofore been illiterate. But I also see those children, that "motley juvenile throng," who had never before encountered such a vision as Isadora, as the first young generation after the revolution, who knew nothing except the problem of survival—and who were not merely surprised by the gramophone and records, but "astonished and wide-eyed" at Isadora's performance and dancing lesson. Actually, I see all Russians, old and young, perplexed by Isadora preaching beauty and dancing to those who were hungry and in rags. And finally her generous gesture of giving the children white bread and sweets, the taste of which they most probably had forgotten since the beginning of the world war, is also not without its sad ironies.

After a day's stay in Narva, the train finally brought its passengers to Petrograd, where they had another free day before they were to proceed to Moscow, their destination. The sight of Petrograd, the capital Isadora knew from her previous visits, with the palaces and buildings scarred by the civil war, with its empty

* *Isadora Duncan's Russian Days*, by Irma Duncan and Allan Ross Macdougall.

shops and people dressed in rags, depressed Isadora and her companions. Hoping to find Moscow, the new capital, in better condition, and at any rate to end what had begun to seem like an endless journey, they boarded the train once more. Instead of fourteen hours, which used to be the time required for the run between the two cities, it took twenty-four. This was due to the frequent stops at stations where passengers from all levels of Russian society, from peasants to high government officials, had been waiting for days for an opportunity to get on board the overcrowded trains. In this way, the trip from London to Moscow took eleven days before it was completed at four in the morning at the Nikolaevskaya station on July 24th.

There was no official reception committee or government representative at the station to welcome Isadora. In fact there was nobody at all to greet her and take her and her party to a place where they could rest after their long journey. Not only was Isadora indignant at such treatment but all three authors who recorded Isadora's arrival in Moscow in minute detail have voiced their wrath at the lack of that common courtesy that should have been extended to her by the Soviet government.

"After all, she *had* come to Russia as the *guest* of the Soviet Government. Her comings and goings, even in the most obscure places in Europe and America, always caused a stir among the population and now here she was, the world-famous invited guest of a great government, and they had not even sent a porter to meet her, or tell her where to go!"*

One has to forgive these non-Russians and ascribe their indignant remarks to ignorance. It is clear that their appreciation of the general situation in Soviet Russia was still obscured by their own glamorous and idealistic project, which in Isadora's mind had more or less attained the proportions of a divine mission. On the following day they learned what happened and why they were not met with the fanfare they considered due them. But as they stepped down from the train at four o'clock in the morning, to all who noticed them they were merely three females, obviously foreigners, who could not speak the language. In Russia foreigners were always looked upon with a slight suspicion, and therefore it was extremely lucky for Isadora and her friends that their train

* Duncan and Macdougall, *Isadora Duncan's Russian Days*.

companion, the diplomatic courier, helped them in their first attempts to find a hotel.

They were also lucky in that, while the three were sitting in an open car waiting for the courier's inquiries at the hotel, Isadora was recognized by Florinsky, who was a frequent visitor at Isadora's cottage in Long Beach. Florinsky, who posed as being one of those few aristocrats who had somehow escaped the "revolutionary cleansing out of the parasites of society," was feeling rather chipper. At this early morning hour, still dressed in his evening clothes, he had just returned from a dinner party at the Turkish Embassy—and he was still smacking his lips over the chicken broth, fried chicken, white bread and butter, wines, and excellent Turkish coffee. He invited Isadora's party to his room where he served them breakfast. Later he succeeded in getting them a room at a nearby hotel.

Since it was Sunday and all the government offices were closed, Isadora could only reach Lunacharsky on the following day. The forty-six-year-old Anatoly Lunacharsky belonged to the intellectuals of the ruling hierarchy. A Social Democrat in his youth, at the age of thirty he had joined Lenin in Switzerland and, under his supervision, worked as a journalist for several communist newspapers. After the end of World War I, he returned to Russia and was appointed Commissar of Education. He was a man of wide education, an exceptional orator, an expert in the arts and in Russian history, as well as in Western European literature. But as a literary critic, he periodically committed "mistakes," which he was able to correct with the "comradely help" of other members of the Communist party, and so was allowed to retain his post as Commissar.

Although Isadora had not met Lunacharsky personally, she was no stranger to him. He had seen her dance in Paris in 1913 and had reported his admiration for her art in his article in the monthly magazine *Theatre and Art,* which was later included in his collected writings, published in 1924. But being well acquainted with Isadora's temperamental behavior, he had not expected her to persist in her decision to come to Russia, and certainly never imagined that if she did come she would arrive on schedule. Thus he was surprised to hear that she was already in Moscow, and he telephoned Ilya Schneider. Since the revolution, Schneider had been connected with the press department of the People's Commissariat for Foreign Affairs. Later he became a journalist and critic, wrote librettos for ballets—a field of particular interest to him—and, at the time of Isadora's arrival, he was a close friend of Ekaterina Geltzer, of the Moscow Opera, *the* chief ballerina in Soviet Russia.

"We expected Isadora Duncan to arrive in three day's time," Lunacharsky telephoned Schneider. "But she arrived unexpectedly yesterday and a room was found for her at the Savoy Hotel, which is far from comfortable and partly in ruins. Besides, it seems to be infested with rats and bedbugs. Isadora Duncan and her companions went out during the night and walked about the streets sight-seeing until morning. While we are looking for other quarters for her, do you think it would be possible to install her temporarily in the apartment of Yekaterina Vasilievna Geltser, who is touring the provinces and who, I understand, has asked you to keep an eye on her apartment? I have already sent Flaxerman to the railway station, where Isadora Duncan, her pupil Irma, and her maid are getting out her luggage. I would like you to go to Geltser's apartment, arrange everything for her there, and look after her for the time being."

If Irma and Jeanne were still indignant at the government's failure to provide Isadora with a distinguished reception, they must soon have been at least partly appeased, for before the day was over Isadora had managed to stir up some of the Moscow population. After exhausting themselves by walking around the Kremlin walls and along the boulevards, they returned to their hotel, hoping to lunch there. In the dining room, at a long round table, they joined a group of a "dozen or so grimy, unshaven men. They wore their hats and coats and audibly supped out of tin bowls a dark, greasy-looking soup, eating the while great hunks of black bread. They were Comrades!" Thus Irma and Macdougall sarcastically describe Isadora's first meeting with the Russians.

"She greeted them cheerfully, 'How do you do, *Tovarishti*,' giving them her most sweet and ingenuous smile. But the *tovarishti* went on eating, after having glanced up sidewise for a moment—the time to take in this 'comrade' in a 'Callot Soeurs' creation—and then went back to the serious business of lapping up the soup."

Did Isadora and her companions actually expect these men to go into conference with them about the meaning of the revolution, or act as if they were all at Fouquet's on the Champs Elysées, gossiping of the latest scandal in Paris society?

And Isadora must have inspired some curiosity among the

Moscovites when a six-foot-high pile of trunks, hampers, hatboxes, and suitcases was brought to Geltser's apartment. The fact that her luggage was available once more gave Isadora an opportunity to change from her traveling clothes and go for a walk again, "to see and be seen." This time she was dressed in a black satin jacket, which shone like leather, and a white satin waistcoat with a red border, which she had had made by Paul Poiret especially for her journey to Russia, later sold under the name Poiret *à la Bolchevique*.

And upon her return to her new domicile, after having been refreshed by several cups of hot tea and an omelet—the latter at that time a luxury item in Russia—she was ready to meet Schneider, her first communist benefactor. Following Lunacharsky's orders, he managed the feat of catching up with Isadora's luggage somewhere between the railway station and Geltser's apartment.

Schneider remembered Isadora from the time when, as a boy in his teens, he had seen her on the stage as a slim figure in a light tunic—and once offstage, when she arrived with Stanislavsky in a sleigh in the court of the Moscow Art Theater. "To me Isadora Duncan was the personification of extraordinary femininity, grace, poetry, the counterpart of which I never expected to see again," Schneider wrote in his book. "Now I had an unexpected impression: she looked monumental; her head covered with the reddish copper of smooth, thick, short hair sat proudly on a regal neck. Before me sat a great artist, the reformer of the art of the dance, the 'queen of gesture,' as she was called, of whom Auguste Rodin had said 'she took that force from nature which does not go under the name of talent, but of genius.' "

After showing her her new domicile, Schneider left Isadora with her first visitor—Konstantin Stanislavsky, the old friend whom she had not seen since his last visit in Paris, when he had lunched with her and Paris Singer. A lifetime ago, Isadora thought, so much had happened since. Stanislavsky had aged; like others, he had suffered privations during the war and the revolution. He complained of the constant difficulties he had with his new projects, but which he hoped to show in Germany and perhaps even in the United States. "My dear, great artist," Isadora was supposed to have said to him, "you are faced with this dilemma; either you must consider your career at an end and commit suicide, or you begin a new life by becoming a communist!"

Isadora had never said a truer word than when, on announcing her decision to go to Russia, she had stated emphatically that she was neither a politician, nor a Bolshevik. Indeed, she never understood a thing about communism; as for the difference between *Bolshevism* and *Menshevism*, or any other "isms—these were mere words to her. But she loved the word *tovarish*, comrade, which in its exotic sound symbolized to her "*Liberté, Egalité, Fraternité,*" and she insisted on being called *tovarish* Duncan instead of Miss or Mlle. Duncan. In fact, Isadora was told in Paris that, since the monetary system had been abolished in Soviet Russia, the word *tovarish* had a magical power and that any driver of vehicles still functioning would oblige her with his services and take her free of charge to her destination. Not having brought any money with her, Isadora paid for this naïve notion by being forced to walk through the streets of Moscow.

She did not approve of Stanislavsky's latest experiment of staging Tchaikovsky's opera *Eugene Onegin*. Isadora was always against opera. "A music drama is impossible," she maintained, "because it requires a combination of speech, song, and dance, an impossible mixture." "You must do bigger things than that," she is supposed to have said to Stanislavsky. "The *Bacchae* of Euripides, for instance. I have always dreamed of you directing this tragedy with Eleonora Duse playing the role of Agave, while I, with my pupils, danced the chorus."

Isadora was speaking with an enthusiasm which belonged to 1908, not to 1921. For the new state she so ardently admired, and which was indeed creating a new life, and a new attitude toward art, was not at all neoclassical in its orientation. But it was not long before she had her first real encounter with the communists, the leaders of the party, at a reception to which she was invited.

Delighted with such an opportunity, she dressed herself to suit the occasion in her red tunic, draped with her scarlet cashmere shawl in which she usually danced the *Marseillaise*, and over her hair, turban-like, she wound a red tulle scarf. Florinsky escorted her to the mansion that had formerly belonged to Kharitonenko, a wealthy sugar merchant, where the supposedly "small and rather intimate official reception" was held. As Isadora entered and saw the gilt furniture, Gobelin tapestries, painted ceilings, shepherdesses and marquises, and heard a young woman accompanying herself on the piano sing a French *bergerette*:

Jeune fillette
Profitez du temps,
Les violettes
Se cueille en printemps;
La, la, la, la, la. . . .

she was so shocked that she could not move. But the applause, the cries of "Bravo," and men greeting her in excellent French, woke her up to the stark reality of the scene. There, at a table laden with food and wines, the likes of which she had not seen since she had come to Russia, men and women attired in evening clothes sat at supper. Far from being dressed like Tolstoy and Gorki in Russian blouses and high boots, as she had imagined, indifferent to heat, cold, or hunger, or any material sufferings, and living like early Christians entirely in the realm of the spirit, they represented instead the familiar bourgeois ideal in their dress and in their manners. It was a sight that she could not pass over without comment.

"Comrades," she is supposed to have addressed the assembly, "you have made a Revolution. You are building a new, beautiful world, which means that you are breaking up all that is old, unwanted, and decayed. The break-up must be in everything—in education, in art, in morals, in everything in life, in dress. You have succeeded in throwing the sugar kings out of their palaces. Why do you preserve the bad taste of their buildings? Throw out of the window the fat-bellied, thin-legged armchairs and these fragile golden chairs. On all your ceilings and in all your pictures are Watteau shepherds and shepherdesses. That girl sang very charmingly, but during the French Revolution she would have had her head cut off. She's singing a song of Louis XVI! I had hoped to see something new here, but it seems all you want are frock coats and top hats to be indistinguishable from other diplomats."

And she stalked out of the house. The account of this speech, although it cannot be taken verbatim—for in some versions Isadora called her listeners "bourgeoisie in disguise, the usurpers"—seems worthy of acceptance because it was later much discussed in communist circles.

Although there is no record explaining in what language Isadora delivered her address, since she knew no Russian, one has to assume it was in a mixture of English, French, and German; her audience, nevertheless, seems to have understood the message, for Lunacharsky later wrote a long article in which he did not fail to refer to the incident.

> . . . What aim did she [Isadora] have in coming to Russia? The main aim was an emotional one. She came to Russia . . . to organize in this country a big school of a new type . . . Duncan believed with all her heart that, in spite of the famine and the lack of necessities; in spite of the backwardness of the masses; in spite of the terrible seriousness of the moment and the consequent preoccupation of the government officials with other vital questions, a beginning could be made with her ideas . . . . Her vision reaches far. She is thinking of a large government school with a thousand children. She is willing for the moment to begin with a smaller number. . . .
>
> At present, Duncan is going through a phase of rather militant communism that sometimes, involuntarily, makes us smile. [Here Lunacharsky tells of Isadora's remark to Stanislavsky.] In another instance Duncan was asked by some of our communist comrades to a small, one might say, a family fête. She found it possible to call their attention to their bad communist taste, because of their bourgeois surroundings, and their behavior, which was far from the flaming ideal she had painted in her imagination. It would have developed into a small scandal, if our comrades had not understood how much originality and charm were contained in the naive criticism which was in substance true.
>
> The People's Commissariat of Education greets Russia's guest and believes that, on the occasion of her first public appearance, the proletariat will confirm the greeting. Duncan has been called the *Queen of Movement*, but of all her movements, this last one—her coming to Red Russia in spite of being scared off—is the most beautiful and calls for the greatest applause.

Such was the beginning of Isadora Duncan's Russian sojourn. Her decision to go there had aroused much animosity toward her when it was first announced. Later it excited much curiosity, and finally it caused her to be branded as "Red" and "Communist," especially in the United States. Indeed, all the subsequent misfortunes in her life were often blamed on this adventure.

Chapter XXX

One glance at Isadora's new lodgings would have been sufficient to convince the least sensitive observer that Geltser's apartment was perhaps the last in the whole of Moscow that should house Isadora even temporarily. Isadora herself thought that it was the height of irony—though quite unintentional—that she should be installed in the home of one she might well have regarded as the most brilliant among her adversaries, in that world of the ballet and ballerinas that she had fervently hoped the revolution would have done away with, along with all that remained of the Tzarist regime.

Geltser's apartment was a veritable showplace, a museum, filled with mementos of a brilliant and highly successful career that had spanned almost fifty years. Her collection of exquisite and delicate Dresden china pieces and bibelots, which for years had adorned every available space in rooms filled with antique furniture, was all useless bric-a-brac in Isadora's opinion. The dainty figurines of shepherds and shepherdesses dancing minuets, or blowing kisses to each other, irritated Isadora beyond measure. Afraid of breaking the precious objets d'art, Isadora did not dare move freely in the apartment. And one day she did accidentally sweep one of the crystal lamps from the table with her shawl—a veritable drama, making her further stay in the apartment impossible, at least as far as her nerves were concerned.

Instead of three days, however, Isadora's sojourn in these surroundings had already lasted more than two weeks. Fortunately, it was summer and, while the commissariat was trying to find a place large enough to serve as Isadora's home, as well as her future school, Isadora, Irma, and Jeanne were moved to a peasant's hut inhabitated by a solitary old woman on Vorobyovy Gory—the Sparrow Hills, well known in history. From there Napoleon had seen Moscow for the first time, the key to his final glory, so he believed, but which brought him disaster instead.

No less impressed than the French emperor by the magnificent panorama, Isadora had dreams of the usefulness of the beautiful countryside that were different from those of Napoleon. "It is here," Isadora told Schneider, "amid this greenery, that a great popular theatre without walls and without a roof ought to be built. There is the *stage* of the ancient Greek theatre, on which the performances would take place. And there," she pointed at the green slope, "is a natural amphitheatre—seating thousands of spectators."

Not all of Isadora's grandiose visions were fated to be discarded as products of an extravagant dreamer; in that very place, some ten years later, the open-air theater of the Gorky Central Park of Culture and Rest was built, with seats for an audience of twenty thousand.

"And there," Isadora finally said, pointing toward the stone building at the top of the slope, "is a good house for my school."

While enjoying her walks with Schneider in those hills, she met Nikolay Podvoysky, Lenin's close friend, and during the October Revolution the chairman of the Military Revolutionary Committee in Petrograd.

Podvoysky was the second man from the communist hierarchy whom Isadora met face to face and she did not waste a minute in explaining her ideas to him and telling him how impatient she was to start the work for which she had come to Russia. Podvoysky knew no language but Russian, and Isadora knew only a few words of that tongue. Accordingly, their long conversation, with questions, answers, interruptions, and explanations, had to be carried on through Schneider's translation of Isadora's German, usually mixed with some French and English words. Schneider has recorded the gist of Isadora's long speech to Podvoysky:

"During the last few years," Isadora said, "my thoughts were with Russia and my soul was here. Having arrived here, I feel that

I am on the path which leads to a kingdom of universal love, harmony, comradeship, brotherhood. . . . I despise riches, hypocrisy, and those stupid rules and conventions in which I had been forced to live. I want to teach your children and create beautiful bodies with harmoniously developed souls who, when they grow up, will show their worth in everything they do, whatever their chosen profession. It is wrong to predetermine the future profession of a child, too young to either discuss it, or choose it. I want to teach all children, but not to make them into dancers. A free spirit can exist only in a free body, and I want to free these children's bodies. My pupils will teach other children, who in their turn will teach new ones, until the children of the whole world will become a joyous, beautiful and harmonious dancing mass. . . . I feel that, since Christendom, Bolshevism is the greatest event . . . destined to save humanity. But . . ." and Isadora complained of the slow progress being made in confronting the still existing conventions with this ideal, and of the delay in her own work that was to contribute to it.

"Oh, Isadora, Isadora," Podvoysky replied, "you were born a hundred years too soon. You have come too early into this world."

"Oh, no," Isadora interrupted him, "you must give right now, immediately, to your people, happiness for all the misery which Russia has gone through."

"Isadora, Isadora," Podvoysky tried to explain, "we have only begun to cut the marble blocks and you already want to give them shape with your fine chisel. Let me give you this advice. Go to the workers, go into their districts, to their clubs. Start to work with small groups of children, show to their parents—the workers—the results of your work. And afterwards go ahead and open your large school and then the workers themselves will bring you their children. Then," Podvoysky laughed, "let Lunacharsky stand in line to get a ticket to see your performance. . . . Succeed in gaining from the workers recognition of the importance of your work. Go through narrow paths, through working districts, to come out on a highway. It will be a long and difficult road that you will have to travel towards recognition and success.

"Tell her," Podvoysky said to Schneider, whose translation could barely keep pace with the speed and excitement of their conversation, "tell her that difficulties do not stop people but merely urge them on, and that there are no difficulties which cannot be overcome. She will, I am sure, come up against many difficulties, but she must not lose courage, she must not complain, and she must not be surprised. She will be helped, as we, too, were helped. As for her—we need her."

Many years later, in 1945, Podvoysky interpreted that last remark more fully when he disclosed that in 1921, as Leonid Krasin's suggestion of inviting Isadora was being discussed, the question of the practicality of having Isadora and her school during those difficult years for the country had been brushed aside by Lenin, who declared "we need her, need her assistance in the work of our cultural revolution."

Podvoysky himself was organizing his own project—directing the naked soldiers, as he called them, the athletes, boys and girls, who were being trained in gymnastics and for whose performances, upon his orders, the Red Stadium mentioned earlier was being built in the Vorobyovy Hills, not far away from the spot that Isadora wanted for her school.

Podvoysky suggested to Isadora to join him in his work, but as much as she admired him, she gently declined, for her ideas were always opposed to gymnastics. She preferred that he join her in a plea for more speedy action in finding a place where she could organize her school. And this he did. He virtually became the moving spirit in solving the organizational problems of Isadora's school, a commissar whose orders had to be carried out, even by Lunacharsky. He told Schneider to write down a message for Isadora: "We need a heroic art, a show of struggle against difficulties, and our achievements. She can have also something of the 'happy spirit,' but don't let her forget that 'our happiness is hard and grim; it is happiness built upon a bonfire.' "

To Isadora's surprise, she was finally installed in the house of another ballerina from the Moscow Ballet. Alexandra Balashova, while not of Geltser's caliber as a ballerina, had an extra charm in her favor—she was the wife of the multimillionaire Ushkov, owner of tea plantations. Ushkov's name is familiar to those acquainted with Serge Koussevitsky's contribution to music as conductor and music publisher—he was married to one of the Ushkovs. In any case Ushkov had acquired the mansion from the original builder, Pyotr [Pierre] Smirnoff, whose name is world famous in a more popular field than the fine arts: vodka distilling.

After the revolution, Balashova had emigrated to France, and her mansion was confiscated by the government and had been turned over to different offices. Now, thanks to Schneider's and Lunacharsky's energetic soliciting, the Commissariat, with the full approval of Podvoysky, assigned the mansion to Isadora and her future school. As Schneider describes it:

> The entrance to the house was flanked by two squat columns; in a recess was a heavy oaken door. The lower floor had a large entrance hall, with two huge, cold marble benches along the walls. A wide staircase of white marble led to the upper hall with balustrade and rosewood pillars.

> Straight ahead and to the right were the two "Napoleonic" ballrooms, an oblong one with columns of grey marble, and a large square one with a balcony. On the walls of the two rooms hung huge, heavily framed battle paintings, with full-length portraits of Napoleon in the foreground. Next to the square ballroom was the North drawing room, its walls covered with flower-embossed pink satin. Next to this was the "oriental" room, the walls and ceiling of which were decorated with stucco mouldings.

> All the doors of the house were huge mahogany double doors with bas-reliefs of Napoleon and Josephine, and bronze ornaments. To the right of the hall was a dining room; a sombre room with ebony-paneled walls, a similar ceiling, and a high musicians' gallery. Through the "Gobelin corridor" was the entrance to the boudoir.

When Schneider showed Isadora the former ballroom, now the bedroom of Balashova, which was to be Isadora's, Isadora sank into an armchair, unable to control her laughter: "A quadrille!" she cried, *"Changez vos places!"* Isadora's amusement was prompted by a strange coincidence. While looking for a place to live in Paris, Balashova had been shown Isadora's little house in the rue de la Pompe, which, with its rather austere furnishings, was a far cry from the palatial one she had left in Moscow.

Fortunately for Isadora's taste, there was no furniture left in Balashova's mansion. This gave her the opportunity of decorating her new home pretty much to her liking—that is, on the same lines as all her previous studios, with her blue curtains covering the walls, her carpets for dancing, and low couches instead of chairs. Thus, at the end of August, their life began at number 20 Prechistenka, for such was the name of the street in which the mansion stood.

At first there were official visits inquiring about Isadora's needs and comfort. Then the sixty persons who made up the organizing committee for the school held conferences, drinking tea for hours on end. Isadora was bored by the inactivity and frustrated by the constant postponement of the date for the opening of the school. "I only want black bread, and *kasha,* but I want one thousand children and a large hall," she pleaded over and over again. This, she was told, was a utopian idea. All Lunacharsky could offer was forty children, who could live in the house, which was still far from being properly equipped. But Isadora "kept after them, Lunacharsky, Schneider, Podvoysky, and the sixty-member committee," following her own precept which I heard her recite so often: "In this world, if you want anything done, you must keep after *them* whoever *they* are." Finally, three months after her arrival in Russia, in the middle of October, the school opened its doors.

From about one hundred children, only half were chosen, and, until the school was officially opened on December 3, these children came from their homes every day for their lessons. Although it was not the number of children she had hoped for, still she was told this was a mere beginning—others would come—it was only the dawn of her lifelong project. She must remember Podvoysky's advice not to be surprised, not to lose courage, and not to complain.

And so when Lunacharsky asked her if she would give a performance during the celebration of the fourth anniversary of the Russian Revolution, on November 7, Isadora was delighted to have her first public appearance connected with that date. The newspapers' announcement of the forthcoming performance referred to the "world-famous artist who had courageously left a crumbling, capitalistic Western Europe" to come to Russia to work with the children of the New Republic.

On the night of the festive gala, the three-thousand seat Bolshoi Theater, was filled to capacity; the wooden barriers separating the loges had to be removed to give every inch of space to the crowd of spectators, who had already filled the long corridors throughout the theater. Then the whole house became silent, and one could only hear the whispered name "Ilych . . . Ilych . . . Ilych . . ." (the affectionate way the Russians referred to Lenin by his patronymic, omitting his first name, Vladimir). Accompanied by Dzershinsky, an officer of the secret police, Lenin walked into the government loge and, smiling, lifted his hand in a friendly gesture toward the audience which responded with what seemed like never-ceasing applause.

Then the lights were dimmed and, before the curtain was raised, Lunacharsky stepped forward on the stage and briefly spoke of Isadora's art and the content of the program of her evening's performance.

After Tchaikovsky's Pathétique, Isadora appeared in the *Marche Slav*. Her interpretation of the latter, which she had introduced in public performances in London and Paris, was even more poignantly felt by the Russian audience as it watched a chained slave, symbolically representing the Russian people, who, after valiant struggles, broke his chains and overcame his oppressor. "It was not dancing in the ordinary technical sense," *Izvestiya* reported in its front-page article on the following day: "It was the most beautiful interpretation in movement and miming of a musical *chef d'oeuvre;* and also an interpretation of the Revolution—the music of a hymn to a monarchy, paradoxically enough, sounding revolutionary.

"The thrill of the evening came at the closing number of the program, when, after her solo performance to the first stanza of the *Internationale,* the audience saw Irma Duncan come from a corner of the bare stage, leading a little child by the hand, who was followed in turn by another and another—a mass of children in red tunics moving against the blue curtains, then circling the vast stage, and finally surrounding with their youthful outstretched arms the noble, undaunted and radiant figure of their teacher.

"The audience sprang to its feet, and with one mighty voice sang fervently the words of their hymn; they seemed like a great antique chorus celebrating the heroic gestures of the central figure on the stage. And no one failed to see that Lenin, keeping his eyes on the stage, stood in his loge and sang the *Internationale* with the rest of the audience."

A month later, when at Ivy Litvinov's request, Isadora repeated her program for an audience of workers and peasants, Mme. Litvinov wrote to her, "Your *Marche Slav* was something no one can ever forget! Seeing you, I lived a hundred years of agony and slavery, but came out into the sunlight at last. But I am still trembling. . . . I have never even dreamt of such a human, living relation between artist and audience. Now you have really given the Moscow proletariat something for their very own. It was a lovely public—all soldiers and women with handkerchiefs on their heads. . . ."

Isadora had known successes and triumphs in her art, had seen men and women in her audiences moved to tears and refusing to leave the hall until they called her yet once more upon the stage. She also claimed, as so many other foreign artists have done, that no other audiences in the world express their enthusiasm as rewardingly as the Russians—and yet all that was obscured when she was told that, after she had completed her *Marche Slav*, Lenin rose in his loge and, applauding, cried in a loud voice, "Bravo, bravo, Miss Duncan."

Chapter XXXI

But Isadora's happiness was short-lived. In her opinion her finest hour had been her triumph at the gala performance in celebration of the Russian Revolution, when at last she had given her art free to the people—something that had always been her aim, so that she now believed that she was at the glorious beginning of the fulfillment of her cherished ideas. But this dream was soon dealt a mortal blow. Lunacharsky called upon her a few days later to explain to her the new economic policy of his government. NEP (the initials of New Economic Policy), permitting business to go back to its former conditions of buying and selling, allowed the theaters to charge for tickets—thus putting an end to Isadora's free-of-charge performances for the people. Furthermore, since Isadora's performances would bring her an income sufficient, so they believed, to carry on her school, the funds promised for maintaining it were withdrawn, leaving only the mansion as the government's single gift to Isadora for all her efforts and future plans.

Thus, after only six months in Soviet Russia, Isadora was again faced with the same old predicament. Without financial support from private persons or from the government, she was to carry all the responsibilities of her grandiose plan, relying solely on her own resources. She asked herself, what, then, was the difference in her situation in Russia from what it had been in Western Europe? The difference was obvious—Russia was going through what she herself called childbirth pains; the country was still in a completely disorganized state. But what Isadora and her school, including the staff of fifty people, suffered from most was the lack of necessities, first of all food and fuel to keep them warm. And yet Isadora decided to remain in Russia.

Years later, when Isadora often spoke to me of those times, I asked her to account for her decision to stay on in Russia rather than return to Western Europe—a choice that no doubt affected the rest of her life. Without any hesitation, and speaking most emphatically, she said that, although saddened by the disappointment of her hopes, she had quickly recovered from the shock, and never wavered thereafter about her new problems. She simply took to heart Podvoysky's warning: "Difficulties do not stop people but merely urge them on; . . . there are no difficulties that cannot be overcome; she must not lose courage, she must not complain. . . ."

Was she afraid, if she returned to Paris or London, of hearing "we told you so," of acknowledging defeat? Isadora merely smiled. "My life was a constant defeat. I became immune to it a long time ago. No, no," she went on with sudden enthusiasm. "If you must know, it was a choice for me between seeing all those depraved, sugary sweet women crying around me, 'Oh, Miss Duncan, you are so wonderful . . . you remind me of . . . my mother used to tell me . . .' and the images of men such as Podvoysky—and he was not the only one—who said 'tell Isadora she can have her happiness in her performances, but not to forget that our happiness is hard and grim and built on a bonfire.'

"No, no," Isadora shook her head, "I couldn't even have hesitated. The very air there was different; it was exhilarating, you had to admire those Russians who, having rolled up their sleeves, so to speak, were going to make a happier place of this world. And you could see that nothing, nothing, neither cold nor hunger, would stop them, and you simply had to join them."

Besides, she also hoped to find escape in Russia from the constant reminders of her personal tragedy, which pursued her not only in familiar places but in the form of "sympathetic" expressions in people's eyes, which stabbed at her heart.

Isadora added, "I immediately gave three performances to sold-out houses at the Zimin theater, a hall larger than that of the Bolshoi, and with the first money I earned in Soviet Russia, I bought a

Christmas tree and presents for all my children in the school. The joy of seeing them decorating the tree with me would have repaid me for all my misgivings, so . . . don't ask me whether I have regretted remaining in Russia."

Isadora need not have finished her recollections because, shortly after Christmas, she met Sergei Essenin, a meeting which led to the major chapter in her years in Russia.

If Isadora had deliberately tried, she could not in all Russia have chosen for her companion a man with a more complex nature than Sergei Essenin. Even today, more than forty years after his death, after the publication of his collected poems, which were first ridiculed and then praised, and after his life has been minutely traced and analyzed, he still remains a baffling personality in the annals of Russian literature.

When they met, Sergei Essenin was twenty-six years old, a mere "youngster" in the eyes of some Westerners, and perhaps no more than a kid on the present American scale. But Essenin at that age had already lived through more than one life. He was born on October 3, 1895, into a poor peasant family in Constantinova, a village in the Ryazan province. In such families, many children were born and many died, and only Sergei and his two younger sisters survived: Katherine was five years and Alexandra fifteen years younger than he. When Sergei was thirteen, his father Alexander went to a nearby town to work in a butcher shop. Only years later, after the revolution, when the private ownership of stores was abolished and the country was suffering from famine, had Alexander returned to the work of a peasant in his native village.

Sergei's mother was illiterate; in her later years, in order to enjoy her son's poetry, she made several unsuccessful attempts at learning to read. She was, however, endowed with such a remarkable memory that she could recite some of his poems by heart merely from having heard him read them. After four years in the village preparatory school, Sergei was sent to live with his grandfather, some sixty miles away, where he was placed in a second-rate parochial school with the aim of his eventually becoming a school teacher. Thus he never worked in the fields with the rest of the peasants. Instead, he engaged in battles with boys of his own age, winning bruises that sent him back to his first attempts at writing poetry. At seventeen, he graduated from school and went to Moscow where, while trying to introduce his work into literary circles, he worked in the printshop of a well-known publishing firm as an assistant to the proofreader.

Lunacharsky described him thus at this point in his career: "Essenin came from the village not as a peasant, but as a sort of village intellectual. He was wearing a regular brown suit, a high starched collar, and a green tie. With his golden curls, he was like a pretty doll. He was extremely depressed—he was a poet, but no one wanted to understand this, the publishers refused his work. His father kept reproaching him for not doing the work a peasant should do, but instead wasting time scribbling little poems, and spending his salary on buying books and magazines without giving a thought to his future."

To his co-workers, both men and women, he appeared conceited and arrogant and he was very much disliked. However, Sergei became very much attached to Anna Izryadovna, a young woman four years older than he, who was working as a proofreader in the same printing workshop. To her he read his poems, with her he attended lectures at Shinyavsky University, and a year later Izryadovna bore him a son. "Here I am a father," he proudly announced to her. Six months later he went through a civil marriage ceremony with her. He was a very tender parent, "quickly got used to his son, loved him, and, rocking him to sleep, always sang to him." "You, too, always sing songs to him," Izryadovna quoted him in her short memoir.

But, although some of his poems were published during 1913 and 1914 in *Mirok*, a children's magazine, he dreamed of "wealth and fame." In May of the same year he went to St. Petersburg, "seeking good luck," as he said. There, almost as soon as he got off the train, he met Alexander Blok, his favorite poet, and through him, Sergei Gorodetsky, Zinaida Gipius, and other already well-known poets.

"I saw Essenin right at the beginning of his arrival in St. Petersburg," Maxim Gorki later wrote to Romain Rolland. "He was short and delicately built, with golden curls, dressed like Vanya in *A Life for the Tsar* [Glinka's opera], blue-eyed and shining like Lohengrin. He was welcomed by his confreres as a gluttonous person might seize a strawberry in January. They began to praise his poems in an exaggerated and insincere way, as hypocrites and those who are envious know how to do. At that time he must have been about eighteen. At twenty he wore on top of his curls a popular and *à la mode* bowler hat and resembled a clerk in a pastry shop."

Essenin was constantly invited to the salons of St. Petersburg society. With the shrewd practical sense that went with his background, he quickly understood what role he was supposed to play in those salons. The habitués schemed to have Essenin presented at court as a sort of rare and entertaining specimen, and they diligently cultivated him with that aim in mind. But the domesticating process was not very successful.

He learned that to be admitted into the city's literary circles, he would have to adhere to certain rules as well as pass through certain modes of introduction, and he lost no time in adjusting himself to them. He found it easy to pretend to be the tinsel-like lad the literary gourmets wished to see in him.

A few years later, when he felt he had sufficiently established himself, he visited another poet, Anatoly Mariengoff, one of his closest friends, at his publishing office, and, placing a yellow bag of pickled cucumbers on a table covered with manuscripts, he advised his friend on the way to a literary career. Mariengoff quotes Essenin in his *Reminiscences* as follows:

"You cannot just helter-skelter get into Russian literature. One has to play a clever game and use a most delicate policy. You are going to find it very difficult. You cannot do it dressed in lacquered little shoes and with your hair parted just so, one little hair next to another. How can it be done without the absent-mindedness of the poet? Who ever flies in the clouds in well-pressed trousers? Who is going to believe it? And it is not a bad idea to pretend to be a little fool. We, here in Russia, just love such little fools. . . . You must give every one his pleasure. Do you know how I have been climbing to Parnassus?" And Essenin roared with laughter like a boy. "Here, my friend, one has to be very sly. Let them, I thought, each of them, think 'I introduced him into Russian literature.' It pleases them, and I don't give a damn. Was it Gorodetzky who introduced me? Let it be Gorodetzky. Kluev?—Kluev. Sologub with Tchebarevskoy? Of course, who else? In a word— Merezhkovsky with Gipius, and Rurik Ivanov, and Alexander Blok . . . all of them. And all those 'oohs' and 'ahs,' 'How remarkable!' 'A genius!' But I have kept myself as modest as I could. Like an innocent virgin I have blushed at every praise, and from mere shyness have not dared to look anybody in the eye. What fun!" Essenin laughed. By that time he had abandoned forever his typically Russian peasant's short coat, his embroidered Russian blouse, and his boots *à l'accordéon*, and, pointing at his American shoes, he said, not with that false sincerity of which he had become a master, but truly sincerely said: "Do you want to know the truth—I have never worn such boots or such an overcoat, as I did when I first showed myself to them. I told them I was going to Riga to work on the waterfront rolling barrels. 'I have nothing to eat, no way of earning my living,' I told them. 'Just happened to be in St. Petersburg waiting for my group of workers to get organized.' Ah, what utter rubbish about those barrels—I came to St. Petersburg to gain worldwide fame and a bronze monument." [Pushkin's monument in St. Petersburg.]

For a while Essenin became silent—one could only hear him crunching the cucumbers, dripping the juice on a manuscript on the table, which he nonchalantly brushed aside with the sleeve of his jacket. His blue eyes suddenly became an angry gray. His temples grew red. "And then," he continued, "during the following three weeks they began to drag me from one salon to the other to sing for them indecent limericks, accompanying myself on the accordion. Just for the looks of it, at first they would ask me to read some of my verses—and after one or two, they hid their yawns with their fists. Ah, but when it comes to the indecent stuff, you can carry on a whole night with it . . . Oh, how I despise them all!"

Two months later Essenin returned to Moscow, but Izryadovna said he had grown somehow different—still gentle and thoughtful, but not the same man who had gone off to St. Petersburg. Restless, he visited his family, then in the autumn stopped in Moscow long enough to suggest to Izryadovna to join him in going to St. Petersburg. But finally he left by himself, saying, "I'll return soon. I won't live there a long time."

In St. Petersburg, Blok warned him, "I have the feeling that your path is not going to be easy, and in order not to lose your way, you should not be in a hurry, nor become nervous. Sooner or later one has to give an account of his every step, and to take steps now is very difficult, especially in literature."

Blok was alluding to the many factions in the literary life of Russia at that time—there were the so-called symbolists, mystical anarchists, neo-Christians, futurists, imagists, and still others. Aside from these, there was a group of poets and writers that had gathered around Gorki, but Essenin did not succeed in being accepted into Gorki's circle, and so eventually (1919) he was willing to be classified as one of the imagists.

And, indeed, the literary life was not simple, as Blok had warned him. Especially not for Essenin, who was determined to preserve the healthy, almost folklorish style of his verse, which he had brought with him, so to speak, from his village, and not let it be influenced either by the different trends of the various literary circles, or by the *mondaine* life he led in Moscow and Petrograd. He was very much attached to his parents, and his two sisters, and he never failed to spend some time visiting them—usually during the summer—and observing the rapid destruction of his patriarchal village crushed by an "iron guest," as he called the industrialization of the country. He had hoped that the October Revolution would bring a *muzhik's* heaven all over Russia, and instead he saw "a steel stallion conquering a live stallion." He felt he was no longer the village poet, but the *last* village poet. His mission, to which he must dedicate all his energy, was to conserve in the subject matter of his poems a complete lack of eroticism, and to maintain the folkstyle.

In addition to writing and publishing his poems in magazines, he took every opportunity to introduce them publicly by reading them at literary gatherings, which were frequently held in both cities. While he was considered one of the imagist group, he himself kept his independence from any ties, saying that he "did not wish to be tied hand and foot." For the same reason, he did not either then or later join the Communist party, although, among the artists and writers, he certainly was the one who had an indisputable qualification for membership—he was of proletarian background, the most valuable virtue in the codex of the party. In this connection, I have in my possession a copy of an official document stating that Sergei Essenin was *bespartiny*, a person who does not belong to any political party.

It was said in Russia that Pushkin "thought in verse," that Mayakovsky "loved in verse," but that Essenin lived "excited by his heart and his verse."

Some of Sergei's literary colleagues, as Gorki had remarked, praised his poems and told fairy tales to the effect that it was not necessary for him to work at them because, they said, "the verses flowed from his lips like water from a brook." Others were more skeptical and teased him about his genius: "Hey, Sergei," they would say to him, "you just loaf about the streets of Moscow, don't you? When do you write your poems?" "All the time, always," he would reply.

And indeed this was closer to the truth. It was not unusual for a friend calling on him wherever he happened to be living at the time to find him lying on the couch with his hands behind his head, either silent, or occasionally murmuring a few words. "Don't bother me," he would wave away the unexpected caller, "I am writing." Or, if the poem was completed in his mind, he would, before saying another word, sit his friend in a chair, recite the poem to him, and demand his critical reaction. Only when the poem was composed more or less to his satisfaction would he write down the first draft, and then, if he felt it necessary, he would do further work on it for hours. His family was accustomed to prepare a work table for him in one corner of their hut and to leave him undisturbed. Or he would go fishing alone in the nearby river, for, as he said, "One can go fishing for hours, perhaps even days, forgetting everything." He was referring to the inspiration he derived from this quiet occupation.

His poems were as uneven and erratic as his nature. Gorki was not the only one who thought that Essenin's poems were written in a bold, sweeping style, with clearly defined images, sincere and remarkably touching. Essenin succeeded in giving human and emotional qualities to animals and to inanimate objects. But sometimes, carried away by his momentary mood or impressions and unable to control himself, he would give vent to his temper and damn past and present conditions in Russia, calling his compatriots, whom he held responsible for the shortcomings of the age, "revolting burglars, charlatans, and imposters." While these outbursts were overlooked by government officials, who regarded him as a mere "hooligan," unworthy of serious attention, his attitude found little favor with the publishers.

Although he had told Izryadovna that he would return soon, that he was not going to live long in Petrograd, he actually returned two years later, in January 1916. In 1917, not particularly concerned with the Soviet marriage and divorce procedures, he married Zinaida Reich, a talented young actress and an exceptionally beautiful young woman. He had two children by her, but a little over a year later he parted from her, as he wrote in his short biographical notes, and from then on began his nomadic existence—common to all Russians, he claimed, during the period between 1918 and 1921. He traveled as far south as the Caucasus and Persia, visited the Crimea and Bessarabia, as well as the steppes of Orenburg, and went as far north as Archangelsk, the Solovki Islands, and the Murman Sea.

By the time he had finished his wanderings, brought home chiefly by his love and concern for his family, and his anxiety over the fate of his village, he had begun to lose his youthful, almost cherubic looks and resembled rather a Moscow loafer who tried to find solace in the bohemian life of the city or in inciting brawls.

Such was Sergei Essenin when Isadora met him. She knew almost nothing about him and his life—either then or later.

There are several published versions of the Isadora-Essenin meeting, each suggesting either the importance of their subsequent feelings for each other or the frivolous character of a mere love-adventure. But some of the quotations from their supposed conversations, given as if the authors had been present and taken stenographic notes, are so un-Russian that they cast doubt upon their authenticity. I prefer to trust Ilya Schneider's report, for he actually brought Isadora to the party at George Jakuloff's, the well-known Moscow painter of theatrical scenery, where Schneider himself met Essenin for the first time, spent the evening there, and later took Isadora home. The only quotation used in all the various versions of this first Isadora-Essenin meeting seems to be authentic. Isadora constantly repeated *"Zolotaya golova!"* (golden head) as she kept tousling his blond curls when, after having been introduced to her, Essenin knelt by the couch on which Isadora was reclining in her usual way. Since these words nearly exhausted Isadora's extremely limited Russian vocabulary, and Essenin did not speak any other language, their evening together passed not in conversation but in Essenin's reciting his poems to her. "He recited his poems to me," Isadora later said to Schneider. "I didn't understand a word, but I heard that there was music in them."

Isadora did not realize how prophetic these words were about her whole subsequent relationship with Essenin.

As the party was drawing to a close, Schneider took Isadora home in a cab with Essenin, who never let her hand out of his. Isadora usually insisted on fast driving, but this time she did not seem to mind the slow pace at which the sleepy cab driver was taking them back to Prechistenka. Nor did she ask for Schneider's assistance in translating the conversation she was carrying on with Essenin. But at one point in their trip, Schneider realized that the sleepy coachman had by mistake driven them around a church three times: "Hey," Schneider said to the coachman, "Are you marrying us—you have driven three times around the church like three times around the lectern."

"Married us!" Essenin laughed. Schneider translated everything to Isadora, and she, not laughing, slowly pronounced in French, *"Mariage!"*

Years later, perhaps because she knew that her reminiscences about her life in Russia would not meet with derision from me, she often spoke to me about that period. When she described her first meeting with Essenin (in a way similar to the account to be given later by Schneider in his book), and I remarked that her driving in a carriage with Essenin so much resembled her trip to Potsdam with Craig that it must have startled her, she said, "It really should have. When I come to think of it, you are right. But at that time it brought something else to my mind. You see, before I sailed for Russia from London, Mary Desti took me to a fortune-teller. As you know, those women always predict long voyages, and troubles that you are bound to overcome. But when she said I was going to get married, I lost my patience—probably for the first time with a fortune-teller. You know I just love them. And so I pulled Mary away from her. And what do you think? As we were going down the stairs, the woman ran after us screaming: 'You'll be married. And within a year.' "

"And did you think that night in Moscow that you were sitting next to your future husband?" I asked.

"Certainly not," Isadora said, "but I could not help remembering the fortune-teller's words."

Chapter XXXII

Nor was Essenin thinking of marrying Isadora at that time. He had
been married twice, but neither of those experiences seemed to
have altered his highly individual and independent character or in
any way influenced his mode of life. In fact, he did not mind at
all that, after he had left Zinaida Reich and she had married the
well-known stage director Vsevolod Meyerhold, she had taken his
son by Izryadovna into the Meyerhold household to be brought up
with the children she had had with Sergei. Although he did not
feel responsible to either of his wives, he remained on friendly
terms with them, and even with Vsevolod Meyerhold, with whom
he enjoyed discussing literature.

He did, however, have an almost abnormal love for his own
family, who throughout his life remained his first concern. Perhaps
because as a boy he had refused his father's request that he work
in the village and thus help earn the family's livelihood, he always
felt financially responsible for them. He took it for granted that
it was up to him to look after their welfare, and to give his sisters
an opportunity for the education he himself had been denied.

Thus his real home always remained the family's hut in the
village, to which he returned every year, even if only for a short
visit; his homes with his wives were simply living quarters, such as
he had often shared with his unmarried friends. It was not unusual
that he did not move into Isadora's apartment but instead continued

to share one room with Mariengoff, which was more of a home to him because there he kept most of his belongings and his clothes. But if he was not yet in love with Isadora, he certainly was very much attracted to her, although because of the lack of a common language their means of communication were extremely limited.

While Isadora would use German or French words in place of Russian, which meant no more to Essenin than if she had spoken to him in Chinese, Sergei addressed Isadora in Russian with remarkable authority and with the conviction that he was being perfectly intelligible. "You are an imagist," he would say to Isadora and, if Isadora looked bewildered, he would explain by saying, "You are the revolution."

But unless Schneider was present and could translate to him what Isadora wanted so much to tell him about her art, her school, her ideas of the role of the Russian revolution, Essenin remained completely ignorant of Isadora's ideals and mission. Except for the names of a few famous composers, which he could not miss in literature, he knew nothing about them or their works, nor was he interested in finding out; he sincerely disliked serious music—it bored him—and loved only Russian folk songs. He never went to a concert or the opera, and except for the Moscow Art Theater, the theater per se did not interest him; and if, occasionally, he would go to a motion picture, it was only because, he said, it was so simple to go in or out of the hall. But he was very impressed by Isadora's performances, never missing a single one, and either watching it from the hall, or from the wings backstage. He especially loved her interpretation of the *Marche Slav*, the obvious meaning of which he could not miss and which led him to repeat to Isadora, "You are an imagist," and to bring a whole group of his imagist colleagues with him to Prechistenka to meet Isadora.

Isadora, on the other hand, did not have the vaguest idea of the various trends in contemporary Russian literature. She could never participate in discussions with Essenin's friends. In fact, she was convinced that the bookstore that Essenin and Mariengoff operated for a while was a nightclub and was eventually closed on government orders because at that time no liquor was allowed to be sold.

During more than one such visit with his group of friends, Isadora would continue to entertain her own guests in the studio. When the noise from the adjoining room where Essenin and his friends were enjoying themselves became too disturbing, Isadora would ask them to join everybody in her studio and offer to dance for them. But, while impressed by her public performances, seeing Isadora dancing in a more intimate atmosphere both bored and repelled Sergei, despite the fact that she was interpreting a Chopin waltz or prelude as an expression of her love for him. Whether because he was embarrassed by so frank a public exhibition of her emotions toward him, or because he neither understood the music nor the meaning of the dance, he would interrupt her roughly and declare that he himself could do a better dance. Thereupon, accompanied by the clapping of his friends and the wailing of the accordion, which his friends always seemed to have with them, he would launch into one of the typically Russian folk dances.

Strange as it may seem, the delight of Sergei's group with his dance and the utter bewilderment of Isadora's own friends, who had only a few minutes before been deeply moved by her dancing of Chopin and Schubert, did not even embarrass her. Isadora was falling in love with Essenin with all the passion of a woman who was past forty. There is a striking similarity between Isadora and Essenin's love affair and that of George Sand and Frédéric Chopin.

George Sand was an eminent French author whose works had wide influence, not only in France but also on the novelists of other countries, including Dostoyevsky. While convinced that love affairs were things of the past for her, and that she should devote the rest of her life entirely to her art, George Sand fell in love with Chopin. She was eight years older than he; Isadora was fifteen years Essenin's senior.

Although in these cases the emotions of both women were as passionate they had been when they were younger, maternal feeling played no small part in their attitude toward their lovers—not always with happy results. George Sand's taking the ailing Chopin on a romantic escapade to the island of Majorca, and Isadora Duncan's insistence on a turbulent tour to introduce European culture and even the United States, to Sergei Essenin, brought disaster to their respective relationships.

Both women preferred not to be conscious of the difference between their ages and their lovers', but both men were well aware of it and did not always succeed in keeping their embarrassment to themselves. At the same time the young men were ambitious for their public careers, and no doubt they did not fail to appreciate the extra glory reflected upon them by the glamorous reputations of their consorts.

And yet they strove to preserve their independence, and even to assert the superiority of their art. This often took the form of a masculine rebellion against the too obviously motherly attitude of their older companions.

It is doubtful that Chopin ever read any of George Sand's works, just as Essenin never really understood the meaning and the significance of Isadora's art, but both women were at least sympathetic to the works of their lovers. George Sand, Chopin, Isadora, and Essenin were all distinct artistic personalities; but while George Sand and Isadora were women of the world, Chopin and Essenin were essentially provincials. And yet both women were convinced that through patience and love they could overcome the diversity of their characters, beliefs, and tastes, and even their attitudes toward their art and work.

While George Sand could communicate with Chopin in French, Isadora and Essenin, lacking a common language, were forced to reduce their exchange of thoughts to the most primitive level. But what both women seemed to have failed to realize was that they were, from beginning to end in these attachments, mere foreigners to their lovers—basically strangers—and that was the main barrier in their relationships.

George Sand wrote in her autobiography that she and Chopin had been strangers; in his letters to the Countess Potocka (recently discovered and published), Chopin admitted that he could love only a woman of his own nationality. In the same way, Essenin consistently showed his belief in his national superiority by his patronizing treatment of Isadora, especially in public. She mistakenly ascribed this behavior to his exotic Russian nature, and it even seemed to have a stimulating effect on her love for him.

It was a challenge to her femininity to conquer, if not with her art, then with her personal charm. She believed that some of Sergei's odd ways and the roughness of his character were due not only to his background, but also to the influence of his bohemian friends, and that a change to a more civilized atmosphere would be a helpful beginning. She was delighted when Essenin, who had come to see her off as she was taking a train to Petrograd to give performances there, was persuaded to come along with her just as he was, without any luggage or even a change of linen.

Isadora's hopes that the comforts of the Hotel d'Angleterre, the once luxurious hotel where she had stayed during her prewar visits to the former capital, would give Essenin his first taste of a different life, were dashed by the deplorable economic conditions prevailing in Petrograd as in Moscow. She had managed to reserve a suite in the now dilapidated establishment, which could offer them nothing better than an icy temperature in their rooms and food as bad as that of Moscow, with practically no hotel service to speak of.

Thus, the stories later gathered by Macdougall about Essenin "having already discovered that traveling with an internationally famous artist gave him a sort of *cachet*, and he had a free hand about ordering what he wanted when he wanted . . . that he was often found sprawling before a varied collection of empty bottles, and that more than once he was forcibly carried back to their rooms, after he was found wandering about the public halls naked and drunk," were pure fiction circulated in Moscow by those friends who disapproved of Essenin's affair with Isadora, and who regarded their first trip together as evidence of a more serious relationship between the two than they would have liked to see.

Actually, not until Anatoly Mariengoff and Sergei had the bookstore, where they occasionally entertained their customers—mostly writers and artists, like themselves—could Essenin have been accused of what is called "drinking." There was a time during those first years of the revolution when the sale of liquor was forbidden. But, of course, there were always ways of obtaining it, and especially at the *Pegas' Stoilo* (Pegasus's stall) a café frequented by Moscow intellectuals. There Sergei's friends saw to it that he was plentifully supplied with vodka, on credit if necessary, for a sober Essenin was not as much use to them as a drunken one who could act as the leader of their noisy and riotous band.

It would be naïve to think that Essenin did not understand their scheme, but he loved to amuse people, and if his drunken state could offer such diversion, he was ready to play his part—by drinking enough to smell of liquor, and behaving as if he were drunk. But it would also be naïve to think that Sergei always managed to remain the perfect master of the situation and keep himself within the limits of sobriety. Still his behavior far from justified his reputation as an alcoholic, which pursued him to the end of his life.

Like any other liquor, vodka seems to have a variety of effects on people—some become amorous or sentimental, others simply sleepy, and some are driven to violence. Essenin belonged to the last category. Well aware of it, Isadora tried to substitute champagne for vodka, imagining that it would not produce the same effect, but the hotel's wine cellar had long since been emptied of every kind of liquor, and Isadora's and Essenin's first trip together was far from being a caviar and champagne banquet.

It was, however, memorable and significant for entirely different reasons.

Her second performance at the Maryinsky Theater was reserved for the workers of Petrograd, and especially for the sailors from the naval base at Kronstadt, with the seamen from the cruiser *Aurora* predominating. These sailors had a legendary reputation, not only because of their daredevil exploits during the crucial moments between victory and defeat on the first day of the revolution, but because their cruiser had moved into the Neva and forced the immediate capitulation of their adversaries by turning its guns upon the Winter Palace.

Isadora was about to finish her performance of Tchaikovsky's Pathétique, when suddenly the whole house was plunged into complete darkness by a fault in the electric power system, which seemed to be difficult to locate and repair immediately. As would happen in any theater under the circumstances, protests, catcalls, and whistlings filled the hall, which held over three thousand spectators, while Isadora remained in the center of the stage as if frozen. Ilya Schneider, who usually accompanied her to her performances, happened to be backstage and fortunately was able to find a lantern with a candle in it. He handed the dim lamp to Isadora.

"It was chilly on the stage," Schneider later described the scene. "I picked up Isadora's red cloak and put it over her shoulders. In her red cloak, holding the lantern high above her head, which she raised challengingly, she looked like some revolutionary symbol. The audience responded with a thunder of applause. Duncan waited for it to subside."

Since it was apparent that the unexpected interruption of the performance might take some time, Schneider translated Isadora's request to her audience: "Comrades, please sing your folk songs."

Thus, while Isadora held the lantern high above her head, at first haltingly but very soon no longer hesitating, the audience filled the hall with full-throated renditions of the well-known revolutionary songs.

"Tears ran down Duncan's cheeks as the songs grew louder and increased in intensity. Light gradually returned to the chandeliers of the auditorium; reddish at first, then yellow, sunny, and finally blindingly white it flooded the huge theatre and the gigantic chorus, which rose slowly with the light, shook the auditorium with the last refrain: 'from our bones a stern avenger will arise, who will be much stronger than we. . . .' At the same time, Duncan flung off her red cloak and the curtain slowly descended. Not even the most talented producer could have thought of such a climax," Schneider concluded.

Later, when telling the story of that evening, Isadora claimed that she was more thrilled than she had been upon her first hearing Gluck's *Orfeo* or Beethoven's Seventh Symphony, for this mass music, rising from simple men, was a more glorious, elemental power and far more moving than any instrumental music.

But speaking to me about it, she confessed to an even more important aspect of that particular evening. No one in that vast audience was as enthusiastic as Essenin. Now, at last, he had witnessed and understood every moment of it. He heard the songs that were so dear to him, knowing every one of them by heart, and he was proud to join the *Aurora* sailors in singing them. And he saw Isadora holding the lantern in a heroic gesture so long that it would have cramped any sailor's hand. He was proud of her.

Isadora told me that later he loved describing the whole evening in all its details and did not conceal his impression that he was not a mere spectator but was himself a part of the performance. "He was still completely overwhelmed, when he came backstage to see me," Isadora told me. "He was radiant, his eyes were burning. He looked as if he were in a trance, or still seeing some kind of vision. I have never seen him look as beautiful. When he put his arms around me and repeated several times 'Sidora . . . Sidora . . .' I felt for the first time that he really loved me." ("Sidora" was the way in which Essenin affectionately shortened Isadora's name.)

But upon their return to Moscow, Isadora soon realized that Essenin's friends were intriguing against their union. They felt that

Essenin's involvement with Isadora would keep him away from his activities in their literary enterprises, and they even devised a scheme to get him abroad, hoping that perhaps a short separation would be sufficient to break his relationship with Isadora. A friend of the imagists, who was going to Persia on a government mission, was to take Essenin along with him. They knew that Essenin had always been anxious to visit the country of Omar Khayyam. He arrived at the station to bid his friend farewell a few minutes before the train's departure, and, unaware of the scheme, was hoisted into the already moving train before he realized that his friends had arranged this unexpected journey to Persia. However, two days later, Essenin returned to Moscow, having ended his voyage in Rostov, cursing everyone for playing such a trick on him.

Undaunted by this failure, the well-wishing friends managed to secure Lunacharsky's help in getting Sergei to go abroad. Whether or not Lunacharsky knew their true reason, or believed that it would be good for Essenin as a poet to "broaden his horizon" by visiting West European countries, he actually procured (February 10, 1921) from the Commissariat of Foreign Affairs an official permit for Essenin and Ruryk Ivanev, another imagist, to travel abroad. And the two poets would have gone to Italy and France for an unspecified length of time had not Soviet Russia moved into the Caucasus to "sovietize" the Democratic Republic of Georgia. In this way, Ivanev had an unexpected opportunity to return to Georgia—he had been forced to leave the country in the past, and was now eager to resume his ties there, rather than go to Western Europe. Without his companionship, Sergei was not particularly anxious to make the trip, even if he were provided with another friend. Or was Essenin not yet ready to leave Isadora?

Isadora, on the other hand, was just as anxious to get Sergei away from the dangerous influence of his friends, and had her own plans for taking him abroad.

But, in order not to leave the school without her guidance for an unpredictable length of time, and also without any financial support, which, so far, she had managed to provide, she conceived of what she thought was a splendid scheme.

She was personally acquainted with a large number of Americans who were members of the American Relief Organization, and her *grossartige Idee*, as she referred to it, was aimed at the dollars they would have to pay for the high-priced entertainment she planned to supply. This "brilliant festival" was to start in the large ballroom with a performance by the children of the school, to be followed by Isadora's dancing in her own studio a few numbers to the music of Chopin and Scriabin. But, since Isadora's own understanding of what was "truly Russian" did not differ very much from that of the Americans on whose favor she counted, she insisted that the second part of the evening should be a party at which blini* would be served to the accompaniment of gypsy singing and dancing.

Such a program was more appropriate for the luxurious entertainment given in Isadora's honor by Paris Singer at their residence in Versailles than for a school, no matter how financially sound such a scheme might be. "All America wants is money, money, money, so let them spend their money themselves," Isadora is supposed to have explained to Schneider, who, as the recently appointed director of the school, was reluctant to carry out her project. "You will never attract them by the charm of dancing children, nor by Chopin and Scriabin," Isadora insisted.

On hearing about it, Lunacharsky telephoned to Schneider: "The notice you issued has met with an unfavorable reception by our Party leaders. I must warn you that everything you do should be kept within the limits of the strictest decorum. I shall hold you personally responsible for any cases of drunkenness within the walls of the school."

Indignant at the obvious order for the cancellation of the *grossartige Idee*, Isadora wrote Lunacharsky: "Dear Comrade, The words 'within the limits of strictest decorum' do not exist in my vocabulary. Will you, please, explain what you mean? Yours, Isadora Duncan."

In a letter to Schneider, which Lunacharsky asked to be translated to Isadora, he patiently explained that apparently Isadora was not aware of "the old Russian habit of associating gypsies and pancakes with vodka, and that there was no possible guarantee that someone would not bring vodka with him." While Isadora still grumbled that "one of the most progressive men in the world, one of the most prominent Bolsheviks, should talk about the 'limits of the strictest decorum'!" even Essenin, whom everybody had expected would welcome being the master of ceremonies at such a

---

*Pancakes served with caviar and similar delicacies only during Lent in Russia, and not at any other time of the year, as is done elsewhere.

party, had strongly objected to Isadora's project, basing it on the same reason—"the association of gypsies and pancakes with vodka."

Having thus failed in her idea for a practical solution to the financial problems of her school, she suggested to Lunacharsky that she go on a tour through Western Europe and the United States, and take along with her a group of her pupils, as well as the necessary attending staff. Essenin, so she imagined, would be included in one or another capacity. Having received Lunacharsky's tentative approval, Isadora cabled to her former manager, Sol Hurok, in New York, asking him to arrange dates for performances.

It was too late for Hurok to arrange the tour during the spring season, but he offered to do it in the fall. But while he was negotiating with Isadora, and Lunacharsky with Soviet Government officials for permission for Isadora's school children to be allowed to go on such a tour, something utterly unexpected happened which speeded up the date of Isadora's departure from Russia.

As we have seen, when bored with everything else, Isadora, half in earnest and half for pure amusement, liked to consult fortune-tellers. On this particular night she played at the ouija board with Schneider. When the mysterious wandering of their fingertips finally settled down on the letters D.O.R.A., Isadora almost fainted—it was the name of her mother, and, as Isadora knew that her mother was ill and staying at Raymond's home in Paris, the ouija board could only be announcing bad news. And, indeed, the next morning, Isadora received a telegram informing her of her mother's death on April 12, 1922. (She had been cremated and buried in Père Lachaise.)

Her first impulse was to fly immediately to Paris, but her American passport, which she, like all foreigners, had had to surrender upon her arrival in Russia, was not to be found in the complicated web of the Soviet bureaucratic system. Her immediate departure had to be postponed, but now, full of premonitions about Essenin and herself, and the fate of her school, and feeling generally restless, Isadora told Lunacharsky that she had decided to leave Russia without waiting for permission to take her school children along with her, but that she would like to take Essenin. She used Lunacharsky's own argument—it would be good for Essenin to broaden his horizons as a poet by visiting foreign countries, learning something about their people, and above all their art treasurers.

According to all the published reports in books and newspaper articles, Isadora took the most unprecedented step of her life and broke her sacred vow by suddenly marrying Essenin because she was influenced by the well-known difficulties Maxim Gorki had had in New York when he arrived with his lifelong companion, M.F. Andreyeva, the famous actress, to whom he was never legally married. Nothing of the kind had influenced Isadora's decision, so she told me. She did know of Gorki's case, as she did of a similar one which had also happened in New York in 1908, that of Alexander Scriabin, the Russian composer. But Isadora's fighting spirit, far from succumbing easily to the American authorities, would rather have welcomed an opportunity to ridicule the moral backwardness and hypocrisy of American public opinion for condoning such incidents, but Lunacharsky was to make marriage a condition of Essenin's permission to leave.

Isadora quoted Lunacharsky to me: "We have great faith in Essenin as a poet. We value him a great deal. And you know how they feel in the West, and especially in America about us—the Bolsheviks. He'll be exposed to all sorts of dangers, including physical ones. Who is there to defend or protect him? As you also know, we are not even recognized by some countries, including America; we have no embassies. . . ." Isadora asked Lunacharsky, "What can I do? I, a woman?" He answered, "You are a world-famous artist. Your name would be his protection—that is, if he were Isadora Duncan's husband."

While Isadora busied herself with preparations for her departure, working with the twenty-five girls in her school (who, she hoped, would soon follow her abroad), on the programs planned for the tour, Essenin had to put his personal affairs into some kind of order. Lunarcharsky helped by getting him a passport for travel abroad, as well as the special document issued to a person sent on an official mission.

In a letter from Essenin addressed to Lunacharsky, dated March 17, 1922, Sergei requested permission to travel to Berlin for three months, giving as his reason that he would seek publication of his own works abroad, as well as those of some of his friends. In the fifth volume of Essenin's complete works, published in Moscow in 1968, it is stated that such permission was denied him, presumably because on December 12, 1921, the Commissariat of People's Education had decided against granting such permission because it was considered financially unprofitable to publish Russian authors abroad.

However, I have in my possession, from Isadora's library, copies of a document which definitely did grant Essenin, on April 3, 1922, official permission to travel abroad:

"Following the decision taken by the Commissariat of the People's Education in reference to travel abroad, Sergei Essenin is allowed such an official trip to Germany for the duration of three months. The People's Commissariat of Education asks all the representatives of the Soviet Government, military as well as civilian, to give Sergei Essenin every assistance."

Apparently, once Essenin left for Germany for further travels and for a much longer period than three months, the document would have been more of an obstacle than a help to him and so he never made use of it in any case.

On the day before the registration of their civil marriage, Isadora asked Schneider to do her a favor. Still not able to locate her American passport, she had to be content with a sort of *laissez-passer* issued by the French officials, and, pointing to the date of her birth, she asked Schneider to do a "little correcting" on it. "It's for Essenin," she said. "We don't feel this difference of fifteen years in our ages, but it is written down here and tomorrow we have to hand our passports into the hands of strangers. It may be unpleasant for him. I shall soon have no more use for this passport. I shall get another."

Thus, when on May 2, 1922, they were issued their marriage certificate, next to Essenin's age of twenty-seven, Isadora's was given as thirty-seven. Also, they had chosen to use a double name, "Duncan Essenin," which amused Sergei so much that, as soon as they left the office, he began to announce to everybody, "Now I am 'Duncan!' "

Chapter XXXIII

Isadora's only honeymoon was no less bizarre than her marriage; she barely saw her husband. The day of their departure was set for May 12, and, while Isadora went about calmly making arrangements for their voyage, Essenin behaved as if he were being taken, at least, on a trip to the moon. The two weeks left for him to attend to everything before leaving Russia were far from sufficient, so he thought, and in his excited, almost hysterical state, he brought even more confusion into his never too well organized affairs. Isadora never knew whether he spent his nights at Mariengoff's, his more or less official domicile for the past few years, or in the room of one of his many imagist friends, or took a quick trip to see his family. He would rush in and out of Prechistenka bringing packages and suitcases, some containing his books and manuscripts, others his clothes, with vague but imperative orders either to store them or to include them in their luggage—only to change his plans a few hours later, or on the following day, and take everything back to Mariengoff's, or to some other friend's room.

His most serious concern was his family, and first of all his sister Katya. During the past few years he had taken complete charge of her life and her education in Moscow, and now he worried about leaving her. He instructed Mariengoff to take care of her, but also wrote letters to other friends asking them to assist Katya in all her needs. In addition to the money he left for this purpose with Mariengoff, he included some funds which he was able to obtain from his publishers, in his letters to friends.

All this could have easily been accomplished had he not increased his excitement by taking part in the bon voyage parties that were constantly being given him by his friends. How to carouse with his friends and still keep sober for arranging his affairs was a problem Sergei did not easily solve at that time.

When, loaded with useless luggage, he arrived at the airport, he was a nervous wreck, for besides being exhausted by the past two turbulent weeks, he was terrified of flying. Unlike Isadora, who had already flown many times in Western Europe and had enjoyed it, Essenin had never been in an airplane before.

Isadora had reserved rooms for them at the Hotel Adlon in Berlin, one of the luxurious hotels where she had stayed in the past, and had ordered a Buick five-seater to be used on their trips in Europe, for she hated traveling by train. Elegantly dressed in her gray flannel traveling suit, she arrived at the airport carrying a luncheon basket which contained two bottles of champagne and a few lemons. "Sucking a lemon and a little champagne would prevent Sergei from getting airsick," she explained. She was followed by a bus, the only one available at that time in Moscow, which brought her pupils to watch her departure. The bus carried a large sign: "A free spirit can exist only in a free body! Duncan School."

The hectic scene at the airport, which was the beginning of a series of dramatic events during their journey, and during their lives thereafter, fortunately was spared one extra touch by the punctuality of the German pilot of the small Junker plane into which Isadora and Essenin had finally settled down. Just as the plane started toward the runway, two well-built men came rushing toward the plane. These were emissaries sent by Mariengoff and other imagist friends to catch Essenin and prevent him by force from making the flight with Isadora. But they arrived a few moments too late. They could only join Isadora's pupils, who, having never seen a plane leave the ground before, looked rather dispirited, pale, and unusually quiet, with raised heads and wide-opened eyes, as the plane became a small black speck on the sparkling blue horizon.

Thus Isadora had taken a step against which she had been warned over and over again. She did not realize, she had been told, the problem of uprooting a peasant from his soil, and the risk and responsibility of such an adventure. But Isadora had turned a deaf ear to all such misgivings. Essenin, she said, was a sick man who needed the care of a specialist, perhaps even medical treatment at one of the spas in Germany. Isadora meant a cure for his drinking. As a poet, moreover, he should not be denied an opportunity to broaden his knowledge of the world. She did not have a moment's hesitation in what she was undertaking, for she expected to lead Sergei by the hand, so to speak, as she would one of her pupils.

What Isadora never understood was that her problem child had his own ideas about this trip. First of all he was not going "to be taken" by Isadora or anyone else, anywhere, at any time. If he was to go abroad it was because *he*, Sergei Essenin, wished to do so for his own reasons, and it was for him, and no one else, to decide how long he intended to be absent from Russia. In fact, he wrote to the friends whom he had asked to look after his sister, that he would be back in two months, not later than the end of July; obviously, at that time he did not include in his plans a journey with Isadora to the United States.

Also, he resented the feeling provoked by the imagists, who warned him that once he was out of Russia, he would be reduced to an insignificant pawn, among Isadora's other admirers. He knew that Mariengoff was leading the intrigues against his relationship with Isadora, as Mariengoff, himself a poet and recently married, had been against all of Sergei's marriages. "He made me leave Zinaida Reich," Sergei said with a touch of regret in his voice. But this time Mariengoff's and the imagists' predictions touched the most vulnerable spot in Essenin's character—his ego. If anyone thought that he would play second fiddle to Isadora, they would have a great surprise coming to them. Such were his reflections as he contemplated his sojourn in Western Europe.

He was well briefed by the imagists about a "Home of the Arts," a sort of literary club in Berlin, which had its premises at the Café Leon, and which was frequented by those Russian intellectuals abroad who were sympathetic toward Soviet Russia. They even published their own newspaper, *On the Eve*, and, having at least one friend among these men in Berlin, Alexander Koussikov, a former imagist, Sergei wrote to him, instructing him to make the necessary arrangements for an "Essenin evening" at the "Home of the Arts," "Put announcements in the newspapers in both German and Russian about the forthcoming event," he wrote in his two-line letter to Koussikov.

In the first few words Isadora had spoken to the reporters after she and Sergei had settled down at the Hotel Adlon, she was supposed to have said: "I love the Russian people, but it is very comforting to return to a place where one can have warm water, napkins, and heat. Not that the Russian people believe in giving up luxuries! On the contrary, but they believe in luxuries for all, and, if there is not enough to go around, then everyone must have a little less."

While Isadora was enjoying her return to Western comforts—fresh sheets, hot water, breakfast in bed, and prompt hotel service—Essenin was on his way to the "Home of the Arts." It was to be his debut among the West European intellectuals, and he had his own idea of how to present himself at this event. Contrary to his usual habit of never informing anyone about his intentions or where-abouts, this time he told Isadora where he was going and asked her to join him there within an hour or so. Then, dressed in his old wornout Moscow business suit and his white canvas tennis shoes, he adopted the air of a shy and extremely modest young man as he entered the hall. With as much dignity as he could muster, he ac-knowledged the audience's welcoming applause and began to read his poems. They were enthusiastically received, but this was only the first part of his planned performance. No sooner had he sat down than the waiter told him that Isadora had arrived. He went out to meet her and then, no longer with a serious mien but happily smiling, led her on his arm into the hall. Once the enthusiastic wel-come for Isadora had subsided, she proposed that everyone in the hall sing the *Internationale* in Essenin's honor. However, the chorus who joined Isadora and Essenin's singing was soon drowned out by boos and shouts of "Down with them!" from a group of White Russians who happened to be in the café. This only spurred Sergei to his final act: he jumped on a chair to shout, "With your silly booing you won't stop us from singing," and later he read his poems again, and was enthusiastically acclaimed once more.

Over a year later, upon his return to Moscow, Essenin said to his friends: "Did I raise hell there because I was drunk? Not at all. Was it so bad? Not at all. I raised hell for our Revolution!" For the Essenin-Isadora appearances practically became a standard performance, with colorful variations, during their journey—especially in the United States. And yet, the Soviet Government had neither suggested nor authorized a propaganda mission. In fact, it caused much embarrassment to the Soviets, and especially to Lunacharsky, who had entrusted Essenin to Isadora to keep him "within the limits of the strictest decorum."

Contrary to many so-called authoritative statements, Essenin was not the first Soviet citizen who had been allowed to travel abroad, and who had obtained his permission on business grounds through Lunacharsky's good offices. There were many such artists, actors, and musicians, who were well known in Russia, Italy, France, and Germany. Not all of them had left Russia with the intention of returning, but, while often referred to as Bolsheviks, they nevertheless attended to their own business of exhibiting their art, and thus caused neither embarrassment nor trouble for the Soviet Government.

Sergei Prokofiev was a good example of such a case. With Lunacharsky's personal help, he left Russia as early as 1918 and went to the United States where, although at first even his compositions were stigmatized, he eventually won a public for his art. Of course Essenin must have realized that the products of his own art, poetry, even if translated, could not reach the public at large as music can. Essenin was not Alexander Pushkin, the author of "To the Slanderers of Russia," or Alexander Blok, the author of "The Scythians." His lyrical poetry had nothing in it that was revolutionary in the simple political sense. And yet, if Lunacharsky thought that, for his personal protection, Essenin needed to be Isadora Duncan's husband, Sergei himself thought that for his personal prestige he ought to claim to be the representative of Soviet Russia. And, since it would not do to whisper this message, it had to be proclaimed, and as loudly as possible.

Hence his attitude was belligerent from the first day of their arrival in Germany—too soon for anyone to acquaint himself with an entirely different race, its mode of life, its general point of view. Essenin was belligerent not only toward Germany, of which he had so far had merely a glimpse, but toward the whole of Western Europe. "Let us show them our big, fat Russian backside," he liked to say.

Proud as he was at being taken as a representative of the Russian proletariat, of the Russian peasant, he also wanted to show that the *muzhiks* were just as good as any gentleman in Europe. Soon after his first appearance at the "Home of the Arts," a second evening in his honor was organized in the Hall of the Society of Dentists. This time he came carrying a cane, dressed in evening dress, top hat, and a black opera cape with a white silk lining. He behaved with extreme punctilio, although a smirk of utter disdain toward everybody and everything in the festive hall seldom left his lips.

He had managed to sell a collection of his poems to a publisher, and, armed with Isadora's generous carte blanche, he equipped himself with a large and elegant wardrobe, which he could not possibly wear out in a lifetime. He bought everything that attracted his eye in the way of lotions, and he bathed, shampooed his hair, and perfumed himself so much that Isadora was supposed to have remarked: "He is such a child. He had never had these things in his life. I couldn't bear to chide him for it."

But he knew better than to appear in such a disguise when Isadora and he were invited for lunch to meet Gorki and Alexei Tolstoy, the poet (no relation to Leo Tolstoy), who were living in Berlin at that time. Isadora was exceptionally happy to have Essenin meet Gorki, who as a writer and as Lenin's friend was held in the highest esteem in Russia, but she herself would have done better by staying away from that meeting, for Gorki did not approve of her relationship with Essenin.

"Essenin was accomplished by Koussikov," Gorki wrote later, describing this meeting. " 'Also a poet,' Essenin said quietly, in a hoarse voice. Next to Essenin, Koussikov, a rather fresh fellow, seemed to be superfluous. He was armed with a guitar, that instrument beloved of barbers. Most probably he could not play it."

During their lunch, Isadora used a regular water glass for her vodka instead of the customary small jigger, and repeatedly clinked glasses with Gorki, loudly announcing in her faulty Russian: "To the Russian Revolution! *Écoutez*, Gorki! I will dance *seulement* for the Russian Revolution. *C'est beau*, the Russian Revolution!"

Clinking glasses with her, Gorki looked solemn. "This lady praises the Revolution in the same way a theatre lover praises the successful premiere of a play. She should not do it." As a rule, Russians are repelled by the sight of a woman drinking hard liquor. Gorki later wrote:

This famous woman, glorified by thousands of European aesthetes, subtle connoiseurs of plastic art, sitting next to the small, boyish, wonderful Ryazan poet, was the perfect personification of what he did not need. There is no prejudice here, something that I have invented now. No, I am speaking of my impression of that grievous day when, looking at that woman, I thought: how could she feel the meaning of such sighs of the poet as: 'It would be nice, smiling at the haystack, / To munch hay with the snout of the moon. . . .'"

While Gorki should be given credit for correctly appraising Isadora's incapacity for understanding Sergei's works, his fantasy, and the whole gamut of his thoughts, one also has to remember that Gorki simply did not like Isadora.

I saw Duncan on the stage a few years before that meeting, when they used to write of her as a miracle, one journalist declaring quite astonishingly: "Her exquisite body burns us by its blaze of flame." But I don't like and I don't appreciate dancing that is an expression of intellect. . . . At Tolstoy's dinner she also danced, having first eaten and drunk vodka. Her dance seemed to me to depict the struggle between the weight of Duncan's age and the constraint of her body, spoilt by fame and love. These words are certainly not meant to be offensive to a woman. They merely speak of the curse of old age. . . .

Gorki was speaking of a dance that Isadora liked to do, not on the stage, but whenever given an opportunity in a private gathering among her friends. I have seen it myself. With a gramophone record of an Argentine tango as an accompaniment, she would depict an apache struggling with his mistress, a dance that had erotic elements and that concluded with the murder by strangulation of the mistress. I was often astonished at Isadora's amazing lack of tact in this respect, her inappropriate choice of occasion, and her obliviousness to the effect she produced.

"While she danced [Gorki wrote in the same article], Essenin sąt at the table and drank wine, looking at her out of the corner of his eye and knitting his brows. It was perhaps at that very moment that he put those words of compassion into his verse:

> 'They loved you too well,
> They soiled you all over . . .'

"Later Duncan, exhausted, knelt down and gazed at the poet's face with a languid smile. Essenin put his hand on her shoulder, but turned away abruptly. Again I cannot help thinking that at that moment the cruel and pitifully desperate lines must have flashed through his mind:

> '*Why do you look with blue gushing?*
> *Or do you want me to smash your mug?*
> *. . . My dear, I weep*
> *Forgive . . . forgive. . . !'* "

Such a scene, accurately described by Gorki, unfortunately was not an isolated occurrence, but had happened too frequently not to have profoundly influenced Essenin's attitude toward Isadora; instead of feeling proud at being Isadora's husband, he was forced to feel embarrassed by any intimate connection with her. No matter what reasons Isadora might give herself for his attitude, she could not possibly miss the obvious, painful truth about their relationship, but apparently she was willing to pay the price.

Gorki was very impressed with Essenin now that he met him again, seven years after Essenin had come from his village to St. Petersburg for the first time.

Of the curly-headed, doll-like boy, only the very bright eyes remained, and even they seemed to have been burnt out by some too-bright sun. Their troubled gaze often changed its expression as it slid over people's faces, sometimes challenging and disdainful, and, all of a sudden, diffident, embarrassed, and distrustful.

I had the feeling that his attitude towards people was, on the whole, unfriendly. One could see at once that he was a drinking man. There were bags under his bloodshot eyes, and the skin on his face and neck was grey, faded, as though he never went out of doors and slept badly. His hands, too, were restless and limp at the wrists, like the hands of a drummer. Besides, he looked troubled and absent-minded, like a man who had forgotten something very important and could not even remember that he had forgotten. . . .

At Tolstoy's, Essenin was asked to recite his poetry. Gorki wrote:

I felt that his reciting was overwhelming, and it was difficult to listen to him without tears. . . . I wouldn't call it artistic—such epithets don't mean much anyway when it comes to reciting poetry.

His voice sounded hoarse, at times strident. It was hard to believe that such a little man could possess such enormous power of feeling, such perfect expressiveness.

As he recited his poems he became so white that even his ears took on a grayish color. He was waving his arms but not according to the rhythm of the verse, and it seemed that this was how it should have been—the weight of the heavy words varied capriciously. It seemed as if he were throwing them—some under his own feet, others somewhere very far away, and still others into the face of a man unknown to him. Actually, his hoarse voice, nervous gestures, burning eyes—everything was as it should have been in the atmosphere in which he found himself at that hour.

He thrilled me so much that a lump rose to my throat and I felt like sobbing. I remember I just could not say anything nice to him. Besides, I don't think he needed my words of praise. I asked him to read his poem about the dog whose seven puppies were taken away and thrown into the river. "If," I added, "you're not too tired."

"Poems do not tire me," he said, and asked mistrustfully, "Do you like my poem about the dog?"

I told him that, in my opinion, he was the first poet in Russian literature to write about animals with such sincere love and with such skill.

"Yes, I love animals very much," Essenin said quietly and thoughtfully.

I asked him if he knew Paul Claudel's *Paradise of Animals*. He did not reply, felt his head with both hands, and began to read *The Song of a Dog*. When he uttered the last line—"The dog's eyes rolled like golden stars onto the snow"—his eyes, too, filled with tears.

After this poem, one involuntarily thought that Sergei Essenin was not so much a human being as a medium, created by nature entirely for poetry, for an expression of the inexhaustible sadness of the fields, love for everything living, and mercy, which more than anything else is deserved by man. And one felt even more the unnecessary presence of Koussikov with his guitar, Duncan with her dancing, and the whole tiresome city of Berlin, of everything that surrounded this talented Russian poet.

Suddenly he became lonely. He stroked Duncan as he must have stroked the girls in his village, slapping her on her back, and then he suggested: "Let's go somewhere, where there is noise."

This meeting with Gorki was the most important of all during his travels abroad, and Essenin did not miss a single one of Gorki's words of approval or disapproval. He cherished what Gorki thought of him as a poet and as a human being. Gorki's feelings about him were to remain in his subconscious.

Nor could Isadora have missed the significance of Gorki's reaction to Sergei and to his poems, for she knew that Gorki's judgment would influence Sergei far more than that of Mariengoff or his imagist friends. In vain she tried to distract him by offering him sightseeing tours of Berlin, even taking him to see the site of her former school in Grünewald. He remained bored, either brooding or carousing with a group of new Russian friends he had managed to acquire in various cafés—gatherings that inevitably ended in brawls and scandals. But Essenin soon learned one German word, *Polizei*, which had a magic effect on him. On hearing it, he would immediately sober up and become as meek as a lamb.

Isadora told me that since in Russia they used to distract him from acting violent by asking him to sing one of his favorite songs, and that in Germany the word "police" was even more effective, she herself tried a device of her own invention. Once, when she simply could not stop him from breaking everything in their room at the hotel, she suddenly pretended to be drunk and began imitating him and smashing glassware and everything else close to hand. Seeing this, Essenin became perfectly petrified, fell on his knees before her and begged her to stop. "Sidora, Sidora," he murmured. He wanted to call a doctor. "For a while the trick worked," Isadora said with apparent satisfaction.

Now, for the first time, Isadora told me, she began to sense the wisdom in the warnings she had been given against taking him on this journey. For the first time, they were actually living together —it was no longer the same as at her home in Prechistenka Street, where she could call for help—and she was left on her own to cope with the irrational behavior of her husband. She also realized that such a situation would jeopardize the whole project of her tour and the responsibility of taking her school with her. Therefore, instead of trying to deal with the constant chore of restraining Essenin in Berlin—his disgust with the Russian refugee intellectuals and his homesickness were driving him to drinking, so he claimed—Isadora forced him to leave the city with her and go to Wiesbaden, where she hoped medical treatment would restore his equilibrium. And, indeed, his letter to Ilya Schneider shows that Isadora's efforts had at least initial success.

... I am sorry not to have written you for so long. The Berlin atmosphere has played havoc with me. At present, because of my shattered nerves, I can barely drag my feet. I am taking a cure in Wiesbaden. I have given up drinking and begun to work.

If Isadora had not been so scatterbrained and had let me sit down quietly somewhere, I would have earned a lot of money. So far, I have received over one hundred thousand marks and expect another four hundred. But Isadora's affairs are in a terrible state. In Berlin, her attorney has sold her house and paid her only ninety thousand marks. The same thing might well happen in Paris. Her property, her library, and her furniture have been plundered, and her money in the bank has been impounded. She has just sent off to Paris one of her close friends. The famous Paul-Boncour* not only did not help her in any way, but has refused his signature for her visa to Paris. Such are her affairs. . . . But, as if nothing had happened, she gallops by car to Lubeck, or to Leipzig, or to Frankfort, or to Weimar. And I follow her with tacit obedience, for, if I ever disagree she becomes hysterical.

Germany? We'll talk about it later, when we meet, but the true life is not here, but in our country. Here, actually, the sad slow decline about which Spengler** speaks is taking place. Let us be Asiatics. Let us smell bad; we may scratch our backsides in public for every one to see, but we don't stink of putrefaction as they do. Here there can be no revolution of any kind. Everything has reached a dead end, and only an invasion by barbarians like ourselves can save and reform them.

An invasion of Europe is needed. . . .

However, in this letter serious thoughts are not becoming to me.

He devoted the second part of his letter to giving instructions to Schneider about his sister Katya, his main concern. He included a check for her and again, as he did before leaving Russia, asked

* Paul-Boncour was a prominent lawyer, and a member of the Chambre des Députés (1906). He was an old friend of Isadora and Paris Singer.
** Oswald Spengler (1880–1936), German philosopher, author of *The Decline of the West*.

his friends to look after her. He ended his letter by saying that he could tell Schneider a great deal about "their Berlin friends," (he ironically referred to the Russian émigrés) especially about their denunciation of him to the French police to prevent his getting permission for entry into France. "But of all this, some other time," he remarked. "Right now I had better take care of my nerves."

As soon as Essenin began to feel better, Isadora took him to visit the old centers of German culture. She noticed, she recalled later, with what veneration he would walk among the graves of famous poets, that in Weimar he spoke almost in a whisper, and how long he bent over the last page written by Goethe and left on his writing desk. Still, despite everything Isadora tried to show him of interest among the art treasures, in museums, galleries, libraries, and architecture, Essenin always came away comparing them to Russian accomplishments, which in his opinion remained superior to everything he saw about him. In a letter to a friend in Moscow, he wrote:

> . . . What do you expect me to say about the terrible reign of this middle-class morality, which borders on utter idiocy. There is nothing here besides the fox-trot; here they gobble and drink, and then again fox-trot. So far I haven't met a single real human being. Mr. Dollar is very much in vogue; as for the arts, they don't give a damn —for them a music hall is the highest expression of it. . . . Everything here is well-ironed out, the birds sit where they are allowed to sit, the pigs snort where and when they are scheduled to snort, so . . . how can we come with our indecent poetry? This would be really as bad manners as communism. Sometimes I feel I should send the whole thing to the devil and go back home. Let us be beggars, let us have famine, cold, and cannibalism, but at least we have a soul, which here, because of its utter uselessness, is rented to Smerdiakovs.

And indeed, Isadora told me that, in order not to have him desert her, she had to use all her powers of persuasion and promise to overcome the difficulties in the way of their leaving Germany. Usually, Isadora did not have any trouble in obtaining visas for any country, but now as the wife of a Soviet citizen, carrying a "red passport," and with the disturbing newspaper reports of his behavior, a number of foreign diplomatic representatives were reluctant to grant them a visa. Finally, at the end of July 1922, they wrote to Maxim Litvinov:

Dear comrade Litvinov, would you be so kind as to help us get out of Germany to proceed to the Hague? I promise to behave correctly and not sing the "Internationale" in public.

The letter was signed by both of them, "Respectfully yours, S. Essenin. Isadora Duncan."

Finally, by a roundabout way of short visits to Ostend and Brussels, thanks to Cécile Sorel's help at the Ministry of Interior in France, and a stern warning against any political activities, which would be followed by police surveillance, Isadora and Essenin arrived in Paris in the first days of August 1922.

Chapter XXXIV

"If you were to see me now, you would probably not believe your own eyes," Essenin wrote to Schneider, shortly before he and Isadora arrived in Paris. "It will soon be a month since I stopped drinking. I have taken the pledge not to drink till October."

Whether because Essenin knew that in Paris he was under police surveillance, or because he was afraid of a recurrence of the painful attacks of neuritis and neurasthenia caused by excessive drinking, his exceptionally good behavior during the following two months could have been used as evidence against the "exaggerated stories about his drinking." Isadora was so pleased with the change in Sergei that she once again wholeheartedly turned her interest to her art. While in Brussels, on their way to Paris, she had been invited to give ten performances at the Trocadero with her Moscow school. She telegraphed to Schneider to get the Soviet Government's permission for the children to join her in Paris, and Essenin, in his letters to Schneider, urged him to speed the matter along: "Of course you will create a sensation with the school. We are awaiting your arrival with impatience. I, in particular, am waiting for it, for Isadora doesn't understand a damn in practical matters, and it is painful for me to watch this pack of bandits that surrounds her. When you arrive, the air will be cleared. Come! Come!"

Schneider managed to secure Lunacharsky's approval, but his colleagues in the government did not support his decision. Instead of securing permission to have her school go to Paris, Isadora's request jeopardized her future plans because there were no funds for such an expedition, which could hardly have been considered as a part of Soviet propaganda. Isadora's request to have the twenty-five girls sent to Paris was rejected. However, since Sol Hurok offered to pay the expenses of sending the school on a tour of the United States, Isadora still hoped to have them rejoin her in New York. But, according to Hurok, the Soviet Government suddenly declined to give permission for the children to leave the country. "Some of them were only eleven and twelve years old—too young, said Moscow with finality."

"Storms, wind, or snow will never stop me from reaching America," Isadora cabled Hurok, and thereafter she spent the summer with Sergei, taking trips for pleasure and for his "education in the Western World."

In her autobiography *This Is My Affair*, published ten years after Isadora's death, Lola Kinel gives a glimpse of those seemingly happy months in the Isadora-Essenin relationship. While in Wiesbaden, Isadora engaged the twenty-three-year-old Miss Kinel as her secretary. Miss Kinel, who knew both Russian and English, could be useful as a translator for Isadora and Essenin, and also could be a companion to Essenin, who now no longer had his Russian friends. Miss Kinel is to be congratulated in that she was one of the few who not only understood the Duncan-Essenin conversations, but actually understood them as people. She traveled with them to Brussels and Paris, but it is her description of their sojourn at the Lido in Venice that answers the puzzling question of how much true communication there was between Isadora and Sergei, since Isadora still knew only a few words in Russian, and Essenin knew no other language. And yet, with Miss Kinel's help, they managed to have serious discussions on art, discussions which, unfortunately, Essenin invariably turned from abstract to personal.

Always jealous of Isadora's popularity, he would try to assert the superiority of literature over the dance by saying to Isadora that the dance ceases to exist when the dance is ended, while poetry —and he meant, of course, his own—would live forever. "But I bring people 'Beauty,' and 'Beauty' lives forever," Isadora would reply. "Akh, Duncan, Duncan," Essenin would shake his head, as if any further argument was useless.

Kinel also speaks of Essenin's jealousy, provoked by Isadora's admirers. Not quite appeased by Isadora's assurances that some of them were homosexuals, Essenin peeped into their rooms in the hotel where they were staying and, after discovering that the room, usually occupied by two men, had only one bed, was ready to believe Isadora.

On her part, Isadora in her own unreasonable jealousy insisted on never leaving Essenin alone because she believed he was capable of getting drunk, committing suicide, or running away. She refused to understand that Essenin, known at the Lido as "the Russian poet in the white silk pyjamas," could neither escape from the island nor get drunk because he had no money and knew not a word of Italian. Nor could Isadora understand his craving for being alone once in a while, since he was reduced to the constant company of three women, Isadora, Miss Kinel, and Jeanne, Isadora's maid, all of them keeping a watchful eye on every move he made.

Fortunately, all the ensuing scenes usually ended in happy reconciliations.

They arrived in New York in the first days of October 1922.

A great deal has been said and written about this American trip; it has been endlessly discussed by eyewitnesses and others who claim to have been well informed—but personally, analyzing Mr. Hurok's detailed account of Isadora's performances and the Essenin-Isadora sojourn in the United States, I can only regard the whole episode as a slapstick comedy. I must, however, hasten to add that this was not Mr. Hurok's point of view when he wrote about it over twenty years later, and certainly not when, as Isadora's manager, he was involved in what seemed to him "dramatic events." Nor was my opinion shared at that time by the American authorities and the general public.

"This, remember, was 1922," Mr. Hurok wrote. "The wave of reaction to the war, to Wilson, to liberalism, was rolling up in a fearful tide. It was the year when red was the color of evil, and to call a man Bolshevik was to damn his eternal soul, as well as to send his earthly body to jail. Suspicion and mistrust of the Soviet Union are still a force to be reckoned with in this country in 1946. In 1922, it was not suspicion but sheer, unreasoning terror; it was not mistrust but the bitterest hatred. Into the arms of this America came Isadora, fresh from Moscow with her *Bolshevik* husband, smiling, friendly, confiding."

The term "Bolshevik" was then synonymous with "communist," and thus should have been applied to a person belonging to the Communist party, an affiliation that bestowed some privileges but also made the party member an instrument of any and all policies adopted by the party. Although the Communist party had the noble aim of eventually creating heaven on earth, the means adopted to secure this happy result could require of its members a variety of services regarded by the non-communist world as highly dishonorable and even criminal—propaganda, spying, denunciation, and even kidnapping and assassination. It should be clear that at no time in her life was Isadora a Bolshevik—a communist—nor was Essenin, whose highly individual nature prevented him from conforming with anything prescribed by anybody.

But the aureole was too good not to be used by Isadora and Essenin on their journey, especially in the United States, where it was to produce an effect entirely out of proportion to any underlying reality. I don't believe that a more operetta-like script could have been concocted than that followed by Isadora and Essenin from the moment of their arrival to their departure from the country. It is equally obvious that the manufactured sensation played an important, and at times even a predominant, role in the tour, affording the best possible publicity for her appearance—if not from Isadora's viewpoint, then at least from that of her management.

After the *S.S. Paris* had slowly passed the Statue of Liberty, the symbol of the United States, as Isadora explained to Sergei, and finally docked in New York harbor, a swarm of reporters began to question Isadora and Sergei, the latter, of course, not understanding a word. Instead, he handed out an already prepared statement, saying that he and Isadora were not politicians, that they worked only in the field of art, and closing on a note of sentiment: "We believe that the soul of Russia and the soul of America are about to understand each other." Probably the message was of Isadora's composition.

The reporters were followed by the immigration authorities, who, not being concerned with the state of Russian and American souls, invited them to Ellis Island. First of all, they had to ascertain whether Isadora and her husband carried with them any material pertaining to the "overthrow of the American Government," or any form of Communist propaganda. Since such things could have been concealed in their luggage, every piece of it, including all the printed material, and Essenin's books and manuscripts, as well as musical scores, were minutely inspected and set aside for further examination. Even Hurok, who tried to be helpful, did not escape the suspicious eyes of the defenders of liberty. He was stripped naked to make sure that he was not concealing dangerous propaganda in the form of a secret message from the Soviet Government that had already been passed to him by Isadora or Essenin.

Finally, on the following day, after having been investigated by a Board of Review, and subjected to an interrogation that included utterly irrelevant questions such as, "What do you look like when you dance?"—to which Isadora naturally answered that she had never seen herself dance—they were released.

Later, upon his return to Russia, in an article entitled "An Iron Mirgorod,"* Essenin gave his impressions of his visit to the United States, and in a few lines referred to the experience on Ellis Island: "As soon as we were seated on the hard benches, a heavily built man with a round head, on which a fringe of hair was brushed upwards, came in carrying documents. 'Look,' I thought, 'this is Mirgorod. Now any minute a pig will run in, grab a paper from the table—and we are going to be saved.' "

On Ellis Island, however, Essenin could not communicate his amusement to Isadora, for at this moment Isadora and Essenin, who stood silently by, were "found innocent, not guilty," as Isadora said. And so she and Essenin were allowed to leave "the Island of Tears," as Ellis Island is known in Russia.

As if taking a leaf from the book of her "little brother Raymond," who would have made the most of such an opportunity for publicity, Isadora, dressed in her handsome Paris suit with wide yellow and orange stripes, and an orange blouse, over which she wore a cape, waved away all taxicabs. Leading an ever-increasing throng of the curious, she walked in her soft red Russian boots all the way from the Battery up Broadway, Fifth Avenue, and then Park Avenue to her suite at the Waldorf-Astoria. Panting, her

* Gogol's masterpiece *The Inspector General* is placed in Mirgorod, a town which has ever since symbolized to the Russian people bureaucracy, provincialism, and all forms of corruption.

dangerous husband could barely keep up with her, as he trotted along in this unusual parade.

Hurok's prior announcement of Isadora's appearance at Carnegie Hall "had fallen curiously dead—the box office men at Carnegie Hall had little to do, but now, thanks to the United States Government and the New York newspapers, three performances were sold out within the next twenty-four hours."

Essenin had to sign a written statement that he would not sing the *Internationale* during their stay in the United States. Isadora, although she had promised Hurok to leave speeches to the politicians and to occupy herself only with her dancing, still could not refrain from addressing her public after each performance.

In judging her tour in the United States, and accepting as natural the tribute paid her as a great artist, one cannot, however, miss the utter monotony of her speeches to her audiences, the amazing reaction of the public and the local authorities, and eventually that of the government itself.

In New York, after asking America to give her a school, she ended her speech on a rather mild note with an appeal for good will toward Soviet Russia. "America has all that Russia has not!" she announced. "Russia has things that America has not. Why will America not reach out a hand to Russia, as I have given my hand?"

But the two scheduled performances in Boston, following her three appearances in New York, signaled the eventual wrecking of Isadora's tour in the United States. Her choice of programs and her performances never drew anything but respect and enthusiasm for her art, but her speeches to her audiences regularly caused riots and these were reported in an exaggerated manner by the press.

Although Isadora once more promised Hurok to refrain from making speeches and he, in turn, had reassured the local authorities, in Boston Isadora made one of her most inflammatory—even abusive —speeches.

From the stage of Symphony Hall, pointing at the replicas of Greek statues all around, she cried, "Those are not Greek gods—they are false and you are as false as these plaster statues. . . . You once were wild here! Don't let them tame you." And she proceeded to give the speech on her favorite subject, which, with slight variations, she repeated at every opportunity. "If my art is symbolic of any one thing, it is symbolic of the freedom of woman and her emancipation from the hidebound conventions that are the warp and woof of New England puritanism. To expose one's body is art; conceal-ment is vulgar. When I dance, my object is to inspire reverence; not to suggest anything vulgar. I don't appeal to the lower instincts of mankind as your half-clad chorus girls do. I would rather dance completely nude than strut in half-clothed suggestiveness as many women do today on the streets of America. Nudity is truth, it is beauty, it is art. Therefore, it can never be vulgar; it can never be immoral. . . ."

And waving her red silk scarf above her head, she cried: "This is red! So am I! It is the color of life and vigor. . . . You don't know what beauty is!"

"And then she tore her tunic down to bare one of her breasts and cried out, 'This—this is beauty!' " according to a newspaper report which was probably not an exaggeration, unlike the more sensational assertions that she stripped herself naked. The prim and proper Bostonians hurriedly left the hall, but the Harvard University students cheered, and the newspapers carried the headlines:

RED DANCER SHOCKS BOSTON
ISADORA'S SPEECH DRIVES MANY FROM BOSTON HALL
DUNCAN IN FLAMING SCARF SAYS SHE'S RED.

To add to an atmosphere already overcharged with excitement and animosity, Essenin insisted on participating in the drama gen-erated by Isadora. Ever since their arrival in the Unted States, he had realized that, despite Isadora's efforts to focus public attention upon her genius husband, he was being ignored. In New York, there was nothing resembling a "Home of the Arts," such as he had found in Berlin, where he could recite his poetry and talk to in-tellectual refugees curious about Soviet cultural affairs. In fact he was reduced to the company of the two Russian men whom Isadora had brought along with them—one as her secretary, and the other expressly to keep Sergei company. Thus his activities were cut down to one continuous shopping spree, buying articles en masse to take back to Russia.

But he craved attention. Since Isadora's performances were his only opportunities, he certainly tried to make the most of them. In Symphony Hall, he appeared in his loge dressed in a colorful Caucasian costume, the Georgian national dress which he, a Russian, was not entitled to wear unless it were meant as a masquerade. He wore a black coat with cartridge loops on either breast, a sort of Cossack's uniform, a large silver dagger dangling from his belt, high soft black boots, and a large fur hat. He was a sight no one in the hall could have missed, but having been caught up in the general hubbub in the hall created by Isadora's speech, he rushed backstage where, after opening the window, he waved some kind of red material (later described as a red flag) and shouted in Russian something that was later interpreted as equivalent to "Long live Bolshevism!"

His childish behavior allowed the newspapers to add to their already exaggerated reports, overlooking the fact that even if Sergei's window act had managed to catch the attention of a few passing Bostonians, they could not have understood a word he said.

Nevertheless, the reports of these theatrical shenanigans resulted in the issuing of an order by James Curley, the mayor of Boston, to deny Isadora a license to appear again in Boston. "In view of the duty the city owes to decent elements, I beg to say that this suspension after the recent disgraceful performance by the dancer, will continue as long as I am Mayor."

The Boston incident set the tenor of the rest of Isadora's tour— she danced to sold-out houses and made similar inciting speeches to excited audiences in Chicago, Milwaukee, and Indianapolis, each time provoking similar reactions from the mayors of these cities: "That Bolshevik hussy doesn't wear enough clothes to pad a crutch," Billy Sunday cried from his pulpit. "I'd like to be Secretary of Labor for fifteen minutes, I'd send her back to Russia and her Gorki. . . ." And the Honorable Lew Shanks, Mayor of Indianapolis, did not miss the chance to give his statement to the press, as Macdougall reports:

Isadora ain't foolin' me any. She talks about art. Huh! I've seen a lot of these twisters and I know as much about art as any man in America, but I never went to see these dancers for art's sake. No, sir, I'll bet that ninety percent of men who go to see those so-called classical dancers just say they think it's artistic to fool their wives. . . . No, sir, these nude dancers don't get by me. If she goes pulling off her clothes and throwin' them in the air, as she is said to have done in Boston, there's going to be somebody getting a ride in the wagon.

((329))

Isadora continued her tour wherever her performances had not yet been canceled: Kansas City, St. Louis, Memphis, Cleveland, Baltimore, and Philadelphia. She was not of a fiber that would crumple under intimidation or the criticism of illiterate mayors; belligerence only spurred her on to express her contempt for those who insisted on defaming her art, and on treating her as a mere instrument of Soviet propaganda.

"Three Departments, the Department of Justice, of Labor, and the State Department have begun a court inquiry to find out the relationship of Isadora Duncan to the Soviet Government," was a newspaper report that made Lunacharsky laugh, but which Isadora could not brush off as inconsequential because it was further reported that the departments in question were collecting evidence about "the Bolshevik propaganda being carried on by the well-known dancer Isadora Duncan . . . red propaganda that would lead her to Ellis Island for deportation to Russia."

Still, even such a threat was less troublesome than her personal problem—her husband. The American way of life was not only not suited to Essenin's character, but its effect was absolutely demoralizing. He could not manage to do any work. He could spend just so much time on shopping. There were no cafés where he might spend hours talking to friends—if he had succeeded in finding any, which he had not. Since Isadora's entourage was the only milieu left to him, it was for that very reason the only one where he could give vent to his abundant energy. But as much as Isadora sincerely desired to focus all possible attention on her husband, she could not provide her poet with an audience that could understand his poetry, or join him in a discussion of the arts, or simply entertain him with pleasant conversation. Isadora told me that he sensed her efforts to put him forward, and saw through the benevolent expressions of her friends, which were meant more to please Isadora than to show an interest in Sergei. His resentment of his position as second fiddle incited him against Isadora. Curiously enough, Isadora tried to explain to me that, as much as he was proud of her public performances, he was extremely irritated by her dancing for an intimate circle of friends, loudly expressing in vulgar Russian his criticism and disapproval, something that led to frequent fights with other persons who tried to subdue his outbursts of temper.

If by some ill chance he was drunk on bad prohibition liquor, then his violence knew no limits—he would smash everything in the apartment and behave as if he were ready to hurt everybody, including Isadora. Isadora would have lost her friends if Mary Desti, ever helpful, had not set everybody's mind at rest by diagnosing Essenin's behavior as the effects of epilepsy, an illness from which, she knew, all Russians suffered.

Wearied by constant persecution in the press, threats from the authorities about her alleged propaganda mission, and suffering a veritable hell in her life with her husband, she gave two final performances at Carnegie Hall, on January 13 and 15, 1923, before sailing back to Europe.

"I really ought not to say a word to you newspapermen," Isadora is reported to have told the reporters who came to see her off. "You have succeeded in ruining my tour, when I hoped so much to earn enough money to take back to the starving children in Moscow. . . . Your papers have devoted whole columns to reprinting details about my personal life during my tour: what I ate, what I drank, whom I associated with, but never a word about my art. . . . If I had come to this country as a great financier to borrow money, I would have been given a great reception, but as I came as a recognized artist, I was sent to Ellis Island as a dangerous revolutionist. I am not an anarchist or a Bolshevik. My husband and I are revolutionists. All geniuses worthy of the name are. Every artist has to be one to make a mark in the world today. . . . Materialism is the curse of America. This is the last time you will ever see me in America again. I would rather live in Russia on black bread and vodka than here in the best hotels. You know nothing of Food, of Love, of Art. . . . So good-bye, America! I shall never see you again."

Isadora's language was naïve, but the sentiments they expressed were just—and tragic. Who were the losers, as a result of the treatment accorded Isadora on her last tour of the United States? Was it really necessary to stage so absurd, ignominious, and cowardly a reception by the representatives of one of the most powerful countries in the world of one of their own greatest artists? Can it be believed that a dancer's speeches, appealing for the foundation of a school—even if accompanied by criticisms of Philistinism and puritanism—could be set down as Bolshevik propaganda, provoking inane statements from mayors and other public officials? Can it be

believed that a boy in his twenties brandishing some sort of red rag
(for where on the spur of the moment could he find a red flag in
Boston's Symphony Hall?), and allegedly blabbering about Bolshevism in a language no one could understand, could set three departments of the United States Government shaking in their boots?
Does it seem reasonable that the fate of the American way of life,
of popular sovereignty, and free institutions was put in jeopardy
by Isadora's speeches and Essenin's antics? Or was it that, rather
than behave with dignity and thus take the wind out of Isadora's
and Essenin's efforts at incitement, journalists and officials, hungry
themselves for sensation, preferred to join the cast of this slapstick
comedy?

Shortly before her death, at the time when Isadora was still
engaged upon her memoirs, I was present at a dinner party celebrating in advance the forthcoming publication of her book. One
of the guests, half seriously and half in jest, offered her a short trip
to the United States. "They would love to see you when your book
comes out. And you know, you love America." "Yes, I do," Isadora
said without a moment's hesitation. "But . . ." and she lowered her
head. Then she spoke again, in a voice that shook a little, and said,
"I am not wanted there." Everyone present saw her tears.

It is embarrassing, it seems to me, that we must give credit to
Golos, a quite worthless New York Russian newspaper of the period,
for a statement published soon after Isadora's death:

> The time will come when freedom-loving Americans will throw the
> Statue of Liberty, that symbol of so-called freedom, into the sea, and
> raise in its place a statue of Isadora Duncan, who was the personifica-
> tion of true freedom and who called for the brotherhood of nations.

Chapter XXXV

Had Gorki been better informed about Isadora's life with Essenin, perhaps he would have been less harsh than to comment that "one could easily imagine that Essenin regarded Isadora as a nightmare that he was used to, and no longer frightened him, but still depressed him." Perhaps Gorki would have recognized that this talented peasant-poet, of whom he had also said, "it was unbelievable that this little man possessed such immense power of feeling, such capacity of perfect expression," had by his irrational behavior turned Isadora's life with him into a waking nightmare. The violence of his outbursts of temper in the United States had the reverse effect of anything he might have hoped. Far from bringing the American public's attention to him as a great poet from Soviet Russia, his behavior only proved that he was an unnecessary, unpleasant, and disturbing adjunct in Isadora's already difficult situation. In France, where Isadora had no immediate prospects for public appearances, Sergei's antics had no public platform, and therefore they were reduced to a personal, family ambiance, which in France traditionally is of neither state nor police concern. But, unfortunately, Isadora, on the verge of nervous collapse after the difficult months in the United States, telegraphed to Mary Desti, in London, asking her to come to Paris to help her cope with Essenin.

Among all of Isadora's friends, Mary Desti was the least suited for the role of confidante to the couple. The very sight of this obese, loud-mouthed, middle-aged woman repelled Essenin. When he understood that she referred to him as a madman, insisting that his behavior stemmed from epilepsy, and that he was a dangerous individual with an urge to kill, she had the effect on him of a red rag on a bull. Mary Desti's constant warnings to everyone that Essenin intended to kill Isadora were groundless, the alleged stories of his "brandishing a revolver" were fictional—never in his life had Essenin held a firearm in his hand. However, to Paris hotel managers, already embarrassed by the three unusually noisy guests, the threat of a murder provided an excuse to be polite but firm in cutting short their stay.

But the worst insult Sergei had to suffer was to learn that, when Isadora begged Mary Desti to treat him with respect, saying that he was as great an artist as she herself, Mary Desti had burst out into contemptuous laughter. Once more he was wounded in his most vulnerable spot, this time by one of Isadora's most intimate friends. "As long as I was playing the buffoon, they kissed my arse, but when it came to recognizing me as I really am. . . ." He wanted to return to Russia. But Isadora was not well, they had no more money, and so he agreed to go to Berlin. He was to be accompanied by Jeanne, Isadora's maid, who, while living with Isadora in Russia, had learned enough Russian to be able to communicate with Essenin. Isadora was to join him as soon as she felt better, and then, together, they would go back to Moscow.

The following four months were the most hectic in Isadora's adventurous life. No sooner had she settled down to recuperate from her recent ordeals with Sergei—and to attend to some business that would provide money for their trip back to Russia, and perhaps for appearances in Paris—than telegrams began to arrive from Sergei, urging her to come to Berlin at once. One of these, written in a mixture of English and Russian, said: "Isadora Browning darling Sergei lubish moya darling scurry scurry."

It would have been unlike Isadora not to give this message a free dramatic interpretation: "Isadora, Browning* will kill your darling Sergei if you love me my darling come immediately hurry hurry." At the time, Isadora was ill, with a high fever. Nevertheless, she borrowed money from friends and money lenders, hired a car,

* Referring to the firearm.

and accompanied by Mary Desti, raced to Berlin to prevent Essenin from committing suicide over their short separation.

Their reunion was marked by parties, with food and champagne *"pour tout le monde"*—that is, for a band of Sergei's Russian friends whom he had already collected in Berlin—but Gorki and Alexei Tolstoy, as well as others of the intellectuals from the "Home of the Arts," were conspicuously absent. These carnivals, moreover, almost never ended peacefully. Sergei's band of hangers-on, with their guitars and balalaikas, stimulated him to engage in brawls, and Isadora's pleas for restraint were fruitless. As for Mary Desti, Sergei would have been well advised to supply her with a gigolo for her more pressing needs, for her role of policeman only incited him to an almost routine violence—upon their return to their hotel rooms he would smash everything in sight.

Isadora suffered over these escapades, and yet she also derived a certain satisfaction from them, and this contradiction has to be understood as part of a mechanism for escaping the torturing memories that assailed her whenever she was in Paris. But the borrowed money was soon spent. Isadora's business affairs, such as selling or renting her little house on the rue de la Pompe, or selling the furniture, or pawning some valuable paintings still in her possession—all to raise enough money for their return to Russia—had to be attended to in Paris.

They left Berlin, hoping to smuggle Sergei into France despite his "red passport," which no longer carried a French visa. Their departure in an open car, piled on all sides with Sergei's friends, who were to accompany them part of the way, provided the last tableau of Isadora's excursion to Berlin to save her husband from suicide. For as the car gathered speed, the couple wanted to jettison the ballast, and therefore Sergei's companions were dumped one by one by the wayside.

In Paris, after camping out in several elegant and expensive hotels from which they were graciously evicted either for nonpayment or because of Essenin's occasional "scandals" which brought the police, Isadora finally was able to move into her own house on the rue de la Pompe. There she hoped to find the tranquility of home. But it was not to be. They had no money for housekeeping expenses. It was not funny when they had to ponder, "What are we going to eat today—this sofa or that desk?" And no matter how impromptu the lunches and dinners, Isadora insisted on having guests at what she called "intimate parties," serving lobster and *champagne nature*, which she explained was cheaper than any other kind of good wine.

And yet it was during those unorganized, uncertain days that Isadora actually saw Essenin work. Of the twelve poems dated 1925, none were directly written to Isadora, although at least five of them had a few lines that could have been inspired by her.

She told me that while he was working he never drank anything but tea. In fact, once in Moscow, when he found one of his imagist friends working in a room in which there was an unmade bed, and with his face unwashed, Essenin told him that he himself could not work in such disorder. "I am never drunk when I work."

In Paris, Isadora told me, he loved to work sitting either in bed or at a table, wearing the Sulka pajamas Isadora had given him, in which he refused to sleep, but left carefully folded on a chair near his bed.

While in Paris, he heard from his sister Katya that their old house had burned down. It had happened when Sergei was in the United States, but they had not known where to reach him. He wrote later:

> *I loved that wooden house,*
> *Stern wrinkles glimmered in its timber,*
> *Our stove so wildly, so strangely*
> *Howled in the rain-swept night.*

He was working on "Confessions of a Hooligan," a poem written in 1920; he was revising it because someone had offered to translate it into French.

At about this time, purely by chance, I met Essenin. He was sitting with Nikolai Zagorsky, a friend of mine, on the terrace of the Café de la Paix near the Opéra, and, as I passed them, my friend called me to join them. I knew nothing about Essenin except that he was supposed to be a talented poet, that he had married Isadora Duncan, and that he left a trail of scandals, fights, and brawls wherever he went. Therefore, I was rather surprised to see this immaculately dressed young man, small, and rather delicately built. I also noticed his well-kept hands—there was nothing of the peasant about him. Nor would I call him beautiful, as many Americans have since done. He looked to me like one of a thousand Russians with curly blond hair and blue eyes .

Even after all the intervening years, I still remember our conversation practically verbatim, not because it was my first meeting with Essenin, but because of the fascinating theme of his discussion with my friend, into which he immediately drew me.

"You are a musician," Essenin said to me with an air of having known me all my life, "and that is exactly what I need in convincing your friend here that the reading public at large doesn't know how to read a book."

"Why so?" I asked him.

"Because they read everything, except perhaps very short poems, piecemeal. They start a novel today, and then keep at it at intervals of days, weeks, and even months—tablespoon-wise."

"And?" I asked, trying to fathom what he meant.

"Ah," he said, "I am so glad you are musician," and his eyes were actually sparkling. "Please tell me how you listen to one of Beethoven's or somebody's symphonies, or what do you call them—sonatas?" Obviously, musical terms were of no concern to him—he concentrated solely on the theory he was trying to convey to my friend and me.

"Do you listen to the first part of it today and then come back for the second part some other time?"

"Certainly not."

"Well, then," he said leaning closer to me. The expression of his face had completely changed—the charming friendly smile was gone, he squinted his eyes as if he were ready to exact vengeance for a crime I had just committed. "Why would you do it to a novel? Why? Aren't they both creative works? Aren't both supposed to say something to you from the author? How can you tell what he is trying to say to you if you constantly interrupt him, and leave him on your shelf for weeks?"

"But a symphony never lasts any longer than an hour, usually much less."

"Ah, so it is a question of the time you are willing to sacrifice to the author of the novel? Besides, wait a minute, how about your operas? I heard that that German, Wagner, am I right, has an opera that goes on for six hours. Of course I wouldn't know what he is talking about after the first hour any more than after six. Besides all this yelling of hi-ho, ha-ho, which is supposed to be poetry, I don't understand, but that is beside the point. Yet, you, a musician, who understands all of it, would sit through six hours of such a work, but would not give that much time to a novel."

"But to read some novels would take much longer than that. What do you do then?"

"What do you do? You go to bed with a glass of tea next to you and read until you finish it."

"But suppose it is something like Dostoevsky's *Brothers Karamazov*, or Tolstoy's *War and Peace*"? I asked him.

"It doesn't matter, the length is of no importance. Apparently they needed that much time in order to tell you what they had to say to you."

"Ah but some, in fact most, of the people who would like to read your way have to work, they are occupied with other things."

"Yes, that is true," he said, "I guess it would be better for them to leave reading until they have time for it. You see," he smiled, and then became serious, "there is a good reason for it, an emotional reason, and you can draw an analogy with listening to music. Now, let me suggest to you—try and read Dostoevsky's *Idiot* in one swallow, and let us see how you are going to feel after you have finished it. You will never get the true impact of this work until you do it that way. Although I am sure you have read it, perhaps even more than once, you have never noticed that Dostoevsky himself never calls Prince Mishkin an idiot until practically the end of the novel, and that is terrific. No one can miss that incredible impact. Do you see what I mean?"

Later, as he and Zagorsky were talking about their friends in Russia, I noticed with what indifference Essenin looked at the passers-by; in fact he often became silent, and when he finally said *"Akh toska, kakaya toska,"** I knew that he was thinking of Russia. "You know," he said to me, "homesickness is a profession, a Russian profession." I have heard since that he liked to say this, and especially at that time when he had to wait for Isadora to wind up her affairs one way or another so that they could at last go back to Russia.

After Essenin's death, Isadora often spoke to me about him, and I told her of my meeting with him and of our conversation. I

* *Toska,* an untranslatable word suggesting melancholy longing.

felt that she was less interested in the experiment of reading a novel at one gulp than regretful that, because of the language barrier, she could never have had such discussions with him—never could learn much about him.

"Unfortunately," she admitted, "I could only intuitively feel his genius."

"Perhaps that wasn't enough," I began, and Isadora must have guessed what I was going to ask her.

"No, talent, even genius, is not enough. There is still a man with whom you live, share your life."

"And so, what made you leave him?" I finally asked her.

"I had decided to leave him long before I actually did. But I never told anybody about it."

"Did anything happen? Did he do anything to you?"

"Yes. A terrible thing." Isadora started to weep, and I wished I had not asked her, for I knew that what she was going to tell me was so intimate that she could hardly bear to speak of it.

"Yes. I made a terrible mistake in taking him out of Russia. I should have listened to them, to his friends. Or were they his friends? They were so much against me. They were right. He couldn't live outside of Russia. He needed them, their following, like an audience.

"He had already become difficult when we first came to Berlin. But that was mostly in public—at home he was very sweet to me. I suppose you wouldn't believe it, because of all the scandalous stories about him, but he really was a very gentle, sensitive boy. He wouldn't hurt a fly. Ah, but he was so proud. Sometimes I wondered if he knew that he was a great poet. Everybody was telling him that. I guess he never heard enough of it. And, I, I couldn't praise everything he wrote. I mean, of course, I did, but he wasn't so stupid—he could tell that I really didn't know what I was talking about. How could I? I didn't understand his poems unless Schneider or somebody else was right there and translated them to me. And even then, I could only understand the story, the subject, but not the way he said it, his expressions, his descriptions. He knew all that and it irritated him. You know that in Moscow he almost never wrote at Prechistenka. Whatever he wrote at that time, he wrote at the homes of his friends. You see, the minute he finished writing, he had to read it to somebody, he had to have their reaction. He had been doing it with everybody, and of course with every woman he had lived with . . . and here I was as if I were deaf and dumb. I was of no use to him.

"Well," Isadora started again after a short pause, while perhaps reflecting whether she should speak of it at all. "Here in Paris he had to work at home, there was no other place for it. He didn't have any friends—I mean Russians. You probably have heard how some of these White Russians beat him up in a Russian restaurant, tore his clothes off, and threw him into the gutter in his underclothes. It was a big scandal. He was taken away by the police, they were going to put him in an insane asylum. I had to promise anything to save him. He, too, the poor boy, was afraid that they would lock him up. He stopped drinking. My friends, whom we always had in for lunches and dinners, bored him—there was no rapport between them. You understand what I mean. He wanted to go home, to Russia, he was lonely, desperately lonely. He began to work. I could hear him in his bedroom loudly declaiming or muttering something to himself, and I made everybody tiptoe in the house. I don't believe he even noticed it, he was too much wrapped up in himself, in what he was doing. Except when he was annoyed with my friends; then he would take it out on me. But I was used to that.

"And then, one evening he came into my bedroom. He carried some sheets of writing paper—it must have been a poem he had just finished writing. He made me sit up in bed and then he read it to me. Of course, I didn't understand a word of it. He tried to explain it to me, but it was no use. And I tried to tell him to wait until later, tomorrow, when somebody could translate it to me. But that wasn't what he wanted. He left the room, and then kept coming back bringing other poems and again reading them to me. Then, without looking at his papers, he recited one or two poems, and each time would ask me *"Ponimaesh?"* And, of course, I had to say I didn't understand. Then he said: *'Gorki, ponimaesh Gorki? Berlin Gorki, Tolstoy . . . Gorki lubish maya sobaka. Gorki ochen lubish.'* " In her faulty Russian, Isadora was quoting Essenin as saying that Gorki loved his poem about a dog. "And then he recited the poem to me, perhaps even with more feeling than I have ever heard him recite anything, or at least it seemed that way to me.

"I knew the poem, it was translated to me even before he recited it to Gorki. He had written it a long time ago, I think during the war. It is about a bitch, whose seven newborn puppies were taken away and drowned by her master, how later at night she mistook the moon appearing over the roof of her master's hut for one of her puppies. I wept, and when he finished I asked him: 'Now Sergei, tell me what would you say if such a thing had happened to a woman?' 'To a woman?' he frowned, covering up the tears he himself had shed in reciting the poem. 'A woman?' he repeated. He suddenly spat on the floor, 'A woman is a piece of shit! *Sobaka . . . sobaka . . .*' he repeated, and walked out of the room, shouting something I did not understand.

"I never knew why he chose to read this poem to me. I am sure it was not intentional. He was in an excited state, he needed an appreciative audience, and he was sure that at least this poem was one of the few that I knew. But—you may think I am unreasonable —from that moment on I knew I could never live with him, with any man who could say such a thing. Every time I looked at him, I heard these words. I was and still am sure that it never occurred to him how much he had hurt me—he was thinking of his *sobaka*. That was when I decided to take him back to Russia and to leave him forever."

Shortly after the time of this incident, Isadora managed to rent her house in the rue de la Pompe. What was left of the furniture was sold, along with a few paintings and pieces of sculpture, and the robes and suits especially designed for her by Paul Poiret a few years before. The books in her library, some of which she had collected even before leaving the United States for the first time, were piled in a heap in the attic.

As the train was leaving the station, taking a happy Essenin home, Isadora waved au revoir to Mary Desti, who had promised to join them in Berlin in a few days. She had "agreed to come to Russia to reorganize Isadora's school there," so she said. She later complained that Essenin saw to it that she was refused a visa to Russia by the Russian Embassy in Berlin. She never saw him again.

On August 5, 1923, after an absence of almost fifteen months, Isadora and Essenin returned to Moscow. It has been reported that Essenin, after getting off the train, actually fell down on his knees and kissed the soil of Russia. Irma and Schneider, who had come to meet them, were far more concerned with the first words they heard from Isadora. She said in German, the language she used when speaking to Schneider, "I am bringing this child back to his country, but I will have nothing more to do with him."

Chapter XXXVI

But few decisions lead directly to their goal. Love is not a tap that can be turned on and off at will. Isadora loved Essenin. She told me that many times on awakening after one of his stormy brawls, he would find her sitting by his bed, gently stroking his forehead. Perfectly sober, he would ask her in all the foreign words known to him, why did she put up with him? How could she? And with tears in his eyes, he would kiss her hands. "Ah, Sergei, you are too young to understand it," Isadora would say to him.

Thus the threatening words about parting with Essenin, announced with a definitive air as he and Isadora stepped from the train, were more a signal of what was to happen in her life with the poet than a statement of accomplished fact.

They left their unusually large assortment of luggage, which included an array of the fancy trunks and suitcases Essenin had collected during their trip abroad, to be transported to its final destination at Prechistenka. The party—Isadora, Essenin, Irma, and Schneider—then decided to drive directly to Litvinovo, a village some four hours away, where Isadora's Moscow school was vacationing.

Isadora could not have wished for a more colorful reception than the one she received when, after their car had broken down, forcing them to walk the remaining mile and a half through a thick forest in the dark, they were met by the lights of torches carried by the children, who had come to welcome them. Encircling the travelers, they danced the party to the house. After letting Isadora and Essenin have a good night's rest, they gave them a performance on the following morning that entranced Isadora and delighted Essenin so much that he kept slapping his knees and laughing like a boy. They spent several happy days at Litvinovo, but when the autumn rains set in, Essenin insisted on returning to the city and Isadora went with him. It was then that this seemingly peaceful life with her husband met its final crisis.

The "scandal" was provoked by Essenin's behavior. If left to her own judgment, Isadora would most probably not have attributed to it the entirely disproportionate significance given it by her friends. Ever since their American trip, Essenin had been accused by them of stealing money from Isadora—in fact, of stealing so much that, despite her large earnings during her tour in the United States, she had been forced to borrow money from friends for their return trip to France.

There are several versions of the discovery and proof of Essenin's dishonesty, each varying in the items of place, time, and the amount involved. His extravagance had always centered on his wardrobe, which he began replenishing in European fashion almost immediately upon their first arrival in Berlin. This had continued in France and reached a paroxysm of desire for more and more clothes in the United States, where their abundance and originality completely turned his head. For the most part idle, as the chronicle of his life in America shows, his sole occupation was the shopping spree. Having already acquired everything possible for himself, he bought everything that caught his attention for distribution among his friends in Moscow. Although Isadora did not know the exact contents of the handsome trunks with fancy locks, she never questioned him nor argued with him about the wisdom of his purchases; she took his extravagance with a good-humored attitude of "the child has never had anything like that in his life," and she cheerfully paid the bills. For after all, he was her husband. And she had not married him with the French provision of *séparation des biens;* Essenin, on his own resources, could not have gone even as far as Berlin. But all the stories of Essenin's dishonesty point either to a metal box, or a small briefcase, depending on the version, which he would not let anybody touch. Isadore was supposed to have said that, with his manuscripts, he kept a loaded revolver, with which he would kill anybody who dared to open it.

But it was opened, according to Mary Desti—in New York, before their departure for France. Instead of the loaded revolver, she and Isadora found money in crumpled bills, as well as a mass of coins, all in American currency. Essenin's loot amounted to close to two thousand dollars. This is according to Mary Desti, who never missed a chance of making Essenin out to be a despicable blackguard.

"Isadora made money on that tour, as I should know," Hurok wrote in his book, *Impresario*. "Yet she had to borrow money, I have been told, to get back to Europe.

"If this is true, the answer lay hidden in the beautiful trunks that Essenin took to Moscow. In these trunks, which he would not permit even Isadora to touch, were stuffed hundreds, thousands of dollars' worth of expensive clothes and luxurious trifles—the child gone wild, or the peasant greedy, in the great wide world.

"There were even Isadora's own beautiful gowns and lingerie. She returned to Moscow with scarcely more than the clothes on her back. The rest, she said, had strangely disappeared, or been lost in their travels. She found all her lost wardrobe in these handsome, heavy trunks of Essenin's."

But according to Irma, this discovery happened at Prechistenka when, upon their final arrival at home, they were unpacking their luggage. It resulted in a tug-of-war between Essenin and Isadora—he claiming this or that dress or gown she had given him for his sister Katya, and Isadora protesting that it was meant as a present for Irma. This petty and ugly scene ended with Sergei's slamming the door as he left the house, not to return for several days.

Since time immemorial men have married women with money and have spent their wives' fortunes on admirable purposes or else on perfectly foul ones. Hurok, as an impresario, should be in the best position to know that a whole tribe of great artists would have gone unknown if their careers had not been promoted with resources provided by their wives.

From the contents of his trunks, it is obvious that he did not "invest" the supposedly stolen money in jewelry or other costly objects, which he hoped to realize on later, but that in these trunks were his new clothes and Isadora's own costly gowns, which surely

Essenin did not buy for Katya, or have copied for his friends in Russia.

If there was anyone in the world who never cared for material things it was Isadora Duncan. But this ugly scene, and Essenin's disappearance for days, knowing full well how worried she would be, once more brought to her mind the inevitability of the end of their relationship. She became so quiet, so resigned to everything, that Irma insisted that only a cure at one of the spas in the Caucasus would revive her. She and Schneider decided on Kislovodsk, Schneider promising to follow them in a few days, because he was determined to find Essenin.

While Irma and Isadora were packing, Schneider sent all three men who worked at the school in search of Essenin. Later in the day the doorman returned assuring him that Essenin would come back very soon. "*They** are perfectly sober," the man said, and indeed Sergei, visibly upset, rushed into the house asking Schneider what had happened.

"Isadora is leaving, leaving you for good."

"I must see her," Essenin insisted.

A momentary reconciliation followed, Essenin promising to follow them with Schneider to Kislovodsk in a few days, and meanwhile agreeing to Isadora's demand that he spend the nights at Prechistenka.

Essenin kept his promise for the first two nights, but on the third night he arrived accompanied by a group of friends, to whom he gave most of the presents he had brought with him in those handsome trunks with the fancy locks. He told Schneider that he could not go with him to Kislovodsk because he was busy organizing his own magazine for which he had been promised the necessary funds, but that he was going to write Isadora and explain everything.

There was never a better cure for Isadora's *crises de nerfs* than her work. A tour of the well-known spas in the northern Caucasus was arranged, to be followed by performances in Batum on the Black Sea, before returning to Moscow. The tour was successful, even if at times her treatment of Tchaikovsky's *Marche Slav* needed protection from the local secret police because the audience misunderstood Isadora's use of the former national hymn in the composition as counterrevolutionary.

But Essenin did not join her as he had promised. On the train

* The servants of the old regime referred to their masters in the plural.

from Baku to Tiflis, Schneider was asked by a stranger if Isadora Duncan happened to be on board—he had a letter for her from Essenin, who had told him that Isadora was somewhere in the Caucasus. In his letter, Essenin promised to meet her in the Crimea, if she would come there after completing her tour in the Caucasus. Why in the Crimea? Isadora wondered as she reread the letter.

> Dear Isadora,
> I am very busy with publishing matters and cannot come. I often remember you with all my gratitude to you. From Prechistenka, I moved first to Kolobova and now I have moved again to another apartment which Mariengoff and I am buying.
>
> My affairs are excellent.
>
> I never expected a great deal.
>
> I am being given a lot of money for my publishing business.
>
> I wish you success and health and less drinking.
>
> Regards to Ilya Ilyich [Schneider.]
>
> With love,
>
> S. Essenin 29, VII, Moscow

Isadora was right in her suspicion that nothing had come of Essenin's enthusiastic plans. For some time Essenin had insisted that he had reached the age when a writer or a poet should spend more time on editing a magazine than on writing his own works, and before Schneider had left Moscow to join Isadora in Kislovodsk, Essenin boasted to him that he had been summoned to the Kremlin, and that he would be given all the necessary financial assistance for his project—hence his "affairs were excellent," as he wrote to Isadora.

But the project never materialized, and Essenin was very much affected by his failure. To the last days of his life, he never gave up the idea of having his own magazine, but each unsuccessful effort on his part only further taxed his already shattered nervous system.

Meanwhile, when Isadora discovered that the small boat taking them from Batum to the northern ports of the Black Sea was to stop at Yalta, she insisted on disembarking there, for she still believed that Essenin would come to meet her in the Crimea. She had

Schneider telegraph to the school and to Essenin that they were in Yalta, and on the following day two telegrams arrived from Moscow.

In vain Schneider tried to intercept one of the telegrams addressed to Isadora. Dated October 9, 1923, it said: "Do not send more letters or telegrams to Essenin. He is with me. He will never return to you. Galina Benislavskaya."

No message could have dumbfounded Isadora, or Irma, or Schneider more, for they had never heard the name of Galina Benislavskaya. To clarify the puzzling situation, Schneider telegraphed Moscow asking whether Essenin was aware of Benislavskaya's telegram.

Obviously shocked by the blow, Isadora tried to conceal her pain, taking long walks along the seashore with Schneider, discussing her plans for the winter season, but in the evening on returning to the hotel she could no longer control her anxiety about the reply to Schneider's telegram.

The laconic, unsigned reply said: "The contents of the telegram are known to Sergei."

As Isadora slowly walked up the stairs toward her room, she met Irma, spoke to her, and then handed Schneider her telegram to Essenin, which had been composed by the two women. "Received telegram probably from your servant Benislavskaya saying not to send any more letters or telegrams to your address have you changed your address please explain by telegram love you very much Isadora."

But Isadora never received a reply to her telegram, for on the following day, October 12, she, Irma, and Schneider left for Moscow.

Years later, according to Schneider, when Isadora, Essenin, and Benislavskaya were no longer alive, Schneider discovered Essenin's reply to Isadora's telegram, which had been sent to her at Yalta on October 13. It seems that in Essenin's first draft of his reply he had said: "I told you in Paris that in Russia I would leave you. You unnerved and incited me. I love you but will not live with you. Now I am married and happy. I wish you the same. Essenin."

In her diary, which Schneider read after her death, Benislavskaya said that Essenin had shown her that first draft of his telegram, but that he had said, "If I am to put an end to it, I had better not mention love, etc." and that turning the page over, he wrote in blue pencil: "I love another. I am married and happy." And he signed it in large block letters "Essenin."

Essenin, of course, was not married to Galina Benislavskaya, nor was she responsible for the telegram which had been sent in her name. In fact, she remarked in her diary, the offensive tone of the telegram was entirely alien to her. Who then was Galina Benislavskaya?

A young woman, she was one of Essenin's closest friends. He had never been in love with her and, in fact, had brutally told her so in a letter in March 1925: "Dear Galya,* you are near to me as a friend, but I never loved you as a woman." But Galya had accepted her position in Essenin's life—she loved him deeply and selflessly. Their friendship dated from long before Essenin met Isadora. She silently endured his marriage to Isadora and his travels abroad. When Isadora left for her tour in the Caucasus, Essenin moved into her apartment and even brought his sisters Katya and Shura to live with them. Benislavskaya devoted herself to taking care of his literary business with publishers, and Essenin trusted her more than anyone else. But he never mentioned her to Isadora or to anyone connected with Isadora. If Isadora had known anything about Galina Benislavskaya, jealousy might have seemed out of place, and there would have been no wounded pride. But as it was, now a new element had entered her already strained relationship with Essenin, and, as it seemed to her, had been interfering with it for some time: a strange woman. More distraught than ever, she wanted to get to Moscow as soon as possible.

At one of the railway stations on their way, Schneider bought the latest issue of the popular magazine *Krasnaya Niva* (Red Neva), and found in it a recent poem by Essenin. He translated it to Isadora, and Isadora sincerely believed that the poem had been written to her. Even the first two lines of the poem:

> *You are just as simple as all of us,*
> *The hundred thousand others in Russia*

did not shake Isadora's conviction. It was fortunate for her peace of mind that the issue of the magazine which Schneider had bought was not from the first printing, which carried the name of Augusta

* Diminutive of Galina.

Miklashevskaya, to whom the poem was dedicated. In Moscow, however, the mystery was soon clarified for Isadora. It was widely rumored that Sergei had fallen in love with the thirty-two-year-old Miklashevskaya, an actress at the Kamerny Theater, and an exceptionally beautiful woman.

Essenin had met her shortly after his return from abroad. During the early autumn, he saw her every day, took long walks with her through the streets of Moscow or on the outskirts of the city, sharing with her his impressions of his trip abroad. "I behave with you like a schoolboy," he used to say to her shyly. And he wrote and dedicated to her a cycle of seven poems.

Although in her mind Isadora had put an end to resuming her life with Essenin, her decision was still more theoretical than actual. She continued to hope for his return, and deeply distressed by the two recent blows to her pride, she tried to find solace in her work with her pupils, and in preparing two new programs for performances at the Bolshoi Theater. But the final curtain to Isadora's dramatic marriage was to fall after Isadora's first performance at the Bolshoi.

Essenin not only sent a small flowerpot with one flower in it to Isadora, with "From Sergei Essenin" written in his own handwriting, but, while Isadora was performing the *Marche Slav*, he managed to get backstage where, from the wings, he succeeded in watching Isadora dance his favorite composition. To the policemen who tried to remove him from his unauthorized vantage point, Sergei, beating his chest, said, "I am Duncan," as if he were repeating his first words after his marriage to Isadora. When she finished her dance and heard Sergei whispering "Isadora . . . Isadora," and she saw him in the wings, smiling, with his arms outstretched toward her, she cried in a broken voice, "Darling," and fell into his arms.

Essenin insisted that after the performances they all go to supper at Prechistenka, and that they should take Katya along. On hearing still another feminine name, Isadora frowned. "Katya, my sister, my sister," Essenin explained to Isadora. "You know? Katya—genius! She is an artist like you, like Chaliapin, like Duse!" And, as if surprised at everybody's ignorance about his sister's talent, he enthusiastically explained: "Katya sings! Ryazan songs! But how she sings them! It is a miracle! Isadora! You must hear how Katya sings."

During supper, Essenin was very much excited and kept on drinking. Then he demanded that Katya sing. Shyly, Katya sang one song. She had a pleasant but very small voice. Each refrain ended with a strange little shriek. Everybody applauded, but she refused to sing any more. Had the company not been in a rather emotional state, it could have with justice compared this scene with that described in Ivan Krylov's fable, "The Jackass and the Nightingale," known to every Russian schoolboy, in which a jackass prefers the crowing of a cock to the singing of the nightingale.

The abyss that separates different forms of art was too obvious for anyone to miss. With his deeply rooted love of everything born of the Russian soil, Essenin sincerely believed that any example of genuine expression is equal in its intrinsic artistic value to the performances given by Isadora, Chaliapin, or Duse.

But this was no occasion for even a hint at humor. Essenin sat silent, with his hand covering his eyes. Then he filled his wine glass, but when Isadora gently touched his arm, silently imploring him not to drink any more, he struck the table with his fist and walked away. It was a tense moment, for everybody knew that it was leading to one of Essenin's tantrums. And, indeed, on noticing his bust, carved by his friend Konnenkov, he snatched it from the glass cabinet, and, holding the sculpture under his arm, ran out of the house slamming the door, before anyone realized what had happened. That was the last time that Isadora Duncan ever saw her husband Sergei Essenin.

On New Year's Eve 1924, Mariengoff's wife received a telephone call from Isadora inviting her to Prechistenka to spend an evening with her. But, since she already had guests at her home, Mme. Mariengoff suggested that Isadora join them. "Miklashevskaya is here," she told Isadora. "Then I will come right away," Isadora said.

Later, describing her first and only meeting with Isadora, Miklashevskaya wrote: "This was the first time I had ever seen Duncan so close. She gave an impression of being a tall woman. Although tall myself, I had to look up to her. She astonished me by her unnaturally theatrical appearance. She was wearing a transparent pale-green chiton with gold lace, belted by a golden braid with golden tassels. She had on golden sandals and lace stockings. On her head was a turban, adorned with colorful beads. Over her shoulders she had something that resembled a raincoat, or a cape of dark green velvet texture. This was not a woman, this was some kind of theatrical king.

"She looked at me and said: 'Essenin is in a hospital, you should take him fruit and flowers.' Then suddenly she tore the turban off her head, as if to say 'I have made an impression on Miklashevskaya —now I can throw it away,' and she threw the turban into a corner of the room.

"Then she became more simple, more animated. One could never be offended by her—she was much too charming. 'All of Europe knows [Miklashevskaya quotes Isadora in her faulty Russian] that Essenin was my husband and suddenly—he sang about love —to you, not to me! There is a bad poem: *You are so simple like all* . . . That is for you.' "

Miklashevskaya then describes Isadora's chatting in French and Russian about her experience with Essenin abroad. "It was getting late, a long time past the hour to go home," Miklashevskaya ends her report of that evening, "but Duncan did not want to leave. It began to be daylight. We had turned off the electricity. Gray dim light changed everything. Isadora sat bent down, looking older, crushed. 'I do not want to leave. I have no place to go. I have nobody. I am all alone.' "

Chapter XXXVII

The question of what kind of emotions had bound Isadora and Essenin together was raised very early in their relationship and has never been answered satisfactorily. It has been puzzling, not so much because of Isadora's attitude and behavior during one of the most dramatic episodes in her life, but because of Essenin's exceptionally complex character. While his poetry, although not ranking with that of Pushkin or Lermontov in Russian literature, has been given its due as work of a high order, even his closest friends' analyses of Essenin the man are far from adequate. As for his personal, his intimate feelings, he was one of those men to whom an old Russian saying applies: "The soul of a stranger is pitch darkness." His lyric poetry revealed only one side of his unusual personality and actually hindered an understanding of his whole nature.

From everything that has been learned about their union, it is clear that Isadora did love Essenin, for otherwise she would not have paid so high a price for her relationship with him.

In judging Essenin, and especially his intimate feelings, one would do better to ignore completely the opinion of non-Russian commentators. Unable to penetrate into Essenin the man, their supercilious statements were based on a common, erroneous, but in their minds firmly established image: "Russian" is synonymous with "irrational."

Thus, not until a few Russian writers, who had known both Isadora and Essenin during their marriage, had expressed candid judgments in their written reminiscences was there a more or less general answer available to the question of whether or not Essenin loved Isadora.

Sergei Gorodetzky, a well-known Russian poet, who had known Essenin since 1915, when he arrived in St. Petersburg for the first time, wrote, "To judge by my own impressions, it was a deep, mutual love. Only love, only unceasing amazement at the rich imagination of his companion could have kept Essenin so long near Duncan in the languishment of loneliness in a foreign land."

Nikolai Nikitin (1895–1963) wrote in his memoirs that Essenin did not like to speak of his personal life. Once, passing a house, Essenin said to Nikitin, "I used to live here. See those windows. I lived there with my wife during the beginning of the revolution. Then I had a family. I had a samovar like you! Later my wife left me." And that was all he said, and Nikitin never asked Essenin whom he meant, as he did not want to question him about his love affair with Isadora. "Was it merely a pose?" Nikitin wondered. "Did Essenin love Isadora? I think he did. She was a great artist, who was destroying what she considered the false canons of the classical French ballet. And obviously she was a great person. It was not so simple to selflessly come to Soviet Russia, which barely was getting over its historical fires, famine and need . . . to come to Bolshevik Moscow with the desire of selflessly giving her talent. This is not to be compared with the tours of foreign artists today. Only an extraordinary being could have had faith in Soviet Russia. Just remember those years . . . To give up wealth, world-fame; even if it was already on the wane, still that was not easy. She could have lived well and quietly in the West. But, during those years she used to say that she could not live that sort of life. She said that only Russia could be the land of art which was not bought by gold. For many years and right up to her death, Stanislavsky enthusiastically spoke of Isadora. Would not Essenin also have felt the charm of her personality? He often spoke to me about her dancing. Their brief life together proved to be bitter. But I do not know what wormwood had poisoned it."

Schneider, who was one of the eyewitnesses of the Isadora-Essenin love affair, commented in his recollections: "Essenin's love for Isadora began in the same way but developed quite differently. [He meant by comparison with Essenin's feelings toward the other women in his life.] The moment he heard of the arrival of Isadora Duncan in Moscow, Essenin fell in love with her name. After meeting her, the poet gave himself up entirely to his feelings. Later on, a reaction set in. At first, though, the weak shoots of that feeling imperceptibly grew into a great, real, and sensual attachment. 'Is not sensuality part of a powerful and real love?' Essenin said to me one day. 'Are we walking on clouds and not on the earth?' "

To these statements, perhaps one should be added that in my opinion is rather of a parenthetical nature. In all my conversations with Isadora, and especially in discussions about the years she had spent in Russia and her relationship with Essenin, she never mentioned a feeling that has been attributed to her, namely, that Essenin resembled her son Patrick.

Knowing Isadora's relationship with Essenin, as I learned of it from her, I would hesitate to suggest that this alleged mother-son feeling added an extra stimulus to her passionate love for Essenin. And yet I have heard from some of her friends that, although she herself attached no special significance to it, Isadora spoke of this "uncanny" resemblance.

She might have also conveyed this to Essenin, for when speaking of his relationship with her, he mentioned it to Nina Tabidze, the wife of Tizian Tabidze, a well-known Georgian poet, whom Essenin frequently visited in Tiflis.

"When we first met," Essenin said, "Isadora was stunned by my resemblance to her dead boy. This was the main thing that brought us together, but I saw something unnatural in it. Very soon I came to my senses."

In fact, the much-discussed scene between Isadora and Essenin, which was supposed to have caused the final rupture in their relationship, is supposed to have taken place when Essenin found Isadora in her bedroom at Prechistenka crying over the photographs of her children. Essenin, who had seen Isadora cry over the pictures of her children before, this time, so the story goes, tore the album out of her hands and threw it into the fireplace. Essenin was supposed to have shouted at Isadora, "I am your husband—your man," thus betraying, rightly or wrongly, his suspicion of Isadora's possible maternal feelings for him.

With Essenin out of her life, if not out of her thoughts, Isadora welcomed the chance to escape from the scene of her latest distress when Boris Zinoviev, a self-made sort of concert manager, offered to arrange a tour for her in the Ukraine. This happened shortly before Lenin died (January 21, 1924), and the two weeks of national mourning postponed Isadora's departure from the capital. During this period, like the rest of the thousands of mourners, she stood in line for hours to pass into the Union House where Lenin's body lay in state. The sight of the grief-stricken peasants and workers, who were waiting their turn as if frozen by the sub-zero temperature, inspired Isadora's new interpretation of two songs: Lenin's favorite revolutionary hymn and the *Funeral Song for the Revolutionary Heroes*, which she had already heard sung by the sailors from the *Aurora*, during her memorable performances in Petrograd in 1922.

With those two songs added to her usual programs, Isadora toured the Ukraian towns with such success that in Kiev, which at that time had a population of about a half million, she gave eighteen consecutive performances to capacity houses. Despite her insistence on low-priced tickets, her earnings were so high that, like a princess in a fairy tale, she distributed rubles and kopeks among the beggars who ran after her carriage.

Encouraged by her success, Isadora apparently became convinced that she was at last experiencing the beginning of the long-hoped-for mass popularity of her art. Upon her return to Moscow, as if to celebrate this turn in her fortunes, she lavishly entertained her friends and urged both Schneider and Zinoviev to book tours for her through the provinces. Little did she know that they would result in a series of disasters.

Nothing happened remotely resembling the incidents on her tours in the United States, or even in the Caucasus during the previous season. She made no speeches that unnerved the authorities and the press as she had done in the United States. She did not have to have the assistance of the secret police in order to perform the *Marche Slav*, as had occurred in one of the spas of the northern Caucasus. Nor was her own emotional state beclouded by Essenin's erratic behavior. This time her constant disappointments were caused by the inadequacies of the transportation, and, in most towns, by a complete unpreparedness of audiences for her art.

During the short interval between her two performances in Leningrad in May, she agreed to an engagement at Vitebsk, seven hundred miles away. Disregarding the terrible state of the Russian highways and the deplorable condition of motor transport, Isadora insisted on traveling part of the way by car. In the course of that drive, before reaching Vitebsk, she met with an accident which could easily have been predicted.

"I was at first in a daze and told myself that this must surely be the end," Isadora said "I had always believed that my end would come in a motor accident. For a while I lay with the most unearthly stillness all about me. Then I suddenly realized that I had come out alive." Fortunately, neither the driver nor the passengers were seriously hurt, though Isadora was thrown into a ditch filled with muddy water. The performances had to be canceled, the ticket money returned to the audience, and yet this almost prophetic example of what was to come did not prevent Isadora from venturing into even more remote regions of the vast territory of Russia.

Anyone with even the most elementary knowledge of the geography of that country, and its climatic conditions, would have known better than to suggest a tour through the provinces, scorched by summer heat. But to Isadora a boat trip on the Volga River, and the Oriental splendor of Samarkand and mysterious Tashkent, sounded so romantic that, disregarding all warnings about the primitive transportation facilities, she set off with her two companions—her manager and her pianist—on this ill-chosen adventure.

"Here is one more catastrophe," Isadora wrote to Irma (June 20). "We can't get from one town to another!!! And the curtains [Isadora was referring to her famous blue curtains] have not arrived."

But in Samarkand, Isadora felt a little more hopeful. She loved the country—she said that she had never seen flowers and fruit in such abundance. It was terribly hot, but she did not mind the heat as much as she did the terrible sensation of walking about without a penny in a land that seemed like a veritable paradise for the natives —for, she added, "the whites don't know how to live here. . . . If one had the money, there are ravishing scarves and silks—but hélas! We are always hoping for better luck. So far the tour is a tragedy. . . . I don't know what is going to happen next."

Still, despite all the discomforts, Isadora enjoyed visiting the old temple, which combined Chinese, Persian, and Arab cultures, with its wonderful mosaics, and the tomb of Tamerlane, and the old Sartian town. It reminded her of Egypt, and she thought it would have been the sort of place to come wtih Paris Singer and his millions.

On their return to Tashkent, at first her manager and the pianist slept in a theater, while Isadora was "next door in a little house without water or toilet." Later they found rooms in a hotel overrun with vermin. "We are so bitten as to appear to have a sort of illness," Isadora wrote Irma. And yet Isadora was capable of writing to Irma, whom she had left in charge of her school in Moscow, "Courage; it's a long way, but light is ahead. My art was the flower of an epoch, but that epoch is dead and Europe is the past. These red-tuniced children are the future, so it is fine to work for them. Plough the ground, sow the seed, and prepare for the next generation that will express the new world. What else is there to do? We will dance Beethoven's Ninth yet."

Continually stranded on the road, and living with the one hope of getting enough money from their performances for transportation to their next destination, they arrived in Ekaterienburg at the end of July.

"You have no idea what a living nightmare is until you see this town," Isadora wrote to Irma. "Perhaps the killing here of a *certain* family [Nicholas II and his family] in a cellar has cast a sort of Edgar Allen Poe gloom over the place—or perhaps it was always like that. The melancholy church bells ring every hour, fearful to hear. . . .

"No one seems to have any sense of humor. The head of the communists said, 'How could you have played such disgusting music as Liszt or Wagner!!!' Another said: 'I did not at all understand the *Internationale*!!!'

"Our two performances were a fiasco and, as usual, we are stranded and don't know where to go. There is no restaurant here, only 'common eating houses' and no coiffeur. The only remaining fossil of that name, while burning my hair off with trembling fingers, assured me there was not one *dama* left here—they shot 'em *All*.

"We saw the house and the cellar where they shot a *certain* family. Its psychosis seems to pervade the atmosphere. You can't imagine anything more fearful."

Finally, by way of Vyatka and Perm, fighting their way through hotel rooms with bedbugs, mice, and other aggravations, the *Sterbende* (dying) Isadora, as she signed her last letters, returned to Moscow at the end of August 1924.

But the "dying" Isadora was quickly revived when, upon her arrival at Prechistenka, she saw from the balcony about forty of her children cheering her. As they danced the *Internationale* for her, Isadora, waving her red scarf, wept with joy: "What do my hardships matter after this; these children dancing and singing in the open air with fine, free movements?"

"They dance beautifully, but they are almost always hungry," Isadora commented in her letter to Allan Ross Macdougall in Paris. "However, they have great spirit. They live on *kasha* and black bread, but, when they dance, you would swear they were fed on ambrosia.

"This summer they went out to the Stadium and taught five hundred of Trotsky's young men* to dance in the open air—it was a beautiful sight to see them in their red tunics and red scarves, dancing and singing the *Internationale*.

"Everyone can say what they please, in spite of the catastrophe and suffering and all, the *idea* of the New World is born here, and nothing can kill it."

But Isadora's selfless dedication to her cause and her contribution to the *idea* of the new world could not be maintained without financial support for her school—even *kasha* and black bread are not given away free in Russia. All her efforts to earn the most modest sums through her own performances, all the tours she had recently undertaken, had proved futile. "The communists and the working men, who had no money to buy tickets, insisted upon coming *free*, saying, as I was a communist, I should dance for all the comrades—which I would be very pleased to do," Isadora said of her tour, "and the *new bourgeoisie*, who have the money to buy tickets, cordially detest me."

Once more she believed that to resolve this financial problem she would have to go back to Western Europe. She succeeded in getting a contract for two performances in Berlin, which were to be the beginning of her tour in other countries.

Before leaving, however, Isadora gave what she thought was

* Trained by Nicolai Podvoysky.

going to be her farewell performance of the season. For the first part of the program, she composed dances herself and taught them to the children, who would join her in a series of dances based on revolutionary songs of the West European countries. But the second part of the evening was reserved entirely for the singing and dancing of Russian songs, leading to a climactic rendition of the *Internationale*, in which they would be joined by some five hundred children with whom Isadora's pupils had been working during the summer. "They danced and sang the *Internationale*, winding down the stage and through the vibrant audience, who joined them in the national anthem, finally cheering and yelling themselves hoarse in appreciation of the dancing children and their inspirer," as the Moscow newspapers enthusiastically reported.

But the success of the evening did not simply end with the press praising Isadora's ideas and work. Mme. Kalinina, the wife of the President of the Soviet Union, who was in the audience, came to Isadora backstage, asking her, "What can I do for you?"

"I would like to show the children in these new revolutionary dances to the leaders of the party. I am sure that if they saw them, and saw how wonderful the children are, they would do something to help the school. At least give us a great hall to work in."

"I could arrange a performance in the Bolshoi Theater and invite the leaders personally," Mme. Kalinina said. "Would sometime next week do?"

"I'm afraid not," Isadora shook her head. "I must go to Berlin on Monday morning. I have a performance schedule there."

"Then you shall have your evening tomorrow, Sunday," Mme. Kalinina said without a moment of hesitation. "And I promise you the leaders will be there."

A command performance, whether ordered by a queen or by the wife of the head of a communist state, is a command performance. Not only the leaders en masse, but four thousand Young Pioneers and communists formed a cheering audience such as Isadora had never faced in her whole career as a performer. This time the evening ended not with a speech by Isadora, but with Lunacharsky's coming onto the stage to applaud her and deliver a long address in which he pointed once more to the importance of Isadora's work with the young generation.

Typically, several things happened before Isadora could fly

to Berlin. Apparently, she assumed that just because she meant to take a short trip abroad, visas would be granted to her immediately. But Isadora did not even have a passport—she was registered in Essenin's passport, which, when Schneider asked him for it, the poet could not find. Fortunately, at the last moment, it was remembered that Isadora had once applied for naturalization as a Soviet citizen. An official document confirming her intentions was accepted for a German visa, and after an all-night farewell party following her Sunday performance, Isadora stepped into a plane which was to take her to Berlin via Königsberg, the same way she had traveled almost two years before with Essenin.

That evening, Schneider saw Isadora walking wearily up the stairs at Prechistenka to her bedroom. "We had an emergency landing in Mozhaisk," Isadora explained, "we're flying tomorrow morning. Please make up a parcel with twenty red tunics for me. I promised to drop them for the Mozhaisk Komsomols tomorrow. I spent several wonderful hours with them while the airplane was being repaired. I taught them dancing and free movement in the spiral arrangement of the *Internationale*. All to the music of an accordion. Don't begrudge them the tunics."

The scene at Mozhaisk could well have reminded her of her very first arrival in Russia in 1905, when during the train's stop at Narva she taught a group of village children on the platform of the station.

"Did the pilot curse?" Schneider asked her.

"Terribly. Can you imagine it? He thought that it was because I was his passenger!"

PART SIX

Chapter XXXVIII

Had Isadora been less eager for an immediate journey to Germany and less hasty in leaving Moscow before learning the results of the performances arranged for her by Mme. Kalinina, perhaps her tour in Germany would have taken on a different aspect, and the fate of her school in Moscow might also have been changed. It was not long before she learned that the contracts for her Berlin appearances were fraudulent—she was put up at the Eden Hotel, one of the most expensive hotels in the German capital, but she received no fees for her two performances. And, since there were no further appearances scheduled, she saw little hope of saving herself from a situation into which she had been virtually trapped.

Her audiences were enthusiastic, even if the reviews were more caustic than favorable. The critics declared that she had grown old and fat. Actually, Isadora had never looked better and was in top physical form. In her good-humored way, she advised those who wished to lose weight not to spend money and time on cures at famous spas, but simply to go and live for a while in Soviet Russia.

But the hostile remarks of the critics were the least of her worries. She had no friends in Berlin, and to have her managers jailed would have done her no good. Elizabeth, whom she had not seen for a long time, came to visit her, but she had no money either. And she could not or Merz would not let her find other help for her sister. And so, utterly discouraged, Isadora began writing and telegraphing friends, begging them to extricate her from the hopeless situation.

She constantly wrote and telegraphed to Irma in Moscow for advice, to assist her in finding an impresario who could arrange performances for her in Vienna and Prague—and, of course, for any good news about the school.

At the beginning of October, 1924, she wrote:

Dearest Irma,

It seems my fate in 1924 to be tragically *stranded*. I am still waiting here for something—God knows what—Berlin is simply fearful. Better to sell matches on the streets of Moscow. Here is no spirit; everything congested with patriotism and fatherland. It is awful. . . .

This Europe is quite impossible. I am homesick for the soldiers singing and the children singing and the *Rabochy Narod* [the working class] marching forward. This old world is dead as a doornail. The children here look like Muffins compared to the Russians. I am not, perhaps, competent to explain what has happened *there*, but here *nothing* has happened, and the people have simply stopped. Something must happen before they become alive again. At present here all is dead. . . .

Something else, in addition to Isadora's freely expressed views on post-World War I Germany, seems to have affected the attitude of German authorities about her situation. There appears to have been a mysterious man named Mueller who had met Isadora in Königsberg, and whom she mentioned in her letter to Irma.

"He comes to see me every day and promises to bring money, but brings none. What he has to do with the affair [Isadora meant the management of her performances] I don't know." But apparently the situation—whatever it really was—was sufficient for the newspapers to be "naturally fearfully hostile and treat me as if I had only come here *paid* to make Bolshevik propaganda, which is a very poor joke."

And yet, despite her personal problems, her mind was on her school as much as ever. To arouse interest in her school, she needed some photographs of the children. "I can do nothing for the school without photos. *Without fail*," she pleaded with Irma, "send me at once good photos of the children. I can send articles and photos over the whole world, but unless you manage this, I can do nothing. But I want *Art photos* and not commonplace ones. Why doesn't my 'secretary' write me, what is she doing?"

And returning again to her unanswered questions about the results of Mme. Kalinina's intervention on her behalf at her last performance in Moscow, Isadora asked Irma: "Have you had no answer from Tovarish Kalinina? You should send her a simple letter saying that you *must have* for the school free electric lights, water, heat, teachers, salaries, and *payoks* [rations] for the children, stuff for costumes. Have they given the big room? Everything seems to be standing still—why? I feel like an airplane *'en panne'* . . ." And she closed her letter with: "Please keep me posted what the School is doing and if there is a chance of getting the 'big room.' I. [Ilya Schneider] should go himself to Comrade Kamenieff,* and ask what chance the School in Moscow has for a future."

A month later (November 27, 1924), thanks to the help of two American music students willing to share with her their own meager allowances from home, Isadora moved to a less expensive hotel.

"Dear Irma," Isadora wrote, "Why on earth don't you write? I have had no news from you for *four weeks*. I am stranded in this awful city. I have signed three contracts and been swindled three times. . . . When the time came, the agent didn't have the money for the R.R. tickets. They all are swindlers.

"I cannot move from here! The hotel has refused to serve us food for the last four weeks. An American friend brings me a slice of roast beef a day, but he has no money either.

"Elizabeth has deserted me and gone to visit a rich friend in Vienna. *Her school in Potsdam won't even let me in."*

Actually, when Isadora could no longer remain at the hotel and went to the Potsdam School with her bags, she was met at the door by Max Merz, who told her that Elizabeth had gone away, and that "it was impossible to have Isadora in the school," and that if Isadora had no place to go and no money for food, that it was her own fault.

"I was ill for two weeks with bronchitis, and now to cap the climax, an ulcerated tooth," she continued in her letter to Irma. "I have telegraphed Raymond, but he is in Nice and apparently *can't*

* Kamenev, then a high official in the Communist party.

or *won't* do anything. Germany is the limit, simply fearful. I don't know what's going to happen next. Please write me and tell me your news. How are the children? . . . With love to you and the children. Yours in dying stages, Isadora."

And three weeks later, in desperation, Isadora wrote again:

Dear Irma:
Why don't you answer my telegrams and letters? I have been without any word from you for six weeks although I repeatedly sent *Luft post* [air mail] letters and telegrams. I am frightfully anxious. Were you ill? Does the school still exist? . . .

I may have to return to Moscow, as my permit to stay here expires in a week. *Every country has refused me a visa* on account of my "political connections." What are my *political connections?* Where are my political connections, I would like to know?

I am utterly stranded and lost here in a very hostile city. I haven't a single friend. If I return, is it possible to make a contract for Siberia?

They have even refused me a visa on a contract for Vienna. Perhaps I. [Ilya Schneider] had better get on a plane and come here and save me, otherwise you will soon be sending a wreath for my funeral. But why haven't you answered a single letter or telegram for six weeks?

Love to the children, if they still exist, and to you and to all our friends. Your dying Isadora.

Isadora never did receive a clear, direct answer as to why Irma did not answer her desperate letters and telegrams, nor did Schneider, the director of the school, bother to reply to Isadora's anxious pleas for news of its fate. A year later, mostly through hearsay, Isadora eventually learned something about what had been happening at her school after she had gone to Berlin. But not until Irma's own account was published in her autobiography years later was the true picture of the situation revealed.

"With Isadora's departure," Irma wrote, I started once more to be independently active on the stage, a venture that had been impossible while she remained in charge of artistic matters. I slowly came to the realization that, if I wanted to make a name for myself in Russia, it was now or never."

And then, already referring to the school as "my school," Irma gave the following description of her life after Isadora had gone to Berlin, leaving her in charge.

My daily existence had little of interest to offer me. Shops were bare; moving picture theatres nonexistent; the fashion world dead and buried; balls and parties unheard of. What was there for a young girl to do in search of fun and amusement?

As far as my tastes go, once I'd seen the Bolshoi Ballet, I had had it. I frequently attended the opera, concerts and the theatres during the season. I could, however, get small enjoyment from the plays— mostly classics—until my Russian improved. My usual day started with a late breakfast, brought to me on a tray by my personal maid Ephrosinia, called Frosia for short. I ate all my meals in my room; in front of the open window looking out on the courtyard in the warmer seasons. I would dress and take my daily outing, snow or shine. I preferred riding to walking; dancing as much as I did, I obtained sufficient exercise.

At the corner of Prechistenka and Myortvy Pereoulok (or Dead Alley, so named in the time of the big plague) stood a horsedrawn carriage or, in winter, a sleigh. The *izvozchik* [coachman] Piotr—in a half-somnolent state, patiently waiting for his steady client—would suddenly spring into action the instant I opened the heavy oak door and stepped into the street. I hardly needed to give directions. He knew my initial stop was at *Okhotny Riad* to do some shopping for my dinner. The Hunter's Row had the best game in town. I would select a grouse, perhaps, or a snow chicken, with the customary sour cream to roast it in, and whatever fresh vegetables and fruit could be had—mostly cabbage, onions, and beets, and those tart little apples, yellow and red, called *Antonovka*. From there I continued via the Theatre Square to the Petrovka, where I knew a pastry shop that made excellent little *piroznye*, those cream-filled cakes the Russians love. In those youthful days I had no reason to watch my weight, which always remained the same. And, of course, my purchases were never complete without Malossol caviar, smoked salmon and that other tasty little Russian fish, smoked *kilki*. Sometimes, if I was fortunate enough, I would discover a dusty bottle of *Abrao Durceaux*, that extremely potable native champagne of pre-Revolutionary vintage, much enjoyed by the former tsars.

On my way back over the *Arbat*, a commercial center, I would stop for an appointment with my hairdresser, or continue on to Sofika, where a very good tailor would make me a dress, copied from one I had, or a coat to order. I also frequently stopped at the *Kusnetzky Most* in the hope of finding something to read in English, French, or German, at the only bookstore open to customers. Usually I returned empty-handed, for books in foreign languages, even second hand, were rarer than hen's teeth. By the beginning of 1925, however, conditions had improved sufficiently for people to purchase these things.

At home I would hand my groceries to Pasha, our cook, who ordinarily did all right with them, except once when I brought back that very rare vegetable, asparagus. She apparently had never cooked it before, and served up the stalks without the heads.

Every afternoon I held my dancing classes. First the younger, or beginners' group, followed by my more advanced students. Teaching is more tiring than performing, and I always welcomed the sight of the tall brass samovar, hissing a column of steam to the ceiling, that Frosia had ready for me; with a pot of good black Chinese tea (the best in the world), which the Russians drink out of glasses with lemon and sugar nibbling on the side.

If Irma Duncan's description of her typical day in Moscow could be read purely and simply against the background of Isadora's existence in Berlin at the very same time, one might choose to regard these pages as classics of unconscious humor. But, unfortunately, they clearly reveal Irma's feelings toward Isadora (her foster mother, as she calls her throughout her book) and the attitude Irma had developed, which put an end to the Isadora Duncan School.

It is clear that, having usurped Isadora's place in the school through the accident of her temporary absence, Irma was now busily cutting all Isadora's ties with it—hence her silence during her "foster mother's" desperate months in Berlin. "Isadora, in the interval since her departure and subsequent arrival in Nice, had suffered continuous catastrophes," Irma remarks in her autobiography. "Her Berlin engagement turned into a complete fiasco. She repeatedly sent letters asking for help. But since all my mail had to be forwarded while I was in the Volga district, her letters reached me too late. By the time I could answer, Isadora had left Germany and settled in the south of France."

Irma's tour of the Volga district did not start immediately upon Isadora's departure from Russia, nor would it have taken months for Isadora's forwarded letters to reach Irma anywhere in Russia. But Isadora was completely unaware that she had lost her school to her pupil. Several months later (January 27, 1925), in a letter to Irma, Isadora still showed her complete faith in her. "I appreciate your hanging on to the school. And together we will accomplish something yet. Remember you are the *only* pupil of mine who has understood what I am trying to do in this world. And you are the only one who cares whether myself or our work lives or dies, and it may be that the understanding of *one* will save *all*.

"Can't you possibly manage to send me some pictures of the children?" Isadora still asked Irma, as she had done in her letters from Berlin five months earlier. "Often I could make propaganda and obtain help for you if I had photos. Do try and have some taken, and if you cannot, send me at least some copies of what you have. Also I would appreciate it if you would let me have the dates of your *tournées* and programs. Someone told me you were all on the Volga. I knew nothing of it."

The letter was written in Nice, where Isadora finally landed after having been rescued from her intolerable situation in Berlin by some friends in the United States, who managed to scrape together sufficient funds to have Isadora go first to Brussels, and then, through Cécile Sorel's intervention with the French authorities—whom she persuaded that Isadora was not a dangerous Soviet agent—to Paris. From there, Raymond took her to Nice. He had built a flourishing business for himself, with studios and shops in Paris and Nice, where through his lectures on ancient Greece and the arts in general he assembled a large number of disciples. While living a spartan existence on a vegetarian diet, they were all weaving rugs, making sandals and togas, printing pamphlets and painting posters as collaborators in Raymond's commercial enterprises. A firm believer in his own way of living, Raymond extended to his sister the kind of hospitality that would not tax his business or his housekeeping—Isadora was given one of the hard, sheepskin-covered wooden benches, and occasionally *frutta di mare* to break the monotony of the daily vegetarian menus. Isadora had always been devoted to the members of her family; she had never criticized their ways of living; but as far as she herself was concerned, she could not enjoy shelter at Raymond's for any length of time.

Through the assistance of her friends, she managed to have a small room engaged for her at a *prix d'artiste* in the Hotel Negresco, the most expensive hotel on the Riviera. And, even more important, a small, abandoned theater was made available to her. In no time her grandiose plans revived. Nevertheless, she wrote to Irma:

"The world is a sickening place. I am. living from hand to mouth. My *friends* have all deserted me. The joke of the whole thing is that it is current gossip that I received vast sums from the Soviets. Isn't that beautiful?"

But this gossip, intriguing and even glamorous, which served as a topic for otherwise empty chitchat at parties was not generally taken seriously. However, the rumors that Isadora had been approached by several sensational magazines to publish her love letters had some basis in fact. Indeed, she had offers not only to publish her correspondence, but her memoirs. In reply to all these sudden prospects of earning large sums, Isadora, however, stressed that if she were to write her memoirs, they would be devoted to her art, which was far more important to her than revealing the details of her love affairs.

She hastened to share her news with Irma: "I have some faint hope on the horizon, but nothing is sure yet. I was offered by the Chicago *Tribune* a sum for my memoirs, but afterwards it all turned to *blackmail*, and they wrote fearful articles by way of revenge." The revenge in question was cruel and thorough, for the libelous newspaper campaign against her was almost worldwide—all based on the fact that Isadora had not only not spoken against the Soviets, but had danced the *Internationale* before thousands of the working-class in Berlin. "I am suing the *Tribune*, but the suit does not advance because I have not the funds to launch it. It seems such suits cost a lot of money," Isadora wrote to Irma.

"If I receive the $20,000 promised, I will either come to Moscow in the spring with money, or if you think Moscow hopeless, you can join me in London with sixteen pupils. But *reflect well* which will be the best."

And still completely ignorant of the fact that she was no longer the mistress of her Moscow school, she kept on asking Irma to send her pictures of the school and the children, assuring her that with these she could raise funds for her. "For Heaven's sake write to me," she pleaded in every letter to Irma. "People hardly believe there is a school. Write to me. Tell me what hope is there for the school? Will the house remain? Is anything stable, or is it quicksand?"

Not suspecting any schemes on Irma's or Schneider's part, Isadora felt that the school was doomed unlees the government was willing to assist it. "But you know, being prophetic, I sensed as much when I was last there. Ask Ilya [Schneider]," Isadora suggested, hoping for a practical solution to the problem, "to write me and answer the following questions: What does he advise? Has he any hopes for this summer from Podvoysky or others? Would my return make things better or worse?"

Isadora's return certainly would have been the least welcome eventuality, for once she took matters in hand again, it could hardly be expected that Irma would return to her former position as Isadora's "favorite pupil," nor would Schneider have been pleased to have Isadora interfering with his plans for Irma's tours "the length and breadth of that vast land." And there was no question of Irma's joining Isadora in Nice so that, as Isadora wrote her, "perhaps together we may find some way out," but which Irma looked upon as joining Isadora in her "grandiose, ephemeral and unobtainable plans." It certainly would have been most impractical for Irma to take such a step, since she claimed that once her own professional tours began, "in the end, [she] was giving a hundred performances a year." Even allowing for a good deal of exaggeration —for Irma's figure comes to one performance every three days, including holidays—she obviously had a motive for confirming her separation from Isadora.

Seemingly not affected by her own precarious situation, Isadora apparently was more possessed by her idea of having a school, no matter where, than ever before in her life. She thought that she could create another Bayreuth right there, in the small old theater in Nice, and yet, after meeting someone, who had expressed great plans for going to Jerusalem, she said, "Perhaps we might go there!!!"

She went back and forth to Paris, where, depending on the amount of her friends' bounty, she lodged in a palatial suite at one of the fashionable hotels or in an unheated studio without a bathroom. "Do not speak of my personal affairs," was her optimistic attitude, "we will arrange them one way or another." All that mattered to her was her school.

She had several interviews with Christian Rakovsky, the Soviet Ambassador, seeking his help in bringing some of her Russian pupils to Paris. At the same time she was negotiating with the leaders of the French Communist party to obtain their financial assistance in establishing her school in France. "Let them give me five hundred, a thousand children, and I will make them do wonderful things! . . . If they will give me a thousand children, I will bring my best pupils from Moscow. They will act as monitors of the school, and they will live with me, being nourished and clothed by me. Living among my books and works of art, they will, impregnated by my principles . . ."—which must have sounded like the refrain from an old *idée fixe* to everybody except Isadora.

Chapter XXXIX

After I had met Isadora at a private concert I gave in Paris some months earlier, she asked me to go with her on one of her visits to Christian Rakovsky. It was early spring of 1925. At that time, the rue de Grenelle in Paris was synonymous with everything evil, criminal, and sinister. It was there, behind fifteen-foot walls, that the Soviet Embassy was located. The mere words, "rue de Grenelle," were sufficient for taxi drivers to know your destination, but not until Isadora and I entered the premises of the embassy did she say, smiling at me mischievously, "Now you are done for. Now you are just as red as I am."

These receptions at the Soviet Embassy were the debut of sumptuous parties which in later years became very popular in the capitals of the Western world. Having graciously led us to a small table at this garden party, Rakovsky left us. Most of the guests were persons curious about the proletarian manner of entertaining rather than adherents of the Soviets. Perhaps the ambassador had thought that Isadora, like the rest of his guests, would be content with caviar sandwiches, vodka, and a glass of champagne. But he soon learned that her visit was strictly business. For after quickly appraising the assembled company, Isadora asked me to come with her—she was going to have another conference with Rakovsky. "You must keep after them; the way to get things done in this world is to keep after them," she said. And, indeed, on this occasion I heard Isadora

((373))

present her case for establishing an auxiliary to her Moscow school in Paris, in the most practical terms, and without beclouding the issue with her usual romantic phraseology.

Whether Rakovsky was well informed or not about the state of affairs at Isadora's Moscow school, he promised to use his influence with the government authorities. Later, after Isadora had thanked him for his assistance, Rakovsky took me aside and asked me to try to convey to Isadora, as he himself had apparently been trying to do during all their "conferences," that there simply was no money allocated in the government budget for projects such as hers.

But Isadora was already on her way to discuss her business with a man who was drinking at the buffet. "I suppose Rakovsky told you that they have no money," Isadora whispered to me. "And what about all this?" and she pointed to the tables laden with caviar sandwiches, and bottles of vodka and champagne. "But I must now speak to that man," and she indicated the one person present who was dressed in a cutaway and wearing a top hat. "It is very important," she said. Because Charles Rappaport, always present at such events, had informed her that the man was from the Italian Embassy, Isadora assumed that he was the Italian Ambassador. After being introduced to him, and acknowledging with a sweet smile the gentleman's flattering commentaries on her art, Isadora put her charm into high gear. She spoke to him of her friendship with D'Annunzio, of her love and admiration for Duse, of the unforgettable time she had spent with Duse and Gordon Craig in Florence—all leading to her suggestion that Mussolini should let her establish a school in Italy. "I am going to have my school here very soon," she told the man. "The Russian Ambassador is very kind, he is going to bring my school here. But, of course, I should have schools everywhere. And there is nobody in the world who can appreciate my art more than the Italians. You should give me a thousand children to teach. I will teach all Italy to dance."

For "a highly paid Soviet agent," Isadora certainly showed embarrassing ignorance—she was offering her ideas, which she said were flourishing in Soviet Russia, to a representative of the fascist state. But such trivial details never troubled her.

The man in the top hat looked vague, either because he understood nothing of what Isadora was saying, or because he was puzzled by her suggestion that all Italy would dance. Trying his best not to hurt Isadora's feelings, he told her that, unfortunately, he was not in a position to influence Mussolini. But Isadora was not easily put off, especially when the matter concerned such a vital question as that of her school. "Oh, yes, you can! Don't say no. I know you can." Only much later during the reception did Isadora learn that she had been prematurely happy about having a school in Italy, and that when she was saying, "You know, you can do a great deal for me," she had been speaking not to the Italian Ambassador, but to a very minor official at the Italian Consulate.

Some time had to pass before one could risk annoying her by pointing out her error, but once Isadora had regained her sense of humor, she herself enjoyed mimicking the scene. She could make fun of herself in this way because, despite all her disappointments, she never lost her faith in people's willingness to assist her in her clearly defined, beautiful idea.

"Even from a purely commercial point of view," Isadora repeated to me many times, "I am a living gold mine of art—I am offering it free for exploitation, and yet no one seems to want it. Isn't it incredible?

Following her principle, "The way to get things done in this world is to keep after them," Isadora began her day at that period by consulting her two large address books. And almost every day she would introduce me to some man or woman saying: "This is my most faithful friend. What would I ever do without him! Now, he is going to help me. We all must keep on the job."

And, after repeating to me one of the grandiose schemes she and this friend had been discussing, Isadora would quietly summarize, "All we really need is a little capital." This encouraging remark would drop the enthusiasm of her most faithful friends to its lowest ebb; he or she, or even a group of the faithful, would search their pockets for a few francs with which to tip the waiter who was clearing the table—the lunch itself was being put on Isadora's ever-mounting hotel bill. Then, suddenly remembering an important engagement, they would hurriedly depart, sometimes even forgetting to assure Isadora once more that they were entirely at her service.

To the last days of her life, I witnessed such scenes almost daily in Isadora's hotel rooms or studios, either in Paris or in Nice, the two cities in which she had lived alternatively ever since her return from Russia. Who, then, were these most faithful friends? They were of different nationalities, different ages, and different professions, but with one common denominator—they were almost invariably homosexual, both the men and the women.

Not being an expert in psychiatry, I would not assert as axiomatic that lying, intrigue, and treachery are necessarily characteristic of that third sex, but at the time when Isadora was most in need of firm ground under her feet, her friends did seem to be singularly afflicted with such habits.

Chiefly hoping for some publicity in connection with Isadora's name, they not only gossiped, but managed to get into the press their "eyewitness" reports of events that had never happened. They even misrepresented her political views to such an extent that she had to send a written protest to the newspapers. As a result, on the one hand she was virtually boycotted in Europe, because of her affiliation with the Soviets, and on the other she was accused of criticizing the Soviet Government.

And yet I could understand her tolerating this band of ne'er-do-wells who announced that their art would someday astound the world. For Isadora truly needed a counterbalance to my sober and pessimistic appraisal of her position. And, at least at the beginning of her life in France, after her return from Russia, their companionship kept Isadora distracted from distressing thoughts of "What to do? Suicide, or wait, or what?" which kept her awake at night.

Neither distance, nor weather, nor warnings of the futility of her efforts could induce her to miss an opportunity of meeting somebody who, after having been introduced to her ideas, might possibly patronize her project—"for all we need," Isadora told everybody "is a little capital."

I went with Isadora on one such errand. "We must be nice to her," Isadora kept advising me in the taxi as we were driving to the home of an American of whom Isadora knew nothing except that the lady claimed to admire Isadora's art. But, since she was rich, Isadora already considered her a potential benefactress.

The large, high-ceilinged, luxurious studio into which we were ushered by the maid, was furnished with everything that Isadora lacked in her austere hotel room—grand piano, low couches on a beautiful blue rug, and dim lights from lamps placed at the corners of the room. Our hostess was an overfed, overdressed, bejeweled woman who, despite her considerable weight, floated into the room like a swan on water. "You know, Miss Duncan," she said, after she had completed the ceremony of serving us tea and soggy cakes, "you, of all people, will understand me. For years I wanted to have a studio! But, my family was always in the way. Now, at last, I can live like an artist!"

"But what do you do?" Isadora asked her.

"Oh, I want to live beautifully! I paint! I dance! I sing! I write poetry! And by the way," she added, as if what she was about to add was merely of secondary importance, "you know, Miss Duncan, I believe every child ought to be taught to dance."

"Yes, I have heard somebody else say that," Isadora timidly agreed.

But she did not hear Isadora because she was too preoccupied with showing us her crayon drawings of flowers, which she took carefully, one by one, out of beautiful leather porfolios. "They are very beautiful," Isadora managed to say, as she passed them for me to see. "Ah, but you must look at them this way," our hostess said, and, as she turned the drawings in various directions, she confidentially disclosed, "They are not real flowers, they are fairy flowers; don't you see the eyes in them, don't you see the smiling faces of children?"

Fortunately, Isadora did not hear her last comment because a sudden blast from a gramophone almost drowned the woman's voice —the accompaniment of recorded music was indispensable, she explained, to the proper exhibition of her work. But before our hostess gave us a sample of her dancing, which was obviously coming next on the program, Isadora graciously made her excuses for cutting short our most pleasant visit.

"Oh, I am so sorry," our disappointed hostess said, "because I wanted so much to dance for you. You know, Miss Duncan, you and I, we could. . . ." But although she did not finish the sentence, we could easily guess her words.

Our hasty departure from Mrs. Van Magden's home was not the end of Isadora's acquaintance with the lady. A year later, when Isadora and I were in Nice, Mrs. Van Magden announced through a mutual acquaintance her desire to visit her good friend Isadora Duncan. This time it was up to Isadora to receive the potential benefactress, and I helped her in arranging her large, recently rented studio on the Promenade des Anglais. After the rug had been swept, the couches placed in rows as if to accommodate a large audience, and the tall alabaster lamps lit, Isadora, exhausted, said to me, "If this won't do, I don't know what will. But you must promise me to play for her. I suppose I'll have to dance. Or perhaps she'll dance. I just hope she won't sing."

Mrs. Van Magden did not sing, and fortunately I knew the pieces she asked me to play. However, no sooner did I finish playing the composition of her choice than she would say, "Oh, my brother plays that for me so beautifully." This encouraging remark would soon have ended my recital in any case, but Mrs. Van Magden, having mentioned her brother, now hastened to warn Isadora that that gentleman must never see her in Isadora's company, for he did not understand his sister's artistic aspirations. She also made it clear that it would hurt both her social position and her character to be seen associating with the scarlet woman of America.

Needless to say, not even a hint of financial assistance for Isadora's school project was ever offered by Mrs. Van Magden. But I, who naïvely regarded the lady as a unique example of vulgarity, was destined to witness more than one such scene which, for the sake of her *idée fixe*, Isadora stoically tolerated.

I was at one of the dinner parties that Count Etienne de Beaumont used to give at his home in Paris and to which, among other guests, he invited a few celebrities from the artistic world. Isadora was one of them. As some twenty-five persons took their places at table, I noticed a woman nosily pushing her way to her chair. It was Mary Barnwell, known as Manya, the Russian diminutive for Mary, because of her extravagant nightly behavior at the *boîtes de nuit* in Montmartre, where she freely dispensed among her Russian gigolos the monthly allowance she received from her husband, a New York banker. She could have been Mrs. Van Magden's counterpart—overfed, overdressed, and overjeweled—for these women all seemed to have come off the same assembly line. Mrs. Barnwell was then in her late forties, and it was rumored that in her youth she had been a pretty Follies girl on Broadway. After their marriage, her husband sent her abroad with a generous allowance, and it was said that whenever she needed extra cash, all she had to do was to cable him that she was returning home.

We were about to start our dinner when Mrs. Barnwell's loud

voice broke the few moments of silence during which the guests dipped their spoons into their soup. She had noticed Isadora on the other side of the table, and, in a sudden fury, turning to the count, her host, she proudly announced, "My dear man, if I had known that you would have that red whore here, I would never have set foot in your home."

This bombshell embarrassed the count, and everybody else at the table. Had such a remark been made by a man, he would have been taken by the scruff of his neck and thrown out of the house, but since Isadora's offender was a woman, everyone was speechless. Most of the guests lowered their eyes to their plates, but I was sitting not far from Isadora on the other side of the table, and I looked straight at her.

Only for a split second did her face express shock. Then, smiling, she turned her head toward the butler, and said in her gentle, melodious voice: "Do you have something sweet in the house? I feel the need of it just now."

Extremely sensitive, Isadora was vulnerable to any remarks about herself. Once she was on the stage, either as a performer or making one of her inflammatory speeches, no audience could intimidate her, but when walking on the street, she suddenly would become shy about her appearance, for she was conscious of being recognized by the people who passed her, and she seemed to shrink from them, especially when she heard them murmur her name.

Thus she liked to spend hours in my studio in the Bois de Boulogne. At that time it was outside the city limits, and because it was located in a private estate surrounded by high walls, and one had to pass through a small courtyard and then through a neglected garden before reaching the high-ceilinged bungalow, Isadora referred to my studio as the home of Alice in Wonderland. She enjoyed its quiet. She felt secure, she said, from the intrusion of uninvited guests, but above all from a *huissier*, an official debt collector, for she knew that once she had passed through the gate, my concierge, to whom Isadora was a superhuman being, would neither let anyone else in nor disclose her presence there.

Reclining on a couch, Isadora would listen for hours to my practicing the piano—she said it was an important part of our *"solitude à deux."* However, I learned then, as others had before, about certain limitations in her appreciation of musical literature. She liked the classics, but the music of Ravel or Debussy still failed to inspire her. "It is only the music of the *senses* and has no message for the spirit," she told me, just as she had written several years earlier to her six girls, who were concertizing on their own in the United States. "The gesture of Debussy is all *inward*—and has no outward or upward." But in the symphonies of Beethoven, Mozart, and Schubert, as well as in the scores of César Franck, Tchaikovsky, and Wagner, she found a music which, she said, "goes from the soul in mounting circles."

Our discussions of music never evolved into arguments over our personal tastes. Perhaps I should mention here that the many written references to me as Isadora's accompanist are mistaken. I never was Isadora's accompanist, neither at her public performances or when she danced for an intimate circle of friends in her studio— or at some friend's home, except on a single occasion, of which I shall speak in the next chapter. I played for Isadora during countless hours in my studio, in her studio in Nice, and in her studio apartment in Paris. I played for her the scores that she planned to include in her programs, usually when we were alone. She never made a single gesture while I was playing, but remained concentrated on and quietly absorbed in the music. We never directly discussed this subject; it was a sort of silent understanding between us—I believed that there is an important difference between giving a solo interpretation of a composition and one accompanied by an extra medium. Isadora realized that our collaboration could not be harmonious. She wisely preferred that I remain a musician, a pianist who was always there to discuss music with her, or play it for her enjoyment.

It was during her first visits to my studio that she decided that the bookshelves along the walls of the room would be the safest place for her library, and asked me to rescue whatever was left of it in the attic of her former house on the rue de la Pompe. The loving care with which Isadora cleaned, sorted, and placed the books on the shelves, often interrupting her time-consuming chore by reading to me passages from a volume that evoked memories of her past, showed how much her library meant to her. It also showed her capacity for temporarily isolating herself from the most destructive aspects of her current life, finding a refuge in an abstract world that no doubt renewed her strength to face again the trials of the everyday one. Then she would write to Irma and, still asking for photographs of the school, she would say that she was ready to carry on the "battle." Her hope of sustaining this battle with the money she would gain from her performances at her studio in Nice, as well as from the sums she expected to earn with her memoirs, drew her once more to that city.

But on the evening of December 31, 1925, while she was dressing for a New Year's Eve celebration, she received the shocking news, soon confirmed by a telegram from Schneider, that Sergei Essenin had committed suicide.

During the following days, both the French newspapers and the Russian-language papers published in Paris carried detailed reports of the poet's death, mostly speculating about his motives. The mention of room number five at the Hotel d'Angleterre, where Essenin had put an end to his life, had a special meaning to Isadora. Later she told me that room number five was the one in which she and Essenin had stayed in 1923 when he went to Petrograd with her for the first time, and that one day, looking at the ceiling, he had said to her, "Do you see that hook? That would be the place to hang oneself." "And so that is what he did," Isadora concluded in her Dostoyevskian analysis.

Actually, Isadora knew almost nothing about Essenin's life after they had parted. After she left Russia, she used to say that she had heard Essenin had gone to the Caucasus, where he had become the head of a group of bandits, so that he might portray their true characters in his poems.

She had also heard from "reliable sources" that Essenin had gone to Persia, where he had married a Persian princess. Naturally, none of these romantic stories was true. Essenin had been in the Caucasus several times, but not because of any interest in the so-called bandits; he had formed close friendships with Georgian poets, and he felt that he worked better in Tiflis or in Batum, far away from the distracting life of Moscow. Of the twenty poems written at that time, he judged some of them to be among his best.

He never went to Persia, and he did not marry a Persian princess, but although not divorced, on September 18, 1925, he did marry Sofia Tolstoy—Suhotina, the novelist's granddaughter.

"Don't you think it sounds good: Sergei Essenin married to the granddaughter of Leo Tolstoy?" he said to Schneider, when the two friends met for what turned out to be the last time. But he was not in love with Sofia Tolstoy. In her home, into which he had already moved in June, she tried to normalize his life, but it was not long before he was irritated by all the mementos of the novelist that filled the apartment. He complained to his friends, "In every room, on every wall, is that beard."

Two and a half months later he entered a hospital, not because of insanity, as malicious gossip suggested, but because he was mortally afraid of the police and the courts. Someone had threatened him with a lawsuit, and his sister Katya discovered that, if he entered a hospital for treatment of his nerves, no court proceedings could pursue him. In fact, he was given complete freedom in the hospital; he worked and received visitors, and his favorite dishes were brought to him by his sisters. Then, without saying a word to anybody, he left the hospital on December 22. During the following few days, while still in Moscow, he visited his first wife, Izryadovna, in whose kitchen he insisted on burning some of his papers and manuscripts. On December 24 he arrived in Leningrad.

He took room number five at the Hotel d'Angleterre to be near his friends the Ustinovs, the writer and his wife. He seemed to be in good spirits and said that he was going to start a new life in Leningrad, that he would not drink again, and would return neither to Moscow nor to his wife. He was through with marriage, having married three times, and according to the law, he said, that was the limit. He was not going to write poetry but he was working on a novel, which he would show them as soon as he finished the first part.

But on the following day he appeared to be depressed. Speaking to Mme. Ustinov, he complained of being bored.

"And what about your work?" she asked.

"A boring work," he said, smiling as if he were ashamed of what he had said. "I don't need anybody nor anything. I simply don't want anything. Champagne makes you gay, gives you courage. Then I am capable of loving . . . even myself. Life is a cheap thing, but I guess necessary. But I am God's fife."

"What is that?" Mme. Ustinov asked him.

"It is when a man spends everything from his treasury and does not replenish it. He had nothing to replenish it with, and it really doesn't even interest him. And that is what I am."

On that day, Essenin wrote a short poem in his own blood,

which he drew from his wrist—"In this hotel they don't even have any ink," he explained. This poem he put into the pocket of Wolf Erlich, the poet, saying to his friend, "You can read it later."

On the following morning (December 28), when Mme. Ustinov came to call him for breakfast, she found him hanging from a hook.

The poem he gave to Erlich was published as Essenin's last message:

To a Friend

Good-bye, my friend, good-bye!
You are still in my breast, beloved.
This fated parting
Holds for us a meeting in the future.
Good-bye, my friend, without hand or word;
Be not sad nor lower your brow.
In this life to die is not new;
And to live, surely, is not any newer.

Shortly after his death, I read in a Russian newspaper in Paris another poem that was supposed to have been his last. In its content it was close to his conversation with Mme. Ustinov, for the gist of the poem was—I have been given a talent, looks, and every opportunity, but I have recklessly burned it all. Now there is nothing left for me in life.

Isadora was spared all these details, for, even later, when some more information became available, the names mentioned remained mere names to her, since she did not know his friends. But more than a year later, she did hear mention, in that connection, of Galina Benislavskaya, who was supposed to have sent that telegram to Isadora that had caused her so much pain.

Almost a year after Essenin's death, on December 3, 1926, Galina Benislavskaya shot herself on Essenin's grave. "I took my own life here," she wrote in a note left beside her body, "though I know that after this, they will heap even more abuse on Essenin. But that will not make any difference to him, or to me any more. In this grave is buried everything I hold dear."

The news of Essenin's death furnished the French and American newspapers with an opportunity to rehash the old stories about his life with Isadora. She promptly telegraphed her protest to the newspaper agencies:

> The news of the tragic death of Essenin has caused me the deepest pain. He had youth, beauty, genius. Not content with all these gifts, his audacious spirit sought the unattainable, and he wished to lay low the Philistines.
>
> He has destroyed his young and splendid body, but his soul will live eternally in the soul of the Russian people and in the souls of those who love the poets. I protest strongly against the frivolous and inexact statements printed in the American press in Paris. There was never between Essenin and myself any quarrel or divorce. I weep over his death with anguish and despair.
>
> Isadora Duncan

And to Schneider from Paris she wrote in January, "Essenin's death was a terrible blow to me, but I cried so much that I cannot suffer any more and I am so unhappy myself now that I often think of following his example, but in a different way. I would prefer the sea."

Although Isadora often spoke of committing suicide, no one took the threat seriously, for in the next breath she would speak of plans for her school that could only be carried out by an Isadora who was very much alive. Through her acquaintances in the artistic circles of Paris, she had managed to stir up considerable interest in her projects among the members of the French Communist party, projects that varied in magnitude according to the encouragement she happened to receive. She was pleased with a suggestion of having the children from her Moscow school, not only as monitors in the future French school, but to have them give a series of performances under the patronage of the French Communist party, thus serving two purposes: earning prestige for the party and providing initial financial support for the school. If her travel expenses were paid, she was ready to go back to Moscow and bring the children to Paris herself. She kept repeating that she asked nothing for herself but, of course, in that case she would have to go on tours to make money for the school, while she would much rather devote herself entirely "to creating a magnificent social center, instead of little troupes which, by force of circumstances, degenerate into theatrical troupes. If the school can be started in Paris, for the workers' children, I have great hopes. I am ready to make all possible and impossible sacrifices as I have already done in Moscow."

And she sincerely believed that "when the Soviets see what a success the children have, they will surely do something for the school."

Anxious to have another conference with Rakovsky, and most especially with Lunacharsky, who she heard was on a short visit in Paris, Isadora returned to that city. She missed Lunacharsky—he had already gone back to Russia. But a few weeks later, Isadora heard from him about an entirely different matter. Rather late in the evening, Isadora telephoned me and asked me to come immediately to see her: "It is very important, very urgent, and I need your help, please come as soon as you can."

I found Isadora sitting up in bed in her room in the Hotel Lutetia. All sorts of newspaper clippings, old theater and concert programs, books, and what I later learned were manuscript pages of her memoirs, were strewn about the covers on her bed. "Here is a letter from Lunacharsky," she said as she handed me a piece of paper. "Please read it carefully."

Writing in French, Lunacharsky was officially informing Comrade Duncan that, since she was not divorced from Sergei Essenin, but was his widow and his heir, the High Court in Moscow had confirmed her right to his estate. "And here is my answer," Isadora said as she gave me another piece of paper. "I would like to telegraph this to Lunacharsky, and also to the High Court in Moscow—there is the address in Lunacharsky's letter—but it must be in Russian. You know what a mess they can make out of the most simple message. Would you translate it for me? Please."

"Of course," I said.

"But right now. It must be sent immediately," Isadora said, and I knew that in her mind's eye she already saw me driving to the Bourse, where the telegraph office functioned all night.

The messages to Lunacharsky and the Moscow court were identical and read as follows: "I have made one vulgar gesture by marrying. I would not make another by divorcing. Since according to your laws I am the sole heir to Sergei Essenin's estate, I wish to state my wish to have his entire estate be given to his mother and his sisters. Isadora Duncan."

As it turned out later, Isadora's treatment of her legitimate inheritance rights was exploited by her friends to prove the nobility of her character. An entirely fictitious story was widely publicized and was repeated in books written about Isadora after her death. The pattern of the tale was somewhat unimaginative: At that time, when Isadora was practically starving, she had declined to accept an inheritance to which she was legitimately entitled. And to make this information even more impressive, a sum of 300,000 francs was mentioned, supposedly representing Essenin's royalties from his books.

At the time of his death, Essenin did not have 300,000 francs (about $15,000); he was 2,500 rubles in debt to the Soviet Government's publishing house. Four months before his death, Essenin had decided to have a celebration of two marriages—his own to Sofia Tolstoy-Suhotin (officially registered on September 18), and that of his sister Katya to his friend Nikolai Nikitin, the poet. For this occasion, Essenin managed to get an advance for a volume of poems he was later to deliver to the publisher. Otherwise, except for some books and clothes scattered in the homes of his friends, Essenin had no "estate" to leave.

And as for Isadora's "practically starving," this notion derives from the old-fashioned theory that every artist must live in a garret, must starve, must remain a complete failure, until one day, as if he had won the sweepstakes, his work is recognized and he becomes rich and famous—a theory that originated with and is favored by the ignorant.

Except during her life in Russia, where food shortages were endured by everyone, Isadora never missed a meal—and these were of a kind that most people would envy. How her lunches and dinners were paid for is another story, but those who spoke of her starvation should have been reminded that Isadora hated to have her meals alone, and always managed to share them with one or two guests to keep her company. And as incongruous as it may sound, it was these very guests who originated and spread the stories of her "hunger," among them the faithful friends, some of whom, as will be seen in the next chapter, made enough money from their involvement in Isadora's business affairs not only to pay for these meals, but easily to contribute to the settling of Isadora's more pressing debts—matters, of course, that never crossed their minds.

Chapter XL

There was one friend of Isadora's, however—the only one to the best of my knowledge—who fully deserved Isadora's remark, "What would I ever do without her?"—though this rhetorical question, unfortunately, was one with which Isadora indiscriminately greeted almost anybody who called on her in those trying days. The friend was the same Ruth Mitchell who had emptied her purse to pay for Isadora's passage back to Europe when she and her seventeen girls were stranded in New York in 1916.

"Now everything will be all right," Isadora would say to me, cheerfully waving a cablegram announcing Ruth Mitchell's arrival in Paris. And, indeed, "Aunty Ruthy," as we nicknamed her, with utter selflessness and a largesse limited only by the extent of the "little capital" that she could save up in a year in the United States, paid Isadora's debts, and on this occasion bought an open Mathis four-seater and took Isadora on a most pleasant journey to the Riviera.

In Nice they discovered a large old wooden barn which Isadora was certain she could transform into a studio. And, as if to show what she meant by "all we need is a little capital," with her ingenuity and with Aunty Ruthy's financial assistance, Isadora created a small the-ater at the far west end of the Promenade des Anglais. No. 343 Prome-nade des Anglais became known as *Studio D'Isadora Duncan*. Just as in the case of my studio in the Bois de Boulogne, one had to pass

((387))

through a courtyard before entering the building. The large, high-ceilinged room had been divided into two parts. One of these sections, which was slightly elevated, could have been used as a stage, but Isadora preferred to reserve it for the audience. Instead of chairs, there were twelve couches—actually box springs with mattresses—covered with soft bois-de-rose velvet. Isadora's long, voluminous blue curtains, which for almost twenty-five years had formed the background to her performances, covered the walls, and, with the thick blue carpet, muffled sound in the interior. The indirect lighting from the tall alabaster lamps contributed to the feeling of serenity and beauty.

Together with a small apartment, less than a few minutes' walking distance from the studio, which Isadora had rented for herself, this place became her general headquarters from which she either sent out SOS signals or a whole list of additional new projects.

After Ruth Mitchell had paid the rent in advance for several months, presented her Mathis to Isadora, and spent all her "little capital," she went back to New York—for such was the pattern of her yearly visits to Isadora.

"My plan is that you should come here on a visit as soon as possible," Isadora wrote to Irma about her latest idea for her school. "We could start here a *paying school* à la Elizabeth, and take pupils from America to board, etc. You could bring one or two of the older girls as co-teachers. By spending six months here and six months in Moscow, we could join the ideal and the material."

Still unaware of the fact that she had lost her Moscow school, she wrote: "Dear Irma, if you will be faithful, I still feel we may arise and conquer the earth and knock all these sham schools and sham disciples to smash. But the time is going and I am like a wrecked mariner on a desert island yelling for help." Isadora closed her letter with still another project of hiring the opera house and orchestra in Marseilles for a series of festival performances if Irma could bring twelve of the oldest pupils. "I press you to my heart, dear Irma. Let us hope for the future. Isadora."

In her autobiography, Irma disclosed her reaction to Isadora's letters. "This left me in a terrible quandary. Torn between my love and loyalty to her on the one hand, and my work and further career mapped out in Russia on the other, what was I to do? Such a division of my labors as she outlined in her letter was impractical. Since she relied entirely on my help, either one school or the other would suffer because of my absence. I have often asked myself in retrospect: By deciding ruthlessly to tear up the roots in Moscow and throw in my lot with her—since I could not do both—could I have been in a position to prevent her tragic, premature demise? I doubt it, for fate has a relentless way of catching up with its victim marked for death."

Irma had no intention of joining the "wrecked mariner on a desert island yelling for help," for in summarizing her decision, she said in her autobiography, "For over a year, ever since our unprecedented, enthusiastic reception by the public on our Volga tour, we had planned a similar undertaking for Siberia. Under no circumstances could I cancel it now."

I do not know whether Irma ever directly answered Isadora's many desperate queries, but I do remember that Irma came to Paris early in 1927 and lunched with Isadora (Irma speaks of this meeting in her memoirs). Nonetheless, to her last days Isadora believed the school in Moscow was still hers.

Irma eventually went on her tour to Siberia, and even to China, and Isadora's hopes of building a theater in a year or two—"a Bayreuth by the sea," as she said—had joined her other pipe dreams.

She did, however, manage to give several performances at her studio, the first of a series "celebrating Good Friday," as she said, with a program of sacred music. "It was a great success," she wrote to Irma (April 17, 1926). "A hundred tickets were sold at a hundred francs a ticket and great *stimmung* and enthusiasm. The studio was *lovely* with alabaster lamps, candles, incense, heaps of white lilies, and lilacs." It reminded Isadora of the old days when, in collaboration with Walter Rummel, she gave such "concerts" at her home on the rue de la Pompe. But by the time the pianist, the florist, and all the "small expenses" connected with the decoration of the studio for these performances, were paid, Isadora was left practically penniless. The winter season on the Riviera was drawing to a close, so she turned her interest to writing her memoirs, for she was convinced that she could solve her financial problems once and for all in that way.

Since she repeatedly said that she was not a writer and would not even know how to begin her memoirs, she took the advice of her friends and engaged a stenographer to whom she began to dictate her life story. I had met Miss Nickson, a middle-aged English spinster, and could easily have predicted the short duration of this collaboration. "It is worse than having a governess," Isadora complained to me. "She keeps interrupting some of my inspired and colorful description by her Oh's and Ah's. 'Miss Duncan, you don't really mean to say this . . . you simply cannot.' Can you imagine it? What am I to do?" Isadora continued almost in tears as she picked up one of Miss Nickson's typewritten pages and asked me to read it.

"Since she was recommended to me, I cannot stop, or I'll hear the Greek chorus of my friends screaming at me that I am lazy, that I don't want to do anything, but have everybody do things for me. Oh, what am I to do?"

I suggested that for a while she skip her personal reminiscences and dictate to Miss Nickson her history as a performer. "Oh that's a wonderful idea." Isadora felt better immediately. "I could even take her with me to Paris to continue there. If she just wouldn't wear those rusty black dresses. When I try to dictate something to her and then I look at her, it depresses me so that sometimes I forget what I was going to say."

But Isadora's enthusiastic recollections of her career, which inevitably included some of her ideas about her art, doomed her first attempt at selling her memoirs to a publisher. Upon her return to Paris, she went back to the Hotel Lutetia, where for a reduced price she was supposed to live *en pension*. This means of economy only boomeranged in Isadora's case, because since she found it much too depressing to take her meals alone, she always invited one or two guests. And often, disregarding the high prices of extras from the table d'hôte, to which she was entitled, she would order them to please her companions. That her hotel bill was rapidly mounting to a height from which only another Aunty Ruthy could rescue her— and there was no other in her new entourage—did not really seem to worry her. She was convinced that her friends, who claimed to have powerful personal influence with American publishers, would soon sell her memoirs for thousands of dollars, and that the bill resulting from her extravagant manner of entertaining them would seem a bagatelle. She distributed copies of the typed chapters among these friends, and to persons who claimed to be literary agents— only to receive a unanimous verdict: they were "too arty." Her memoirs must reveal scandals in her love life, and, of course, should include her love letters.

This stopped the progress of Isadora's memoirs for a while and brought to her the stark realization of her situation. No wonder that, whenever I succeeded in cheering her up, she would refer to the Hotel Lutetia as the *Lusitania,* which had been sunk in the Atlantic during World War I.

And, already overburdened with anxiety about her plans for her school, for keeping her studio and the little apartment in Nice, and maintaining her daily existence in Paris, she was informed that unless a sum of ten thousand francs were paid, her house in Neuilly would be sold at public auction. This sum represented several mortgages and innumerable bailiff's fees, having grown from three thousand francs, which Isadora had borrowed in 1922. She had five days in which to raise the money, and, not knowing to whom to turn for help, she made an appeal through the press. The Paris newspapers came out with long columns describing Isadora's plight, and to everybody's surprise painters and sculptors donated their works to be sold for Isadora's benefit, actors and actresses, music hall performers, and scores of art students generously contributed according to their means—and thus at least temporarily saved the only property Isadora could call her own. Because the greatest tragedy in her life, the loss of her children, had taken place when she lived in that house, Isadora had tried for years to sell it, but the property was now rented to a soap and perfume manufacturer who had a long lease. There was also a pending lawsuit, originally brought by a previous tenant, in addition to mortgages—all of which diminished the property's market value to a fraction of its real worth.

But encouraged by the response to Isadora's appeal, the "faithful friends" organized a committee whose aim was to prevent the sale of the house and to collect more money in order to build artists' studios on the premises, which, when rented, would pay for the upkeep of Isadora's school. The committee provided an excellent excuse for constant meetings, at which the female members and the "boys" exchanged the latest gossip about their respective clans in preference to discussing the practical aspects of their project. In addition to drinks, sandwiches, "*Oh, ma chérie,*" and "*Oh, mon cher,*" a poetry reading was an almost obligatory part of the evening's entertainment. Isadora was not invited to all meetings, but only to those which were considered important.

Since Isadora's reports on the business at hand were far from satisfactory to her lawyer, M. Paul-Boncour, whom the committee kept in the background, he asked me to accompany Isadora to one such committee meeting, for he was anxious to know how the sixty thousand francs, collected after Isadora's appeal to the press, had been spent, as well as what was happening to the other thousands of francs that had since been donated.

As if it had been planned that way, that particular evening was saturated with entertainment by the artistically stirred female guests. Georgette LeBlanc, Maurice Maeterlinck's wife, was the chosen star on the program. The poem that she was to deliver was the latest written by her female lover, and LeBlanc had to be implored for a long time before she consented to oblige the company.

It is indeed unfortunate that neither Isadora nor I could remember the poem, except that claiming an affinity to Pierre Louÿs' *Chanson de Bilitis* it described the young woman's head facing her beloved's pelvis. "*Et tes jambes comme l'Arc de Triomphe,*" was the passionate outcry in this poem that Isadora and I retained from that evening. In fact, we left the aphrodisiac atmosphere, as Isadora called it, shortly afterward. Once outside, Isadora took a deep breath of the evening air, tossed up her gray felt hat, and dramatically declaimed: "*Et tes jambes comme l'Arc de Triomphe.*" Then laughing she added: "I would like to hear what Paul-Boncour would say to that? Didn't he want us to find out about the money that was spent?"

Until the last days of her life, whenever she was depressed, it was sufficient for me to quote this sentence from the poem to make Isadora smile and, at least for a moment, forget the thought that troubled her. But at that particular time, I sensed that there was more on Isadora's mind than amusement over the "realism" of the poem. And, indeed, my suspicion was not farfetched.

For the first time since the days when, in the theatrical company of Loie Fuller, Isadora had witnessed Lesbian courtships, she was now confronted with a rather delicate situation. She could not now, as she had done in her early twenties, telegraph her mother to come to her rescue when one of the members of Loie Fuller's entourage attacked her. Nor, having spent her life in the company of male admirers, was she experienced in fending off the advances of passionate females without hurting their feelings. And yet she knew that all her projects, the fate of her school, and her house had been entrusted to this society, and that she would have to use extreme diplomacy in personal matters that were entirely alien to her nature.

It was also made clear to her that, while the committee painted for her a future life of blissful security, her current needs were none of its business. In this way, a contract for her memoirs, with a substantial advance, was her only hope.

Had the process of writing her memoirs, the negotiations over them, and their subsequent publication not given rise to so many false accounts, I should have preferred to omit the names of the authors of these fictitious stories rather than accord them the undue honor of a mention in a book about Isadora Duncan. But, since in this book my aim is to set straight the record of Isadora's life and work, I feel compelled to suspend this chronicle long enough to give an analysis of the overall situation surrounding her memoirs, and to which I can testify from personal knowledge.

I should say at this point that I knew quite well practically all the persons at that time connected in one way or another with Isadora, and especially those authors of books and articles written after her death. An exception was Mr. Sewell Stokes, who said in his book, *Isadora Duncan, An Intimate Portrait,* that Isadora had introduced us in Nice; I have no recollection of that introduction and I have certainly not seen Mr. Stokes since that time. A number of these authors speak of me in the most flattering way, and yet choose to disguise me under invented names, which do not exist in any language, and probably testifies to their ignorance of Russian. The trouble with most of their reports concerning me is simple—I have not been in the places or lived in the hotels or apartments where their accounts put me, nor did I utter a single word of the sentiments attributed to me. Otherwise, I found their accounts of me fascinating, and even informative.

Isadora's entourage of flatterers, profuse in optimistic predictions and promises, swearing eternal loyalty, and engaging in the most complicated intrigues and deceptions, bewildered her already exhausted mind. At the same time, it forced her, *faute de mieux,* to play the game and believe in what she knew was unbelievable.

She found no difficulty in dealing with male homosexuals. In fact, she thought that their coquetry, their flirtations, and their fits of jealousy, even if they did not always seem real, were at least touching; with her motherly attitude, she was ever ready to comfort the one who was abandoned by his mate. Somehow, she always had such couples at her side—at her expense they kept her company in Paris and Nice.

Of the two fairly worthless young men whom she called *"mes petits pigeons,"* Walter Shaw was supposed to act as Isadora's secretary, and also to take down her dictated memoirs instead of Miss Nickson, who had finally been dismissed. I never saw a single line written by him, and, as a secretary, his functions never went beyond handing Isadora the bills for their drinks, lunches, and dinners.

Marcel Herrand was a pretty, doll-like boy, who dreamed of becoming an actor, but whom meanwhile I sometimes found sobbing in Isadora's arms about the infidelities of Walter Shaw. Except for malicious gossip about Isadora, which they exchanged with their Lesbian colleagues, they were harmless and caused Isadora no particular anxiety. Since they were useless for any practical purposes, their relationship with her was limited to escorting her on her trips to Nice, as well as to restaurants when Isadora had the money to pay the bills; discreetly, they kept away when she had no cash.

After Isadora's death, they left no traces of their friendship with her. It was different in the case of Allan Ross Macdougall, who in 1916 had accompanied Isadora on her short trip to Cuba. Although his functions as her secretary ended upon their return to the United States, he continued to see Isadora fairly frequently in Paris, and on one occasion in Nice. Immediately after Isadora's death, he went to Russia where, in collaboration with Irma, he compiled from Isadora's letters and Irma's reminiscences a book I have already referred to, *Isadora Duncan's Russian Days.* In that memoir, Macdougall, otherwise extremely discreet, bestowed upon himself the title of *"the"* friend of Isadora. It would have been as harmless as many similar statements that have been advanced throughout history if Macdougall had not made it the basis for claiming for his reports an incontestable authenticity. In the preface to his later book, *Isadora, a Revolutionary in Art and Love,* published some thirty years after the one written in collaboration with Irma, he says of Isadora: "An international legend during her own star-crossed lifetime, there has since grown up around her name and artistry a confused and luxuriant thicket of myths, misinformation, and complete misconception." Yet, except for his discovery of facts about Isadora's early background, through his personal researches, he drew his information from her memoirs—in which he himself thought Isadora "sometimes strayed from the austere road of truth into romantic bypaths of exaggeration . . . and into the never-never land of fantasy"—as well as from hearsay, gossip, and such misinformation as only Mary Desti could offer. Thus he himself added to the confused and luxuriant thicket of myths, and so forth. More than six months before Isadora's death, he stopped his visits to her. It came about in this way.

One afternoon Macdougall walked into Isadora's apartment unannounced, and, after a quick glance at a large framed photograph on the piano, he shouted: "Isadora, who is your new lover, the handsome young man I see here?" Isadora and I were on a small balcony overlooking the studio, so that Macdougall could not see us. Realizing what had prompted Macdougall's question, Isadora made a sign to me to be quiet. A few seconds later, we heard Macdougall tiptoe out of the room. He never came back. What was it all about? In that photograph on the piano, he had suddenly recognized himself—the handsome, elegant, slender young man of 1916, no longer discernible in the slovenly, froglike, aging Macdougall.*

But it was an entirely different matter for Isadora to deal with the rest of her new entourage, which, with the exception of Mary Desti and Ruth Mitchell, was entirely Lesbian. Isadora did not adhere to the Frenchman's contention that Lesbianism is merely "*amusant*," but felt toward it the revulsion of a normal, healthy woman. In any case, she had to be on guard against its effects in her own life. After Isadora's death, however, her Lesbian acquaintances indulged themselves by publishing stories entirely fabricated by their special kind of imagination. In this connection it will be remembered that there is a long list of women "in whose arms Frédéric Chopin died."

As for Mary Desti's *Isadora Duncan's Life, the Untold Story*, it can be dismissed for its unreliable information. It was composed by an illiterate megalomaniac, who, imagining herself as Isadora, claimed to have inspired and directed the writing of Isadora's memoirs and finally had them published. But that is mild compared to the com-

---

* Since he had no further contact with Isadora, his account of the last six months of her life is based on hearsay and conjecture.

ments on Isadora's memoirs which appear in Mercedes de Acosta's *Here Lies the Heart,* an autobiography. It reads like the New York telephone directory because of the quantity of names mentioned, but fails to live up to the comparison in the quality of its information. Claiming that, after trying nine publishers, she had "fairly browbeaten" Tommy Smith, one of the editors of the Boni and Liveright publishing firm in New York, into giving Isadora a contract and two thousand dollars advance, de Acosta states: "Poor Isadora! How she struggled and suffered over the book. Many days I locked her in her room and only let her out when she slid a number of finished pages under the door."

I have never read a sillier lie. But it should not surprise the readers of de Acosta's autobiography, which in the main is a tasteless chronicle of her sexual conquests over practically every illustrious female film star—with even an insinuation that Isadora was not among the unlucky ones who had missed her favors.

Her reference to Isadora's imprisonment is meant to imply a proximity in their living quarters, which was never the case. It also suggests a certain intimacy in their relationship—and a complete misconception of Isadora's character. Isadora Duncan was hardly the woman to submit to writing her memoirs in the manner described by de Acosta.

It was a general practice of those of Isadora's friends who wrote about her after her death to avoid mentioning important facts and even to omit one another's names, either out of a desire "to get even" or to emphasize their own importance in relation to Isadora. Thus de Acosta claims to have sold Isadora's memoirs to Boni and Liveright, the American publishing firm, while actually it was William Bradley, the literary agent, who succeeded in getting the contract for the book.

But it was most unfortunate indeed that she did eventually get hold of Isadora's manuscript, for her free editing of it supplied Isadora's life story with de Acosta's own interpretation, especially obvious in the characterization of the men who were close to Isadora. But she, as well as Desti, Macdougall, and others who wrote about Isadora, must at least be given credit for stating that Isadora, although influenced by their advice, actually wrote the original draft of the memoirs by herself. After the unsatisfactory attempts at dic-

taking them to Miss Nickson, Isadora relied on her own literary ability—which was far from up to her task. She did not have the *"derriere,"* the *Sitzfleisch*, the discipline that Blasco-Ibáñez once remarked about when warning her of the first requirement for writing a serious book. In addition to the lack of this professional quality, Isadora was constantly interrupted by more pressing demands.

No sooner had her house in Neuilly, which she already called the future temple of the dance, been saved from an immediate sale, than there was the problem of her studio in Nice, on which she depended for her performances to keep herself alive, as she said. Josephine, Isadora's maid, kept sending her alarming letters about her impending starvation—a word which was in constant use by everybody, including Isadora, in connection with any of her daily problems—and usually enclosed unpaid bills which threatened the sale of Isadora's last personal possessions. And there was the ever-mounting bills at the Hotel Lutetia.

As graciously as she could, Isadora declined several propositions to live for "economy's sake" with one or the other female member of her entourage, even at a time when, in the autumn of 1926, her health finally broke down under the constant nervous strain. She was suffering from an internal hemorrhage, which the efforts of her doctor failed to check. Only complete rest could save Isadora's life, and that, according to her doctor, she could find only in her little apartment in Nice in Josephine's care, and near the studio that contained those precious possessions that were still left to her.

Chapter XLI

"You need not be in any hurry," Isadora said to me, as we were preparing for a trip to Nice. "You don't know what a Greek chorus of creditors will greet us there." We were to drive down to the Riviera in an open car, despite the freezing December temperature. Lotte Yorska—at one time supposedly a well-known actress, but during the period of which I speak, active among the members of Isadora's entourage—after having had her invitation to Isadora to "come live with her," gently declined, was nevertheless not yet resigned to joining her similarly unsuccessful sisters-in-arms. Far from being discouraged, she kept up her faith in the ultimate success of her designs and in fact, concocted some kind of plan to give joint performances with Isadora on the Riviera. For this nebulous enterprise, she was willing to invest a little money in paying Isadora's bill at the hotel, and she lent her chauffeur for the trip to Nice.

Had Isadora not been as ill as she was, perhaps her unusually robust constitution could have survived traveling in an open car through bitter winds in a sub-freezing temperature. But by the time we reached Lyons, she was in such a state that the doctor whom I called in to see her feared for her life. She was hemorrhaging continually. The doctor could not predict when Isadora would be able to continue the journey. Like Isadora's doctor in Paris, he felt that she needed a long and complete rest. The driver was sent on to continue the trip by himself, while Isadora, who lay prostrate in her hotel room, finally agreed to be taken by train the rest of the way to Nice.

When we finally arrived, Josephine led us into the little apartment holding a candle in her hand. Because of the unpaid bills, the electricity had been turned off, nor was there any wood in the fireplaces. But it was typical of Isadora, not only not to betray her concern about facing discomforts in her weakened condition, but to try and cheer up her old and faithful maid. "Don't you worry, Josephine," she said to her. "We've come home, and everything will be all right. And you can talk Russian again. But we must go to the studio right away."

The studio was just as cold as the apartment, but Isadora was instantly happy—she was once again among the things she cherished most, once again in an atmosphere that was sacred to her, instead of facing the pink walls of her hotel rooms. She put a record on the old gramophone, and we listened to Beethoven's Ninth Symphony. It was three o'clock in the morning before she realized how tired she was from the trip, and we went back to the apartment.

Obeying doctor's orders and protected from the intrusion of creditors, Isadora would rest immobile for hours on a chaise longue on the balcony, facing the meager December sun and the vast span of the sea, while Josephine would come to my room, obviously hoping that her complaints would be better understood when expressed in Russian.

She was a small, frail, gray-haired woman, who still looked more like a governess than a maid—for a governess she had been in aristocratic Russian families, for most of her life. Her kind expression behind her glasses would grow stern when, losing patience with Isadora's largesse, she would speak of some of Isadora's callers. "Madame knows we have no food, and yet she always invites people for dinner," Josephine grumbled. She had received no salary for months, but she was devoted to Isadora and would not think of leaving her; apparently, however, she needed to unburden herself. Despite Isadora's reputation as a rank communist, she always maintained a certain dignified distance in her relationship with her servants— even with Josephine, who had been with her for almost three years. Isadora would merely listen to Josephine and make no comment on her woes. But to me she said, "When the memoirs are finished, and we'll be rich, I am going to buy Josephine a cottage and two Angora cats—Josephine loves cats—and she can sit on cushions and have her nails manicured."

Whenever she felt a little better, Isadora would go to the studio to do some exercises—it was good for Josephine, and especially for the creditors, to know that Madame was preparing a performance which would bring in some money. But she was still very weak, and would soon lie down to rest on one of the couches, saying, "There is no use in those exercises, not for me. I never was an acrobat, even in my youth. I have always been the poorest of all professional dancers in the usual sense, although when I was very young, I, too, used to throw spears at imaginary gods."

The fact that she was reclining on a couch, and remaining almost immobile while listening to recordings, could easily give an erroneous impression of Isadora's way of passing the monotonous days of her recuperation. Actually, she was "working"—creating in her mind the dances that were to be on the program of her future performance. Unfortunately, this inspiring occupation was cut short when Isadora received a telegram from Yorska canceling the joint concerts with Isadora and calling her chauffeur back to Paris. In vain, Isadora awaited Yorska's explanatory letter. She never heard from the lady again.

In fact, Isadora received no letters from her faithful friends in Paris. She knew nothing of the committee's activities, of the pending sale of her house, nor the results of the promised negotiations about her memoirs. "Oh, well," Isadora shrugged, "what can you expect from them? But there is one thing they can't take away from us." I could see a vengeful gleam sparkling in her eyes. "Tonight is New Year's Eve, and they cannot stop us from celebrating. Let's see how much money we have left. And let's have blini—Josephine is an expert at making them. And, of course, we must have a bottle of champagne."

Isadora looked very happy mingling with the gay crowds making their last purchases for the evening's feast, and, at home again, only once, when we were sorting all the purchases on the dining room table in front of a delighted Josephine, did Isadora's holiday mood change. As if a black cloud had obliterated everything before her, the charming childish smile suddenly gave way to a grim expression in her eyes. "Perhaps this will be our last New Year's Eve," Isadora whispered.

Later we told Josephine that we would go into town to watch

the celebration and return shortly before midnight for our supper.

We did go into town and walked through the gayly lit streets, and Isadora almost danced all the way back to the apartment, but we did not have the blini. Under the impression that it was flour, Josephine used pea soup, and because it would not "rise," she presumed that Madame had bought the wrong kind of flour. Josephine, very much chagrined, explained to us her disappointment. We met the year of 1927 by supping on old canned goods and a few glasses of champagne.

Next morning we received the invitation to what must have been a sumptuous party—an invitation which on the previous day had been delivered to the wrong address.

Not superstitious except when, more for fun than seriously, she would occasionally blame the number 13 for any misfortune, now in real earnest she spoke of our unfortunate celebration of the New Year as a bad omen for 1927. She let her imagination dwell on all sorts of calamities. Isadora, who with superb nonchalance could face any of her creditors and, in fact, make them ashamed of themselves for bothering her with such trifles as long overdue bills, had now become almost panicky whenever she heard the ring of the doorbell.

The apartment had to be given up, Josephine had to go to a home for the aged, and, because Isadora was not yet ready to give up her studio, we moved to two small rooms in a cheap pension nearby. "All this is a mistake," Isadora kept repeating to me. "Who is going to pay a hundred francs for a ticket if he knows that Isadora Duncan lives in such a dump?"

And she could not keep secret her presence in Nice. She was recognized on the streets, and before long the small dining room on the ground floor of the pension was crowded every evening with Isadora's friends and the friends of Isadora's friends. The reports that were circulated about our giving a series of joint performances at her studio were unfounded, for never once did Isadora even take these guests to her studio, and certainly she never danced for them. If she welcomed these gatherings at all, it was only because in her depressed state of mind they offered some distraction, some escape from reality, which at times she did not seem able to bear any longer. However, one of these impromptu evenings, ending as usual with a dinner charged to Isadora's now steadily mounting bill at the pension, did cause serious trouble.

On that particular night at the dinner table were Countess Linda de Monici and her friend Captain Patterson, a retired English officer, Mary and John, a young couple whose last names nobody seemed to know, and Alice Spicer and her lover Ivan. Except for the Countess de Monici and Captain Patterson, who were Isadora's frequent guests in Paris, Isadora had never met the rest of her company; I could only tell her that Alice Spicer, a beautiful American woman in her thirties, was an old friend of mine, whom I had not seen for a long time, and that I knew nothing about her escort.

The dinner was unusually peaceful—there were no violent arguments, nobody got drunk. Ivan, who did not use his last name, was supposed to be a Russian, although from the way he spoke the language, I would have taken him for a member of another nationality. He called himself an independent film producer who wished to talk business with Isadora, but during dinner he remained silent most of the time. Whether Isadora was bored and simply wanted to stir up some excitement, I do not know, but she suddenly insisted that Miss Spicer was not drinking enough wine. When I suggested that she let the young woman alone, Isadora, out of pure deviltry, kept filling Alice Spicer's glass and forcing her to drink, until it was quite obvious that she would be sick on the spot.

Since no one seemed to care, and unaware of what I was provoking, I helped Miss Spicer to the bathroom on the second floor, and later told her to rest in my room. Then I returned to the dining room where the Countess de Monici, calmly sipping a glass of champagne, said to me, "See what you have done? Run to the beach. Isadora tried to commit suicide." I thought she was joking, but since, except for the countess, everybody else seemed to have gone to the beach, I too went there to see what was really going on. And, indeed, I had hardly walked part of the way down, when I met Captain Patterson leading Isadora in a dress that was now drenched with sea water.

Not having had any experience with suicidal persons, and seeing Isadora bashfully smiling, as if to say, "See what you have done?" all I could say was that she was taking the chance of catching her death of cold, and, taking her firmly by the hand, I led her to her room. If in the process of urging Miss Spicer to drink, she had got tipsy herself, the cold sea water must have partially sobered her up, for she obediently changed into warm clothes and only said meekly that she was resolved to commit suicide by jumping out of the window. Knowing her sense of humor, I told her that, since her room was not high enough for her to kill herself, she would only make a mess, which would be a rather poor climax to her more romantic first attempt, and certainly unworthy of a great artist. With this heartless sermon, I locked her in her room.

When, half an hour later, I looked into Isadora's room to make sure that the drama of the evening had ended, I found her peacefully sleeping, well wrapped in warm blankets.

But the drama had not come to an end. On the following morning, everything was as peaceful as if nothing had happened. Alice Spicer and Ivan departed early in their little Citröen car; after breakfast, I found Isadora cheerfully chatting with reporters, who had unsucessfully tried to reach her the night before. Isadora must have been weaving the most fantastic stories for their benefit. I overheard only a sample in the conclusion of one of them, in which Isadora said, "We murdered Alice Spicer and buried her body in the courtyard back of the house."

Isadora's name was too famous for the newspapers to miss an opportunity for a sensational front page story, and the most incredible reports of Isadora's attempt at suicide were published. Their fictional character was so obvious that the books on Isadora written after her death did not dwell on this episode, except for that of one author, René Füllop-Miller, who wrote the epilogue to a German edition of Isadora's memoirs (published by Amalthea Verlag in 1928), which actually was more of a free adaptation than a translation, indeed was described on the title page as "worked over."

After describing Isadora's performance at the Mogador in Paris, which incidentally was not to take place until some seven months later, Füllop-Miller wrote the following account of this incident:

Then she drove to Nice and took with her the young Russian pianist Seroff. Once again a love-affair began, only this time, it came to a tragic end much too soon. One evening, during a dinner in which several young American women took part, suddenly Seroff, ghostly white, jumped from his seat; one of the guests had kissed a young girl. The pianist suffered from an attack of delirium and, without saying a word, broke all the plates and glasses on the table, including the lamps. This outburst left Isadora with no illusions that she had any hope for his love. In despair, she ran after her beloved, who had disappeared into his room with the young American girl. Faced with a closed door, Isadora threatened to commit suicide. Seroff simply laughed at her.

Then she made herself up as if she were going to dance, and in the moonlit evening walked toward the sea. With her arms lifted high above her head, she walked deeper and deeper into the water. An English officer, who saw her, ran after her and pulled her back. Laughing, Isadora was supposed to have said to her friends: "That would have been a beautiful scene for a film, don't you think?"

Six months after Isadora's death, when I was in Berlin, I saw the German edition of Isadora's memoirs and, for the first time, read Füllop-Miller's epilogue. It was so full of inaccuracies that in the law suit I brought before the Berlin court I could have demanded that the entire epilogue be scrapped, but I asked only that the page on which Füllop-Miller described the episode in which he mentioned my name and my behavior be omitted. It took two years for the court to decide in my favor, but whether the books already in circulation were recalled and the page actually removed, I never knew. However, seven years later, purely by chance, I met Füllop-Miller in Vienna. He was extremely apologetic, and told me that, unfortunately, he had relied on newspaper reports and unreliable gossip.

No wonder that the accounts of that evening, of which Füllop-Miller's was merely a sample, caused the committee taking care of Isadora's affairs in Paris to abandon its work, and even to stop the occasional minimal financial assistance to Isadora as loans against an advance for her memoirs. I had spent all the money I had, and with practically none left in Isadora's purse, one night upon returning home, we found ourselves locked out of our rooms at the pension. Waving the newspapers at us, in which, in addition to a description of the by then famous evening, there was a list of a number of her debts and unpaid hotel bills, the proprietor refused us even our clothing unless his bill was paid immediately. It was late at night and raining, but Isadora took this added situation as if she had expected it and was only surprised that it had not happened a long time before. "Well, she said to me, "we must go to the Hotel Negresco. There is no use my going to a cheap place, they don't know me." And as we were driving to the hotel in the old Mathis, she added, "It's no use people trying to make me economize. You can't make an elephant ride a bicycle."

((404))

Following her own logic, and especially her own understanding of simple arithmetic, Isadora insisted that it was just as cheap to live in a hotel such as the Negresco, where she had credit and was charged a *prix d'artiste*. However, after two days of arguing, I succeeded in persuading Isadora that my own account of the whole situation might reverse the committee's attitude, and I took a train to Paris.

However, I was wrong. Upon my arrival, I went to see Alfredo Sides, who had been playing a major role on the committee. I knew far more about him than he thought I did, and therefore his attempts at impressing me were wasted. Alfredo Sides was a dubious character, even in the opinion of his close friend, Mercedes de Acosta. Although a French citizen, his true origin was unknown, for at different times he implied that he was a Turk, an Italian, a Spaniard, and he spoke all those languages equally well. He insisted that he preferred women to "those terrible males with their black cigars," but actually he was favored by the homosexuals of both sexes. His profession was similarly indefinable—he claimed to be a connoisseur, and had in his possession some valuable objets d'art. His connection with Isadora's committee he based on his assertion that he had been her lover, alternating the date of this close relationship according to the person to whom he was making the disclosure. But Isadora, speaking of him, called him a rug merchant, such as one sees on the streets of Paris, carrying his wares on his shoulders. Nevertheless, since the committee, predominantly Lesbian, had entrusted Sides with carrying on the business part of all negotiations concerning Isadora's house in Neuilly and the plans for her school, Isadora warned me to be careful with him.

My visit was very short. Wearing a silk-embroidered dressing gown and hold a safety razor in his left hand, apparently to show me that I was intruding on his more pressing business, and adjusting a monocle with his right hand, he made his entrance into the salon of his apartment on the rue Gît-le-Coeur, which overlooked the Seine with a view of Notre Dame. He said: "I will do everything for Isadora's school, but, if she were dying across the street, I would do nothing for *her* whatsoever." This profound announcement was brief and to the point. Wishing him good day, I left him still adjusting his monocle.

The few members of the committee I was able to contact preferred to believe the newspaper reports, and, having already been warned by Sides, either spoke in vague terms about the approaching date of the sale of Isadora's house or suggested consulting Sides on all financial matters concerning Isadora. Finally, I called Cécile Sorel, Isadora's only true friend in Paris that I knew, and told her of Isadora's desperate situation. In Sorel's opinion, as in my own, only Isadora herself could stir the committee to action, and I had to promise Sorel that I would never tell Isadora or anybody else that it was she, who with the assistance of the Negresco directors, was to provide Isadora with a train ticket to Paris.

Not more than ten days had passed since I had left Nice and arrived in Paris, and yet Sewell Stokes, in his *Isadora Duncan, An Intimate Portrait*, managed to spin out a romantic tale that would leave any reader with the impression that at least several months had gone by, during which this "intimate portrait" was developed.

Actually, Stokes said in his book that he never saw Isadora again after she went back to Paris. Accordingly, I am inclined to applaud his confession: "Of the inadequacy of the portrait I am aware." For that reason, I was surprised to hear, in connection with the most vulgar television documentary about Isadora thus far, produced by the BBC in England, that Sewell Stokes was Isadora's close friend during the last years of her life.

I never heard Isadora mention either his name or that of his friend, who in his book is indicated as G——. In *Isadora Duncan's Russian Days*, Macdougall discloses the identity of G——, saying "Gabriel Atkin, a charming English artist, and his friend Stokes, an English journalist, who were hanging about Isadora for material for one of the chapters in his book on Riviera personalities. . . . Atkins was to do caricatures for the book."

Although Macdougall does not provide his readers with any evidence of Gabriel Atkin's charm, and Stokes keeps him completely silent in his book, I gained the impression that the two young men, who were, as Macdougall said, "hanging about Isadora," were another two pigeons such as Isadora had in Marcel Herrand and Walter Shaw. And, although Stokes lacked the essentials for quoting Isadora accurately—a good musical ear and at least a fair memory—I do not doubt that, during those ten days, when Isadora was not only anxious about her affairs in Paris but desperately lonely, she said to her new friends, "You two are saving me from foolish things, because I cannot bear to be alone."

Isadora's telegram to me saying, "Telegraph the news," was followed by one equally laconic: "Meet me tomorrow at the station." She did not indicate the hour of her arrival, but remembering that she had said on several occasions, "You cannot make an elephant ride a bicycle," I inquired which was the *train de luxe* among the ones due from Nice, and calmly waited for Isadora to descend from it.

As she stepped down onto the platform, she asked me to give the porter fifty francs, for, she said, he had paid for her dinner aboard the train.

Chapter XLII

Isadora refused to go back to the Hotel Lutetia. It had brought her nothing but bad luck, she said, referring to it again as the *Lusitania*. She said she would like to try the recently opened Studio-Hotel in the rue Delambre in Montparnasse. That the small hotel was located in back of the Café du Dôme, which, with La Rotonde, the Sélect, and several others, served as a constant residence for the artistic society of Paris, as well as for hordes of American expatriates, did not interest Isadora in the least, for contrary to gossip, she never set foot in any of these bohemian locales during the many months of her last sojourn in Paris.

But her apartment, a sort of duplex, consisting of a studio and bathroom on one floor and a bedroom and small balcony overlooking the studio on the second floor, became a center of the most feverish activities from the moment she had settled herself in these, her new general headquarters. From morning until the late evening hours, Isadora had to receive the various callers, for, although most of them simply wasted her time and what was still left of her energy, she believed she could not risk missing a chance of something important connected either with the sale of her house or with a contract for her memoirs. Their business might be local gossip, which did not interest Isadora, the latest vague information about the donations to save her house, which she could never comprehend, or a reminder to include in her memoirs this or that particular story, which only further confused Isadora's already disorganized plan of work, or to provide an occasion to meet somebody who for years had waited for an opportunity to express personally her admiration for Isadora's art.

So far, the memoirs existed in snatches, some parts still in Isadora's own hand, more disconnected notes than a consecutive narrative, others already retyped. "Well, I have written twenty thousand words, and I'm still a virgin," she used to say to those who kept inquiring about the progress of her memoirs. And, although there was actually very little of her memoirs ready to show to prospective publishers, Isadora had received several offers for serialization of her manuscript. This, she was assured, meant a great deal of money—perhaps even more than the actual publication of her book, and certainly far more than any advance on the future royalties she hoped for in connection with a book contract. When, at last, she heard that a group representing an American magazine was coming to see her "on business," she became just as excited as when we previously had expected Mrs. Van Magden's visit at Isadora's studio in Nice.

"We simply cannot lose this chance," Isadora kept repeating, as she was arranging the specially bought flowers in one or another vase to create the right atmosphere for the occasion. "And you," Isadora said to me, putting her hands on my shoulders, "you must, you know what. . . ."

"Behave myself?" I asked.

"No, no. You must promise me to play for me when I dance for them. Yes, just this one time. It is very important."

On that evening, Isadora gave strict instructions to the porter to keep everybody away from her apartment except the group of guests she was expecting. We had almost given them up when, at about ten o'clock in the evening, several men and women almost knocked down the door as they piled into the studio. Many a time I had seen Isadora's inherent dignity have a calming effect on people's noisy and boisterous behavior, but this time it failed completely.

Dressed in evening clothes, they had obviously come from "doing Paris." Giving free reign to their humor, they chose and moved armchairs to suit their comfort. After sinking into them, one of the men, taking the long cigar from his mouth, shouted at his perplexed hostess: "Hey, listen, Isadora, talk to us about art."

"Yeah, Bill, that's a good one," another said.

Isadora would have asked them to leave had the realization of her desperate financial situation not induced her to deal diplomatically with a prospective purchaser of the serial rights to her memoirs. Before she had a chance to say a word, her noisy visitors demanded that she dance for them.

At this suggestion, Isadora smiled and said she would, if I would play something first to get everybody into the proper mood. I do not remember what I played, but my choice must have been the wrong one, for I was soon interrupted by their comments: "Oh, stop that! Play us some fiery Russian stuff, Sarnov. . . . Or is it Saraf? Say, Jim, I can never pronounce those Russian names. You *are* Russian, aren't you? Don't you know any fiery Russian stuff?" And, to the general hilarity of his friends, he began to kick his legs and clap his hands, indicating the rhythm of his imaginary Russian dance.

Fortunately for Isadora, her guests had brought with them their taxidriver—presumably to demonstrate their true democratic spirit. He was quiet, showed good manners, and seemed to be genuinely moved by her dance a few minutes later. To control herself in what was becoming an unbearable situation, Isadora addressed herself entirely to him, for he was the only one who did not interrupt her with rude remarks when she spoke of the freedom she should be enjoying in creating beauty instead of telling the American public the insignificant details of her love affairs.

Then, after she merely indicated with a few gestures the dance she had composed to the memory of the Russian revolutionary martyrs, she tried to explain to him in words what she was trying to express in her dance. She spoke of men who had died for him and the freedom of his children in the fight against the "white-livered bourgeoisie," she spoke of Lenin as the only savior of humanity, and the more she was interupted with rude and mocking remarks from her guests, the more "revolutionary" her impromptu political discourse became, until everybody was shouting at the same time, "So you want a revolution?" "Communism?" "Vive la France!" "We had better get back to the good old U.S.A." And out the door went the serial rights.

Exhausted, Isadora almost fell onto a couch near her. "Did you hear those females saying: 'Oh, Miss Duncan, your memoirs must be thrilling! We're so anxious to read them!' What they need are pornographic pictures, and the bordels they all visit to learn something about love-making. Oh . . . the hell with them anyway! People say I drink. Well, how can one face them without it?"

In connection with Isadora's remark, "People say I drink," I would like to join those who knew Isadora well enough to say that she was not an alcoholic. I never saw Isadora drunk and, in fact, having heard about her drinking, I was rather surprised by proof to the contrary when we arrived in Nice at the end of 1926. While at that time Isadora was recuperating by spending many hours lying on a chaise longue on the balcony, I, looking for a book, opened a wall cabinet which I had taken for a book cupboard. To my surprise, all the shelves were filled with liquor of every description. Although Isadora knew about it, she never "helped herself," because, she said, since I did not drink, she would not drink by herself. And that is hardly a drinking person's philosophy.

But since I gave up arguing against that generally accepted myth a long time ago, I was very glad to see the following statement in Irma Duncan's autobiography:

> I must interrupt my story here to point out and correct some popular misconceptions. In all my life with Isadora, I never attended a so-called "orgy," staged either by her or by anyone else, as the newspapers loved to misrepresent. A champagne party and supper, where guests dance, cut funny capers, and generally enjoy themselves in public cannot exactly be termed an "orgy"! That happened every day in the social world I used to know and is a festive occasion most people have enjoyed at least once in their lives.

> Outside of an occasional cocktail before meals, none of us girls, nor Isadora, ever indulged in drinking or especially craving hard liquor. Our European tastes were conditioned to wines. Only in her late forties, after her marriage to a Russian and under his malign influence, did she acquire a habit for stronger stuff. But no one could ever honestly accuse her of becoming an alcoholic in her last years. That, to my certain knowledge, represents a gross calumny.

I have also watched Isadora's dear friends filling her glass to to help her "forget," or "to be in a better mood," or for whatever reasons they may have concocted not for Isadora's sake but for their own. Just as in the case of Sergei Essenin, whose friends preferred for their own amusement to see him drunk rather than sober.

Fortunately for Isadora, who was too depressed to write a single line of her memoirs after the "serial rights visit," William Bradley, the literary agent, arrived from New York with a contract for her book. According to its terms, the two-thousand-dollar advance was to remain in Bradley's hands and be doled out to Isadora at his discretion upon his receiving from her a certain number of pages of her manuscript. She was also to receive another five hundred dollars if she completed the manuscript by the end of May. This, of course, was an absurd clause in the contract, for it would have been impossible even for a professional writer to "finish" a manuscript the beginning of which had not yet been properly organized.

"It is not very good," Isadora said referring to the contract, and especially when she spoke of the manner in which Bradley, whom Isadora called "my ten-percent man," was authorized to deal with *her* money. "But I have signed it," she said, "and now I must go on and finish it. I have never yet put my signature to a contract that I didn't carry out."

And Isadora did begin to work in earnest, but erratically, either because she was not in the "proper mood," or was not "inspired," or because she was interrupted by her friends who brought her good or bad news, or would not come to see her for days in order to leave her undisturbed. Then, in desperation, she would announce to me that she could no longer stand looking at the pink walls of her studio room, and that she simply must, *"pour changer les idées,"* go to a theater, a motion picture, or even a circus.

There took place during this period at least three events, to my knowledge, with which Isadora's name was connected, at first in the press and later in the books written about her. The first of these was Charles Lindbergh's landing in France, May 21, 1927, when, according to Mary Desti's version, Isadora "stood all night at Le Bourget and harangued the crowd of French people at different times when they began to lose hope, saying he would arrive and then, almost suffocated and torn to pieces by a terrific crowd when he finally landed, she marched all the way back to Paris triumphant. . . . In the next few days, she was brought down to the lowest depths by the loss of two young French aviators, Nungessor and and Colli, Nungessor being a very dear friend of ours."

Nothing remotely resembling Desti's description had happened. Shortly before May 27, Isadora received a check from Augustin as a birthday present, and Isadora, especially lonely on weekends when "everybody" was going away, decided to celebrate her birthday a week earlier on May 21 by going for luncheon to her favorite restaurant at Chantilly. Before starting on our way in a car that Isadora had hired for the occasion, we, like everyone else in Paris, heard that an American aviator was on his way across the Atlantic. His name was mispronounced and misspelled, for the name "Lindbergh" did not sound American to anybody. Since only two weeks before, on May 8, 1927, France had been saddened by the loss of Nungessor and Colli, who, crossing westward, had perished in the Atlantic, Isadora was not particularly eager to go to Le Bourget, although it was only a short distance from Chantilly. But, as our excursion was one of those *"pour changer les idées,"* and watching a crowd of people awaiting the aviator's arrival would serve that purpose, we drove to Le Bourget, and climbed to a small terrace on the top of a building that served as an observation point for the arrival and departure of planes. There were at most about twenty or so French people, who applauded several French planes, which were doing loops over the field for their benefit. With cheers of *"Vive l'aviation Française!"* the crowd seemed to express its opinion that, since Nungessor and Colli had failed, it was a mistake to believe that an American could succeed in such a feat. As they expressed their feelings even more loudly and Isadora and I were the only two speaking English in the group, far from "haranguing the crowd," Isadora whispered to me that perhaps it would be wiser for us to go down to the restaurant on the ground floor.

It was getting late in the evening, and perhaps after we had dined at the restaurant we would have left rather than hear any sad news. But suddenly it was announced that the American plane had been seen passing over England and was momentarily expected at Le Bourget. Everybody rushed to the door, which I pushed open, for the policeman who was guarding it was looking up in the air. A plane circled the field, more powerful projectors were turned on, and then we could see the small aircraft on the ground, toward which a crowd, trampling over our feet, was rushing.

We saw someone being carried on people's shoulders, but we did not know whether it was Lindbergh or somebody impersonating the aviator for safety's sake. For a few minutes later, on another observation tower, we saw Myron Herrick, the American Ambassador, accompanied by a young man waving an aviator's helmet, acknowleding the wild cheers of the crowd, this time including those of Isadora, who, in a patriotic gesture, threw her hat in the air.

Isadora was not as patriotic when the case of Sacco and Vanzetti, the two alleged anarchists condemned to death for killing two men carrying a payroll, stirred world opinion. The adamant attitude of Governor Fuller of Massachusetts, who held the fate of the two men in his hands, despite the pleas of mercy from all over the world, only gained an ever-increasing number of sympathizers for Sacco and Vanzetti. Pinning the newspaper photograph of the governor on the fireplace in her studio, with her own comment written in red lipstick, "Down with the Philistines!" Isadora opened her studio to daily meetings of the Sacco and Vanzetti sympathizers and their general discussions on the cruelty of the American laws, and the Philistinism and backwardness of the country. Not satisfied with these rather peaceful discourses, Isadora insisted on going to a great many protest meetings, which were being held all over Paris.

At one of these when I arrived to join her, I found Isadora being quietly but firmly led away by a policeman, who said to me, "Monsieur, please take Isadora home." The policeman's calling her by her first name had an immediate effect. She smiled at me as if to say, "See how well the people know me." On the way home, she sat quietly in the taxi, lost in thoughts that I felt had no connection with the Sacco and Vanzetti case. But in her studio, while taking off her coat, she showed me her wrist and said: "Look what he did!" She was ready to cry over the slight blue bruise, left by the policeman's firm grip when he pulled her away from the protesting crowd. I could not help thinking of the difference between Isadora's timid femininity and the false opinion of her as a potential American Danton.

As a rule, Isadora was not successful in her public interventions. At that time, while still preoccupied with the fate of Sacco and Vanzetti, she saw in the Paris newspapers short reports about certain Borodins, who were to be executed in China. Neither the newspaper reports, nor the circulated rumors made clear whether the married couple—the Borodins—were Russian or American, but stated that they were accused of spying in China, under the disguise of visiting their daughter, who was a member of Irma's group of touring dancers.

This was enough to make Isadora decide to protest to the Chinese Ambassador and demand the immediate release of the Borodins. Brave in threats, Isadora was timid when called upon to follow them with action, and she asked me to accompany her to the Chinese Embassy. Contrary to various published versions of Isadora's intervention on behalf of the Borodins, which were worthy of cheap cloak-and-dagger mysteries, our visit to the embassy was not particularly dramatic.

After making an appointment to see the ambassador, I asked Isadora to reread the news reports in order to deliver her protest in a coherent way, for it was obvious to me that she was as ignorant about the Borodins' case as everyone else who had read the nebulous newspaper comments. "Just imagine," Isadora would cry out as she paced up and down the room, "those yellow people executing a white couple!"

"That would hardly be a diplomatic thing to say to the Chinese Ambassador," I suggested, but Isadora gave me such a look for my advice, that, wishing her good luck, I said nothing more.

At the embassy, we were immediately ushered into the ambassador's office. As we walked into the room, Isadora was completely thrown off her guard, as she told me later, because neither the room nor the ambassador resembled in the least what she had expected to see. Instead of an Oriental atmosphere, such as she had always seen in motion pictures on Oriental subjects, instead of being greeted with great ceremony by an ambassador dressed in a fancy kimono, and being offered luxurious cushions to sit upon, she found a room bare of any ornament, and that looked like any other office of a high official, with a large desk at one side of the room. The Ambassador, dressed in a double-breasted blue suit, rose, and pointing to chairs near his desk, said in French, "I am delighted to see you. To what do I owe the honor of your visit?"

Isadora was much too nervous to deliver her protest speech, which she had been rehearsing over and over again at home. Instead, she began to address the ambassador by telling him about her school in Moscow, and that it was *she* and not Irma who should have taken her pupils on a tour in China. Although the ambassador quietly listened to her, it was obvious that, not having been advised as to the true reason for Isadora's call, he was bewildered by her talk until she mentioned the name of the Borodins. Then, at the first opportune moment—not to sound as if he were interrupting her—he smiled, leaned on the table toward Isadora as if he were about to tell her something very confidential, and said: "May I first say that to us, and I don't mean only to myself but to all of us, you are an extraordinary being. And I am not speaking of you only as a performer on the stage. No one looks or even walks like you. You have an unforgettably melodious voice. You represent to us harmony and beauty. But politics. . . ." He shook his head. "You should not soil your beautiful hands with politics, so . . . may I ask you both to join my daughter for tea."

Isadora's notion of Oriental courtesy, gained from the films she had seen, must have been satisfied when, as he finished the last sentence, the French doors leading into an adjoining room were opened, and there stood the ambassador's daughter, quiet and dignified, dressed in her traditional national dress, buttoned up to her neck. She was young, beautiful, and spoke faultless French without the slightest accent.

There was not much else that Isadora could do but accept the gracious invitation, and, since the Ambassador's daughter told Isadora that she knew Princess der Ling, who was Isadora's pupil when she first came to Paris, the conversation during tea was devoted to the arts, and predominantly Isadora's own art.

Isadora was so enchanted with her charming young hostess that she did not notice that the ambassador, on the pretext of showing me the beautiful garden from the window, took me away from the tea table for a few minutes. Nor could Isadora part with the young girl without tears and kisses.

"Well, how did you like the tea pary?" I asked Isadora, as we drove back to the rue Delambre.

"Oh those Chinese, you certainly have to hand it to them."

"You mean the Borodins?" I said, as if I were finishing her sentence.

For a moment Isadora looked annoyed. But, as I did not want to spoil her enthusiastic impression of the Chinese girl, I told her what the ambassador had asked me to reveal to her, and I quoted him: "By the time Madame Duncan returns home, a telegram will be on its way to intervene against the execution of the Borodins."

"Oh, no, when did he say that?" Isadora asked, very much excited.

"When he was showing me their garden. Only he asked me to tell it to you later."

"Oh, those Chinese. . ." Isadora sighed with the satisfaction of one who had successfully completed her mission.

"Yes, the yellow race—" I began, but Isadora stopped me from teasing her further.

Chapter XLIII

Isadora was not told until months later about the sale of her Neuilly house, which supposedly had taken place in November 1926. In fact she was always left with the impression that it was not a final sale, and that, for a certain sum, it could be bought back. She was also told that it had been sold at public auction at a fraction of its true value, and the sum of 300,000 francs was mentioned, mysteriously resembling the supposed sum of 300,000 francs that Isadora had refused to accept from Essenin's estate.

But somehow she never received a penny from this sale, nor could she nor her lawyer Paul-Boncour ever find out what had happened to the money. So many versions were offered that a person far more experienced in financial matters than Isadora would have given up his inquiries. Then again, she occasionally received small sums from her friends, which were not sufficient to assure her a month's living, and which she spent "recklessly." "Recklessly," Isadora laughed. "And what have I done? Look at me. For weeks I haven't had any money to have my hair washed. I was a sight, like an old witch. I bought a few cosmetics, toothpaste, a few flowers to brighten up this room, and now I haven't got a penny again. And they call that reckless." Perhaps because of this precarious income, having or not having money now meant less to Isadora than ever before.

As always, Isadora would hail anyone who assisted her financially as her only true friend and savior. Richard Buhlig, an American pianist whom she had not seen since Bayreuth, was one of them. He gave Isadora several thousand francs with which to pay her hotel bills, and Iasdora insisted on celebrating the occasion by going out to dine with him.

At first, the idea petrified Buhlig, for he already saw Isadora choosing an expensive restaurant, inviting several of her friends to join them, and, of course, ordering the champagne to "celebrate the occasion." Therefore, he was greatly relieved when I met them just as they were going out, still discussing their plans for the evening. He quickly decided that, by inviting me to join them, he would have in me a sort of safety valve to control Isadora in her sudden extravagant decisions. My assistance, however, did not go any farther than the suggestion of a very inexpensive Swedish restaurant within walking distance of the hotel. To my surprise, Isadora immediately agreed, saying it would be "fun to try it."

As we were chosing our menu, we heard a loud thumping of Liszt's Second Rhapsody on an old upright piano in a corner of the room. Now Isadora did not like any kind of music played while she was having her dinner. She used to say that she could not combine the two, listening to what was being played, and enjoying her dinner—it spoiled her appetite and gave her indigestion. However, when the bespectacled young pianist in a worn-out suit learned that Isadora Duncan was in the restaurant, he came up to our table and asked her if she would like to hear him play something else.

I expected Isadora to thank him and say, "Perhaps later on," as she usually did, but this time she opened her purse and handed the pianist all the money she had been given by Buhlig and, with tears in her eyes, mumbled that she wished "she could do more." One can easily imagine the effect this generous gesture had on Isadora's "only true friend and savior."

"Now look at him," Isadora said, "look at his furious expression. I suppose you," she said to Buhlig, "disapprove of it. Now listen to me. This boy, like any of you pianists, must have spent all his life practicing the piano for six or eight hours a day, denying himself all the pleasures his friends were enjoying. He believed he would be another Paderewski. Well, he did not become another Paderewski, and he never will. These several thousand francs would mean a great deal to him. And as for me—I could have paid my hotel bills, and now I won't. It doesn't matter. But, if you don't understand this, I won't even sit at the same table with you."

As an example of Isadora's human qualities, I have told this story many times, but, to my surprise, I found the reaction of my listeners almost always critical of Isadora, especially among those who prided themselves on being patrons of the arts. In any case when during those months in the spring of 1927, she did receive small sums from William Bradley as she kept delivering the pages of her manuscript, and some money for a serialization in a British magazine, she spent them just as "recklessly," and lost practically all her former benefactors.

The committee, whose functions should have ceased with the sale of Isadora's house, kept on holding their meetings, now with a new project in view: to arrange a performance for Isadora—for only in Isadora's resuming her public appearances could they see any solution to her problems. It always remained a mystery where Cécile Sartoris, a member of the committee who now became Isadora's manager, procured the funds necessary for promoting Isadora's matinee. Since she had not given any performance in Paris for years. it had been agreed upon that the occasion should be promoted in a manner worthy of Isadora's fame. But by the time Cécile Sartoris had reserved the Théâtre Mogador and the Pasdeloup Orchestra under the direction of Albert Wolff, one of the foremost French conductors of the period, there was hardly any money left for publicity. Also, July 8, the date of the performance, was not particularly well chosen, for it was at the end of the theatrical and concert season.

Always ready to be reasonable and helpful where financial matters were concerned, Isadora told her manager that she could save money on rehearsals—she would need only one, a dress rehearsal, on the day before the concert. This, instead of pleasing Madame Sartoris and her friends of the committee, alarmed them and provoked unfortunate gossip: Isadora can no longer dance!

When Isadora heard that her relatively short program was serving as further material for malicious gossip, which was affecting the sale of tickets, she enlarged it several days before the matinee. In the first part of the program, she added César Franck's *Redemption* to two Schubert compositions: the Unfinished Symphony, and the *Ave Maria*. To the all-Wagner program of the second part, she added her well-known interpretation of the Bacchanale from *Tann-häuser*. But the programs had been already printed, and Isadora was told that it was too expensive to redo them. This was an extra annoyance to her, already critical of the lack of publicity and the unprofessional activities of her manager.

Except for those who participated in Isadora's performances, not many ever witnessed her rehearsals, which indeed were most unusual. On the afternoon scheduled for the dress rehearsal, I accompanied her to the Mogador, and she went at once to the theater's gallery. From there, for a while, she watched the men of the orchestra taking their places on the stage. Then she went down to greet Albert Wolff, who was standing at the conductor's desk waiting for her to begin the rehearsal. The orchestra was about to clear a space for her, but Isadora shook her head and told them it would not be necessary—all she needed, she said, would be a chair placed near the first violins and the conductor's desk. Whispering to Wolff, she asked him to play Franck's *Redemption*, and without taking off her cape or hat, she remained immobile in her chair listening to the music. In fact, after the orchestra finished playing the composition, Isadora still sat motionless in the silent theater, while Wolff waited for her further requests. Then Isadora walked up to him, thanked him, bowed graciously to the orchestra—and that was the end of the dress rehearsal. And she performed triumphantly on the following day.

Some eleven years previously, during her South American tour, she had performed an even more astonishing feat when she was preparing for a performance in São Paulo. She was going to include in her program Beethoven's Pathétique sonata which she had heard many times but which in contrast to the *Redemption* she had never really studied. At her rehearsal with Maurice Dumesnil, her pianist, she asked him to play the sonata for her. Sitting in an armchair near the piano, she had listened to Dumesnil's playing, and then asked him to play it again. "She retained throughout this repetition the same attitude of thoughtful concentration, and at the end, seemed satisfied," Dumesnil said in the book he later wrote about their tour. "However, she said: 'If it isn't asking too much, would you mind playing it once more?' and, of course, I did so most willingly. 'Thank you,' she said after I struck the last chord. 'This time I have it.' "

The orchestra and Albert Wolff must have been just as mystified as Dumesnil by the mysterious process that enabled Isadora to assimilate the music and devise her choreography in such a short time.

To the last days of her life, Isadora retained that uncanny musical memory, which permitted her to remember by heart all the choreographic details of her interpretation.

As Isadora had anticipated, the amateurish management was far from achieving a packed house on the day of her performance. But distinguished members of the artistic world and Isadora's faithful old admirers made an enthusiastic audience nonetheless. Her interpretation of Franck's *Redemption* was monumental, and her *Ave Maria*, with maternal arms lulling an imaginary babe, was so personal and so heartrending in its simplicity that it provoked unashamed sobs throughout the audience. At the end of the performance she was cheered and called back to the stage again and again. Perhaps she was expected to make a speech, as had been *de rigeur* after her previous public appearances. But she made none.

It seemed to me as if the whole audience were trying to pay its respects to Isadora, so dense was the crowd moving toward the door leading backstage. I overheard Éduard Schneider, Duse's biographer, saying to a friend, "Duse should have seen this performance." When I finally reached the door, I felt Cécile Sorel's hand on my arm. "She is absolutely exhausted," Sorel whispered to me. Sorel had been one of the first to see Isadora in her dressing room after the performance, and now was on her way out of the theater. "Take her home, but not to the rue Delambre, to your studio. Let her have a good rest. Telephone me later. Bring her to me for dinner, but without those noisy women."

It would have taken several policemen to rescue Isadora from the adoring clutches of her passionate female admirers, led by the Countess de Monici, and Mary Desti with a bottle of champagne in her hand.

Two days later, after the constant congratulatory telephone calls and the waves of visiting admirers had subsided, and I was alone with her, she spoke to me of her own feelings about the performance. From the way she had suggested that we should spend the evening in my studio and not in her apartment, where she would be frequently interrupted by telephone calls and perhaps by unannounced visitors, I presumed that she had something important on her mind. I felt that it was going to be one of those evenings of *solitude à deux*, when she would think aloud, so to speak. It seems to me now that I remember the occasion in detail.

"Have you your car with you? Well, then, let's go right now. Take that picnic basket there on the balcony. We can get something on the way."

Within a few minutes we were driving toward my studio, but, since I was taking the shortest way to it, Isadora said, "Oh no, don't go through those ugly streets."

"I thought you told me that you didn't mind the ugly streets as long as we could tell each other interesting stories?"

"No, no, not tonight. Let's go through the Champs Élysées."

"But you will tell me interesting stories?" I asked, as I turned the car around to drive toward the Tuilerie Gardens.

The streets, hotels, and shops evoked memories from her past: the Hotel Meurice where she had kept open house during the war before going on her South American tour, the Sulka shop where Essenin insisted on buying more shirts and pajamas than he could wear in a lifetime, the American Embassy in front of which she had joined the protesting crowd during the Sacco and Vanzetti case.

Then, still thinking about Essenin, she said, "You know, you Russians are so different—no two of you are alike. Perhaps those leaders of the Communist party are, they are so bound by the same idea, but I have never met any of them, except Lunacharsky. I only met artists and musicians, and they were all poets. Lunacharsky is a poet too. You canot understand art unless you are something of a poet yourself, have some vision, imagination."

Then she suddenly interrupted her own trend of thought. "There is the rue Boissy d'Anglas. Do you remember how, in that nightclub, le Boeuf sur le toit, you asked me to dance with you? I was sitting with Mrs. Russell. She had brought me there to meet an American banker who, she was sure, would be helpful with my school. But he only spoke of facts and figures, wrote things down in his notebook, but understood nothing of my ideas. Then he went to speak to somebody at another table, and you and Anna Pavlova came to our table to say 'hello.'"

"Of course I remember," I interrupted Isadora. "I barely knew you, and it was Pavlova's idea to speak to you."

"And you were so embarrassed. You didn't know what to talk to me about, especially since Mrs. Russell took Pavlova aside to tell her something she didn't want me to know, and so you asked me to dance. And at first I refused, and then I asked you why you wanted to dance with me, and do you remember what you said?"

"Of course—" I started to say, but Isadora laughed and said, "You said that, if you could say that you had danced with the two greatest dancers of our time, Pavlova and myself, who could ever doubt that you were a good dancer? And you did say that you weren't. Now that was a poet speaking, it was something D'Annunzio might have said."

"D'Annunzio? Why D'Annunzio?" I asked.

"Oh, most men would say to me something like, 'Your hands are like rose petals,' but it took someone like D'Annunzio to say, 'Your hands are so beautiful—they are created by Michaelangelo.' I told Pavlova what you had said and she laughed too. You see, we artists understand each other immediately, but when we have to speak to a banker—oh, let's not talk about it."

Before we arrived at my studio, we bought our cold supper at a small *charcuterie*. "It is going to be like our New Year Eve's supper. Poor Josephine, I often wonder how she is. I must go to see her when we go to Nice. But those blinis; how could she use pea soup for flour? It was a bad omen for this year."

I tried to brush aside her superstitious forebodings by reminding her of the great success of her recent performance. "Yes, success, success," Isadora said, after she took a sip of white wine. "Well, at least, I know what I have learned myself." She then spoke at length about something that she had been repeating throughout her career —that just as words have certain meanings and express certain thoughts so do gestures sometimes express things whose meanings cannot be conveyed in words. She said that one of the grossest misconceptions is the idea that a shock of pain, or deep grief, should be shown by the hand clutching the heart. "What does the heart have to do with it? It may suddenly beat faster, but actual pain, physical pain, your heart does not feel. Pain strikes your stomach, or even lower—*that* is where it hurts. How many in an audience would understand that gesture, since they expect you to clutch your heart?

In fact I hate to think what interpretation they are apt to give to my way of indicating sudden grief, physical pain.

"But," Isadora smiled, "and I am very happy about it—for the first time I have achieved something I have been striving to do all my life. And I am not sure I can explain it in words, and yet I simply have to talk about it. For two days I have been thinking of nothing else, but how can I talk about such things with people who keep repeating to me, 'Oh, Isadora, darling, you are so wonderful, you were marvelous. . . .'

"That is why I wanted to talk to you without interruptions. Please forgive me if at first it won't be clear, I'll try to explain."

In the course of the long evening's conversation that followed, Isadora often interrupted her remarks to ask me to play portions of Franck's *Redemption* and Beethoven's Seventh Symphony in order to illustrate her meaning. Perhaps the essence of the artistic discovery she meant to communicate to me was best expressed in the words that follow—words that struck me forcibly at the time, and which I believe are very nearly verbatim.

Isadora told me that ever since she had watched Ellen Terry's and Duse's acting, she had learned that the true expression of tragedy lies, not in the actress's raging on the stage, or harassing the audience with wild screams, but, on the contrary, in remaining absolutely mute and immobile when stunned by a sudden blow of fate.

"I understood that a long time ago," Isadora said, "but how to have the audience too feel it in the same way the actress does? How to make the audience stop breathing? How to hold three thousand people hanging with you on that one note which you musicians mark in your scores with a fermata—meaning you can hold it as long as you like? Yes, to have your audience remain breathless as long as you yourself remain on the stage mute and immobile. That is true art, and I believe at that matinee I achieved it for the first time."

Chapter XLIV

The financial result of her performance at the Mogador was far from impressive; it was again more of a *succès d'estime*. But with a new conception in mind for her interpretations, Isadora was already planning future programs. Just as she had previously chosen Franck's *Redemption* as a vehicle for the monumental expression of her art, so now she believed that Liszt's Dante Symphony would provide her with the best opportunity for further development of her ideas. To familiarize herself with the score, she often asked me to play it for her.

Traditionally, after July 14 (Bastille Day), Paris begins to be deserted; most of Isadora's friends were going to the Riviera for a long summer vacation, and Mary Desti, who always had her own schemes to promote Isadora's fun and work, urged her to go to Nice. Since Isadora had spent all of the money received from her performance at the Mogador and the small sum for the British serial rights to her memoirs, which had arrived in time to pay her hotel bills, Isadora and Mary Desti accepted an invitation to go to Nice by car with Alice Spicer and her friend Ivan.

Ivan was planning to make a film of this journey with Isadora, a project which she considered far too amateurish to be taken seriously, but Desti's enthusiasm for it prevailed. I did not accompany them on this trip for, knowing the four members of the party, I was convinced that the journey was not going to be pleasant. Instead, I promised Isadora to join her in Nice, where I would go by train a few days later. I was not mistaken in my premonitions. Before they had reached Lyons, halfway to Nice, Mary Desti and Isadora quarreled with Alice Spicer. Isadora insisted on making it a leisurely journey, with stops for lunches and dinners in attractive inns on the road, while Alice, who was driving the car, claimed that she had to be back in Paris within a few days and refused to waste time. She ended their constant arguments by presenting Isadora and Mary Desti with two second-class railway tickets so that they might continue their journey by train. Indignant at such treatment, Isadora wanted to engage a taxi to drive them all the way to Nice, but Mary managed to find a private car whose chauffeur was willing to accept her postdated check.

Although I left Paris by train after their departure from that city, I reached Nice before they did. Upon their arrival, Mary Desti's major concern was to find some money to cover the check she had given the driver, a check on an account whose funds had long since been exhausted. This was quite symbolic of the sort of existence in store for her and Isadora.

I had witnessed similar situations before in Paris and in Nice— debts beginning to accumulate with no prospect of paying them —but this time, Mary Desti came up each day with a new plan for procuring on credit the bare necessities for the day's existence, or for getting some money from friends. As soon as Isadora's arrival was known, old and new friends were constantly visiting her. She and Mary passed their days among these friends, on the beach or at lunches and dinners, or entertained them at the Hotel Negresco, where she and Isadora were staying, because they were going to "do things for Isadora." It was good for their credit at the hotel, Mary Desti explained. "People mustn't think we have no money."

After the first look at this absurd situation, I felt that I could be of no assistance to Isadora. She herself admitted that under such circumstances she could not concentrate on the work she was planning to do—preparing a new program for another performance or even a series of performances in Paris. But it took me two days of arguing with her before I succeeded in convincing her that it would be wiser for me to return to Paris and see what could be done for her there.

I spent barely ten days in Paris trying to find out whether another performance could be arranged at the beginning of the winter season. Cécile Sartoris, who had managed Isadora's performance at the Mogador had not yet returned to the city, and Albert Wolff, the conductor, asked me to wait a few days longer before he could suggest a date for the performance. While I was thus forced to be patient before sending any encouraging word to Isadora, I received several letters and telegrams from her, desperately urging me to "keep after them."

It is most unfortuate that in her book, *The Untold Story*, Mary Desti let herself be carried away into the most fantastic fiction in giving an account of what took place during the eight days after my departure from Nice. And what was even more unfortunate is that her account has been considered authentic enough to be repeated, with some variations on the original theme, by magazines and newspapers, as well as by the authors of books written about Isadora—including Macdougall, who surely knew Mary well enough not to trust her spoken or written word.

I will mention here only three of Mary Desti's stories, which apparently made Macdougall remark at this point in his book, "Things, it seemed, were going to brighten up." According to Mary Desti, she had gone to see Paris Singer, who was in his villa Des Rochers at St. Jean-Cap Ferrat, and Singer had promised financial assistance to Isadora. This fiction was followed by another—a gay luncheon with Robert Winthrop Chandler, an American painter, and, more important for the purposes of Mary's inventions, a member of the millionaire Astor family—at which luncheon the forthcoming marriage of Isadora to Chandler had been announced. Finally, as if this were not enough to fill a week, Isadora was supposed to have planned a new amorous adventure with a young Italian who owned a Bugatti car. As an appropriate background to al these events, Desti gives a minute account of the sumptuous luncheons and dinner parties to which she and Isadora were constantly taken.

But on September 14, I received the following letter from Isadora, dated September 11, which obviously contradicts Mary's description of Isadora's situation in Nice.

> Darling Vitia*
> Why no letter?
> No telegram?

* Diminutive of Victor.

Nothing from you—

I was very anxious until Ivan said he had seen you in Paris & you were quite well—I miss you dreadfully—we are in a H— of a fix here—Mary insisted on leaving that nice hotel* where we had credit & coming over here where we have none—& the result is we have nothing to eat—& no way of getting out unless I can sell the furniture here [in her studio]—so I can't very well wish you here under such deplorable circumstances—

Did you rescue trunk & papers from Alice's Studio?

Did you see Cécile? We are in the dark as to whether Hussard has made the mortgage or not [on Isadora's house in Neuilly]? Mr. Schneider could not place the book [Isadora's memoirs with the publishers in France] and has gone to Italy—our only hope is the American serial—but no word yet—

If nothing else turns up—I will sell everything here & return to Paris—This place seems to be a *Jonah*—Do write—& tell me what you are doing—& what your plans. . . . . I hope you are not starving as we are—

Ivan's plans seem vague and he evidently has no money—I have not seen Alice & after her horrid treatment of us I don't want to—She seems to do nothing but run the car like a female flying Dutchman—

Are you living in your Studio—are you playing beautiful music —Think of me & play Scriabin—perhaps you will be nearer to my spirit when the body with all its material nuisance is not there—

There are a few inspired moments in life & the rest is Chipuka**

I kiss you tenderly with all my love

Isadora

Even had I not already known of the desperate state of her mind from the letters and telegrams I had received since I had returned to Paris, I would have been deeply moved by her letter, which contained no word of self-pity but calm despair and a gentle

* The Negresco.
** Nonsense, in Russian.

sorrow. I composed as cheerful a message as I could, telling her to come to Paris, and took it to the post office. I was going to telegraph the few lines I had written, but when I handed the paper to the clerk I discovered that I had left my wallet at home and had only a few francs in my pockets, not enough to pay for the telegram. I was about to go home to fetch the money when the clerk who read my message called me back. "Monsieur," he said, "this goes to Isadora. Even if she gets your telegram today, she won't be able to leave Nice before tomorrow. So . . . why don't you send it as a letter—she will get it tomorrow morning. It will do just as well," and he handed me an envelope to write Isadora's address.

Next morning as I walked through the garden of my studio, my concierge, handing me my mail, looked at me strangely. Her face twisted with pain, she barely managed to say, "Don't you know what happened?" before she burst into sobs. "When? What happened?" I asked her, not having the slightest notion of what she was referring to. "But, Monsieur, perhaps I should not tell you?" "Oh, stop it, what is it?" "Isadora was killed last night," she said, covering her face with her hands. "What nonsense," I said, "Who would want to kill Isadora?" "*Pauvre, pauvre Isadora,*" she continued to cry. "Nobody killed Isadora. It was an automobile accident. You had better get a newspaper."

The front pages of all the newspapers gave the most confusing reports. Some of them described the accident as if Isadora had been knocked down on the Promenade des Anglais by a speeding car. Others spoke of a speeding car that caught her shawl as she stood on the curb, and dragged her to her death. One eyewitness, who claimed to have been sitting on the terrace of the Café de France, reported that the accident did not take place on the Promenade des Anglais but on the corner of the rue de France and the Boulevard Gambeta, far away from Isadora's studio.

When I had returned home, Raymond Duncan telephoned and asked me to go down to Nice with him. In the afternoon we met at the station, but we were told all the seats on the train to Nice were sold. We were prepared to go standing up all night, when a young Chinese student came up to us. He showed us a ticket he wanted to sell; Raymond bought it. "I have another one," the Chinese student said, smiling shyly, "but I am not sure you would want it." "Why not? What's wrong with it?" I asked. "It was my friend's ticket, but he committed suicide. You wouldn't want to travel on a dead man's ticket, would you?" Raymond looked at me. "Are you superstitious?" "Even if I were," I said, as I bought the ticket, "I would use it this time. The worst has already happened."

In Nice, we were met by Walter Shaw and a few of Isadora's new friends, whom I did know, and were taken to the studio. Walter handed me my letter, which had just arrived. As I started toward the studio where Isadora's body was placed on a couch, a Frenchwoman, a stranger, stopped me: "You will be glad that you did not see her," and her husband nodded his agreement. It seems that Isadora's neck was broken and her nose smashed. It was at this moment that I saw Paris Singer crossing the pebbled courtyard and entering her studio.

Later, Raymond and I went to see the car and to hear from the driver the true details of the accident.

The car had been left near the spot where the accident had occurred. It was a racing machine of Italian make—Bugatti. I immediately recognized the red coachwork, which I had seen once when I was in Nice before my return to Paris. A thought flashed through my mind that perhaps I, better than anybody else, could tell the origin of the accident. Once, while Isadora and I had been taking a walk through the streets of Nice, we stopped in front of a shop where cars of various makes were displayed in a large window. Our attention was caught by this red Bugatti racing car.

"There," Isadora said to me, "is the car you should have, and not your old jalopy—so bourgeois for a young man." (Whenever Isadora wanted to express her disdain for something, she used the word "bourgeois," which she had learned in Russia, where, after the revolution, the word was applied to everything the new regime found unacceptable.)

I told Isadora that I hated fast and noisy driving in such cars, and that my poor eyesight would prevent me from handling it properly.

"And I just love fast driving. I would love to have a ride in a car like that." I suggested that such a ride could easily be arranged—either she herself, or Mary Desti, or one of her other friends, could call on the proprietor of the shop and tell him they wanted to buy the car, and the man would be glad to give a demonstration of his Bugatti. There would be nothing unusual about it. "So that is what happened," I thought, as the young Italian garage mechanic, who had been sent to take Isadora for a drive, came up to Raymond and me and told us what had occurred.

After he had finished his work at the garage, at about nine in the evening, he had come to Isadora's studio to pick her up for a short drive. It was a rather chilly evening and both Mary Desti and Ivan suggested to Isadora that she wrap herself in a cape, or something warm. The driver, who spoke a sort of Italianized French, told us that he had offered Isadora his leather jacket, although it was not too clean, he added apologetically. But Isadora refused everything offered her and just wrapped herself in her shawl as she walked to the car. This racing machine was very low, with its two seats practically on the ground. The driver's seat on the right side of the car was a little forward of the other, and the two rear wheels were nearly on a level with the occupant's shoulders.

"Adieu, mes amis. Je vais à la gloire!" Isadora shouted to Mary Desti and Ivan, who were standing in front of the studio. Once seated, Isadora again settled the shawl around her neck and shoulders, unaware that the heavy fringe had fallen into the spokes of the wheel at her side—for the wheels had no mudguards. As the driver set the powerful motor in motion, the very first revolution of the rear wheels broke Isadora's neck. Death was instantaneous.

In a drizzling rain, Mary Desti, Raymond, and I boarded the train that was taking Isadora's body for burial in Paris. In a drizzling rain three days later, she was buried. On the morning of September 19, many of Isadora's friends and admirers gathered at Raymond's home in Auteuil where her body lay in state. Before the flower-covered coffin was put into the hearse, Raymond draped one part of the coffin with a large American flag, and Mary Desti rearranged the red ribbons of the scarlet gladioli so that everyone might see the gold-imprinted legend, *The Heart of Russia Weeps for Isadora.* This tribute did not come from the representatives of Soviet Russia —is was ordered by Mary Desti herself.

The long trek to the Père Lachaise cemetery had to be rerouted, for it was the day on which the American Legion was having a parade in Paris, and the funeral procession could not go through the Champs Élysées. The enforced detour reminded me of the evening when, walking Isadora home to the studio-hotel in the rue Delambre, we had to go through the streets on the Left Bank instead of the out-of-the-way Champs Élysées. "Never mind," Isadora had said to me, "Of course the Champs Élysées is more beautiful, but if we tell each other good and amusing stories, we won't mind missing the Champs Élysées." And so, as if reviewing Isadora's life in Paris, the cortege passed through the Champs de Mars, from which, across the bridge, one could see the two-towered Trocadero where Isadora had triumphed dancing the *Marseillaise*, then, beyond the Pont d'Alma, the Théâtre des Champs Élysées with the marble bas-reliefs of the dance by Bourdelle—the sculptor's tribute to Isadora's art. As the procession turned to go down the rue de Rivoli, it was stopped for a while by a passing regiment of *Chasseurs Alpins*, which was on its way to protect the American Legion from the radical sympathizers of the recently executed Sacco and Vanzetti.

It would have pleased Isadora's sense of humor, I thought, if she could see the bemedaled French officer on horseback, who led the regiment, saluting with his uplifted saber, and the standard bearers lowering their tricolor flags and regimental colors as they passed the hearse carrying the body of one who had raised her voice in defense of Sacco and Vanzetti.

Then the cortege passed the Châtelet Theater, where she had enjoyed great success until her performances were interrupted in 1913 by the death of her children. Further on was the Gaieté-Lyrique, where she had danced with her girls in 1909. The procession continued through the Place de la Bastille toward Père Lachaise. Several thousand mourners awaited the cortege at the entrance to the cemetery.

Isadora's body was cremated; the ashes were to be placed next to those of her children. During the final ceremony in the small chapel packed with sobbing mourners, Ferdinand Divoire, a well-known poet, delivered a moving oration, which was followed by a baritone singing Beethoven's *In Questa Tomba Oscura*. When, after the death of her children, Isadora visited Duse at Viareggio, Isadora had heard Duse sing this song:

> *In this dark tomb*
> *Let me be at rest.*
> *When I was living,*
> *Then it was you should have*

Thought of me,
Oh, ungrateful world!

Schubert's *Ave Maria* was sung, and finally Bach's Aria in D Minor from the D Minor Suite for Violin was played. I had heard Isadora say many times that she would like her spirit to hear this aria as it left the earth. Perhaps Isadora's spirit would have left this earth even more happily if she had witnessed the scenes that we of the cortege saw as we passed through the crowded cobblestoned markets. The women selling vegetables, and the men busy repairing the street, stopped their work. They lifted the children to their shoulders so that they should remember the funeral of a great artist. Crossing themselves, they wiped away their tears, and murmured, *"Pauvre Isadora, pauvre Isadora. . . ."* It seemed to me as if the people were repeating in chorus the words of my concierge as she told me of the accident, an echo resounding through all of France, through all the world.

Bibliography

De Acosta, Mercedes, *Here Lies The Heart*. New York: Reynal & Company, 1960.

Craig, Edith and St. John, Christopher, *Ellen Terry's Memoirs*. New York: G. P. Putnam's Sons, 1932.

Craig, Edward, *Gordon Craig, The Story of His Life*. New York: Alfred A. Knopf, 1968; London, Victor Gollancz, 1968.

Craig, Edward Gordon, *Index to the Story of My Days*. New York: The Viking Press, Inc., 1957; London: Hulton Press, 1957.

"Dance Magazine Portfolio." *Dance* Magazine, Vol. XLIII, No. 6 (June 1969), pp. 51–59.

Desti, Mary, *The Untold Story, The Life of Isadora Duncan, 1921–1927*. New York: Horace Liveright, 1929.

Dumesnil, Maurice, *An Amazing Journey*. New York: Ives Washburn, 1932.

Duncan, Irma, *Duncan Dancer*. Middletown, Conn.: Wesleyan University Press, 1966.

Duncan, Irma and Macdougall, Allan Ross, *Isadora Duncan's Russian Days*. New York: Covici-Friede, 1929.

Duncan, Isadora, *My Life*. New York: Horace Liveright, 1927.

Duncan, Isadora, *Memoirs*. Zurich-Leipzig-Wien: Amalthea-Verlag, 1928.

Duncan, Isadora, *Tanz Der Zukunft*. Leipzig: E. Diederichs, 1903.

Essenin, Sergei, *Complete Works* (5 vols.). Moscow: Khudozestvenaya Literatura, 1966.

Fokine, Vitale, *Fokine*. Boston: Little, Brown and Co., 1961.

Genthe, Arnold, *As I Remember*. New York: Reynal & Hitchcock, 1936.

Haskell, Arnold, *Diaghileff, His Artistic and Private Life*. New York: Simon and Schuster, 1935.

Hurok, Sol, with Ruth Goode, *Impresario*. New York: Random House, 1946.

Kinel, Lola, *This Is My Affair*. Boston: Little, Brown and Co., 1937.

Kschessinska, Mathilda, *Dancing in Petersburg: Memoirs of Kschessinska*. Garden City, Doubleday, 1960.

Bibliography

Lunacharsky, Anatoly, *Memoirs*. Moscow: 1967.

Macdougall, Allan Ross. *Isadora: A Revolutionary in Art and Love*. New York, Thomas Nelson & Sons, 1960.

Prokusheva, U. L., *Collection of Reminiscences of Sergei Essenin*. Moscow: 1965.

Schneider, Ilya, *Moi Vstrechi s Esseninym*. Moscow: Sovietskaya Rossia, 1965.

Schneider, Ilya, *Isadora Duncan, The Russian Years*. London: Macdonald and Co., 1968.

Sorel, Cécile, *Les Belles Heures de ma Vie*. Monaco: Editions du Rocher, 1946.

Stanislavsky, Konstantin, *My Life*. Moscow: 1926.

Stokes, Sewell, *Isadora Duncan, An Intimate Portrait*. London: Brentano's Ltd., 1928.

Vospominaniya ob Essenine. Moscow: Moscovsky Rabochi, 1965.

Index